D0948621

EDUCATIONAL ENVIRONMENTS and EFFECTS

THE NATIONAL SOCIETY
FOR THE STUDY OF EDUCATION

Series on Contemporary Educational Issues
Kenneth J. Rehage, Series Editor

The 1979 Titles

The Principal in Metropolitan Schools, Donald A. Erickson and
Theodore L. Reller, Editors
*Educational Environments and Effects: Evaluation, Policy, and Pro-
ductivity,* Herbert J. Walberg, Editor
Research on Teaching: Concepts, Findings, and Implications,
Penelope L. Peterson and Herbert J. Walberg, Editors

The National Society for the Study of Education also publishes Year-
books which are distributed by the University of Chicago Press. Inquiries regarding all publications of the Society, as well as inquiries
about membership in the Society, may be addressed to the Secretary-
Treasurer, 5835 Kimbark Avenue, Chicago, IL 60637. Membership
in the Society is open to any who are interested in promoting the investigation and discussion of educational questions.

EDUCATIONAL ENVIRONMENTS and EFFECTS

Evaluation, Policy, and Productivity

Edited by

HERBERT J. WALBERG

University of Illinois at Chicago Circle

McCutchan Publishing Corporation
2526 Grove Street
Berkeley, California 94704

ISBN 0-8211-2259-2
Library of Congress Catalog Card Number 78-62101

Printed in the United States of America

Cover design and illustration by Catherine Conner, Griffin Graphics

Series Foreword

The current Series on Contemporary Educational Issues includes two companion volumes that deal directly with classroom instruction. The first of these, *Educational Environments and Effects: Evaluation, Policy, and Productivity,* edited by Professor Herbert J. Walberg, brings together a number of studies that provide data on the effects of environmental influences on educational achievement. Professor Walberg's wide knowledge in this area and his continuing interest in it have made him familiar with studies undertaken not only in the United States but in other countries as well. The investigations reported here, which deal with environments outside the school as well as with various aspects of the environment within the classroom, have been initiated with a view toward providing a deeper understanding of the often subtle and certainly complicated relationships between environmental influences and the learning that occurs in schools.

The second volume, *Research on Teaching: Concepts, Findings, and Implications,* edited by Professor Penelope L. Peterson and Professor Walberg, continues the inquiry into classroom instruction by focusing on studies related directly to teaching. Like the companion volume, this book draws upon recent investigations that have provided insights helpful in understanding how the actions of teachers influence the outcomes of the instructional process, and it contains reports of studies that have used various approaches in the investigation of teaching. Both volumes have methodological as well as substantive significance for those working in the field of education.

The National Society for the Study of Education is greatly indebted to Professors Walberg and Peterson for bringing together these important studies, and to each of their colleagues who have contributed to them. We are indeed pleased to have these books in the series.

Kenneth J. Rehage

for the Committee on the
Expanded Publication Program of the
National Society for the Study of Education

Contributors

Albert B. Chalupsky, Director, Behavorial Science and Technology Group, and Senior Research Fellow, American Institutes for Research, Palo Alto, California

Gary J. Coles, Senior Research Scientist, American Institutes for Research, Palo Alto, California

H. Russell Cort, Jr., Director of Evaluation Research, Antioch School of Law, Washington, D.C.

David L. DeVries, Director of Research, Center for Creative Leadership, Greensboro, North Carolina

Chad D. Ellett, Director of Assessment for Project ROME, College of Education, University of Georgia, and Associate Director, University of Georgia-State Department of Education's Beginning Teacher Evaluation Project

Joyce L. Epstein, Research Scientist and Director, School Organization Program, Center for Social Organization of Schools, and Assistant Professor of Social Relations, Johns Hopkins University

Barry J. Fraser, Lecturer in Education, Macquarie University, Sydney, Australia

Neal J. Gordon, Assistant Professor of Education, University of Illinois at Chicago Circle

Robert A. Horwitz, Clinical Instructor of Psychology, Child Study Center, Yale University, and Clinical Psychologist, Adolescent Crisis Unit, Clifford Beers Guidance Clinic and Hospital of St. Raphael, New Haven, Connecticut

David W. Johnson, Professor of Educational Psychology, University of Minnesota

Roger W. Johnson, Associate Professor of Curriculum and Instruction, University of Minnesota

Nancy Karweit, Research Scientist, Center for Social Organization of Schools, Johns Hopkins University

William P. Kuert, former member of the staff at Oral Roberts University; to join the staff of a school in Kenya, East Africa

Cris R. Kukuk, Assistant Professor of Sociology, University of Missouri at Kansas City

Daniel U. Levine, Professor of Education, University of Missouri at Kansas City

Sara Lawrence Lightfoot, Associate Professor, Department of Social Policy, Graduate School of Education, Harvard University

Jeanie Keeny Meyer, Research Associate, Police Department, Kansas City, Missouri

James M. McPartland, Codirector, Center for Social Organization of Schools, and Associate Professor of Social Relations, Johns Hopkins University

Kevin Marjoribanks, Professor of Education, University of Adelaide, Australia

Rudolf H. Moos, Professor of Psychiatry and Behavioral Sciences and Director, Social Ecology Laboratory, Stanford University and Veterans Administration Hospital, Palo Alto, California

Stephen L. Murray, Senior Research and Evaluation Associate, Northwest Regional Educational Laboratory, Portland, Oregon

Colin N. Power, Professor, School of Education, Flinders University of South Australia, Bedford Park

Sue Pinzur Rasher, Assistant Education Specialist, Office of Evaluation Research, College of Education, University of Illinois at Chicago Circle

Robert E. Slavin, Associate Research Scientist, Center for Social Organization of Schools, and Assistant Professor of Social Relations, Johns Hopkins University

Nick L. Smith, Senior Research Associate, Northwest Regional Educational Laboratory, Portland, Oregon

Richard P. Tisher, Professor of Experimental Education, Monash University, near Melbourne, Australia

Herbert J. Walberg, Professor of Human Development and Learning and Research Professor of Urban Education, University of Illinois at Chicago Circle

Wayne W. Welch, Professor of Educational Psychology, University of Minnesota, and Director, Minnesota Research and Evaluation Project for the National Science Foundation

Richard M. Wolf, Associate Professor of Psychology and Education, Teachers College, Columbia University

Contents

Introduction and Overview

Herbert J. Walberg

Educators are usually environmentalists. Heredity bears on achievement in education and success in life; but, because its influence is difficult to estimate or to alter, educators concentrate on designing and bringing about environmental contexts, processes, and interventions that seem likely to maximize each student's learning. For this reason, the subject of this book as suggested by the title, *Educational Environments and Effects,* is one of the central concerns of educational research workers, policy makers, and practitioners.

Two humanistic questions recur in the history of education: What are the ends of education? And, do the educational means, that is, manipulations of the environment, justify the ends? These philosophical questions concern values, morality, and ethics. Modern psychology and the social sciences raise additional questions: Can the ends and means of education be measured? Do the presumed means in fact cause the ends, and, if so, to what extent or how productively? Although all of these questions are important, and remain incompletely answered, this book primarily addresses empirical questions concerning causality, estimates of relation, and productivity.

On these questions, education follows medicine, agriculture, and engineering. The physician wants to know recovery rates in groups of patients subjected to several drugs or treatments and possibly in an un-treated control group; the agronomist estimates the yield in response to varying amounts of fertilizer and rainfall; and the process engineer seeks to find the effect of control settings on output. Similarly, educa-tors are increasingly searching for answers to empirical questions con-cerning causality. After estimates of causal relations have been made, policy can be formulated within an explicit, objective, rational frame-work; and an approach intended to maximize achievement and other educational outcomes can be specified. Or, if costs of feasible, alterna-tive approaches and the levels of the required outcomes are known, the most efficient approach can be recommended.

Judging from the accumulated research, however, such causal rela-tions and objective policies are not readily available in education. It is by no means clear, for example, that the two chief determinants of operating expenditures for schools—class size and the usual teacher qualifications, such as experience and training, on which salaries are based—are, other things being equal, consistent and strong determin-ants of scores on achievement tests or of other measurable outcomes of education. If not, then policies and decisions with respect to these costly variables must be based on wisdom, tradition, guesswork, or au-thority but not on systematically applied scientific principles.

Why is it comparatively difficult to estimate and replicate causal ef-fects in education? A number of reasons are discussed in subsequent chapters, but several deserve mention here. First, educators in differ-ent classes, schools, and systems often place different emphases on goals of education, and, even when the goals are similar, educators employ different means to accomplish them. Such variations make comparison difficult, if not arbitrary. Moreover, measures are un-available for many worthy goals, such as integrity and courage, and measures of other goals, such as creativity and moral development, lack adequate reliability and validity. Even goals that can be mea-sured reasonably well, such as skill in reading or mathematics and knowledge of such subjects as science, social studies, and English, are indicated by a great number of uncalibrated, incomparable tests; and such incomparability can invalidate research and evaluation. Finally, it is often difficult to assign students experimentally at random to al-ternate environments and courses of instruction; and nonexperimental research with incomplete statistical control can make causal infer-ences with regard to policy questionable.

In spite of these and other difficulties, it still seems reasonable in a democratic society to raise skeptical questions about the effectiveness and efficiency of our public agencies, including the schools, rather than to place complete trust in tradition or expert opinion. With respect to effectiveness, democracy assumes an educated citizenry; if education can be improved by objective means, so much the better for society and individuals. With respect to productivity, if education is the largest industry in the United States (involving nearly all the people at some time during their lives and perhaps a quarter or a third at any given time), then even small gains in productivity can bring about immense savings, including conservation of those precious resources, time and energy of both educators and students.

Public interest in educational effectiveness and efficiency has been growing since the 1970s. On November 14, 1977, *Time* reported that from 1962 to 1976 the cost per student in the public schools rose from $400 to an inflation-adjusted $750. During that same period the scores for national samples of students who took a college entrance examination, the *Scholastic Aptitude Test,* fell from 470 to 430 on the verbal section and from 500 to 470 on the mathematics section. One week earlier, on November 7, *Newsweek* also noted the decline in scores on the *Scholastic Aptitude Test,* and reported that, for the period from 1972 through 1977, the total professional staff in all public schools in the United States increased by 8 percent and the cost per student rose 21 percent with correction for inflation, while the number of students and the number of schools had fallen 4 percent. I do not mean to imply that scores on the *Scholastic Aptitude Test* should be considered the only outcome of interest or that cost per student is the best indicator of efficiency. What I am suggesting is that raising questions about the effectiveness of schools seems not only reasonable but timely.

PURPOSE

This book is not meant to achieve consensus or to produce definitive answers to questions concerning educational policy. The chapters bring together a variety of exemplary analyses in evaluation and research. What they have in common, in my view, are: explicitness about the evidence; a causal approach to the analysis; and relevance to educational evaluation, policy, and productivity. To quote my letter of invitation to the contributors:

I have been thinking of this project for several years; and, since several investigators have recently completed major studies, research programs, conceptual analyses, and literature reviews, this is a good time to bring the work before a wider audience, especially educational policy makers and practitioners. . . .

Obviously, the field has no universal paradigm, and it would be useful to have a variety of approaches laid out for readers to compare and contrast and to draw implications for subsequent theory, research, and educational application. . . .

The major themes of the chapters should concern theoretical conceptions, substantive research, critical review, and especially educational implications and applications. Because policy implications require causal inferences, either speculative or confirmed causal relations should be made explicit; they might concern the impact of either inputs on educational environments or environments on outcomes.

The authors of chapters are free to define theoretically and operationally these and other domains and the variables within them, but they should make clear the assumed causal relations among them and, from these relations, determine how education might be improved. Instrumentation and methodology obviously should be mentioned for the reader to examine the justification of the empirical findings, but these are secondary and might be concisely summarized, and the reader should be referred to prior publications for details.

Two points should be added: First, I chose to solicit a large number of varied, concisely written chapters rather than a smaller number of highly detailed, lengthy treatments. Thus, the reader may examine the summary evidence, causal argument, and implications of a variety of approaches and can pursue any of these in greater detail through extensive references at the ends of the chapters.

Second, the response to my invitation was twice as great as I had expected and resulted in a sufficient number of chapters for two books of substantial length. I am grateful to Penelope Peterson, who agreed to collaborate in editing a companion volume that treats the teacher as a major factor in the learning environment. The second volume, entitled *Research on Teaching: Concepts, Findings, and Implications* is being published simultaneously in this same series.

OVERVIEW

Home Environments

It is often said that the influence of the home on learning is greater than that of the school. If this is so, in what specific ways does the home environment promote learning? Can the home environment be changed to increase learning? What are the optimal relations between home and school? How does television affect the child's development?

Kevin Marjoribanks, in "Family Environments," analyzes and sum-marizes sociopsychological research on the quality and quantity of interactions of parents and children and their influence on children's intellectual and emotional development. He shows the immense im-portance of the parental role in children's learning and suggests that school-based programs for parent education should be encouraged and that they should be firmly based on the accumulated research in this field.

Sara Lightfoot, in "Families and Schools," stresses the irony that these two institutions, which engage in complementary tasks, are often in conflict with one another and with the larger society. She argues that mothers and teachers, caught in devalued roles in our society, are asked to raise children in the service of individualistic and competitive goals they do not share. Only a profound redefinition of cultural norms, she concludes, will establish more productive relationships and more satisfying lives for those who choose to play these socializing roles.

Neal Gordon, in "Television and Learning," broadly reviews the popularity of television and the effects of this pervasive medium on learning, as well as its specific impact on such outcomes as aggression, prosocial behavior, passivity, and cognitive development. He con-cludes by pointing out a number of ways that parents and teachers can use television more effectively in promoting learning and encouraging positive attitudes and behavior.

Sociopsychological Environments

What social and psychological forces influence the social environ-ment of the classroom group and subgroups or teams within the class? How do aspects of environment, including both the climate or morale as well as social groupings within the class, affect learning? Also, can the schools as organizations and teachers within these organizations be encouraged to develop more productive and cohesive classroom envi-ronments? These and other questions are considered in this section.

Rudolf Moos, in "Educational Climates," reviews the history, scope, and current status of work in this field, including his own research program. He finds that three dimensions—relationships, personal growth or goal orientation, and system maintenance and change—characterize classroom and other social groups and that these con-structs and measures of them can serve as the empirical basis for socio-psychological diagnosis and educational intervention.

David Johnson and Roger Johnson, in "Cooperation, Competition, and Individualization," state that the ways teachers set goals and students interact with each other during instruction exert powerful effects on learning and socialization. The authors summarize the evidence on how the three modes of goal-interaction structures affect ten instructional outcomes and suggest ways that structures conducive to learning may be readily implemented in school classes.

Richard Slavin and David DeVries, in "Learning in Teams," summarize fourteen experimental studies of student teams in which members cooperate with one another but compete as teams with other teams within the class. Although there are some theoretical and practical variations in the ways the teams are formed, the overall results suggest a number of positive effects that team learning has on achievement, mutual concern, and intergroup relations and friendships.

Chad Ellett and Herbert Walberg, in "Principals' Competency, Environment, and Outcomes," review the development of paradigms for research on school administrators and the development of competency-based assessment and training programs. Using a theoretical model of the school organization, they trace the empirical correlations of principal competencies, the morale of the teaching staff, the social environments of classes, and learning outcomes

Instructional Environments

This section, which focuses on the impact of curriculum and instruction on the social environment and educational outcomes, raises such questions as the following: How have classroom environments in the nation changed during a recent period? Does the subject matter exert a characteristic influence on the way students perceive their classes? Can an environment-assessment approach illuminate aspects of curricular evaluation?

Wayne Welch, in "Curricular and Longitudinal Effects on Environments," analyzes changes in sampled schools in fifteen states over a four-year period. He interprets increases in formality, organization, and goal direction as a movement back to the traditional classroom from the activist-permissive innovations of an earlier period. These changes, perhaps surprisingly, are accompanied by increased student satisfaction.

William Kuert, in "Curricular Structure," surveys the research on the differences in student perceptions between classes in different subjects. A strikingly consistent, three-fold curriculum typology emerges: a convergence-divergence dimension distinguishes mathematics and English; a substance-syntax dimension separates science and social studies from mathematics and English; and an objectivity-subjectivity dimension characterizes the differences between science and social studies. From such an empirical typology, psychologists might ask curriculum workers if mathematics can be presented divergently or social studies more objectively or whether such features are completely inherent in the subject matter.

Colin Power and Richard Tisher, in "A Self-Paced Environment," document how innovative curricular materials in science affect student perceptions and classroom behaviors by using a sample of science classes in Australian schools. In contrast to many curriculum researchers who have restricted measurement of outcomes to conventional achievement tests and have revealed limited effects, Power and Tisher show sharp changes in cohesiveness, diversity, goal direction, humor, fact stating, and usage of materials while using the new materials. They also explore the links between teachers' values, students' perceptions, and cognitive and affective outcomes.

Barry Fraser, in "Evaluation of a Science-Based Curriculum," uses another Australian sample to determine the relative weights of aptitude, instruction, environment, and their interactions in accounting for such outcomes as interpreting information, critical thinking, and attitudes toward science and inquiry. As others have found, aptitude carries the greatest weight, but social environment also predicts outcomes, and environmental measures reveal important differences in student perceptions.

Russell Cort, in "A Social Studies Evaluation," characterizes the effects of *Man: A Course of Study,* a National Science Foundation-sponsored middle-school course, and of initial student characteristics and classroom process and climate measures on a variety of cognitive and affective outcomes. Student aptitude carries the greatest weight in accounting for outcomes, but environmental and course effects are also significant. Among other findings, experimental students absorbed a great deal of factual information and concepts and liked their classes better than control students did.

Gary Coles and Albert Chalupsky, in "Evaluation of Innovations," report on a three-year study involving 30,000 students. They examine the effect of different innovative educational experiences on ability and the achievement of basic skills. Test performance of students does not appear to be strongly or consistently related to innovative practices; performance is, however, related to time spent by students on the subject and to qualifications of teachers.

Robert Horwitz, in "Effects of the 'Open Classroom,'" reviews and summarizes the literature on the effects of "open" classrooms, also known as "informal" or "integrated-day" programs, as compared with traditional instructional approaches. The overall results on such criteria as academic achievement, self-concept, curiosity, and creativity suggest that open programs are more beneficial. There are, however, several mixed results and nonsignificant differences between open and traditional classrooms.

Joyce Epstein and James McPartland, in "Authority Structures," find that teachers in open schools allow students to work simultaneously on separate assignments, choose their own assignments, and study on their own for extended periods more frequently than do teachers in traditional schools. Students in open schools are found slightly more self-reliant and positive in their attitude toward teachers, but there is no difference, in their analysis, between groups in terms of academic performance.

Macroenvironments

Of the most promising curricular and teaching effects, which emerge as the closest correlates of achievement in the United States? How does achievement vary across census tracts in large cities and the fifty states and covary with socioeconomic indexes? And, are lower socioeconomic indexes found in some regions linked to poor educational services?

Richard Wolf, in "Achievement in the United States," analyzes the data from the International Study of Educational Achievement that bear upon learning environments and effects in this country. Home background and instructional time prove to be the strongest, most consistent correlates of achievement, but a number of other factors, such as measures of the learning environment and teacher preparation, are found to be educationally significant.

Daniel Levine, Chris Kukuk, and Jeannie Meyer, in "Poverty in Big Cities," analyze the relation of poverty indexes and middle-grade reading achievement in Chicago, Cincinnati, Cleveland, Houston, Kansas City, and St. Louis. From 50 to 90 percent of the variance in achievement can be accounted for by neighborhood socioeconomic and poverty indexes such as "percentage of households with 1.51 or more people per room," but "percentage of black households in the neighborhood" has little effect on school achievement beyond that accounted for by other indexes.

Herbert Walberg and Sue Rasher, in "Achievement in Fifty States," relate percentage of failure on the military draft test to population and education indexes. Smaller percentages of children in the public schools and larger pupil-teacher ratios are associated with higher test failures. The states fall into five geographical clusters, and those with populations characterized by lower socioeconomic status and higher percentages of minority-group members in the population also tend to have poorer educational services.

Research Methods

The chapters discussed above present a number of cases of statistically and educationally significant effects from which it seems reasonable to draw policy and practical implications. In my view, such effects and implications may be seriously considered because the authors employed one or more of the following: accumulation of findings and replications in programmatic research; careful planning of single large-scale studies on the basis of past research; and advanced measurement and analytic techniques in executing the methodological phases.

Even so, the authors themselves note various major or minor flaws in their research and point to more compelling designs and data that would prove useful in further validating, probing, or refuting their conclusions. Since the authors treat the substantive issues related to the topics of their respective chapters, it seems fitting that the last section address in general the methodological problems of educational-effects research and set out recommendations on relating theory, analysis, and evidence to educational policy and decision making for future work.

James McPartland and Nancy Karweit, in "Research on Educational Effects," treat two general methodological issues: the limited range of natural variation in the environments of the schools, and the problem of separating school from nonschool effects in the presence of overlap of the two types of effects, especially in nonexperimental research, that is, investigations with nonrandom assignment of students to educational treatments. Educational researchers often confront both confounding and limited variation in searching for effects. The authors set forth a number of design and analytic techniques that should help to overcome these problems.

Stephen Murray and Nick Smith, in "Causal Research on Teacher Training," describe a causal-modeling approach to the analysis of the effects of programs designed to help teachers improve classroom environments for learning. The approach calls for drawing the presumed causal paths of such factors as biographical characteristics, training variables, attitudinal gains, and classroom impacts. The empirical analysis assesses the paths and either validates the program or yields formative insights on improvements that appear to be required. Their chapter shows how researchers and practitioners can work together to gain a better mutual understanding of educational causes and effects.

CONCLUSION

Since the time of Plato and Aristotle, educational thinking about the role of the environment in learning has occasionally swung toward extremes. The last two decades provide examples: the optimistic hopes and claims of the 1960s seem to have been crushed in the 1970s. It has seemed to me, and it appears to be confirmed in the chapters that follow, that a moderate outlook is more constructive. Twenty-five centuries of humanistic insights may already have accumulated a large fund of balanced educational wisdom. Even so, each generation may have to rediscover old truths; indeed, each educator may need to come somewhat independently to certain conclusions and decisions by reflection and personal experience.

Whatever the amount of wisdom and the means of arriving at it, startling breakthroughs, as exemplified by the notable discoveries in agriculture, medicine, and engineering, are not likely to emerge in education. There are no panaceas; nothing will quickly double educational productivity. Progress is likely to come in small steps, and to achieve them will require enduring effort on the part of practitioners and research workers. The following chapters point out some of the steps that require continuing efforts on the part of both groups.

Science, in its completion and by some definitions, puts attempts to gain systematic knowledge in the public domain. In this respect, it can help educators by putting insights to empirical tests and by providing a record of the results that are open for examination, criticism, and exploration of possible implications. The record of research has its barren spots and inconsistencies, and what it suggests as educationally beneficial for one time or place may not be so for another; but, in the long run, it will be the best resource for making educational practice more systematic and productive.

PART ONE
Home Environments

1. Family Environments

Kevin Marjoribanks

Educators agree that family environment is one of the most important influences in the development of a child's cognitive abilities and
affective characteristics. Only now are we beginning to understand
how family environment affects behavior. Much of the research on
family environment has assessed learning environments in terms of
such global social-status indicators as occupation of the father and income of the family and such sibling constellation variables as size of
family and birth order. Gross variables have, however, accounted for
only small percentages of variance in measures of affective characteristics, and they have only low to moderate concurrent validities in relation to cognitive performance. At the same time, global classificatory
environmental variables have failed to reflect the dynamics of the
learning environments that families create for their children. As a result, much of the environmental research in education has had little
functional or diagnostic value for teachers, student counselors, or
educational administrators. This chapter examines family environments in terms of proximal sociopsychological variables that can be
manipulated in parent-teacher programs in an effort to make family
learning contexts more stimulating for children.

CONCEPTUAL FRAMEWORK

In developing a theory of personality, Murray suggested that, if the behavior of individuals is to be understood, then it is necessary to devise a method of analysis that "will lead to satisfactory dynamical formulations of external environments,"[1] and an environment should be classified by the kinds of benefits or harms that it provides. If, according to Murray, the environment is potentially harmful, individuals attempt to reject it or defend themselves against it. If the environment is potentially beneficial, individuals usually accept it and try to interact with it. The directional tendency of the environment implied in Murray's framework is known as the press of the environment. Each press is defined as having a qualitative aspect, which is the kind of effect that the environment has or might have upon an individual, and a quantitative aspect, which is the effect that the environment has on different individuals or on the same individual at different times. Murray distinguishes between an alpha press, "which is the press that actually exists, as far as scientific discovery can determine it," and a beta press, "which is the subject's own interpretation of the phenomena that he perceives."[2]

In his own research Murray concentrated on the beta press of family environments, and it was not until 1964, when Bloom and a number of his doctoral students examined the environmental correlates of cognitive and affective measures, that a definite "school" of research emerged to measure the alpha press of family environments.[3] In what might be designated the "Chicago School" of environmental research, Bloom defined the environment as conditions, forces, and external stimuli — whether physical, social, or intellectual — that provide a network surrounding, engulfing, and playing on the individual. While it is acknowledged that some individuals may resist the network, only extreme and rare individuals are likely to avoid or escape environmental forces completely. Thus, Bloom conceives of the environment as a shaping and a reinforcing force that acts upon the individual and suggests that "such a view of the environment reduces it for analytical purposes to those aspects of the environment which are related to a particular characteristic or set of characteristics."[4] That is, the total environment surrounding an individual may be described as being composed of a number of subenvironments, and, to understand the development of a particular characteristic, it becomes necessary to

identify in that subenvironment those press variables potentially related to the characteristic. Assessments of environmental press variables
have been made by defining the variables using sociopsychological
process characteristics. In interview schedules the process characteristics have generally been assessed by obtaining measures of particular
behaviors or attitudes within the family.

As the research of the Chicago School was progressing, another set
of investigators, loosely termed the "British School," emerged. Although the members of the British group did not consciously adopt
Murray's concept of the alpha press nor generally use Bloom's model
of subenvironments of press variables, their research can be interpreted in terms of those constructs. The studies examined here are considered to be representative of research into family environments undertaken by both schools.

THE CHICAGO SCHOOL

In the initial studies of the Chicago School, Dave[5] and Wolf[6] examined the relationship between family environment and measures of
academic achievement and intelligence, respectively. Both investigations used the same sixty children, thirty-two girls and twenty-eight
boys. The children averaged eleven years of age and were selected
from nineteen schools within one system in Illinois. Wolf used the
Henmon-Nelson Tests of Mental Ability to assess children's intelligence and identified three press variables that were hypothesized to be
related to the intelligence scores. The three press variables, "press for
achievement motivation," "press for language," and "provisions for
general learning," were defined by thirteen process characteristics.
The characteristics formed the framework for the construction of a
semistructured interview schedule that was used to elicit responses
from the mothers of the children in the sample. Each process characteristic was rated on a seven-point scale and a score for each press variable was computed by totaling the ratings on the relevant process
characteristics. When the three press variables were combined into a
predictor set, they were associated with 49 percent of the variance in
the intelligence test scores.

In Dave's study the academic achievement of the children was assessed using the *Metropolitan Achievement Tests*. Out of the total set
of conditions and processes that constitute family environment, Dave

identified a specific component, which was labeled "educational environment of the family." The educational environment was defined by six press variables: "achievement press," "language models," "academic guidance," "activeness of the family," "intellectuality in the home," and "work habits in the family." These variables were defined by twenty-one process characteristics and a nine-point rating scale was devised for each characteristic. Scores on the six press variables were obtained by averaging the ratings on the relevant process characteristics, and an index of the educational environment of the family was computed by totaling the scores on the six press variables. When the variables were combined into a predictor set, they had different relations with performance in different academic subjects. For example, the environment was related to over 50 percent of the variance in scores for solving problems in arithmetic, reading, and word knowledge, but only to 31 percent of the variance in arithmetic computation scores (see Table 1-1). The order of importance of the predictability of the six press variables also differed from subject to subject. In the case of word knowledge and reading, for example, achievement press was the most important variable in a stepwise regression analysis, while for problem solving in arithmetic the most important variable was intellectuality in the home. Thus, as Dave suggests, while factor analysis indicates that less than six press variables might be quite sufficient for the measurement of the educational environment of the family, the results show that "if one is interested in the prediction of subjectwise achievement, one might even find more than six variables desirable on the environmental measure, so that different combinations of variables measured by the same instrument could be used for the optimal prediction of specific-subject achievement."[7]

The family environment measure devised by Dave has been used in other cultural settings. Dyer, for example, examined the family environments of sixty eleven-year-old children from Port of Spain, Trinidad.[8] The environment measure was associated with a large percentage of the variance in academic achievement scores and generally related moderately to intelligence. In a study of sixty eight-year-old Irish children from a socially disadvantaged area of Dublin, Kellaghan found that the Dave measure accounted for moderate to large percentages of the variances in scores on tests of arithmetic, Irish reading, and English reading, but associated with less of the variance in intelligence scores.[9]

Differing Mental Abilities

In studies of Canadian children, Mosychuk[10] and I[11] moved beyond examining global intelligence scores and investigated the relationship between family environment and sets of ability measures. Mosychuk studied the scores on the *Wechsler Intelligence Scale for Children* (WISC) for a hundred ten-year-old boys from Edmonton. A schedule that assessed ten different aspects of the family environment was used in interviews with mothers. The ten process characteristics were labeled: "academic and vocational aspirations and expectations of parents," "knowledge of, and interest in, the child's academic and intellectual development," "material and organizational opportunities for the use and development of language," "quality of language in the home," "female dominance in child rearing," "planfulness, purposefulness, and harmony in the home," "dependency-fostering overprotection," "authoritarian home," "interaction with physical environment," and "opportunity for, and emphasis on, initiating and carrying through tasks." Factor analysis of the scores on the ten measures produced four factors that may be considered as press variables: "aspirations-planfulness-harmony," "authoritarian-overprotective," "activity-environmental interaction," and "female language." The first environmental factor had moderate concurrent validities in relation to the WISC verbal, performance, and full intelligence scores, while the other press variables had low to negligible relation to the WISC scores. When the ten WISC subtest scores were further analyzed, the four factors that emerged were defined as: "reasoning," "general memory," "verbal-symbolic," and "perceptual-motor-spatial." A significant canonical correlation of .57 was obtained between the four press variables and the four WISC factor scores.

In a study of eleven-year-old boys from southern Ontario, I examined the relations between the family environment and scores on tests of verbal, number, spatial, and reasoning ability. Approximately five hundred boys were tested, using first the *California Test of Mental Maturity* and then the *SRA Primary Mental Abilities Test* (1962, revised edition). The first test-taking situation was used to establish examiner-examinee rapport, to ensure that all the boys were able to understand the test instructions, and to establish as far as possible uniform test-taking situations. The boys were assigned to two categories, one classified as middle social status and the other as lower social status. The social-status classification was based on an equally weighted

combination of the occupation of the head of the household and a rating of his (or her) education. As far as possible, two parallel pools of
boys were formed. The purpose of the substitute pool was to provide a
set of alternate families that could be included in the study if families
from the first pool did not agree to participate. The final sample consisted of ninety boys and their parents classified as middle social status
and ninety-five classified as lower social status. Both parents from
each family participated in the interviewing sessions. The family environment schedule used in the interviews assessed eight variables identified as press for achievement, intellectuality, activeness, independence, English, a second language, and father or mother dominance.
In general, the press variables had moderate to high concurrent validities in relation to verbal and number abilities, low to moderate concurrent validity for reasoning ability, and low to negligible validity for
the spatial scores. For example, in regression models the eight variables were associated with approximately 50 percent of the variance in
verbal and number ability scores and 16 percent of the variance in
reasoning scores, while the relationship to spatial ability was not
significant.

Canonical correlations were computed between the four mental
ability scores and measures of both the global environment variables
and the eight press variables.[12] The first two canonical correlations
were significant, and, when the relations between the environment
measures, the mental abilities, and the two canonical variates were
plotted, it was found that, with respect to the first canonical variate,
verbal and number abilities and, to a lesser extent, reasoning ability
were more closely associated with the environmental press variables
than spatial ability.[13]

After removing the variance of the first canonical variate from predictors and criteria, the emphasis on the second variate revealed that
the social-status indicators and press variables were significantly related to differentially developed abilities. High ratings on press for English, father's occupation, press for a second language, and, to a lesser
extent, press for activeness and father dominance were associated on
the second variate with high scores on verbal, reasoning, and spatial
abilities, but with lower scores where number ability was concerned.
The two-language press scales reflected, in particular, a measure of
parent-son interaction in activities such as reading, conversations after
school and during meals, purposeful teaching of vocabulary, and the
correction of syntactical errors in language use. The press for active-

ness scale measured parent-son involvement in both academic and nonacademic situations, while the father dominance scale gauged the father's involvement in a son's activities.

The second canonical variate suggests, therefore, that the differential development of verbal, reasoning, and spatial abilities in relation to number ability might be facilitated in homes characterized by high parent-son interaction. The result is consistent with Bing's finding that mothers of high-verbal boys (boys who had high-verbal scores in relation to number and spatial ones) in comparison to mothers of low-verbal boys provided more stimulation in early childhood, were more critical of poor academic achievement, provided more storybooks, and let the boy take a greater part in conversations at mealtime.[14] Bing suggested that, for boys, differential verbal ability is fostered by a close relation with a demanding, intrusive mother. Honzik also found that a close mother-son relationship related significantly to the development of boys' verbal ability.[15] For optimal verbal ability, Honzik proposes that a boy first needs a close relation with a mother, followed by a close relationship with a male model who not only achieved himself but who is also concerned about his son's achievement. The results of my study suggest that an overinvolvement with parents may impede the relative development of divergent number ability.[16] Similarly, Bing found that divergent number ability was fostered in homes that allowed boys a considerable amount of uninterrupted free time and encouraged independent experimentation. Ferguson and Maccoby found, in addition, that boys with higher number ability (in relation to verbal and spatial abilities) seem to have been discouraged from being overly dependent on their parents.[17] Thus it is possible that environmental press variables may encourage the development of some abilities and leave others relatively underdeveloped.

The results of studies of the Chicago School that have been discussed are summarized in Table 1-1. All of the studies indicated that it was possible to move beyond the use of global classificatory family environment variables, such as social-status indicators and family structure variables, and to assess the family environment using sociopsychological press variables that have high predictive validity in relation to children's cognitive performance. All of the studies discussed so far are limited to an analysis of the correlates of cognitive measures, but the environmental correlates of affective characteristics were also examined by the Chicago School.

Table 1-1

**Relations between family environment and measures of
cognitive performance: The "Chicago School"**

Study	Sample	Criterion measures	Multiple R	$100R^2$
Dave (1963)	Eleven-year-olds in Illinois (N = 32 girls, 28 boys)	*Metropolitan Achievement Battery*		
		Word knowledge	.79	62.2
		Reading	.73	53.1
		Arithmetic problem solving	.71	50.3
		Word discrimination	.69	48.1
		Language	.68	46.8
		Spelling	.61	37.2
		Arithmetic computation	.56	30.9
Wolf (1964)	Eleven-year-olds in Illinois (N = 32 girls, 28 boys)	*Henmon-Nelson Test* Intelligence	.70	49.0
Dyer (1967)	Eleven-year-olds in Trinidad (N = 15 girls, 15 boys of middle social status)	*Iowa Test of Basic Skills* Total achievement	.67	44.9
		Lorge-Thorndike Test		
		Nonverbal ability	.32	10.2
		Verbal ability	.11[a]	1.2
	Eleven-year-olds in Trinidad (N = 15 girls, 15 boys of lower social status)	*Iowa Test of Basic Skills* Total achievement	.78	60.8
		Lorge-Thorndike Test		
		Nonverbal ability	.51	26.0
		Verbal ability	.39	15.2
Kellaghan (1977)	Eight-year-olds in Dublin (N = 30 boys, 30 girls)	*Stanford-Binet Scale* Intelligence	.51	26.0
		Cattell Tests		
		Culture-fair ability	.35	12.3
		Nonculture-fair intelligence	.50	25.0
		Marino Word Reading	.63	39.7
		Irish Word Recognition	.60	36.0
		Schonell Mechanical Arithmetic	.55	30.3
Mosychuk (1969)	Eleven-year-olds in Edmonton (N = 100 boys)	*WISC*[b]		
		Verbal	.39	15.2
		Performance	.32	10.2
		Total	.42	17.6

Table 1-1 *(continued)*

Relations between family environment and measures of cognitive performance: The "Chicago School"

Study	Sample	Criterion measures	Multiple R	$100R^2$
Marjoribanks (1972)	Eleven-year-olds in southern Ontario (N = 185 boys)	*SRA Primary Abilities*		
		Verbal	.71	50.4
		Number	.71	50.4
		Spatial	.26[a]	6.7
		Reasoning	.40	16.0
		Total score	.72	51.8

[a]Correlations not significant at .05 level.

[b]Only the relations between one environmental press variable and the WISC scores have been shown.

Sources: Ravindrakumar Dave, "The Identification and Measurement of Environmental Process Variables That Are Related to Educational Achievement," unpub. diss., University of Chicago, 1963; Patrick B. Dyer, "Home Environment and Achievement in Trinidad," unpub. diss., University of Alberta, 1967; Thomas Kellaghan, "Relationships between Home Environment and Scholastic Behavior in a Disadvantaged Population," *Journal of Educational Psychology* 69 (1977): 754-760; Kevin Marjoribanks, "Environmental, Social Class, and Mental Abilities," *Journal of Educational Psychology* 63 (1972): 103-109; Harry Mosychuk, "Differential Home Environments and Mental Ability Patterns," unpub. diss., University of Alberta, 1969; Richard M. Wolf, "The Identification and Measurement of Environmental Process Variables Related to Intelligence," unpub. diss., University of Chicago, 1964.

Affective Characteristics and Cognitive Performance

Weiss investigated the relations between family environment and measures of achievement motivation and self-esteem for twenty-seven boys and twenty-nine girls from a community in Illinois.[18] The children averaged approximately eleven years of age. The subenvironment for achievement motivation was defined by three press variables: "generation of standards of excellence and expectations," "independence training," and "parental approval." The subenvironment for self-esteem, in turn, was assessed by "parental acceptance," "evaluation of child," and "opportunities for self-enhancement." The three measures used to assess each of the affective characteristics were a self-report, a rating by the child's current teacher, and a projective technique.

The interview schedule for parents contained three categories of questions: those asked of the mother alone, those asked of the father alone, and those asked of the mother and father together. Rating scales were developed for each question so that the verbal responses could be translated into scores. The results indicated that the relations between the environment and affective measures depended upon the criterion used (see Table 1-2). As Weiss suggests, by extending the range of individual characteristics studied by the Chicago School from the cognitive area to the affective domain, the study supports "the thesis that a sub-set of the total environment can be identified and measured for individual personality characteristics."[19]

Table 1-2

**Relations between family environment and measures of
affective characteristics: The "Chicago School"**

Study	Sample	Criterion measures	Multiple R	$100R^2$
Weiss (1969)[b]	Eleven-year-olds in Illinois (N = 29 girls, 27 boys)	Achievement motivation		
		Self-report		
		Girls	.27[a]	7.3
		Boys	.57[a]	32.5
		Teacher rating		
		Girls	.54[a]	29.2
		Boys	.66	43.6
		Projective technique		
		Girls	.70	49.0
		Boys	.81	65.6
		Self-esteem		
		Self-report		
		Girls	.72	51.8
		Boys	.47[a]	22.1
		Teacher rating		
		Girls	.79	62.4
		Boys	.80	64.0
		Projective technique		
		Girls	.43[a]	18.5
		Boys	.65	42.3
Keeves (1972)	Eleven- and twelve-year-olds in Australia; (N = 215)	Achievement		
		Mathematics	.58	33.6
		Science	.59	34.8

Table 1-2 *(continued)*

**Relations between family environment and measures of
affective characteristics: The "Chicago School"**

Study	Sample	Criterion measures	Multiple R	$100R^2$
		Attitudes		
		Toward mathematics	.29	8.4
		Toward science	.14	2.0
Marjoribanks	Twelve-year-olds	*Otis Intermediate Test*		
(1978)	in Australia;	Intelligence		
	(N = 120 girls,	Girls	.33	10.9
	130 boys)	Boys	.43	18.5
		Enthusiasm for school		
		Girls	.19[a]	3.8
		Boys	.33	10.9
		Academic self-concept		
		Girls	.36	13.2
		Boys	.24[a]	5.9
		Friendliness of school		
		Girls	.25[a]	6.3
		Boys	.31[a]	9.4
		Dislike for disruptive behavior		
		Girls	.23[a]	5.4
		Boys	.33	11.1
		Educational and occupational aspirations		
		Girls	.36	13.3
		Boys	.44	19.4
		Commitment to school		
		Girls	.36	12.7
		Boys	.28[a]	7.7
		Academic orientation		
		Girls	.16[a]	2.7
		Boys	.25[a]	7.3

[a]Correlations not significant at .05 level.
[b]Correlations in the Weiss study have been corrected for unreliability of measures.

Sources: John P. Keeves, *Educational Environment and Student Achievement* (Stockholm: Almqvist and Wiksell, 1972); Kevin Marjoribanks, "Family and School Environmental Correlates of School-Related Affective Characteristics: An Australian Study," *Journal of Social Psychology,* in press; Joel Weiss, "The Identification and Measurement of Home Environmental Factors Related to Achievement Motivation and Self-Esteem," unpub. diss., University of Chicago, 1969.

Two studies of Australian children, one done by Keeves[20] and the other by me,[21] have examined relations between the family environment and measures of both cognitive and affective characteristics. Using a simple random sample of 242 children in their final year of elementary school, Keeves examined the environmental correlates of children's scientific and mathematical achievement and their attitudes toward science and mathematics. The family environment was assessed when the children were in their final year of elementary school and in their first year of secondary school. The measures of achievement and attitude were administered at the end of the first year of secondary school. Five attitudinal and four process variables were assessed in the family environment schedule. The attitudinal variables were: "father's and mother's attitudes toward child's present education," "father's and mother's ambitions for the child's future education and occupation," and "parents' hopes and aspirations for themselves." The process variables were: "relations between home and school," "use of books and library facilities," "provision of help with formal schoolwork," and "arrangements made for tackling home assignments." Principal component analysis was used to construct an environmental press score for each of the two general family dimensions. The results (see Table 1-2) indicated that, when attitudinal and process variables were combined into a predictor set, they were moderately related to achievement in science and mathematics and had lower concurrent validity in relation to the attitude scores.

In a study of 550 twelve-year-old Australian children, I examined the environmental correlates of intelligence scores and measures of school-related affective characteristics.[22] Family environment data were collected from interviews with the parents of 250 children, 130 boys and 120 girls. Where possible, two parallel pools of families, based on social-status background, were formed. The purpose of the substitute pool was to provide a set of alternate families that could be used in the study if families from the first pool did not agree to participate. Family environment was assessed using six press variables: "parents' expectations for the child," "expectations for themselves," "concern for the use of language within the family," "reinforcement of educational expectations," "knowledge of the child's educational progress," and "family involvement in educational activities." The interview schedule was an adaptation of a previous instrument.[23] Besides the effort to obtain a measure of the intensity of the present family environment, the schedule attempted to gain a measure of the cumulative nature of the environment. That is, besides asking how much education parents expected the child to receive, the schedule also asked how long the expectations had been held. Factor-scaling techniques were used to examine the structure of the six press variables.[24] Scores on the items that made up each of the variables were factor analyzed using principal component analysis. After eliminating items affected by other factors, where factor loading was less than .40, the remaining items were refactored, producing six factor scales that all had theta reliability estimates greater than .80. Measures constructed by Barker Lunn[25] and by Sumner and Warburton[26] were used to assess children's school-related affective characteristics. Seven factors were generated from a principal component analysis of the responses to the schedules, and they had theta reliabilities ranging from .70 to .87. The seven affective characteristics were identified as enthusiasm for school, academic self-concept, perceived friendliness of school, dislike for disruptive behavior, educational and occupational aspirations, commitment to school, and academic orientation. Factor scores on the seven characteristics were computed for each child. The general intellectual ability of the children was also measured using the *Otis Intermediate Test*. When the environment variables were combined into a predictor set, they were associated with a low percentage of the variance in scores of intellectual ability, and they had differential relations with the affective measures (see Table 1-2).

The findings from the studies of the Chicago School reflected in Tables 1-1 and 1-2 show that, in general, the environment measures have moderate to high concurrent validity in relation to academic achievement, low to moderate concurrent validity in relation to intelligence test scores, and negligible to moderate relationships when compared with measures of affective characteristics. As Bloom suggests, there have been some major exceptions in the predictive power of some measures, "especially with personality and attitudinal measures. We still have much to learn about how to measure some environments — and some characteristics."[27]

THE BRITISH SCHOOL

The results of studies in British settings are presented in Table 1-3, and they show that family environment measures are moderately rela-

Table 1-3

Relations between family environment and measures of cognitive
performance and affective characteristics: The "British School"

Study	Sample	Family environment measures	Criterion measures	Multiple R	$100R^2$
Fraser (1959)	Twelve- to fifteen-year-olds in Aberdeen, Scotland (N = 427)	Reading habits of family	Intelligence	.28	7.8
			Achievement	.33	10.9
		Parents' attitudes toward education and future occupation of child	Intelligence	.30	9.0
			Achievement	.39	15.2
		Impression of home environment	Intelligence	.39	15.2
			Achievement	.46	21.2
Wiseman (1967)	Eleven-year-olds in Manchester, England (N = 186)	Preferred age of leaving school	Total achievement[a]	.41	16.8
		Child's reading		.34	11.6
		Parents members of library		.34	11.6
		Prefer grammar school		.31	9.6
		Whether parents read		.29	8.4
		Number of books in home		.27	7.3
		Complaints against teacher		-.24	5.8
Peaker	Junior cohort (seven-year-olds) in England (N = 1,053)	Total family environment score	Reading		
			Girls	.46	22.0
			Boys	.51	26.0
	Middle cohort (eight-year-olds) in England (N = 1,016)	Total family environment score	Reading		
			Girls	.44	10.0
			Boys	.45	20.0
	Senior cohort (eleven-year-olds) in England (N = 1,023)	Total family environment score	Reading		
			Girls	.57	32.0
			Boys	.67	45.0
Marjoribanks (1976)	Plowden senior cohort (eleven-to fifteen-year-olds) in England (N = 396 girls, 383 boys)	Family environment measured during first survey	Intelligence		
			Girls	.30	9.0
			Boys	.34	11.6
			English		
			Girls	.49	24.0
			Boys	.45	20.3

Table 1-3 *(continued)*

Relations between family environment and measures of cognitive
performance and affective characteristics: The "British School"

Study	Sample	Family environment measures	Criterion measures	Multiple R	$100R^2$
			Mathematics		
			Girls	.50	25.0
			Boys	.45	20.3
			Aspirations		
			Girls	.48	23.0
			Boys	.45	20.3
			Locus of control		
			Girls	.23	5.3
			Boys	.21	4.4
		Family environment	Intelligence		
		measured during	Girls	.27	7.3
		second survey	Boys	.29	8.4
			English		
			Girls	.48	23.0
			Boys	.45	20.3
			Mathematics		
			Girls	.46	21.2
			Boys	.45	20.3
			Aspirations		
			Girls	.45	20.3
			Boys	.46	21.2
			Locus of control		
			Girls	.25	6.3
			Boys	.26	6.8

ᵃTotal achievement represents a combination of scores for intelligence, arithmetic, and English.

Note: All correlations significant beyond the .05 level.

Sources: Elizabeth Fraser, *Home Environment and the School* (London: University of London Press, 1959); Stephan Wiseman, "The Manchester Survey," in *Children and Their Primary Schools,* ed. Bridget Plowden (London: H.M. Stationery Office, 1967), II, 347-400; Gilbert F. Peaker, "The Regression Analysis of the National Survey," in *Children and Their Primary Schools,* ed. Plowden, II, 179-221; Kevin Marjoribanks, "Attitudinal Orientations and Cognitive Functioning among Adolescents: A Further Study," *Educational Research and Perspectives* 3 (1976): 3-16.

ted to cognitive performance. The academic achievement measure used in the study by Fraser was a combined assessment of children's performance during secondary school, while the intelligence test score was obtained during the children's last year in elementary school. The family environment schedule assessed the cultural, material, motivational, and emotional aspects of the children's homes, but the environment schedule was not as refined and detailed as those developed by the Chicago School.[28] In Wiseman's investigation the children were selected from twenty-two elementary schools in Manchester, England. In Table 1-3 the relations represent averages of correlations between the family environments of children, assessed when they were ten years old, and measures of cognitive performance obtained when the children were seven, eight, nine, and ten years old. Only the behavior or attitude items from the family environment schedule that related most strongly with the cognitive scores are presented. As Wiseman indicates, "what is very significant is the presence in the 'top seven' of the four variables dealing with reading, with average correlations with all tests ranging from .272 to .341, and an overall average of .312."[29]

In the Plowden survey, *Children and Their Primary Schools,* the environmental correlates of cognitive performance were examined for three age cohorts of a national sample of English children.[30] The sampling procedure was divided into two stages. First, a stratified random sample taken from all types of government-supported elementary schools in England resulted in the selection of 173 schools. Then a systematic selection of children from the schools produced three age cohorts, each containing approximately a thousand children. The children in the senior cohort averaged approximately eleven years of age; those in the middle cohort, eight; and those in the junior cohort, seven. From an analysis of eighty attitude and behavior items, fourteen press variables were identified by factor analysis. For the results shown in Table 1-3, the press variables were combined into a predictor set in a multiple regression mode.[31]

Four years after the original Plowden survey, the children and their families were surveyed again.[32] In an analysis of the data from the senior cohort, which included 396 girls and 383 boys and where the average age was by then fifteen years old, I examined the relationship between family environment, measured during both surveys, and assessments of the cognitive and affective characteristics of the children made during the second survey.[33] In the latter survey, cognitive performance was measured using the *Alice Heim General Intelligence Test* (AH4), the *Watts-Vernon English Comprehension Test,* and the *Vernon Graded Mathematics Test.* Two scales constructed by the National Foundation for Educational Research were used to measure the children's educational and occupational aspirations and their locus of control (sense of control over the environment).

In both the Plowden survey and the follow-up study, a structured interview schedule was used to gather information about the family environments of the children. In my study, factor scaling was used to construct environmental press variables. Eight variables were identified from the first survey, and nine from the second survey. Both sets of press variables were refactored, and in each case the variables were weighted heavily toward general factors that had theta reliabilities of approximately .85. Two family environment scores for each child were obtained by totaling the scores on the press variables that made up the two general factors. The correlations in Table 1-3 show that the family environment measures were associated with greater variance in the achievement scores than in the intelligence test scores, which supports the Chicago School's findings. Also, the environment related to only a low to moderate percentage of the variance in the locus of control scores but a moderate to large percentage of the variance in aspiration scores. In my study of Australian children, I also found that, from a set of affective characteristics, children's aspirations were most strongly related to family environment (see Table 1-2).[34]

VALIDITY OF THE SUBENVIRONMENTAL APPROACH

In many of the studies that have adopted a subenvironmental approach to environmental research, the construct validities of the environmental measures have been examined by testing the proposition that the measure of the family or subenvironment accounts for more of the variance in cognitive and affective characteristics than other environmental measures, such as social-status characteristics. Generally, it has been found that the global social measures are relatively poor predictors of children's characteristics when compared with the more sensitive parent interview measures of the family environment. Such an interpretation of the relation between social status, family environment, and children's cognitive and affective characteristics has been subjected to trenchant criticism.[35] The criticism proposes that in

many of the studies the concept of social class has been trivialized to
the point where differences in parental attitude are considered separate factors rather than integral parts of the work and community situation of children. With the data from the senior Plowden cohort, I
constructed regression surfaces to investigate relations between social
status, family environment, and measures of children's cognitive and
affective characteristics.[36] Social status was assessed by an equally
weighted composite involving education of the father, occupation of
the father, and income of the family. The family environment scores
that were assessed during the Plowden survey and in the follow-up
study were combined to provide a measure of the cumulative nature of
the environment.

Regression surfaces were plotted using raw regression weights generated from regression models of the form: $Z = aX + bY + $ constant,
where X and Y represent measures of social status and family environment, respectively, and Z represents measures of children's cognitive and affective characteristics assessed during the follow-up survey.
It was found that the two-term equations accounted for as much significant variance in the cognitive and affective measures as complex
equations containing quadratic terms (to test for nonlinearity) and
product terms (to test for interactions). In these more complex models
the raw regression weights between the performance scores and the
quadratic and product predictor terms were not significant. The results indicated that at different environmental levels, the social status
of boys' families was not related directly to performance scores while,
for girls, there were significant direct relations between social status
and performance at each environmental level. From these findings
comes the proposition that the social status of families may have two
separate influences on the cognitive and affective characteristics of
children. First, there is a "contextual effect" in which social status influences the performances of children through its effect on the sociopsychological learning environment that a family creates for its children. The second influence may be labeled the "individual effect" of
social status, which is assessed by the remaining direct effect on children's performances after accounting for the intervening family environment variables. It is possible that the "individual effect" reflects an
interpretation by children of the social-status position of their family
that leads children to adapt their behaviors and performances. My
analysis suggests that, by adolescence, the cognitive and affective

characteristics of boys are related to the contextual effect of social status but not related directly to the individual effect, while girls are influenced directly by both the contextual and individual effects.

The present review of the relations between the family environment and measures of children's performances has shown that it is possible to move beyond the use of gross classificatory variables in defining the family environment by using refined press variables. But my regression surface analysis also suggests that family environment research might become more sensitive and be further enriched if interrelationships between global environment variables and sociopsychological measures are investigated in greater detail.[37] That is, as Halsey suggests,

The association of social class with educational achievement will not be explained by a theory or eliminated by a policy which falls short of including changes in public support for learning in the family and neighborhood, the training of teachers, the production of relevant curriculum, the fostering of parental participation, the raising of standards of housing and employment prospects, and, above all, the allocation of educational resources.[38]

IMPLICATIONS FOR EDUCATORS

The sociopsychological process variables that have been identified in the Chicago and British Schools may be classified into two interrelated learning environments: the technical environment and the affective environment.[39] The technical environment, on the one hand, includes those situations in which children learn items of information, construct systems of thought that organize the information, and develop their linguistic, intellective, and motor skills. This environment may be defined by proximal measures such as press for language and press for intellectuality. From socialization within the affective environment, on the other hand, children develop commitments to different sets of beliefs, values, and attitudes. The affective context may be assessed by variables such as press for achievement motivation and press for independence. Many parent-teacher involvement programs and parent intervention projects have had minimal success in changing children's cognitive performance because they have attempted to change only the affective contexts of families. There has been little attempt to influence both the affective and the technical environments. As the Bullock report on the teaching of reading and other uses of English in British schools suggests, if children are to acquire as wide a range as possible of the uses of language, and, in particular, to learn the dialect of the classroom, then parents must be helped to understand the complex process of language development in their children. In the classroom and in the family,

it has to be recognized that increasing the opportunities for talk with a sympathetic adult will not necessarily develop more complex language forms in children who are unaccustomed to using them. . . . [S]ituations have to be created from which such uses are bound to emerge. The person who plans these situations must have a knowledge of how language works, and the ability to appraise children's language and operate on it accordingly.[40]

If parent-teacher programs are to have meaningful cognitive benefits for the child, educators will need to assist parents in acquiring skills that can be used to create more stimulating technical and affective socialization contexts for their children. Walberg, Bole, and Waxman have provided one of the few evaluations of a program that was aimed at helping parents create conditions in the home to facilitate academic achievement.[41] The evaluation examined the effects, over a one-year period, of an intensified parenting program, initiated and sustained by school staff, on the reading achievement scores of black, inner-city children from a large elementary school in Chicago. A joint school staff-parent steering committee formulated seven goals that were directed at both the technical and affective socialization practices of families. The goals were:

to increase parents' desire to aid children in achieving; to acquaint parents with the means of determining what the child is doing; to increase parents' awareness of the reading process; to establish and/or improve parent-school-community relations; to develop enthusiasm on the part of parents and children toward higher achievement; to work continuously to create a classroom atmosphere that fosters enthusiasm and a feeling that "learning is fun"; and to evaluate the ability of this program as to its effectiveness in reading achievement.[42]

It was found that classes where parents were intensively involved in the program gained an estimated 1.1 grade equivalents in reading achievement, while classes where parents were less intensively involved gained only .5 grade equivalents.

The studies reviewed in this chapter suggest that there exists a set of proximal family environment variables that can be manipulated by educators and parents to promote a child's cognitive and affective development. If parent involvement programs are to be successful, however, educators will have to help parents create environments that encourage technical and affective learning. Educators involved in such programs will need not only a thorough understanding of the structures of the cognitive, linguistic, and affective development of children but also an increasing familiarity with the dynamics of the sociopsychological forces operating within families.

NOTES

1. Henry A. Murray, *Explorations in Personality* (Oxford, Eng.: Oxford University Press, 1938), 16.

2. *Ibid.*, 122.

3. Benjamin S. Bloom, *Stability and Change in Human Characteristics* (New York: Wiley, 1964).

4. *Ibid.*, 187.

5. Ravindrakumar Dave, "The Identification and Measurement of Environmental Process Variables That Are Related to Educational Achievement," unpub. diss., University of Chicago, 1963.

6. Richard M. Wolf, "The Identification and Measurement of Environmental Process Variables Related to Intelligence," unpub. diss., University of Chicago, 1964.

7. Dave, "Identification and Measurement of Environmental Process Variables That Are Related to Educational Achievement," 86.

8. Patrick B. Dyer, "Home Environment and Achievement in Trinidad," unpub. diss., University of Alberta, 1967.

9. Thomas Kellaghan, "Relationships between Home Environment and Scholastic Behavior in a Disadvantaged Population," *Journal of Educational Psychology* 69 (1977): 754-760.

10. Harry Mosychuk. "Differential Home Environments and Mental Ability Patterns," unpub. diss., University of Alberta, 1969.

11. Kevin Marjoribanks, "Environment, Social Class and Mental Abilities," *Journal of Educational Psychology* 63 (1972): 103-109.

12. *Id.* "Another View of the Relation of Environment to Mental Abilities," *ibid.*, 66 (1974): 460-463.

13. Herbert J. Walberg and Kevin Marjoribanks, "Differential Mental Abilities and Home Environment: A Canonical Analysis," *Developmental Psychology* 9 (1973): 363-368.

14. Elizabeth Bing, "Effect of Childrearing Practices on Development of Differential Cognitive Abilities," *Child Development* 34 (1963): 631-648.

15. Marjorie P. Honzik, "Environmental Correlates of Mental Growth: Prediction from the Family Setting at 21 Months," *ibid.*, 38 (1967): 337-364.

16. Marjoribanks, "Another View of the Relation of Environment to Mental Abilities."

17. Lucy Ferguson and Eleanor Maccoby, "Interpersonal Correlates of Differential Abilities," *Child Development* 37 (1966): 549-571.

18. Joel Weiss, "The Identification and Measurement of Home Environmental Factors Related to Achievement Motivation and Self-Esteem," unpub. diss., University of Chicago, 1969.

19. *Id.*, "The Identification and Measurement of Home Environmental Factors Related to Achievement Motivation and Self-Esteem," in *Environments for Learning,* ed. Kevin Marjoribanks (London: National Foundation for Educational Research in England and Wales, 1974), 147.

20. John P. Keeves, *Educational Environment and Student Achievement* (Stockholm: Almqvist and Wiksell, 1972).

21. Kevin Marjoribanks, "Family and School Environmental Correlates of School-Related Affective Characteristics: An Australian Study," *Journal of Social Psychology,* in press.

22. *Ibid.*

23. *Id.*, "Environment, Social Class and Mental Abilities."

24. David J. Armor, "Theta Reliability and Factor Scaling," in *Sociological Methodology,* ed. Herbert L. Costner (San Francisco: Jossey-Bass, 1972), 17-50.

25. Joan Barker Lunn, "The Development of Scales to Measure Junior School Children's Attitudes," *British Journal of Educational Psychology* 39 (1969): 64-71; *id., Streaming in the Primary School* (London: National Foundation for Educational Research in England and Wales, 1970).

26. Raymond Sumner and Frank Warburton, *Achievement in Secondary School: Attitudes, Personality and School Success* (London: National Foundation for Educational Research in England and Wales, 1972).

27. Benjamin S. Bloom, "Preface," in *Environments for Learning,* ed. Marjoribanks, 10.

28. Elizabeth Fraser, *Home Environment and the School* (London: University of London Press, 1959).

29. Stephan Wiseman, "The Manchester Survey," in *Children and Their Primary Schools: A Report of the Central Advisory Council for Education,* Volumes I and II, ed. Bridget Plowden (London: H. M. Stationery Office, 1967), II, 347-400.

30. *Children and Their Primary Schools,* ed. Plowden.

31. Gilbert F. Peaker, "The Regression Analysis of the National Survey," *ibid.*, II, 179-221.

32. *Id., The Plowden Children Four Years Later* (London: National Foundation for Educational Research in England and Wales, 1971).

33. Kevin Marjoribanks, "Attitudinal Orientations and Cognitive Functioning among Adolescents: A Further Study," in *Environments for Learning,* ed. *id.*

34. *Id.*, "Family and School Environmental Correlates of School-Related Affective Characteristics."

35. Basil Bernstein and Brian Davies, "Some Sociological Comments on Plowden," in *Persectives on Plowden,* ed. Richard S. Peters (London: Routledge and Kegan Paul, 1969), 55-83; R. W. Connell, "Class Structure and Personal Socialisation," in *Socialisation in Australia,* ed. Frederick J. Hunt (Sydney: Angus and Robertson, 1972), 38-66; *id.*, "The Causes of Educational Inequality: Further Observations," *Australian and New Zealand Journal of Sociology* 10 (1974): 186-189; A. H. Halsey, "Sociology and the Equality Debate," *Oxford Review of Education* 1 (1975): 9-23.

36. Kevin Marjoribanks, "Educational Deprivation Thesis: A Further Analysis," *Australian and New Zealand Journal of Sociology* 13 (1977): 12-17.

37. *Ibid.*

38. Halsey, "Sociology and the Equality Debate," 17.

39. Charles E. Bidwell, "Schooling and Socialization for Moral Commitment," *Interchange* 3 (1972): 1-27; *id.,* "The Social Psychology of Teaching," in *Second Handbook of Research on Teaching,* ed. Robert M. W. Travers (Chicago: Rand McNally, 1973), 413-449.

40. Alan Bullock, *A Language for Life* (London: H. M. Stationery Office, 1975), 67-68

41. Herbert J. Walberg, Robert E. Bole, and Herschel Waxman, "School-based Family Socialization," unpub. MS, 1977.

42. *Ibid.,* 2-3.

2. Families and Schools

Sara Lawrence Lightfoot

It is ironic that families and schools, although they are engaged in a complementary sociocultural task, find themselves in conflict. Parents and teachers, although they are expected to be natural allies, find themselves, instead, in an adversarial relationship based on their roles as defined by the social structure of society — a relationship that does not, however, necessarily nor primarily result from the dynamics of interpersonal behavior. Historically, there has been potential for conflict among the several institutions involved in the rearing of children. The controversy has assumed a variety of forms and different levels of intensity at specific times, in specific places, and with specific participants. This discussion focuses on three major sources of conflict between families and schools in contemporary society: differences between the structure and the functions of the institutions, disparity in status and power between the schools and the communities they serve, and ambiguous roles and ambivalent competition between mothers and teachers. Most of the analysis focuses on the parents and the teachers of elementary school children (six through twelve years of age). Many of the interactional discussions between families and schools remain constant across grade levels, but different issues emerge as children grow older, become more independent of their families, are more clearly identified with the values and perspectives of their peers, and feel less need for parental protection, guidance, and support.

STRUCTURAL DISCONTINUITIES

Certain of the discontinuities between family and school are endemic to the very nature of the family and the school as institutions, and they are experienced by *all* children as they traverse the path from home to school. Dreeben, for instance, describes differences in the scope of relationships among participants in the family and school environments. In families, interactions are functionally diffuse in that the participants are intimately and deeply connected and rights and duties are all-encompassing and taken for granted. In schools, interactions are functionally specific in that the relationships are more circumscribed and activities are defined by the technical competence and individual status of the participants.[12]

Relationships differ not only in terms of scope but also in terms of affectivity, that is, the quality and depth of personal interactions. McPherson contrasts primary relationships between parents and children with secondary ones between teachers and children. Parents have emotionally charged relationships with their children that rarely reflect interpersonal status or functional considerations.[2] Children in the family, for instance, are treated as special people, but pupils in the school are necessarily treated as members of categories.[3] Clearly, the secondary relationship encouraged by teachers is supportive of a more rational, predictable, and stable social system with visible and explicit criteria for achievement and failure. It does not exhibit chaotic fluctuations caused by emotion, indulgence, and impulsiveness that are often part of the more intimate relationship between parents and children.

The scope and depth of relationships between teachers and children reflects the preparatory, transitional, and sorting functions performed by schools in this society. The roles allocated to children in the schools are evaluated primarily in terms of future status; they do not reflect full membership in the present society. The Parsonian analysis of the unique characteristics of school life traces the relationship between the teacher's evaluation of achievement and the child's later participation in the occupational and political world.

The school is the first socializing agent in the child's experience which institutionalizes a differentiation of status on a nonbiological basis. Moreover, this is not an ascribed status; it is a status "earned" by differential performance of tasks set by the teacher.[4]

For Parsons, therefore, the classroom is a relatively impartial and objective social structure strikingly different from what is often an egocentric, child-centered existence prior to entering school. The classroom is seen as essentially liberating — a place where children can rid themselves of the shackles of sex, family, culture, and race and can prove themselves anew as achievers or nonachievers. (This is obviously a theoretical, rather than an empirical conception of the socialization function of schools. It is based on a normative notion of a static, democratic state working smoothly and effectively, rather than on actual data.)

Following the Parsonian model, Dreeben sees the classroom as a microcosm of the wider society — a reflection of the norms and values of the corporate world beyond school. He suggests that schooling experiences impart to children the norms necessary to sustain "organic solidarity" in society.

The argument . . . rests on the assumptions that schools, through their structural arrangements and the behavior patterns of teachers, provide pupils with certain experiences largely unavailable in other social settings, and that these experiences, by virtue of their peculiar characteristics, represent conditions conducive to the acquisition of norms.[5]

Individuals will supposedly achieve a "meaningful" position in the differentiated society that these "democratic" norms ensure. Although the structuralist conceptions of Parsons and Dreeben are useful in describing the natural and inevitable boundaries that are drawn between families and schools and the continuities that exist between the normative order of schools and the social and economic structures of society, the authors provide little insight into the processes of socialization and accommodation required when children move from one environment to the other. Their analyses do not move us toward understanding how children begin to internalize and integrate the norms of the school environment, nor help us interpret deviance or difference in the response patterns among children. There seems to be an implicit assumption that children will be the passive recipients of the school's normative structure, that their socialization will be complete and irreversible, and that the abrupt shift from home to school will be accomplished smoothly.

The structuralists' conception of social institutions, however, does point to the fact that part of the dissonance between families and schools appears to be related to the growth, socialization, and liberation of children. Conflict emanates from real differences in the sociocultural function of families and schools. Parents, protective and highly invested in their child, see the educational system as competitive and individualistic and seek recognition and favors for their child. These are neither misperceptions of the nature of the educational system nor antithetical to the role of the nuclear family in a hierarchical, materialistic society. Teachers, on the other hand, see themselves as rational and universalistic, creating and sustaining order in a classroom that is flexible and responsive to the special needs of a child but that ultimately equalizes attention and favors. This means the criteria for success within the classroom must be explicit and visible and that children must be socialized to respond to symbols of success and failure in a relatively nonaffective environment.

ISSUES OF POWER AND ASYMMETRY

The conflict and distrust between families and schools intensify when there are differences in status and power within society. The adversarial relationship between parents and teachers in an industrial society can be traced to the historic role of schools as major institutions for social order and social control — an institutional strategy designed to ensure that deviant and threatening strangers would not challenge the status quo. Bowles, the economist, described the transition from a precapitalist society, where the basic productive unit was the family, to capitalist production and the factory system, where the authority structure, prescribed types of behavior, and response characteristics of the workplace became increasingly separate from the family. The schools provided ideal preparation for factory work — discipline, punctuality, and acceptance of authority — based on the illusion that a benevolent government was offering opportunity for all. Actually, American schooling was (and is) a mechanism of social control and a place to inculcate workers with motivational schemes for factory work.[6]

Revisionist historians have echoed Bowles's pessimistic interpretation of the structure and purposes of school culture. In what Tyack refers to as an "excavation for conspiracies," they have searched for sinister and malicious forces behind what appears to be a benevolent and democratic process and have shown schools to have monolithic

and static purposes.[7] Schools were not so much an outgrowth of bene-
volence and goodwill as the result of "coercion." They stand as symbolic expressions of the triumph of an imported "bourgeois morality,"
and they have served as a mechanism for managing the influx of im-
migrants. who were perceived as a threat to the social order.

The school bureaucracy stands as a rigid, hierarchical, impenetrable authority that dictates who teaches, what they teach, how they
teach, and to whom they teach.[8] To sustain itself, the bureaucracy
builds walls against and annihilates any forces that oppose regulation
and order. Katz described the insular, immovable character of the
school culture when he traced the emergence of school bureaucracy.

Because they built the rationale for their own existence and their increasing command
of community resources upon an implausible ideology ever more divorced from reality, educators had to turn inward; they had to avoid a hard look at the world around
the schools and at their own work; they had to retreat into an ideology that became a
myth. By the 1850's educators had helped set the stage for the rigid sterile bureaucracies that soon would operate urban schools.[9]

In a recent observational study done in middle- and lower-class
public schools in New York, anthropologist Leacock noted the strong
class interest of school bureaucracies and the exclusion of community
cultures referred to by Katz and found the same systematic patterns of
discrimination and differentiation described by Bowles. The social relations of the educational process mirrored the social relations of the
work roles into which students were likely to move. There was a clear
difference in rules, expected modes of behavior, and opportunities for
choice. Middle-class students were rewarded for individuality, aggressiveness, and initiative; lower-class students were reinforced for passivity, withdrawal, and obedience.[10] There is, therefore, an illusion of
mobility and assimilation through schooling that creates distance and
hostility between middle-class-oriented teachers and low-class parents,
while in reality the educational system serves less to change the results
of primary socialization in the home than to reinforce and denigrate
them by rendering them in adult form. In other words, poor and minority parents expect that schools will change their child's orientation
toward middle-class life, mothers are made to feel inadequate in preparing children for an uncharted future, and families relinquish the
final remnants of their cultural traditions and familiar social structures.

In *Small Town Teacher,* McPherson documented the different relationships that teachers sustained with parents from varying socioeco-

nomic backgrounds. Teachers identified with the average people in town, felt vulnerable and powerless in relation to the upper-middle class, and considered only the lower class as really inferior to them. Sometimes teachers tried to form temporary alliances with identifiable subgroups of parents who were perceived as being cooperative. Poor parents were sometimes taken into the teacher's confidence when they adopted an obsequious and humble manner. The teachers were viewed as the gatekeepers for their children's social mobility, and teachers appreciated the parents' nonthreatening appreciation. Middle-class parents often became potential allies for teachers because of their shared convictions about the value of achievement and hard work.[11] But, for the most part, teachers felt they could not trust or depend upon coalitions with parents, and they feared that real collaboration might lead to an awkward confusion of rules.

In my own interviews with black teachers in a public ghetto school, I found varying perceptions of the abilities and strengths of poor black parents — ranging from the stereotypic image of parents as shiftless, lazy, uncaring, and lacking ambition for their children to understanding and empathetic views of parents as committed and caring but unable to negotiate the complexities and hostilities of the school system. The latter group of teachers viewed poor black parents as potential collaborators in an educational, cultural, and social enterprise. The teacher's perceptions of parents seemed to be related to her own view of parents as victims of an unjust and racist society (rather than responsible creators of their own helpless condition) and the teacher's identification of her own place on the social ladder, her own sense of power and influence in the occupational and social world.

I lived in a real big ghetto, in a housing project. I was not really hungry or anything, but I know what it is to be a welfare recipient . . . and see my mother sneak out to work. . . . I think I can identify quite easily with people who are lower-class. People who are trying. *My family is the working class* [emphasis mine].[12]

This teacher was expressing both an ideological and political vision of the world and a personal need to identify with her own roots and culture. Part of her identification with the lives of the working class was reflected in her attitude toward parental involvement and participation in the education of their children. Teaching was not considered to be solely within the lofty province of the professional, and learning was not reserved for inside classrooms; instead, the concept of teaching was far-reaching and inclusive and involved the active and critical participation of parents.

No matter what you do as teachers, or what is done as a community, or what is done as a school system, *the parent is the first teacher* [emphasis mine]. Unless black parents come together, there's not going to be much hope for their children. They've got to reinforce, they've got to motivate, they've got to be concerned.[13]

Another distinction made between parent groups by teachers in a progressive, independent school seemed to combine elements of social class, life-style, and attitudes toward child rearing. Ambitious, middle-class parents (both black and white) were seen as aggressive, expecting too much from their children, and obsessed with their children's achievements. Teachers often felt they had to protect such children and themselves from the unrealistic ambitions of the parents and to establish classroom relationships that matched a child's developmental stage. Other noncollaborators were a group of parents who were labeled "laissez-faire" and were seen as possessing a sloppy, overly permissive approach to child rearing. Teachers accused such parents of responding to their children with their heads (that is, looking for the origins and motivations of poor behavior), rather than their hearts (that is, responding spontaneously to children without the benefit of a psychological orientation). In some sense, lower-class parents who demanded order and respect and who did not overintellectualize their responses to children were seen by the teachers as potential collaborators. Teachers appreciated their realistic and objective appraisal of their child's abilities and development, and parents seemed to permit teachers a large measure of autonomy and to show genuine respect for the difficulties and complexities of the role of teacher. The mutual admiration seemed to be a circular and sustaining relationship that was rarely articulated, but deeply enjoyed.[14]

These teacher's voices reflect a wide range of work experiences, personalities, skills, and ideological views. McPherson's teachers worked in a relatively heterogeneous and stable community in a small town where the distinctions of a hierarchical social order were exaggerated. My own research was done in a black ghetto school that was surrounded by decay and the false promise of urban renewal, and the study I did with Carew took place in a relatively progressive, independent school. In these three divergent settings teachers gave different reasons for trusting some subgroups of compatible parents, but they saw parents en masse as threatening. They formed strong bonds among themselves as protection and expected the institution to support their interests against those of parents.

Although the incipient bureaucracy of schools has effectively excluded the powerless strangers of society and teachers' relationships with families often express the prevailing "middle-class efficiency," any explanation of the asymmetry and dissonance between teachers and parents cannot be reduced to contrasts in race and class. The perspectives of teachers in the three studies cited above reveal the origins of conflict to be far more complex and multidimensional. Part of the oversimplified vision of the unequal power between middle-class schools and lower-class families and communities comes from social scientists' preoccupation with describing and analyzing the behaviors of the more powerful mainstream groups in society. McPherson, for example, recognizes that she is only telling half of the story of families and schools when she reminds the reader that she is expressing teachers' perceptions of parent groups, not the actual experiences of parents. For the most part the literature does not present an authentic picture of parents who are in the process of trying to communicate their concerns and cope with the complexities of the school system. "Parents . . . remain nameless and powerless—always described from the position of the middle-class institution, never in relation to their own cultural style or social idiom."[15]

In her account of *The Great School Wars: New York City, 1805-1973*, Ravitch criticizes revisionist historians for the same lack of attention to the aggressive, initiating actions of the less-powerful minority groups. She presents a view of school culture that is dynamic and transforming—a shifting compromise among competing interest groups. Ravitch perceives the structures and functions of schools as evolving out of numerous cultural wars in which disenfranchised elements of the community rose to seize power. The subsequent reorganizations were never quite what the fighting faction had hoped for, but the schools usually did incorporate some modifying concessions. From this historical perspective, therefore, schools are viewed as volatile, political arenas that inevitably support values and norms that are objectionable and alien to someone. "The city's melange of classes, races, religions, and ethnic groups guarantees an ever-present potential for conflict over the distribution of power."[16] Recognizing the productive uses of conflict for the resolution and compromise of cultural and class differences, Ravitch makes an appeal for "Comity"[17]—that basic recognition of differences in values and interests and of the desirability of reconciling those differences peacefully. Even more important, Ravitch's analysis emphasizes the tranforming power of the oppressed groups. They are not viewed as helpless, passive victims who are being silenced and abused by a monolithic bureaucratic system. By their fight for inclusion and participation, they have a significant impact on the nature and direction of a once impenetrable and distant institution. Oppressed and excluded groups are viewed as actors who do more than respond; they engage in forceful, focused action.

Historical and sociological interpretations of the structures and purposes of schools, therefore, shape our view of the relationship between schools, communities, and families. Whether we are guided by the more pessimistic descriptions of revisionist historians or the more dynamic and optimistic analysis of Ravitch, we must recognize the interaction of forces and consider the voices, perspectives, and actions of excluded and ignored groups. Only when we view the asymmetric relationship between families and schools as a dynamic process of negotiation and interaction will we gain an authentic picture of the nature of the conflict and the potential for resolving it.

MOTHERS AND TEACHERS: SUBTLE AND SILENT COMPETITORS

Most of the explanations for intense conflict between parents and teachers have social-class and racial origins. In other words, the "normal" tensions that exist between nuclear families and schools in an industrialized society are exaggerated and amplified when we introduce the experiences of minorities and poor people. Many of the psychological explanations for the need to keep family and school separate, however, do not have a structural or an institutional basis. They rest, instead, upon theories of psychosocial growth that are thought to be relevant to all people.

In *Psychoanalysis for Parents and Teachers,* Anna Freud emphasizes the psychic needs of children and focuses on the differences between child care and child education.[18] Child care is the province of mothers, and it is characterized by an all-giving, nurturant relationship, whereas child education belongs to teachers whose responsibility it is to demand a renunciation of bodily pleasures, a deprivation, an inhibition.

The teacher's role is not that of a mother-substitute. If, as teachers, we play the part of mother we get from the child the reactions which are appropriate for the mother-child relationship—the demand for exclusive attention and affection, the wish to get rid of all the other children in the classroom.[12]

Freud, is, therefore, proposing that the teacher's role be far more circumscribed, objective, and generalized in relation to children in order to escape the dangers of rivalry with mothers, "who are the legitimate owners of the child," by taking a "more general and less personal interest in the whole process of childhood with all its implications."[20] In the same sense, the teacher must not shift into the role of therapist and become dangerously sensitive and responsive to the emotional involvements of the child.

Freud is proposing that teachers become neutralized, objective human beings who avoid creating strong emotional and sexual bonds with children; that the teacher-child relationship be removed from drive-activity and instinctive wishes. Interestingly enough, she assumes that the teachers of young children will be women, but she feels that the teacher's role must be more circumscribed and defined in such a way that she is less seductive, less entrapping to the expressive instincts of young children. Perhaps she must be thought of as less nurturant, less loving, and even less womanly.

The strong and uncompromising words of Freud underscore the critical and dynamic interactions between mothers and teachers and the powerful cultural imagery that surrounds their roles in society. Clarity of boundaries and issues of territoriality are at the center of relationships between mothers and teachers. Although Freud claims that clear boundaries can be drawn reflecting their distinct cultural functions, mothers and teachers, for the most part, experience a profound and subtle rivalry that arises out of the ambiguous and gray areas of responsibility and authority that stretch between family and school.

In an interview I had with an experienced master teacher, she described the often silent warfare that exists at the boundary between family and school. Her penetrating comments are paraphrased below:

Most mothers feel that their areas of competence are quite similar to those of the teacher. In fact, they feel they know their child better than anyone else and that the teacher does not possess any special field of authority and expertise. Especially now, when mothering is often self-consciously learned through reading, when educated mothers are reading books about child care, child development, and "good" parenting, mothers often feel that their knowing and understanding of socialization and development are not primitive and simplistic; not only are they shaped by intuition and emotion, but they are reinforced and confirmed by experts in psychology and education. The combined wisdom of their own deep experience with the child and their knowledge of the contemporary child-rearing literature makes them feel (at one level) as if they have a unique and special perspective. On the other hand, the discrepancies between realities of their daily lives with children and the "expert's" words of advice and warning make them feel great ambivalence about their competence as mothers. The more they know about the potential psychoemotional and intellectual dangers of child rearing, the more inadequate and fearful they feel about their mothering and their child's healthy development. Part of the mothers' difficulty in relating to teachers may reflect the basic feelings of inadequacy and insecurity that they are feeling as mothers. Their self-doubt gets projected onto the teachers. Mothers' feelings of inadequacy are often intensified by the fact that child care may be their only arena of expression. If they fail in the area of socialization and nurturance of children, then they will experience total failure as useful and valuable people. So a great deal of their self-esteem and self-worth hangs on their child's successful transition from home to school and on his achievement through school. The teacher is a threatening figure because her evaluation of the child can enhance or negate the mother's self-image.[21]

The profound disappointments of a mother's empty existence are, therefore, often translated into strained and burdensome relationships with "the other woman" in her child's life. The mothers that tend to cause the greatest turmoil for both teachers and children are those who express their sense of loss by overidentifying with, and living vicariously through, their children. When the child leaves for school each morning, a piece of the mother goes along, and it is extremely hard for the mother to "let go" and permit her child to have a separate, autonomous experience. One way a mother might try to share in her child's world is to probe constantly for information about school. In some sense, the mother's motives are very immature and self-centered. She wants to relive her own childhood (perhaps more happily and successfully the second time around) and every new encounter for her child reminds her of her own childhood. One mother expressed her vicarious needs by dressing her child meticulously and preciously even when she knew her six-year-old would be tussling with her friends, romping in the park, and working with finger paints and clay. In a sense the mother saw in her girl a miniature version of herself, and she wanted to project an adult, ladylike image. Separation from their child seems to be a problem for such mothers. It is difficult for them to disentangle their own motives and needs from those of their child, to see their child as a separate person. Their intrusive presence, their questions, their prodding, their nosiness make even the most secure teacher want to deny them information in an effort to structure an environment that protects the child from the burdensome presence of the parents and gives the teacher some space to establish a new and different adult-child relationship.

Although it seems clear that overidentification is problematic for teachers and dysfunctional to the development of autonomy in children, mothers, who have a more balanced vision of their own independence and their child as a separate being, also talk about the agonies of separation and the very authentic and uncomplicated feeling that they know their child in a way that no one else can. We recognize this special kind of knowing in mothers who are also teachers, who speak of the deeper, more intense attachments they have to their own child and how much more energy and passion are involved in being the parent of one child than the teacher of twenty-five children.

In general, women who are both teachers and mothers seem to experience easier, more fluid interaction between school and family. Their more generous visions of each special role seem to underscore the importance of clarity, understanding, and negotiation as elements of constructive relationships. This mother-teacher relationship is made easier when the woman has a greater knowledge and understanding that she shares a collaborative adult role in the socialization and education of the child and an understanding of the child's role in his or her own development. There is little mystery that shrouds either being a parent or being a teacher, and there is a profound recognition of the complexities of both roles. A sense of relief accompanies the realization that one has a partner and an ally. For the most part, mother-teachers do not experience exclusion from their child's classroom; instead, they feel the easing of an all-too-heavy burden. The productive, collaborative style is not limited to mother-teachers. Other mothers who have fulfilling and satisfying lives (inside or outside the home) also experience a sense of relief when their child forms strong alliances with teachers and peers in school.

Where mothers and teachers are knowledgeable and understanding of each others' special competencies and responsibilities, differences and conflicts in values, attitudes, goals, and styles are to be expected and are often welcomed. These differences lead to bitter antagonism if they are neglected or repressed under a superficial veneer of good will. If they are recognized, articulated, and negotiated, however, there is hope that the differences can be resolved.

One of the great difficulties between mothers and teachers in American society lies in the inability of each to recognize their own needs and their refusal to face the risks and dangers of open confrontation. Women have been socialized to accept and internalize the "subordinate" role—a role that denies the full power of their individuality and unique character and projects their needs onto their husbands and children. In *Toward a New Psychology of Women,* Miller describes the profound limitation of the subordinate role:

A subordinate group has to concentrate on basic survival. Accordingly, direct, honest reaction to destructive treatment is avoided. . . . [A]nother important result is that subordinates often know more about the dominants than they know about themselves. If a large part of your fate depends on accommodating to and pleasing the domi-nants, you concentrate on them. Indeed there is little purpose in knowing yourself. Why should you when your knowledge of dominants determines your life? This ten-dency is reinforced by many other restrictions. One can know oneself only through ac-tion and interaction. To the extent that their range of action and interaction is limi-ted, subordinates will lack a realistic evaluation of their capacities and problems.[22]

Mothers and teachers closely identified with the traditional roles of women in our society have not yet realized the potential strength of collaboration because they have not adequately identified their own skills, resources, and needs. They have not been allowed to be in touch with their own self-definition and identity and that limits their au-thentic interaction with one another.

CONFLICT: POSITIVE AND NEGATIVE FACES

The social science literature on the intersection of families and schools reflects a basic preoccupation with the *negative* dissonance be-tween families and schools. In fact, one finds mention of the intersec-tion of these two institutions only when researchers are analyzing the origins of pathology and deviance in children (that is, issues of cogni-tive deprivation, juvenile delinquency, effects of father-absent families on achievement patterns of children). This chapter has also echoed the themes of threat and distrust. I do believe that hostility, distrust, and unequal power between families and schools cause great anxiety in children and threaten a smooth and constructive transition between the two environments. It is important, however, that we not perceive family-school dissonance as necessarily dysfunctional to healthy child development or destructive to the social fabric of society.

Difference and dissonance are not only historically determined; they are also functional to child growth and social change. Slater argues that, in American society, people have endured a historical pattern of chronic change that has created an "experiential chasm" between par-ents and children.[23] This generational distance has, to some extent, eroded parental authority and wisdom because parents have not experienced what is of central importance to the child. Nor do they possess the knowledge, attitudes, and skills to help them adapt to the conditions of contemporary society. This child-adult discontinuity is viewed by Slater as a natural lever for social change. Schools (and any other nonfamily based collectivity) have served the important function of regulating and modifying parent-child relationships.

One segregates children from adult life because one wishes to do something special with them — to effect some kind of social change or to adapt to one. Such segregation insulates the child from social patterns of the present and makes him more receptive to some envisioned future.[24]

Dissonance between family and school would, therefore, be not only inevitable in a changing society, but it would also help to make children more malleable and responsive to a changing world. Absolute homogeneity between family and school, seen in this context, would reflect a static, authoritarian society and discourage creative, adaptive development in children.

It would appear that parents and teachers are most comfortable with one another when they recognize the validity and necessity of both in the effective socialization of young children in this society. Teachers are, for instance, more at ease with parents who seem to respect the importance and value of the teacher's role, who feel the teacher is performing a critical task, and who respond to her needs for autonomy and control. They have more difficulty with parents who do not seem to value their special competence and skills and who do not differentiate between the demands of the primary relationships within families and the requirements of the secondary relationships within schools.

An underlying theme of possessiveness seems to cause much of the friction between parents and teachers. Parents often view their relationship to the child as one of ownership, and they attempt to extend the years of parental protectiveness and control. This seems to reflect a view of children as property — a commodity owned by nuclear families or a competitive resource that lends potential status to hardworking parents. In this sense, children are viewed as the projection of their parents. When parents defend their children and argue for continuous and ultimate control over their lives, they are also, and perhaps primarily, concerned with protecting their own status in the economic structure of society and assuming some measure of control over their child's projected future.

Conflicting needs and expectations on the part of parents and children create confusion and anxiety within nuclear families and inevitably lead to difficulties in the family's relationship to schools. Parental feelings of ownership and control are further complicated when middle-class, status-seeking parents in this society recognize the need for their child to separate from them in order to achieve success in the world beyond family and school.

> When one joins the values of independence, hope in the future, and mobility, it is easy to understand why the successful separation of the child from his family of orientation and his own willful launching upon a career are both possible and necessary. But the potential and recognized consequences extend to the very nature of relations within the family itself. Consciously the future is optimistically viewed; and the task of the family is to equip the child as effectively as possible in the present with all available means for his solitary climb to better and more prosperous worlds lying far ahead of him.[25]

The ambivalence of parents' possessive and protective relationship toward their child and their equally strong recognition that the child's success depends upon autonomy, mobility, and separation from family is apparent.

The tensions arising between parents and teachers are, therefore, part of the very fabric of competition and materialism present in this society. The school becomes the major mechanism for the standardized competition of human resources: children are viewed as property to be developed, protected, and controlled by parents, and parents, as ambivalent sponsors, must find effective strategies for securing their child's status in some future and unknown society.

It is critical that we distinguish between creative conflict and negative dissonance between family and school. The former, inevitable in a changing society, is adaptive to the development and socialization of children. The latter is dysfunctional to child growth and acculturation and detrimental to families, communities, and culture. It is important that educational practitioners, who are daily engaged in trying to shape and clarify their relationship with parents and community, recognize the positive and negative faces of conflict. Difference and discontinuities between home and school are not necessarily signs of hostility and threat, and they can be potentially constructive in the teaching and learning process. Both teachers and parents should, therefore, be socialized to anticipate and tolerate creative tension, differences in perspective, and opposing value systems. As early as 1934,

Waller noted that the child will experience more freedom of expression and autonomy when different demands are being made by teachers and parents. In *The Sociology of Teaching* he argued persuasively that conflict between families and schools is not only inevitable, but, from the point of view of child growth, it would be unwise for parents and teachers to empathize completely with each other's perspectives.

> Parent-teacher work has usually been directed at securing for the school the support of the parents, that is, at getting parents to see children more or less as teachers see them. But it would be a sad day for childhood if parent-teacher work ever really succeeded in its object. The conflict between parents and teachers is natural and inevitable, and it may be more or less useful. It may be that the child develops better if he is treated impersonally in the schools, provided the parents are there to supply the needed personal attitude. . . . But it would assuredly be unfortunate if teachers ever succeeded in bringing parents over completely to their point of view, that is, in obtaining for schools the complete and undivided support of every parent of every child.[26]

Discontinuities between family and school become dysfunctional when they reflect differences in power and status in society. If the origins of conflict are perceived as being rooted in inequality, ethnocentrism, or racism, then the message being transmitted to the excluded and powerless group (both parents and children) is denigrating and abusive. When schooling serves to accentuate and reinforce the inequalities in society, then it is not providing a viable and productive alternative for students. The message of ethnocentrism is conveyed to parents and children when socialization, acculturation, and learning within schools are defined in the narrow, traditional terms of the dominant culture. Negative and paternalistic messages are communicated when schools begin to assume the total range of familial functions — not just the effort to adapt intellectual and social learning to a changing society but interference with dimensions of primary socialization that usually fall within the family domain. Creative conflict can only exist when there is a balance of power and responsibility between family and school. It cannot exist when the family's role is negated or diminished.

The pessimistic focus on family-school conflict is magnified by the moral tone that pervades much of the literature. The family has always been such a profound and intimate aspect of everyone's experience that it is difficult to avoid projecting one's values, beliefs, and attitudes into the lives and experiences of others. As Levy has pointed out, "down through the years no organization has been the focus of greater moralizing or musing."[27] For instance, one recognizes that pervasive moral tone in social science definitions of family. Lévi-Strauss set forth the classic definition of the family that still prevails in the hearts and minds of contemporary scholars as:

> a group manifesting the following organizational attributes: it finds its origins in marriage; it consists of husband, wife, and children born in their wedlock, though other relatives may find their place close to the nuclear group; and the group is united by moral, legal, economic, religious, and social rights and obligations (including sexual rights and prohibitions as well as such socially patterned feelings as love, attraction, piety, and awe.)[28]

This same definition is also mirrored in the popular imagery of family life and structure conceived in the middle-class mold. Any deviation from the narrowly construed norm is thought to be potentially disruptive to a smooth social order. Mead points out that "the American family pattern is an urban middle-class pattern, although upper-class patterns occur, and lower-class practice deviates sharply from middle-class standards, and rural family life still retains the stamp of an earlier historic period. Films, comic strips, radio, and magazines presuppose a middle-class family."[29] But the celluloid and plastic images of family conflict with the rich and varied reality of family patterns. One of the critical challenges for researchers and practitioners is to escape the definitional boundaries and recognize the adapative and responsive structures that have emerged in our society. They must move beyond the moralizing blinders and pessimistic tradition of social science, beyond "absent fathers" and "cognitively inadequate mothers" in search of a more comprehensive analysis of family-school relations. As long as teachers cling to the ideal middle-class images of family, they will not be able to form constructive alliances with the many families that do not match their unreal images.

In turn, a redefinition of family-school relationships will require that we separate the myths about mothers and teachers from the realities of their lives and trace historical changes in the quality of their relationships. We must search out the roots of their devalued status, the dimensions of struggles and competition between them, and the consonance and integration in their social and cultural roles. Mothers and teachers have been caught in a struggle that reflects the devaluation of both roles in this society, which makes them perfect targets for each other's abuse. They do not dare to strike out at the more powerful groups in this society that are most responsible for their demeaned social and economic position.

Not only do mothers and teachers provide relatively safe and visible objects of discontent for one another and for the rest of society, but they are also involved in an alien task. Both are required to raise children in the service of a dominant group whose values and goals they do not determine. In other words, mothers and teachers socialize their children to conform to a society that belongs to men. Within this alien context, it is almost inevitable that mothers and teachers would not feel an authentic and meaningful connection to their task and not completely value the contributions of one another.

Establishing positive and productive relationships between woman-roles means that the values and goals of our culture, which shape the education and socialization of children, must undergo a profound transformation that reflects more than the competitive and individualistic agenda of a male-dominated society, but also encompasses the special and valuable qualities of women. This redefinition of cultural norms will not only enhance the roles of both mothers and teachers in the eyes of others, but it will also give greater meaning and purpose to those who choose to assume those roles. This will inevitably clarify the various ways in which mothers and teachers can engage in collaborative and supportive relationships.

NOTES

1. Robert Dreeben, *On What Is Learned in School* (Reading, Mass.: Addison-Wesley, 1968).

2. Gertrude McPherson, *Small Town Teacher* (Cambridge, Mass.: Harvard University Press, 1972).

3. Jacob W. Getzels, "Socialization and Education: A Note on Discontinuities," *Teachers College Record* 76 (1974): 218-225.

4. Talcott Parsons, "The School Class as a Social System," *Harvard Educational Review* 29 (1959): 297-318.

5. Dreeben, *On What Is Learned in School*, 84.

6. Samuel Bowles, "Unequal Education and the Social Division of Labor," in *Schooling in a Corporate Society*, ed. Martin Carnoy (New York: David McKay, 1972), 36-64; *id.* and Herbert Gintis, *Schooling in Capitalist America* (New York: Basic Books, 1976).

7. David Tyack, *The One Best System: A History of American Urban Education* (Cambridge, Mass.: Harvard University Press, 1974).

8. Michael Katz, *Class, Bureaucracy, and Schools: The Illusion of Educational Change in America* (New York: Praeger Publishers, 1971).

9. *Id., The Irony of Early School Reform: Educational Innovation in Mid-Nineteenth Century Massachusetts* (Cambridge, Mass.: Harvard University Press, 1968), 159.

10. Eleanor B. Leacock, *Teaching and Learning in City Schools* (New York: Basic Books, 1969).

11. McPherson, *Small Town Teacher,* 139-140.

12. Sara Lawrence Lightfoot, "Politics and Reasoning through the Eyes of Teachers and Children," *Harvard Educational Review* 43 (1973): 215.

13. *Ibid.*

14. *Id.* and Jean Carew, "Individuation and Discrimination in the Classroom," unpub. report, 1974.

15. Charles A. Valentine, *Culture and Poverty: Critique and Counter Proposals* (Chicago: University of Chicago Press, 1968), 80.

16. Diane Ravitch, *The Great School Wars, New York City, 1805-1973: A History of the Public Schools as Battlefield of Social Change* (New York: Basic Books, 1974), 402.

17. *Ibid.,* 402.

18. Anna Freud, *Psychoanalysis for Teachers and Parents* (Boston: Beacon Press, 1935), 40-63.

19. *Id.,* "The Role of the Teacher," *Harvard Educational Reivew* 22 (1952): 231.

20. *Ibid.,* 230.

21. Sara Lawrence Lightfoot, "Teacher-Mothers: Conceptions of the Dual Role, A Pilot Study," unpub. report, Radcliffe Institute, Harvard University, 1976.

22. Jean Baker Miller, *Toward a New Psychology of Woman* (Boston: Beacon Press, 1976), 11.

23. Norman B. Ryder, "The Cohort in the Study of Social Change," *American Sociological Review* 30 (1965): 843-861.

24. Philip Slater, "Social Change and the Democratic Family," in *The Temporary Society,* ed. Warren G. Bennis and Philip Slater (New York: Harper and Row, 1968), 40.

25. Conrad Arensberg and Solon Kimball, *Culture and Community* (New York: Harcourt Brace and World, 1967), 377.

26. Willard Waller, *The Sociology of Teaching* (New York: John Wiley and Sons, 1932), 69.

27. Marion J. Levy, "Some Hypotheses about the Family," *Journal of Comparative Family Studies* 1 (1970): 119.

28. Claude Lévi-Strauss, "The Family," in *Man, Culture, and Society,* ed. Harry Shapiro (New York: Oxford University Press, 1960), 267.

29. Margaret Mead, "The Contemporary American Family as an Anthropologist Sees It," in *Social Perspectives on Behavior,* ed. Herman Stein and Richard Clavard (New York: Free Press, 1958), 21.

3. Television and Learning

Neal J. Gordon

TELEVISION: A POPULAR MEDIUM

The number of people who own and watch television sets argues for the popularity of television. It is appropriate here, then, to begin by considering why it is so popular. For one thing, television asks nothing of the viewer except visual and auditory attention. In many instances only the auditory portion is sufficient if one can judge from the sale of radios equipped to receive the audio tracks of television channels. There is also an interesting example of use of just the visual portion of the medium. A friend of mine who teaches deaf students told me of sign stories her students shared in class. At first she could not follow the stories, even though they had some elements in common with television programs she had seen the night before. It seems that her students, who frequently watched television although they heard nothing, formulated their own interpretations of the programs they saw.

Television requires no effort to turn pages, to follow words sequentially, or to formulate visual images of written material. The programming ordinarily requires no thought on the part of the viewer. Plot formulas generally are similar, and there is little doubt about the outcome of a program. The hero always lives to return the next week;

criminals are always apprehended; and, commercials always arrive to allow for breaks in attention and concentration. Three types of programming—soap operas, quiz shows, and sports—leave room for some uncertainty concerning the outcome, but the formats are predictable.

In addition, television does not directly criticize the viewer. While viewers are encouraged to do things, especially during advertisements (buy this, use that, go here, see that), their reputation does not suffer if they do not follow the recommendations. Instead, the implication is that the viewer is smart enough to accept the recommendation while others who may not yet know of or use a product are likely to have problems.

Television allows the viewer to be the ultimate source of control as well. If the viewer does not like a particular program, the channel can be changed; if nothing appeals to the viewer, the set can be turned off. Viewers also affect programming in that the essential criterion for the continuance of any program is the Nielsen rating. Programs that consistently fail to attract about 30 percent of the homes where televisions are turned on generally are not renewed, even though a 25 percent share could represent 30 million viewers.[1]

Television also provides interesting visual images accompanied by music, dialogue, story lines, and attractive people. Cameras allow close-up views of individuals, music signals emotional tones, and dramatic moments frequently occur. Compared to reading, which is exclusively visual, or radio, which is exclusively auditory, television is more interesting in that it brings both visual and auditory information to the viewer, and does this in a variety of formats (animation, pixilation, slow motion). Also, compared to reading, television is more likely to satisfy a viewer's desire for completeness. It takes longer to read a complete book (that is, to finish it) than it does to watch a complete television program. In addition, the reader must conjure up images of the people and events discussed, whereas television provides images of "real" people and events. In this sense television is oriented toward other people more than reading, where the medium is print rather than images.

Another consideration is that television allows the viewer to participate vicariously in numerous activities, often without the inconvenience of actual participation. For example, if one wanted to attend the Olympics in 1976, it meant traveling to Canada, fighting crowds,

and waiting in lines to see events once. (It is ironic that some large sta-
diums have installed enormous television screens so that spectators also
have the advantage of instant replay.) By staying home and watching
the events on television, viewers can watch the events and have the advantage of instant replay without waiting in line, without expense and
inconvenience, and without fighting crowds.

Because entertainers generally are attractive people surrounded by
equally attractive sets, there is considerable glamour associated with
the television industry. Performers who are or become stars outshine
most of the people with whom viewers ordinarily interact. This often
establishes performers as models for viewers to imitate in appearance
and mannerisms. Watching them can inform one as to what one
should do to be watched by others.

There are other reasons why television is popular. Certainly it does
not require any skills on the part of the viewer.[2] More sophisticated
viewers may receive different messages from the medium than less
sophisticated ones, but everyone, at any age, can use television and
gain something in return. This even includes, as has been mentioned,
those who cannot for some reason watch a set or are unable to hear the
sound. The pervasiveness of television allows one message to reach and
be discussed by millions, and, in this sense, it makes up part of
McLuhan's "global village."[3]

Since everyone can receive something in return and since television
sets are found in 97 percent of American homes, the medium provides
readily accessible, economical entertainment. One buys a set, and it
lasts for some time; there is no need to keep buying materials throughout the life of the set. Favorite programs or special broadcasts are
made available to the viewer at no additional cost beyond the price of
the set. In other words, television is cost-effective.

As for children, the fact that adults watch television makes viewing
more attractive. Because adults do it, this makes it a grown-up,
"mature" way to spend one's time. For both children and adults, viewing television is easy, relaxing, and escapist. It is also noncompulsory.
One does not have to watch it; one can do with it what one wishes.
Compare this with going to school or going to work. One wonders if
the desire to watch television would decrease if it were forced on
people.

This discussion of the popularity of television also demonstrates that
it is an effective medium. The fact that television is both popular

and effective leads us to ask how it affects viewers, for even when all they are seeking is entertainment and diversion, viewers are affected. This chapter is primarily concerned with effects on children and youth.[4]

TELEVISION: AN EDUCATOR

There is little doubt that television can and does educate. It educates during "entertaining academic" programming (for example, "The Electric Company," "Nova," "Sesame Street") and during commercial programming (for example, "Charlie's Angels," "Starsky and Hutch," and "The Rockford Files"). Sometimes the curriculum is deliberately and carefully planned to teach ("Sesame Street"); at other times there appears to be little concern for the explicit and implicit lessons that are broadcast. Despite the intent, the effects are similar: audiences (especially children) imitate, learn, remember, believe, and are affected by what they see on television.

Effects of Television on Children and Youth

A recent guide to the wide range of literature relating to television lists over 2,300 citations, most of which focus on material published since 1960.[5] The guide includes reports on such subjects as the messages of television;[6] the effects on children and youth;[7] television and women;[8] television and the poor;[9] television and decision making about politics and purchases;[10] television and psychological processes;[11] communicator behavior;[12] alternative methodologies for studying television, communication theory, and the research agenda;[13] and current studies. The reason this chapter stresses the effects of television on children and youth is because these are the populations most directly connected with the potential educational application of the medium in the schools.

Extent of Viewing. According to a report in *TV Guide* for April 1977, ninety-seven out of every hundred homes have a television set. The latest figures from Nielsen surveys indicate that in 43 percent of the 71 million homes with television there are two or more sets, with a color set in three-quarters of those homes. During the 1976-77 television season the average household had a television on for slightly more than six hours daily. In the fall of 1976 the television was on for nearly seven hours daily. Although there are 962 television stations in the United States (26 percent of them public), 85 percent of the viewing time of the national audience is concentrated on the three commercial networks (ABC, NBC, and CBS). Independent stations are viewed 14 percent of the time, and only 1 percent of viewing time is spent on the public broadcasting stations.

By the time children enter kindergarten, they will have used more time viewing television than they will later spend sitting in university classes. Children spend more time watching television than going to school.[14] Most children watch two hours or more of television per day.[15] It has been estimated that by the time today's American children are sixty-five years of age, they will have spent the equivalent of nine full years in front of a television set. One writer estimated in 1972 that a typical eighteen-year-old has watched television in excess of 10,000 hours,[16] while, by 1975, the total viewing time of a sixteen-year-old was estimated to be approximately 15,000 hours.[17] Clearly, Americans like to watch television, even though many may publicly criticize the medium.

Programming and Aggressive Behavior. A frequent criticism of television is that it encourages aggressive behavior. In the past twenty-five years there have been seven major congressional hearings concerning the amount of violence depicted on the television screen. A National Commission on the Causes and Prevention of Violence has been formed. Empirical findings from twenty-three investigations, funded at more than $1 million, have been reported to the Surgeon General.[18] In 1976 the American Medical Association, the American Psychiatric Association, and the National Congress of Parents and Teachers all began serious efforts to deal with televised violence.

Perhaps this concern stems from the results of the research that has been done. Generally, in study after study, whether in the laboratory or in the field, findings indicate that televised aggression leads either to an increased proclivity toward violence, a greater tolerance of violence, or a slower reaction toward violence.[19]

The Surgeon General's report offers the conclusion that there is "a preliminary and tentative indication of a causal relation between viewing violence on television and aggressive behavior; an indication that any such causal relation operates only on some children . . . and an indication that it operates only in some environmental contexts."[20] The reason these findings were stated so cautiously was because representatives of the television industry were part of the board making final conclusions and because seven distinguished researchers who had previously reported indications of relationships between aggression and viewing were excluded from participating in the funded projects.[21]

Criticism of the methodologies used in studying the effects of television on aggressive behavior has appeared.[22] It seems that, while most of the experimental studies reveal that witnessing violence can instigate "aggressive" behavior, subjects usually are intentionally aroused and most sanctions against aggression are removed. If, based on this criticism, one defines "aggression" as a naturally occurring behavior, findings indicate either that television violence has no effect[23] or that it affects only initially aggressive children.[24]

There is also an argument that televised aggression serves as a release for the viewer's aggression. This argument, frequently referred to as the catharsis point of view, has been supported by many people for a long time, and there is empirical support for the view that televised aggression does, in fact, lead to reduced aggression among young viewers.[25] There is also, however, considerable empirical support for the opposite conclusion.[26] The net result of the controversy generally leads to the conclusion that "there is little or no evidence of catharsis of aggression through media experience . . . ."[27]

Despite methodological criticism and persistent belief in catharsis, the effects of televised aggression should be clear to all familiar with television economics. A single minute of broadcast time can cost an advertiser as much as $250,000, although $25,000 to $100,000 would be closer to the average figure. Estimates of total income attributable to advertising for the 1976 season were approximately $7 billion,[28] and as far back as 1973 advertising for children alone amounted to nearly $400 million.[29] For that amount of money one expects reasonable returns. The television industry must have been able to convince advertisers that viewers can be persuaded to purchase advertised products and that, therefore, the money spent for commercials will provide reasonable returns. How can the industry argue, on the one hand, that commercials affect viewers and, on the other hand, that programs do not affect them? Since more time is spent on television programming than on advertising (no matter how it seems to viewers frustrated by commercial interruptions), the reasonable expectation is that television programming, like advertising, affects viewers' behaviors and attitudes.

The networks are sensitive to the weight of the empirical data suggesting that televised aggression is a significant cause of concern. Apparently ABC worked hard to revise its presentations in the 1977-78 season.[30] For the first time human consequences of violence — subsequent guilt, economic hardship, social effects — were to be portrayed. Thus, in addition to the traditional and commonplace message that those who are illegally aggressive will be caught and punished, there was concentration on the more realistic human consequences of aggression. The revised portrayals were at least partially the result of the empirical studies cited here.

Another possible result of concern with the effects of television is reflected in the efforts of CBS to concentrate on messages that have social value in their children's programs and to test the effects of those messages on over four thousand subjects.[31] The findings from the network's investigations are generally encouraging in that nearly nine out of every ten children received at least one positive message from programs such as "Fat Albert and the Cosby Kids," "The Harlem Globetrotters' Popcorn Machine," "The U.S. of Archie," "Shazam," and "Isis." In short, the networks have been responsive to criticism. Their efforts may not be as widespread or rapid as many critics would like, yet it is encouraging to see some activity focusing on achieving positive effects.

Programming and Prosocial Behavior. Less empirical work has been done in the area of the effects of television on positive, or prosocial, attitudes and behavior than of the effects of viewing aggression. This is presumably because researchers have been more concerned with the potentially harmful effects of television than with the potentially beneficial effects. Several recent investigations have, however, appeared, and the general conclusion has been encouraging. It appears that children can become more cooperative and nurturant after viewing programs emphasizing these behaviors.[32]

In addition to its effects on behavior, television affects children's attitudes, especially concerning topics where they have had little experience.[33] It has been reported that children who watched "Sesame Street" for two years had more positive attitudes toward members of various races and toward school than children who watched less than two years.[34]

These findings suggest that programmers should attend to portrayals, attitudes, and characters as they are presented on television. In particular, images of women should be reviewed with an eye toward providing a greater diversity of presentations.[35] Rather than focusing on flying nuns, twitching noses ("Bewitched"), ghosts and Mrs. Muir, and female genies; rather than having advertisements for products found in the bathroom and kitchen associated with women; rather than emphasizing a narrower range of occupations for women than men; and rather than showing women indoors and out of business settings more often than men—women should be placed in as wide a range of roles, occupations, and settings as men.[36] How we see televised characters affects our attitude toward appropriate and inappropriate social roles. The importance of this is underscored when one notes that many young children and adolescents often consider television drama an accurate portrayal of reality.[37]

The Influence of Advertising. It has already been established that televised advertising influences viewers. Young children apparently fail to distinguish between the programming and the advertising until approximately the age of six or seven when they begin to make the distinction.[38] Distrust of commercials appears as early as the age of seven, and by the time four years elapse that distrust has grown.[39] Children in the third grade (age eight) are strongly affected by commercials. They make more requests that parents purchase advertised products, and there is a tendency to react aggressively when parents hesitate to purchase the advertised product.[40] The more time children spend watching television, the more advertised products they request. This is especially true among children where the parents have a limited education.[41]

Although televised commercials during children's programs decreased from 225 advertisements in a four-hour review of programming on Saturday morning to 218 advertisements between 1972 and 1973, the pervasiveness of commercials directed toward children is noticeable.[42] The frequency with which the same commercial appears, especially where it involves the use of slogans, jingles, and repetition, is particularly effective in attracting the attention of viewers. In discussions with approximately four hundred mothers of two- to ten-year-olds, investigators found that children recognized advertised products three times out of four.[43] Children apparently do not, however, recognize the disclaimers on the products and may be dissatisfied with the actual products.[44]

Thus, even if children have difficulty reading, they succeed in recognizing advertised products. Once viewers recognize that commercials are distinct from programs, it is possible that they can become accustomed to attending to program material for fixed time intervals. Children's attention spans may then be conditioned by television. A preoccupation with buying, emphasis on the importance of material possessions, and fear of being ridiculed for personal conditions (body odor, oily hair, yellow teeth, dandruff, dirty shirt collars) are also likely to result from televised advertising.

Exemplary Programming for Children. The effects of commercials were noticed by the creators of "Sesame Street," a program for preschool children. Segments of the program, which are short, professionally produced, and varied in style (animation, live action, slow motion), "advertise" various products (the letter "W"; the number "9"). The program is very successful. Children learn from watching, and they enjoy what they see.[45]

In addition to "Sesame Street," the Children's Television Workshop has also been responsible for another successful program, "The Electric Company," designed to help children acquire reading skills. This program, too, has been empirically tested with results indicating that children benefit from viewing.[46]

Commercial networks have also tried to develop programs that not only entertain but also educate. During the 1976-77 television season, for example, CBS introduced "Marlo and the Magic Movie Machine" in five markets. Favorable reviews and ratings encouraged the producers to introduce the program nationally during the 1977-78 season. It is an hourlong, weekly program with a focus on music appreciation, reading, vocabulary, social studies, and practical aspects of science, as well as career awareness. If "Sesame Street" has encouraged commercial networks to produce similar programs, perhaps the message has by now reached commercial programmers who are slowly acting to improve quality in children's programs.

Efforts to improve television are constantly needed. The medium exerts a tremendous influence on American life, but that influence is often to make viewers passive. There is evidence to indicate that young viewers do other things while watching television,[47] yet it is clear that the more time children spend watching television, the less time they are active. Along the same vein, S. I. Hayakawa has said: "For all values television has, one thing you can't learn from it is interaction. Interaction . . . is an experience we all need. What happens to you if you've lost 22,000 hours of practice in interaction—interaction with your relatives, your grandma, your brothers and sisters, neighbors and friends, and so on?"[48]

TELEVISION: AN EDUCATIONAL TOOL

We have established that television provides an educational environment. Once that is clear, it is reasonable to ask what can be done about the effects of television. Others have suggested that one can turn to the government, to legal strategies, to parents, to teachers, and to the television industry.[49] I offer my suggestions to teachers and parents, for, even if television programming were to remain as it is, there is much that parents and teachers can do to affect the impact.

What Parents Can Do

Actively Watch with Their Children. Probably the most important thing parents can do to affect the impact of television is to watch it with their children and to ask the children about what they see, thereby developing in children a critical awareness of the impact of the medium. Children may be asked if they think that a road runner could be hit on the head one minute and completely recover the next minute. Do they think that people recover from injury so rapidly? They may be asked if they think the ambulance always arrives on time, as it does on television. They may be asked if the products we buy are the same as those seen in television advertisements. Or, do products look better on television than they really are? Older children might be asked about character portrayals on television. Do they think all women should stay at home, like Olivia Walton does? Why do they think women are usually shown in the kinds of roles in which they usually appear on television? Are there other things a woman might do besides the things they are seen doing on television? How does a person become a police officer? Do they think the police always catch criminals since criminals are always caught on television? Why, when looters are shown as they were during the blackout in New York, did the camera focus primarily on blacks? Why are all problems usually resolved before the end of a program?

In other words, television can stimulate conversation if parents talk with children and listen to their comments and ideas. Television is an important part of their lives. By listening to their comments, one can learn more about what life is like for them. Occasional questions asked by either parents or teachers familiar with the programs children and adolescents watch can make students more critical of televised programming.

Set Limits on Viewing. Perhaps television is too much a part of children's lives, and parents should restrict a child's viewing. Most research data indicate that not only do parents not restrict their children's viewing, but they allow children to watch whatever they want to watch—often on their own sets.[50] This brings us back to the observation that the more time one spends watching television, the less time is spent doing other things and the more people expect to be passively entertained.

There should be some limits on how much time one spends viewing television, but, when parents restrict viewing, they make television a valued commodity (high demand and lower supply). Just as, when parents say, "Don't read this yet; I think you may be too young for it," they increase a young person's desire to read "adult" material, restricting television may increase the desire to watch it. Despite potential problems, parents should seriously consider placing some restrictions on viewing, and the restrictions should depend on the age of the child.

There is little reason to suspect that young children know there are a wide range of channels on the television unless they see their parents or older brothers or sisters changing the channel. For children younger than five or six, therefore, it is possible to restrict viewing simply by leaving the television tuned into one of the public broadcasting stations or fixing the set so that it is impossible for the child to change the channels. Programs such as "Sesame Street," "The Electric Company," "Zoom," "Mr. Roger's Neighborhood," and "Nova," which are intended for a young audience, are found on the public broadcasting stations.

Older children can sit down with their parents at the beginning of the week and select programs they want to watch for the week. This teaches the children to manage their time, to read (the television listings), to make decisions, and to set priorities. By writing their viewing schedule, they increase their writing skills and learn the value of written contracts for the future.

Adolescents seem to watch fewer programs than younger children.[51] They leave the house more often and listen to other media (radio, records, tapes). Nevertheless, parents might occasionally ask their children to summarize the story lines of programs they have watched, just in the course of a normal conversation rather than as a test. For example, parents could ask, "Did anyone see 'Maude' last night? I missed it and wonder what it was about." These types of discussions are probably unusual, so it is best to introduce them gradually and recognize that it will take time for children to develop the ability to give a complete synopsis of story lines. But the procedure could develop the ability to speak in public, to include important details, and to analyze plots. The more young people do this, the more likely it is that they will discover that most television programming reflects standard formulas (criminals are always caught, problems are always resolved, race and sex roles are stereotyped).

Discussions of restricting viewing imply that all television content is indistinguishable and adverse. In my opinion this is not so. News programs, documentaries, treatments of literature, music, and art, sports, and well-done original drama not only entertain, but they educate positively and lead to stimulating discussions and discoveries. This is important. Parents may want to have their children develop a critical aesthetic appreciation and learn to distinguish between quality and nonquality programming. The more this happens, the more likely it is that the general overall quality of television programming will improve.

Develop Critical Evaluation of Content. Parents may develop aesthetic abilities in their children by asking them why they have selected the programs they are to view. What about the programs is good? Parents may ask what their children think are some of the bad aspects of their favorite programs. Perhaps the children will see nothing negative. If so, nothing more need be said. But each week, if the child prepares the television schedule, the parents might repeat some variation of the question. In time, the question will be on the child's mind, and, from it, children may begin to discover how to evaluate strengths and weaknesses in television broadcasts. Again, patience on the part of parents is needed, for change comes slowly, especially when it is related to something as popular as television.

Send Letters to Networks. Parents can also write to the television networks and to the local stations when they see programming that they really like and request that more be done. And, because the ultimate indicator of what people like on television is the Nielsen rating, parents should stop watching programs that they find objectionable. They can also write to the advertisers of programs that they find offensive[52] or stop purchasing their products. Parent-teacher organizations should invite speakers to discuss the impact of television. Discussion about how to effect changes in programming or how to deal with current programming may follow, thereby increasing public awareness of the educational environment created by television. The National Congress of Parents and Teachers is beginning an organized campaign to improve television. Parents and teachers may want to become better informed of their intended activities by contacting the leaders of their local parent-teacher association. In addition, if parents discuss television among themselves and watch critically, they can set an example for their children.

What Teachers Can Do

Use Television in Class. Teachers can make use of the techniques suggested above for parents, but they are in a position to make even more use of television as a teaching tool. Many teachers do not include television in their teaching programs because they think it is more entertaining than educational. As should be clear by now, television, even when primarily meant to entertain, is an educational environment. Learning does occur from it and, consequently, it can legitimately be included in an instructional program.

Another reason that teachers may not use television is that their schedules are already full with all that is on the agenda to be learned. In that case, administrators and curriculum planners need to be informed of the importance of television and to be aware of how the same educational objectives may be attained with the occasional use of television. The parent-teacher organization might undertake to make educators aware of how television can aid learning.

Teachers may also hesitate to incorporate television into the curriculum because they feel that it is already too much a part of children's lives outside of schools. While that is true, as we have seen, it is also important to realize that children are not critical sophisticated viewers. Teachers can and should help students develop the ability to view television critically. Since there is evidence to indicate that one reasonable way to teach is by meeting students at their interest level and since many students are interested in television, teachers should occasionally use television as a springboard to other discussion.

Refer to Programs in Classes. More teachers can be encouraged to do what many already do: refer to an occasional program that they would like their students to watch at home for subsequent discussion in class. For example, teachers may ask students to watch "Masterpiece Theater," a Jacques Cousteau program, "Nova," or a play. One problem is that some students may not be able to watch the program because they work or because someone else in the family is watching another channel. It is still appropriate to make the assignment, for students who have seen the program can summarize the story line for the class. One can check the historical accuracy of programs in history and social studies classes, assess the credibility of the story line and suggest supplementary reading in English classes, discuss the finances and figures involved in producing a television program or determine how much time in a commercial is devoted to showing the product in mathematics classes, assess the skills necessary to perform televised feats in physical education classes, or discuss product claims in consumer education classes.

Provide an Aid to Reading. Teachers may also include television as part of their reading curricula, as two enterprising teachers in Philadelphia have done.[53] As many teachers are aware, one problem in working with older children who have difficulty reading is to find suitable material. Students who are in the sixth grade but read at a second-grade level often complain that the content of the materials available is too childish. One could turn to things that are not too immature, and television scripts are a possibility. If the school has a videotape player and monitor, it is possible to tape a popular television program, such as "Gilligan's Island," or "Hogan's Heroes." Then the script for the program can be typed from the tape. Students view the entire program in class and become familiar with the content; then they read the script. If they have difficulty, the program can be replayed so that students can check their reading against the televised material. Teachers can also ask students to write their own endings to unfinished scripts. This is not to suggest that television should dominate in the curriculum; rather, it should become part of the materials with which teachers deal.

Other Uses of Television. There are other activities that might make use of television. Viewers can be instructed to look up and define one or two new words that they hear on a television program, and a running log of all the new words can be kept. Viewers can also be asked to go to the library and read about things they see on television. If a program is about life on an island, for example, they can read about life in similar circumstances. If the child has difficulty going to the library, additional materials can be supplied in class.

To help overcome the unrealistic attitudes often portrayed on television, schools can invite representatives of various occupations to visit the classrooms. If children watch an episode of "Baretta," or "Hawaii Five-O," or "Barney Miller," a police officer could be invited to class to compare incidents on the program with incidents in the actual life of police officers. Or the students could watch "Baretta" and record incidents of violence or cooperation, so that a class discussion of who commits violence, why it is committed, and whether it is ever justified can follow.

Students can be given televised scripts and asked to act them out. Some student could pretend to be a famous unidentified television star, and the class could interview the "star" to find out who is "appearing" in class. Students can be asked to prepare their own commercials, which can actually be taped on school video equipment and played back for classroom review. Also, teachers may turn off the sound of recorded programs and ask students to fill in the dialogue and story line. Another activity is to have students write the words shown on television, for most advertisements and program wrap-arounds (the beginnings and endings of programs) have words. The words can then be used in learning to spell. Or teachers can use game shows as a model ("Password," "Jeopardy," "$25,000 Pyramid") and have occasional quiz show contests in class.[54]

Teachers can benefit from attending to some of the reasons why television is popular. As mentioned earlier, these include absence of criticism, allowing the viewer to be the ultimate source of control, and providing interesting visual images in various formats. It is possible in some classes occasionally to allow the children to be the ultimate source of control and decide what the topic for the day will be and how it will be handled. Since most children are accustomed to having adults do this, it may take some time for them to decide what to do. When presenting material in classes, teachers should try various formats, such as films, drawings, and photographs, in addition to verbal presentations. Of course, teachers should carefully attend to the amount and types of criticisms one gives to student performance. Teachers may also videotape activities in later classes and play back the material for the students. In this way students may better understand the "myths" behind television. That is, they may develop an appreciation of how events come to be televised. They may also come to understand themselves better by seeing how they look to others.

This chapter has suggested ways in which viewers may make better use of, and become familiar with, the best of television. It offers hope that, as we become more sophisticated about the use of television, it will in turn become more sophisticated. And, as familiarity with the educational roles and possibilities of television increases, so will the awareness of how to increase the benefits and overcome the shortcomings. Television is unquestionably an educational environment, and it can be used and improved.

NOTES

1. Les Brown, *Television: The Business behind the Box* (New York: Harcourt Brace Jovanovich, 1971).

2. Alberta E. Siegel, "Communicating with the Next Generation," *Journal of Communication* 25 (1975): 14-24.

3. Marshall McLuhan, *Understanding Media: The Extensions of Man* (New York: Signet, 1964).

4. I am particularly grateful for the helpful comments and suggestions that Gerald S. Lesser, Herbert Walberg, and Elaine Barron offered on earlier drafts of this chapter.

5. George A. Comstock and Marilyn Fisher, *Television and Human Behavior: A Guide to the Pertinent Scientific Literature* (Santa Monica, Calif.: Rand Corporation, 1977).

6. Joseph R. Dominick and Millard C. Pearce, "Trends in Network Prime-Time Programming, 1953-74," *Journal of Communication* 26 (1976): 70-80; George Gerbner, "Violence in Television Drama: Trends and Symbolic Functions," in *Television and Social Behavior,* Volume 1: *Media Content and Control,* ed. George A. Comstock and Eli A. Rubinstein (Washington, D.C.: U.S. Government Printing Office, 1972), 28-187; Ronald Slaby, Gary Quarfoth, and Gene A. McConnachie, "Television Violence and Its Sponsors," *Journal of Communication* 26 (1976): 88-96.

7. Aimee D. Leifer, Neal J. Gordon, and Sherryl B. Graves, "Children's Television: More than Mere Entertainment," *Harvard Educational Review* 44 (1974): 213-245.

8. Linda J. Busby, "Sex-Role Research on the Mass Media," *Journal of Communication* 25 (1975): 107-131.

9. Bradley S. Greenberg and Brenda Dervin, *Use of the Mass Media by the Urban Poor* (New York: Praeger, 1970).

10. Anees A. Sheikh, U.K. Prasad, and T. R. Roa, "Children's Television Commercials: A Review of Research," *Journal of Communication* 24 (1974): 126-136; Scott Ward *et al.,* "Effects of Television Advertising on Consumer Socialization," (Cambridge, Mass.: Marketing Science Institute, 1974).

11. Charles K. Atkin, John P. Murray and O. B. Nayman, "The Surgeon General's Empirical Findings," *Journal of Broadcasting* 16 (1971): 21-35; Robert M. Liebert, John M. Neale, and Emily S. Davidson, *The Early Window: Effects of Television on Children and Youth* (Elmsford, N.Y.: Pergamon Press, 1973); Donald Roberts, "Communication and Children: A Developmental Approach," in *Handbook of*

Communication, ed. Ithiel de Sola Pool and Wilbur Schramm (Chicago: Rand McNally, 1973), 174-215.

12. Douglass Cater and Stephen Strickland, *T.V. Violence and the Child: The Evaluation and Fate of the Surgeon General's Report* (New York: Russell Sage Foundation, 1975).

13. George A. Comstock, "The Evidence So Far," *Journal of Communication* 25 (1975): 25-34.

14. Siegel, "Communicating with the Next Generation."

15. Jack Lyle, "Television in Daily Life: Patterns of Use Overview," in *Television and Social Behavior,* Volume 4: *Television and Day-to-Day Life: Patterns of Use,* ed. Eli A. Rubinstein, George A. Comstock, and John P. Murray (Washington, D.C.: U.S. Government Printing Office, 1972), 1-32.

16. Robert B. Choate, "Fair Play for Young Viewers," *New York Times,* September 17, 1972.

17. Siegel, "Communicating with the Next Generation."

18. Surgeon General's Scientific Advisory Committee on Television and Social Behavior, *Television and Growing Up: The Impact of Televised Violence* (Washington, D.C.: U.S. Government Printing Office, 1972).

19. Albert Bandura, *Aggression: A Social Learning Analysis* (Englewood Cliffs, N.J.: Prentice-Hall, 1973); Leonard Berkowitz, "Violence in the Mass Media," in *Aggression: A Social Psychological Analysis,* ed. Leonard Berkowitz (New York: McGraw-Hill, 1962), 229-255; Leo Bogart, "Warning: The Surgeon General Has Determined that T.V. Violence Is Moderately Dangerous to Your Child's Mental Health," *Public Opinion Quarterly* 36 (1972): 491-521; Steven H. Chaffee, "Television and Adolescent Aggressiveness (Overview)," in *Television and Social Behavior,* Volume 3: *Television and Adolescent Aggressiveness,* ed. George A. Comstock and Eli A. Rubinstein (Washington, D.C.: U.S. Government Printing Office, 1972), 1-34; Comstock, "The Evidence So Far"; Anthony N. Doob and Hershi M. Kirshenbaum, "The Effects on Arousal of Frustration and Aggression Films," *Journal of Experimental Social Psychology* 9 (1973): 57-64; Ronald S. Drabman and Margaret H. Thomas, "Does Media Violence Increase Children's Tolerance of Real-Life Aggression?" *Developmental Psychology* 10 (1974): 418-421; R.E. Goranson, "Media Violence and Aggressive Behavior: A Review of Experimental Research," in *Advances in Experimental Social Psychology,* Volume 5, ed. Leonard Berkowitz, (New York: Academic Press, 1970), 1-31; Liebert, Neale, and Davidson, *The Early Window;* Jerome L. Singer, "Influence of Violence Portrayed in Television or Motion Pictures upon Overt Aggressive Behavior," in *The Control of Aggression and Violence: Cognitive and Psychological Factors,* ed. *id.* (New York: Academic Press, 1971), 19-60; Surgeon General's Scientific Advisory Committee on Television and Social Behavior, *Television and Growing Up;* Margaret H. Thomas and Ronald S. Drabman, "Toleration of Real-Life Aggression as a Function of Exposure to Televised Violence and Age of Subject," *Merrill-Palmer Quarterly* 21 (1975): 227-232; Margaret H. Thomas *et al.,* "Desensitization to Portrayals of Real-Life Aggression as a Function of Exposure to Television Violence," *Journal of Personality and Social Psychology* 35 (1977): 450-458.

20. Surgeon General's Scientific Advisory Committee, *Television and Growing Up,* 18-19.

21. Siegel, "Communicating with the Next Generation." For further comments on this research, see also Leifer, Gordon, and Graves, "Children's Television," and Cater and Strickland, *T.V. Violence and the Child*.

22. R. M. Kaplan, "On Television as a Cause of Aggression," *American Psychologist* 27 (1972): 968-969.

23. Seymour Feshbach and Robert D. Singer, *Television and Aggression* (San Francisco: Jossey-Bass, 1971); Alberta E. Siegel, "Film-Mediated Fantasy Aggression and Strength of Aggressive Drive," *Child Development* 27 (1956): 355-378.

24. Aletha H. Stein, Lynette K. Friedrich, and Fred Vondracek, "Television Content and Young Children's Behavior," in *Television and Social Behavior*, Volume 2: *Television and Social Learning*, ed. John P. Murray, Eli A., Rubinstein, and George A. Comstock (Washington, D.C.: U.S. Government Printing Office, 1972), 202-317.

25. Seymour Feshbach, "The Drive-Reducing Function of Fantasy Behavior," *Journal of Abnormal and Social Psychology* 50 (1955): 3-11; *id.* "The Stimulating versus Cathartic Effects of a Vicarious Aggressive Activity," *ibid.*, 63 (1961): 381-385. Feshbach and Singer, *Television and Aggression*.

26. Leonard Berkowitz, "Control of Aggression," in *Review of Child Development Research*, Volume 3, ed. Bettye M. Caldwell and Henry N. Riccuti, (Chicago: University of Chicago Press, 1973), 95-140; Comstock, "The Evidence So Far"; R. F. Goranson, "The Catharsis Effect: Two Opposing Views," in *Violence and the Media: A Staff Report to the National Commission on the Causes and Prevention of Violence*, ed. David L. Lange, Robert K. Baker, and Sandra J. Ball (Washington, D.C.: U.S. Government Printing Office, 1969), 453-459; Robert M. Liebert, Michael D. Sobol, and Emily S. Davidson, "Catharsis Aggression among Institutionalized Boys: Fact or Artifact?" in *Television and Social Behavior*, Volume 5: *Television's Effects: Further Explorations*, ed. George A. Comstock, Eli A. Rubinstein, and John P. Murray (Washington, D.C.: U.S. Government Printing Office, 1972), 366-373; Siegel, "Communicating with the Next Generation."

27. Siegel, "Communicating with the Next Generation."

28. Merrill Panitt, "Network Power: Is It Absolute?" *TV Guide*, February 26, 1977.

29. William Melody, *Children's Television: The Economics of Exploitation* (New Haven, Conn.: Yale University Press, 1973).

30. Gary Deeb, "T.V. Puts Out a Contract for Violence that Really Means Something," *Chicago Tribune*, June 20, 1977.

31. Office of Social Research, Columbia Broadcasting System, *Learning While They Laugh: Studies of Five Children's Programs on the CBS Television Network* (New York: Columbia Broadcasting System, 1977).

32. Lynette K. Friedrich and Aletha H. Stein, "Aggressive and Prosocial Television Programs and the Natural Behavior of Preschool Children," *Monographs of the Society for Research in Child Development* 38, no. 4 (1973): entire issue; Aimee Leifer, "Television and the Development of Social Behavior," paper presented at the biennial meeting of the International Society for the Study of Behavioral Development, Ann Arbor, Mich., 1973; F. Leon Paulson, D. L. McDonald, and S. L. Whittemore, "An Evaluation of Sesame Street Programming Designed to Teach Cooperative Behavior" (Monmouth, Ore.: Teaching Research, 1972); Rita W. Poulos, Eli A.

Rubinstein, and Robert M. Liebert, "Positive Social Learning," *Journal of Communication* 25 (1975): 90-97.

33. Melvin DeFleur and Lois DeFleur, "The Relative Contributions of Television as a Learning Source for Children's Occupational Knowledge," *American Sociological Review* 32 (1967): 777-789; Joseph R. Dominick and Bradley S. Greenberg, "Attitudes toward Violence: The Interaction of Television Exposure, Family Attitudes, and Social Class," in *Television and Adolescent Aggressiveness,* ed. Comstock and Rubinstein, 314-335; Neil Hollander, "Adolescents and the War: The Sources of Socialization," *Journalism Quarterly* 48 (1971): 472-479; Joseph T. Klapper, *The Effects of Mass Communication* (New York: Free Press, 1960).

34. Gerry Bogatz and Samuel Ball, *The Second Year of Sesame Street: A Continuing Evaluation* (Princeton, N.J.: Educational Testing Service, 1971).

35. Busby, "Sex-Role Research on the Mass Media"; Leifer, Gordon, and Graves, "Children's Television."

36. Joseph R. Dominick and G. C. Rauch, "The Image of Women in Network T.V. Commercials," *Journal of Broadcasting* 16 (1972): 259-265.

37. Greenberg and Dervin, *Use of the Mass Media by the Urban Poor;* J. M. McLeod, Charles K. Atkin, and Steven H. Chaffee, "Adolescents, Parents, and Television Use: Adolescent Self-Report Measures from Maryland and Wisconsin Samples," in *Television and Adolescent Aggressiveness,* ed. Comstock and Rubinstein, 183-238; *id.,* "Adolescents, Parents, and Television Use: Self-Report and Other-Report Measures from the Wisconsin Sample," *ibid.,* 239-313; Jack Lyle and Heidi R. Hoffman, "Explorations of Television Viewing by Preschool-Age Children," in *Television and Day-to-Day Life: Patterns of Use,* ed. Rubinstein, Comstock, and Murray, 257-273.

38. Ward *et al.,* "Effects of Television Advertising on Consumer Socialization."

39. Scott Ward, "Effects of Television Advertising on Children and Adolescents," in *Television in Day-to-Day Life,* ed. Rubinstein, Comstock, and Murray, 432-451.

40. Thomas S. Robertson and John R. Rossiter, "Children's Responsiveness to Commercials," *Journal of Communication* 27 (1977): 101-106; Anees Sheikh and L. Martin Moleski, "Conflict in the Family over Commercials," *ibid.,* 152-157.

41. Robertson and Rossiter, "Children's Responsiveness to Commercials."

42. Charles K. Atkin and Gary Heald, "The Content of Children's Toy and Food Commercials," *Journal of Communication* 27 (1977): 107-114.

43. Pat Burr and Richard M. Burr, "Product Recognition and Premium Appeal," *ibid.,* 115-117.

44. Diane Liebert *et al.,* "Effects of Television Commercial Disclaimers on the Product Expectations of Children," *ibid.,* 118-124.

45. Bogatz and Ball, *Second Year of "Sesame Street";* Gerald Lesser, "Learning, Teaching, and Television Production for Children: The Experience of 'Sesame Street,'" *Harvard Educational Review* 42 (1972): 232-272; *id., Children and Television: Lessons from "Sesame Street"* (New York: Random House, 1974). This latter volume provides a fascinating account of the history of "Sesame Street," reviewing its curriculum, discussing finances, and reporting research relating to the strengths and weaknesses of the program. "Sesame Street" has been introduced in several other countries. See Thomas D. Cook and Ross F. Conner, "'Sesame Street' around the World: The Educational Impact," *Journal of Communication* 26 (1976): 155-164.

Other articles in the same issue of the *Journal of Communication* describe experiences with the program in other countries.

46. Samuel Ball and Gerry A. Bogatz, *Reading with Television: An Evaluation of "The Electric Company,"* 2 vols. (Princeton, N.J.: Educational Testing Service, 1973).

47. Robert Bechtel, Clark Achelpohl, and Roger Akers, "Correlates between Observed Behavior and Questionnaire Responses on Television Viewing," in *Television in Day-to-Day Life,* ed. Rubinstein, Comstock, and Murray, 274-344; John P. Murray, "Television in Inner-City Homes: Viewing Behavior of Young Boys," *ibid.,* 345-394; Jack Lyle and Heidi R. Hoffman, "Children's Use of Television and Other Media," *ibid.,* 129-256.

48. S. I. Hayakawa, "Image and Reality," *Bulletin of the National Association of Secondary School Principals* 53 (1969): 42.

49. Leifer, Gordon, and Graves, "Children's Television."

50. Anne H. Adams and Cathy B. Harrison, "Using Television to Teach Specific Reading Skills," *Reading Teacher* 29 (1975): 45-51.

51. Marc Baranowski, "Television and the Adolescent," *Adolescence* 6 (1971): 369-396.

52. Nicholas Johnson, *How to Talk Back to Your Television Set* (New York: Bantam, 1970).

53. Craig R. Waters, "Thank God Something Has Finally Reached Him," *TV Guide* (January 19, 1974), 6-9.

54. Other suggestions for using television in the teaching of reading may be found in Adams and Harrison, "Using Television to Teach Specific Reading Skills," and in George J. Becker, *Television and the Classroom Reading Program* (Newark, Del.: International Reading Association, 1973).

PART TWO
Sociopsychological Environments

4. Educational Climates

Rudolf H. Moos

A school principal tries to develop an alternative school in which students who do not adjust to traditional classrooms can function more effectively. Members of a school board establish an "open plan" school because they believe that a freer and more innovative atmosphere will enhance student learning. A parent, shocked at the lack of emphasis on basic skills in the public schools, waits in line to ensure his child's enrollment in a new "back to basics" program. A school counselor recommends that a shy, introverted child be transferred to a class in which students are friendly, the teacher is supportive, and competition is de-emphasized. A teacher suggests that a hyperactive child might function better in a structured than in an unstructured classroom setting.

Each of these people is responding to the belief that the social environment has important effects on students' satisfaction, learning, and personal growth. Their search for information and their decision making reflect the assumption that one can distinguish different types

Preparation of this chapter was supported in part by NIMH Grant MH16026, NIAAA Grant AA02863, and Veterans Administration Research Funds.

of dimensions of social environmental stimuli, that these dimensions can have distinctive influences on psychological processes and behavior, and that their effects may differ widely from one individual to another. I believe that these assumptions are valid. In this chapter I illustrate the concept and assessment of social climate, discuss the underlying patterns of social climate in educational settings, describe the utility of the social climate concept by drawing on examples from our program of research, summarize evidence suggesting that the social environments of educational settings have important effects, and focus on some practical applications of the information.

THE SOCIAL CLIMATE

Definition and Measurement

How can the "blooming, buzzing confusion" of a natural social environment be adequately assessed? Although many procedures have been developed, much of the relevant empirical work derives from the contributions of Murray, who first conceptualized the dual process of personal needs and environmental press.[1] Murray suggested that individuals have specific needs (for example, needs for achievement, for affiliation, for autonomy, for order) and that the strength of these needs characterizes personality. The concept of need represents the significant internal or personal determinant of behavior, but, as Murray pointed out, this "leaves out the nature of the environment, a serious omission."[2] Murray selected the term "press" to indicate a directional tendency in an object or situation that facilitates or impedes the efforts of an individual to obtain a particular goal.

Pace and Stern extended the concept of environmental press by applying the logic of "perceived climate" to study the "atmosphere" of colleges and universities.[3] They constructed the *College Characteristics Index* (CCI) to measure the global college environment by asking students to act as reporters about that environment. The student's task was to answer "true" or "false" for items covering a wide range of topics about the college (student-faculty relationships, rules and regulations, classroom methods, facilities, and so forth).

Stern later remarked that descriptions of environmental press were based on inferred continuity and consistency in otherwise discrete events.[4] If students in a school are assigned seats in classrooms, if attendance records are kept, if faculty members see students outside of class only by appointment, if there is a prescribed form for all term papers, if neatness counts, among other things, then it is probable that the press at this school emphasizes the development of orderly responses on the part of students. These conditions establish the social climate or atmosphere of a setting. Students' perceptions of this climate or "learning environment" are useful in predicting achievement and in contributing to our understanding of educational processes.[5]

Constructing the Classroom Environment Scale

The steps involved in the construction of the *Classroom Environment Scale* (CES) illustrate the logic underlying the measurement of social climate. Edison Trickett and I used several methods to gain a naturalistic understanding of classroom social environments and to obtain an initial pool of items for a questionnaire. Semistructured interviews were conducted with teachers and students in different high schools. Interviews focused on students' behavior and attitudes toward their classes, on teaching styles, and on how classes differed from one another. Observations of different kinds of classes were carried out in several schools. Popular and professional literature was reviewed to identify characteristics along which classrooms might vary.

Initial dimensions that were salient for students and teachers, and that were conceptually meaningful, were identified on the basis of these data, and test items thought to indicate these dimensions were written. Items were chosen to represent varying degrees of abstraction. With respect to the dimension of student involvement, for example, one of the more behavioral items was "very few students take part in the class discussions or activities" (a negatively keyed item), while a more inferential item was "students really enjoy this class." After the original pool was developed, items were reassigned to dimensions by two naive raters on the basis of independent agreement that they "belonged" to a particular dimension. These procedures resulted in a 242-item initial questionnaire representing thirteen conceptual dimensions.

Data from sixty-four junior and senior high school classrooms representing a wide range of settings were used in constructing several revisions of the CES. Various criteria were used to select items for inclusion in the final form. Each item had to relate highly to its own subscale. The subscales had to show only low to moderate interrelationships. Each item had to discriminate among different classrooms.

Items that correlated with the *Crowne-Marlowe Social Desirability Scale* were deleted. These criteria resulted in the current CES (Form R) consisting of 90 true-false items grouped into nine subscales.

The development of the CES is more fully discussed elsewhere.[6] In brief, the nine subscales have adequate internal consistency (ranging from .67 to .86), show good six-week test-retest reliability (ranging from .72 to .90), and have average intercorrelations of around .25, indicating that they measure distinct though somewhat related aspects of social environments in the classroom. All nine of the subscales significantly discriminate among classrooms. The proportion of subscale variance accounted for by differences among classrooms is generally quite substantial, ranging from 21 percent to 48 percent in one sample of twenty-two classrooms. (The *University Residence Environment Scale* (URES), which is composed of 100 true-false items representing ten dimensions, was derived in an analogous manner from data obtained from students and staff in university living groups.)[7]

There are three parallel forms of the CES: The Real Form (Form R) asks teachers and students (or observers) how they perceive the current classroom social environment. The Ideal Form (Form I) asks people how they conceive of an ideal classroom environment. The Expectations Form (Form E) asks prospective members of a class (or observers) what they think the social milieu they are about to enter is like. The URES and other social climate scales also have three parallel forms.

UNDERLYING PATTERNS OF SOCIAL ENVIRONMENTS

Recent research has shown that vastly different social environments can be described by common or similar sets of dimensions conceptualized in three broad categories: relationship, personal growth or goal orientation, and system maintenance and change. These categories are similar across many environments, although vastly different settings may impose unique variations within the general categories.[9] The dimensions identified in junior and senior high school classrooms and in university students' living groups are listed in Table 4-1.

Relationship dimensions assess the extent to which people are involved in the environment, the extent to which they support and help one another, and the extent of spontaneity and free and open expression among them. Involvement in classrooms, for example, measures how attentive students are in class activities and how much they parti-

social environments

Table 4-1
Underlying patterns of educational settings

Setting	Relationship	Personal growth or goal orientation	System maintenance and system change
Junior and senior high school classrooms	Involvement Affiliation Teacher support	Task orientation Competition	Order and organization Rule clarity Teacher control Innovation
University student living groups	Involvement Emotional support	Independence Traditional social orientation Competition Academic achievement Intellectuality	Order and organization Innovation Student influence

cipate in discussions. Involvement in students' living groups reflects commitment to the residence and the residents and the amount of social interaction and feelings of friendship. Affiliation in classrooms measures the extent to which students work with and come to know each other within the classroom. Teacher support assesses the degree to which the teacher expresses a personal interest in, and is supportive of, the students.

Personal growth or goal orientation dimensions assess the basic directions along which personal development and self-enhancement tend to move in an environment. The exact nature of these dimensions varies somewhat among different environments, depending on their underlying purposes and goals. In junior and senior high school classrooms these dimensions are: task orientation (the extent to which the activities of the class are centered around the accomplishment of specific academic objectives) and competition (the amount of emphasis on academic competition and grades). In university students' living groups the dimensions are: independence (diversity of residents' behaviors allowed without social sanctions versus socially proper and conformist behavior), traditional social orientation (stress on dating, going to parties, and other "traditional" heterosexual interactions), competition (the degree to which a wide variety of activities such as dating and grades is cast into a competitive framework), academic achievement (the extent to which strictly classroom and academic accomplishments and concerns are prominent), and intellectuality (the emphasis on cultural, artistic, and other scholarly intellectual activities).

System maintenance and change dimensions assess the extent to which the environment is orderly, clear in its expectations, maintains control, and is responsive to change. The relevant dimensions in classroom environments are order and organization (emphasis on the overall organization of assignments and classroom activities), rule clarity (emphasis on establishing and following a clear set of rules and on students knowing what the consequences will be if they do not follow the rules), teacher control (how strict the teacher is in enforcing the rules and how severe the punishment is for rule infractions), and innovation (how much students contribute to planning classroom activities and the amount of unusual and varying activities and assignments planned by the teachers).

My colleagues and I have completed work in seven other types of social environments: hospital-based and community-based psychiatric treatment programs, correctional institutions, military basic training companies, social and task-oriented groups, industrial or work settings, and families. We have developed social climate scales for each of these environments. Each of the dimensions (subscales) on each of these scales was empirically derived from independent data obtained from respondents in that particular environment. Our studies have shown that the above three broad categories of dimensions are relevant to each of the environments and are useful in characterizing the social and organizational climates of a variety of groups and institutions.[10]

The overall concepts hold as well for scales developed by other investigators as they do for our social climate scales. Stern identified several major types of dimensions based on extensive research with the *Organizational Climate Index*.[11] The first two dimensions—closeness and group life—appear to be relationship dimensions. Three of Stern's dimensions seem to reflect personal growth, and they are intellectual climate, personal dignity, and achievement standards. Stern's last two factors—orderliness and impulse control or constraint—are system maintenance factors. Other investigators have found conceptually similar dimensions in high school and college environments.[12] Formulating three broad categories of dimensions gives us a convenient framework within which to provide an overview of the utility of the concept of social climate.

Description and Classification

One of the most important uses of information about social climate is to provide a detailed description of how people perceive an environment. For example, the CES and URES can be used to compare the perceptions of different groups of people (for example, teachers and students in classrooms, housing administrators and resident assistants in students' living groups), and to monitor fluctuations in the social climate of an environment over time. The degree of agreement among students and between students and teachers about the social environment of their classroom is an important descriptive characteristic of that classroom.

A more complete description of an environment may be obtained when the Ideal Form of the relevant social climate scale is used, since then the goals and value orientations of different participants are also assessed. What kinds of environments do teachers and students consider ideal? In what areas are the goals of housing administrators, resident assistants, and university students basically similar with respect to students' living groups? In what areas are their goals basically different? How close is the current social environment to what the participants feel is ideal?[13]

The CES and URES can also be completed by observers or other individuals who are not participants in a setting. Parents can fill out the CES on the basis of their observations of their children's classrooms. Teachers can fill out the scale on the basis of their observations of other teachers' classes. A student can fill out the URES on the basis of a visit to a living group. Although the social climate scales assess perceptions of an environment, applicability is not limited to those who are currently participating in that environment.

A more comprehensive approach to description is to construct general classification schemes for classroom learning environments. The need for this approach is apparent from research indicating that different dimensions of classroom environments are related to different classroom outcomes, and suggesting that the congruence or fit between student and classroom characteristics accounts for at least some of the variance in student behavior and development.[14]

We attempted to develop an empirical typology of the social envi-

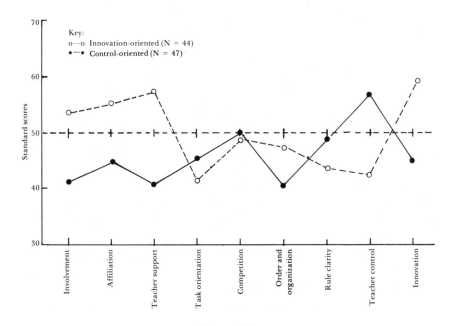

Figure 4-1
Mean classroom environment scale profiles for control-oriented
and innovation-oriented clusters

ronments of junior and senior high school classes from CES data obtained from students in 200 classes representatively drawn from a larger sample of 382 classes. The nine student CES mean scores for each of the 200 classrooms were subjected to an empirical cluster analysis,[15] and five distinctive types of classes were identified: control oriented, innovation oriented, affiliation oriented, task oriented, and competition oriented.

One of the most striking aspects of the results was the identification of forty-seven classrooms (over 23 percent) almost exclusively oriented toward teacher control of student behavior. These classrooms showed a high emphasis on teacher control in the absence of emphasis on any of the other dimensions of classroom environments. Students complained of a lack of teacher-student and student-student interaction, and perceived little emphasis on task orientation or classroom organization (see Figure 4-1). The forty-four classrooms in the next largest cluster, labeled innovation oriented, showed high emphasis on innovation and on all three relationship dimensions, indicating that students perceived moderate to substantial emphasis on teacher-student and

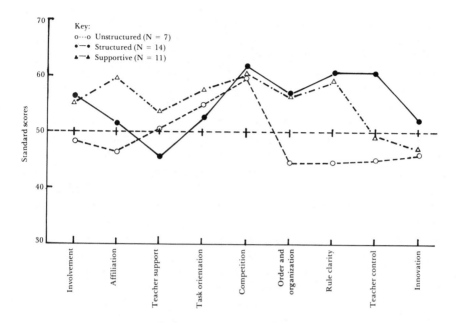

Figure 4-2

Mean classroom environment scale profiles for
three competition-oriented subclusters

student-student relationships. On the other hand, they perceived relatively little task orientation and complained of a lack of clarity in
classroom goals and procedures. In sharp contrast to the first cluster,
they perceived relatively low levels of teacher control (see Figure 4-1).

The thirty-two classrooms in the competition-oriented cluster emphasized students competing with each other for grades and recognition. Three distinct types of classrooms were represented (see Figure
4-2). Although the structured and unstructured competition-oriented
subtypes both showed their highest scores on competition, they were
quite different on all three of the system maintenance dimensions.
The structured subcluster was considerably higher on organization,
clarity, and control, as well as somewhat higher on student involvement. These two subclusters were relatively similar in their emphasis
on student-student interaction and teacher support, indicating that
the degree of teacher control can vary among classes even when the
degree of teacher support does not.

The affiliative competition-oriented subcluster also emphasized
competition, but did so in a context in which students felt friendly to-

ward each other, helped each other with homework, and enjoyed working together. These classes emphasized organization and clarity, but de-emphasized teacher control. This subtype indicates that an emphasis on competition and, to a somewhat lesser extent, on task orientation can occur in a context in which students feel supportive toward one another.

Attempts to replicate studies on different samples of classrooms may often be unsuccessful because of differences in the social environments of the classrooms studied. For example, findings using mainly innovation-oriented classes may or may not generalize to control-oriented classes. Since control-oriented classes emphasize control of behavior to the virtual exclusion of substantive learning, they may not even be appropriate for studies of teacher effectiveness.[16] The development of a typology of classrooms may provide information on the range of environmental variation within which replications of specific findings can reasonably be expected to occur.[17]

Comparison and Contrast

Another major use of information about social environments is to compare different educational settings. For example, how do several mathematics classes taught by the same teacher differ? How do the English classes taught by one teacher differ from those taught by another? How do classes taught by more-experienced teachers differ from those taught by less-experienced ones? Do large classes have more emphasis on teacher control and less emphasis on innovation than small classes? In what ways do coed living groups differ from all-male and all-female living groups?

This type of research is illustrated by a comparison of the social environments of classrooms randomly drawn from five types of high schools: urban, suburban, rural, vocational, and alternative.[18] The clearest differences among the five types of schools occurred between alternative and vocational schools. Alternative schools had classrooms that stressed the interpersonal aspects of student-student and teacher-student relationships, as their underlying ideologies would suggest. They also reflected an antiauthority and anticompetitive quality consistent with their emphasis on personal rather than role-related relationships. Contrary to popular stereotype, however, alternative school classrooms were generally well organized and task oriented. Vocational school classrooms presented a quite different picture. They were lowest in teacher support and innovation and highest in competition and teacher control. In supportive findings, Eash and his colleagues reported that students in an alternative junior high school perceived their classroom environments as higher on cohesion, democracy, and goal direction, and lower on apathy, friction, and disorganization than did students in control schools.[19]

Trickett reasons that alternative and vocational schools may contrast sharply in classroom environments because they have distinct institutional missions.[20] Alternative schools are often developed in reaction to perceived inadequacies in large public high schools, including impersonality and an overconcern with rules, discipline, and academic competition. In the vocational school classrooms, however, there is a more businesslike hierarchical teacher-as-expert environment consistent with an attempt to impart clearly defined vocational skills to students.

Rural, suburban, and urban classrooms also differed from one another in generally expected ways, though they did not provide the sharp contrast found between alternative and vocational schools. Suburban classrooms emphasized supportive teacher-student relationships, stressed order and organization, and, somewhat surprisingly, were below the mean on competition, particularly below the level of competition reported in vocational schools. Quite unexpectedly, urban classrooms were highest on task orientation, and were higher than all except alternative schools in classroom involvement. Trickett notes that systematic differences in classrooms in different types of schools suggest that adolescents undergoing these various "treatments" have different socialization experiences, and, consequently, different socialization outcomes.[21]

Two related uses of information about perceived climate involve testing theoretical predictions regarding the ways in which social environments should differ from one another[22] and monitoring the degree to which the implementation of a new educational program actually affects the social climate of a setting. Relevant studies in university residence groups have shown that novel living-learning environments differ from those of more "traditional" dormitory units,[23] that the social milieus of high-rise megadorms differ from those of low-rise dorms,[24] and that small student suites foster a different type of social environment than traditional dormitory rooms.[25]

Evaluating the Impact

Several investigators have recently emphasized the importance of focusing on educational outcomes other than those assessed by traditional achievement tests, such as cognitive preferences,[26] satisfaction with school,[27] and continuing interest and motivation to learn.[28] Some relevant studies have been carried out with the CES and derive what I think are reasonable conclusions regarding the impact of educational settings, notwithstanding the host of methodological difficulties involved, and they are mentioned briefly here.[29] Since most people believe, probably correctly, that the social environments of educational settings do matter, we need to formulate some tentative conclusions regarding their differential effects.

What do recent studies tell us about the impact of educational environments? Students express greater satisfaction in classrooms characterized by high student involvement, by a personal student-teacher relationship, by innovative teaching methods, and by clarity of rules. Classrooms in which students report a great deal of content learning combine an affective concern with students as people (relationship dimension) with an emphasis on students working hard for academic rewards (competition) within a coherent, organized context.[30] Senior high school physics classes seen as more difficult and competitive (personal growth dimensions) gained more on physics achievement and science understanding, whereas classes perceived as more satisfying and as having less friction and apathy (relationship dimensions) gained more on science interest and activities.[31] Paige found that fifth- and sixth-grade Indonesian students' perceptions of classroom personal growth press were positively related to their end-of-course achievement levels,[32] whereas Walberg, Singh, and Rasher found that student perceptions of all three types of dimensions (as operationalized by classifying scores on the *Learning Environment Inventory* subscales) were significantly related to mean end-of-course achievement scores in general science and social studies classes.[33]

Student input factors in colleges are strongly related to student aspiration and achievement levels. The social environment of the college the student attends is, however, also important. Colleges that emphasize relationship dimensions (for example, faculty-student interaction, peer cohesion) have a positive impact on student satisfaction and morale. Colleges that emphasize personal development dimensions (for example, humanism, reflectiveness, broad intellectual emphasis, independent study and criticism, high standards) tend to facilitate their students' academic aspirations and intellectual productivity.[34]

The clearest conclusion to date is that satisfying human relationships tend to facilitate personal growth and development in all social environments. An emphasis on relationship dimensions is necessary, but it is *not* sufficient. Objective behavioral and performance effects seem to depend on a combination of warm and supportive relationships, an emphasis on specific directions of personal growth, and a reasonably clear, orderly, and well-structured milieu. These environments yield a high expectation and demand for performance,[35] but too much emphasis on personal growth may have certain negative concomitants and result in environments with high rates of absenteeism, dropout, or illness.

For example, Bernice Moos and I found that classes with high absenteeism rates were seen as high in competition and teacher control and low in teacher support. Students in these classes felt they were often clock-watchers, that they needed to be careful about what they said, that it was easy to get into trouble in the class, that passing the class was relatively difficult, that the teacher was fairly strict, and the like.[36] Studies conducted in quite different social settings (senior high school classrooms, university student living groups, psychiatric treatment wards, and military basic training companies) have obtained generally similar results.[37] High-risk settings appear to share certain characteristics, at least as perceived by their inhabitants.

Thus, students may learn more in classrooms that are considered difficult and competitive, but they may also be absent more often from those classrooms. And, since absenteeism is related to making poorer grades and ultimately to dropping out of school, emphasis on competition may encourage cognitive growth in some students while discouraging it in others. This is consistent with Wessman's finding that there is increased anxiety and tension among some of the disadvantaged students who participated in a compensatory education project.[38] It is also consistent with the notion that some students will experience more failure, perform more poorly, and be less self-assured and less motivated in competitive than in cooperative or individualistic class settings.[39] In addition, highly structured educational settings can create considerable dependence on the part of students toward the program. These students may rapidly lose their former high gains when they return to a regular sink-or-swim setting in which they get little individual attention.[40]

The interrelationship of various social-environmental dimensions may critically affect impact. A moderate degree of structure (particularly organization and clarity of expectations) in a class oriented toward student-student interaction or teacher support can, for instance, relate positively to student involvement and satisfaction, and, to a somewhat lesser extent, to teacher satisfaction as well. The degree of classroom structure, however, can become too rigid and nonsupportive. The crucial difference is in the overall context in which the structure occurs since the same "objective" level of teacher control may be perceived as more restrictive in settings that lack emphasis on the relationship dimensions.[41]

An emphasis on task orientation, competition, and teacher control is often rationalized on the basis that students will learn more in such an atmosphere, but the emphasis on student-student and teacher-student interaction may be an important moderating influence on the potential impact of these dimensions. Stress on noncognitive aspects of the environment may facilitate cognitive outcomes,[42] just as stress on maintenance-oriented aspects may facilitate satisfaction and morale.

These considerations have implications for research on the impact of school and classroom, for comparing "open" and "traditional" instruction, and for identifying consistent achievement-treatment interactions. Not only are there several relevant dimensions of classroom characteristics,[43] but the characteristics may interact and alter the potential effects of each. The relationship between task orientation or competition and learning outcomes may vary among studies because other relevant variables, such as affiliation and teacher support, are not taken into account. Although competitive classes can have negative effects on students' self-esteem and continuing motivation,[44] this may not be true of those competitive classes that also emphasize affiliation and support. Future research on the impact of classroom and school environments should focus on these important interactions.

SOME PROMISING APPLICATIONS

One further question requires some attention. How can knowledge about social environments be made practically useful? My recent work has led me to identify several related areas in which a focus on social environments may be useful for evaluating and changing educational settings,[45] three of which are discussed briefly below.

Maximizing Information

The rapid growth of new educational settings has increased the need for more accurate and complete descriptions of the settings. Teachers, for example, know much more about the characteristics of students entering school than students know about the educational programs in the school they are entering. Since the psychosocial or learning environment is usually considered to be especially important, descriptions of educational settings should provide information about this key aspect. Knowledge about the social environment of a setting is relevant to prospective members of that environment, to educational counselors and guidance workers, and to individuals interested in new developments in the educational field. School guidance counselors and students might be better prepared to make effective use of innovative educational programs if they had more complete knowledge of what the programs offered.

Major ways of conceptualizing environments can provide useful guidelines for writing more accurate and complete descriptions, which in turn may help people understand and adapt to new settings. The presentation of information about social environments to their prospective members has been shown to reduce discrepant perceptions and expectations and to enhance successful adaptation in the new environment.[46] One recent application of this procedure is the use of the CES to provide information about the social environments of minischools in an educational voucher program to help parents select the schools they wish their children to enter.[47]

Methods like the CES and URES may be used to specify the psychosocial or perceived climate characteristics of an educational setting. Students, teachers, or outside observers can fill out the scales on the basis of their experiences in the setting. Since most junior and senior high school classrooms and university student living groups have frequent visitors, it would be possible to have some of these individuals complete the relevant social climate scales on the basis of their visits. Descriptions of educational settings should systematically include each of the dimensions in the relationship, personal growth, and system maintenance and change areas.

Facilitating Environmental Change

Feedback and utilization of findings about social climate can facilitate environmental change. For example, the CES allows teachers to define more accurately the type of classroom they have, not only in terms of their own perceptions, but also as it is seen by students. A self-initiated analysis may result as discussion of the real profile leads to interest in the differences and similarities between the perceptions of teachers and those of students. This analysis allows teachers to discuss key areas of concern rationally rather than emotionally. Furthermore, as a natural consequence of such discussions, teachers often begin exploring their own and student ideals and relating these ideals to actual classroom performance. The CES serves as a concrete guideline for discussion. As a result of feedback, teachers can identify specific changes by which to improve their classrooms as suggested by the definition of their own and their students' goals and values.

DeYoung successfully used the CES to effect positive changes in a college sociology-social psychology class.[48] He used information regarding real-ideal class discrepancies from one class, which indicated that students wanted more involvement, greater stress on innovative teaching methods, and clearer notions about the organization and direction of the class, to modify substantially his approach in a subsequent class. For example, students indicated a desire to "get a group together for a project" (affiliation) and to have the instructor "spend a little time just talking with students" (teacher support). Therefore, teams of students were formed to report on specific topics, efforts were made to see students individually to discuss class subject matter and procedures, and grading policies and appeal procedures were clarified in writing, among other changes.

Although the social climate desired by the students in the two classes was virtually identical, there were great differences in their actual learning environments. Students in the second class perceived higher emphasis on all three relationship dimensions, on rule clarity, and on innovation. These differences, which represented the specific areas the instructor had attempted to influence, indicated that it is quite possible to change the learning environment along lines suggested by the CES, given an understanding of the salient features of the classroom setting. The generally positive changes in classroom social climate were linked to greater student interest and participation and a higher student attendance rate.[49]

Some benefits may occur in the process of planning and facilitating classroom change. Students and teachers can untangle and analyze the multiple dimensions of classroom functioning. Important classroom characteristics often overlooked can be systematically called into awareness, such as clarity of expectations regarding class grading policies. Student input can be comprehensively obtained in a manner that makes students feel comfortable and competent. (Although many junior and senior high school students do not feel qualified to criticize a course, they do feel able to act as reporters about its current functioning.) In some behavioral science courses (sociology, social psychology, group dynamics) the issues surrounding the utilization of the CES or URES— analysis of teacher versus student roles, discussion of types of institutional sanctions, and sources of resistance to change—can provide relevant topics for discussion. Instructors can subtly change their perceptions of their own role by beginning to concentrate on their role as a "facilitator" of learning as well as that of "teacher." If students and teachers concentrate their attempts to change their classrooms on a few commonly defined areas, the possibility of confusion or conflicting behavior can be reduced, and change is more likely to take place in an orderly manner. And, finally, involvement can be increased simply because students and teachers are engaged in the common task of changing their own classroom environments.

Such benefits are not, however, assured, and there can be serious resistance to change and other problems during the change process. Nor is it possible to change a social environment toward a "static ideal." Feedback of information is a dynamic, continuing process that may result in changes in the concept of an ideal social environment, as well as changes in perceptions of the real environment. To complicate matters further, students and teachers may not "know" what is best for them and may wish to function in classrooms that tend to maximize immediate satisfaction and comfort rather than basic learning skills and long-range social competence. In general, however, these methods are promising since they concentrate on aspects of settings that tend to be under "local control" (teachers and students *can* change the emphasis on involvement, affiliation, teacher support, task orientation, and rule clarity in their own classrooms) and since they speak directly to people's needs for personal efficacy (this includes actively helping to mold their own environments).

Assisting the Educational Consultant

Information about the social environment may help a consultant gain a better understanding of an educational institution. The consultant's image of an institution consists of observations and speculations about its structure, its functioning, and its dynamics. The CES and URES may provide a valuable input to this working image. The discrepancy between the CES and other information can be the source of new information for the consultant. Furthermore, the measurement-feedback-planning sequence constitutes an assessment of variables relevant to the consultant's task (for example, amount of resistance to change, resources for generating and maintaining innovations, values and priorities of institution staff).

The reactions of staff to data gathering and feedback are valuable clues to the functioning of an institution. How do administrators and teachers react to the idea of evaluating their environments? Is the initial resistance to evaluation understandable in terms of the job and security of counselors and teachers? Or does it reflect a conflict among staff members about the worth of evaluation and classroom change? By a judicious interpretation of the scales, of staff reactions to each phase of the assessment-feedback-planning sequence, and of information that conflicts with the results of the scales, an image of each classroom and of a school as a whole can be generated. This image can then serve the consultant in the same way a good personality assessment serves the therapist.[51]

Although the specific types of educational environments needed depend in part on the types of people in them and on the outcomes desired, the above considerations begin to clarify some of the issues involved. At the least, we need to focus on relationship, personal growth, and system maintenance and change dimensions in describing, comparing, evaluating, and changing educational settings. A more varied conceptualization of the social environments of educational settings may help us transcend sterile debates about the relative merits of "open" versus "traditional" schools, and allow us to design more sophisticated studies that mirror the full complexity of the educational process. We also need to study the mechanism by which educational settings exert their effects,[52] and the extent to which these effects may be facilitated or inhibited by other important life settings, such as those of the family[53] and the factory.[54]

NOTES

1. Henry A. Murray, *Explorations in Personality* (New York: Oxford University Press, 1938).

2. *Ibid.*, 116.

3. C. Robert Pace and George Stern, "An Approach to the Measurement of Psychological Characteristics of College Environments," *Journal of Educational Psychology* 49 (1958): 269-277.

4. George Stern, *People in Context* (New York: Wiley, 1970).

5. Herbert Walberg, "Psychology of Learning Environments: Behavioral, Structural or Perceptual?" in *Review of Educational Research,* Vol. 4, ed. Lee Shulman (Itasca, Ill.: F. E. Peacock, 1976), 142-178.

6. Rudolf Moos and Edison Trickett, *The Classroom Environment Scale Manual* (Palo Alto, Calif.: Consulting Psychologists Press, 1974); Edison Trickett and Rudolf Moos, "Personal Correlates of Contrasting Environments: Student Satisfaction in High School Classrooms," *American Journal of Community Psychology* 2 (1974): 1-12.

7. Marvin Gerst and Rudolf Moos, "The Social Ecology of University Student Residences," *Journal of Educational Psychology* 63 (1972): 513-522; *id., The University Residence Environment Scale Manual* (Palo Alto, Calif.: Consulting Psychologists Press, 1974).

8. Rudolf Moos, *The Social Climate Scales: An Overview* (Palo Alto, Calif.: Consulting Psychologists Press, 1974).

9. *Id., Evaluating Correctional and Community Settings* (New York: Wiley-Interscience, 1975); *id., The Human Context: Environmental Determinants of Behavior* (New York: Wiley-Interscience, 1976).

10. *Id., Evaluating Correctional and Community Settings.*

11. Stern, *People in Context.*

12. Rudolf Moos, *Evaluating Treatment Environments: A Social Ecological Approach* (New York: Wiley-Interscience, 1974), chap. 14; Walberg, "Psychology of Learning Environments."

13. See Moos and Gerst, *University Residence Environment Scale Manual,* and Moos and Trickett, *Classroom Environment Scale Manual,* for examples of social climate descriptions of classrooms and student living groups.

14. William Cunningham, "The Impact of Student-Teacher Pairings on Teacher Effectiveness," *American Educational Research Journal* 12 (1975): 169-189; David Hunt, "Person-Environment Interaction: A Challenge Found Wanting before It Was Tried," *Review of Educational Research* 45 (1975): 209-230; Daniel Solomon and Arthur Kendall, "Individual Characteristics and Children's Performance in 'Open' and 'Traditional' Classroom Settings," *Journal of Educational Psychology* 68 (1976): 613-625.

15. See Rudolf Moos, "A Typology of Junior High and High School Classrooms," *American Educational Research Journal* 15 (1978): 53-66, for methodological details.

16. Elizabeth Cohen, "Sociology and the Classroom: Setting the Conditions for Teacher-Student Interaction," *Review of Educational Research* 42 (1972): 441-452.

17. See Rudolf Moos *et al.,* "A Typology of University Student Living Groups,"

Journal of Educational Psychology 67 (1975): 359-367, for an empirical typology of the social environments of student living groups.

18. Thomas Ellison and Edison Trickett, *Environmental Structure and the Perceived Similarity-Satisfaction Relationship in Traditional and Alternative Schools* (College Park: University of Maryland, 1976); Edison Trickett, "Toward an Ecological Conception of Adolescent Socialization: Normative Environments of the Public Schools," *Child Development,* in press.

19. Maurice Eash *et al., An Evaluation of a New Curriculum Design as a True Experiment* (Chicago: University of Illinois at Chicago Circle, 1975). ERIC:ED 113 373.

20. Trickett, "Toward an Ecological Conception of Adolescent Socialization."

21. *Ibid.*

22. Jim Hearn and Rudolf Moos, "Social Climate and Major Choice: A Test of Holland's Theory in University Student Living Groups," *Journal of Vocational Behavior* 8 (1976): 298-305; *id.,* "Subject Matter and Social Climate in High School Classrooms: A Test of Holland's Theory," *American Educational Research Journal* 15 (1978): 111-124.

23. Charles Schroeder and Charles Griffin, "A Novel Living-Learning Environment for Freshman Engineering Students," *Engineering Education* 67 (1976): 159-161.

24. Brian Wilcox and Charles Holahan, "Social Ecology of the Megadorm in University Student Housing," *Journal of Educational Psychology* 68 (1976): 453-458.

25. Marvin Gerst and Harvey Sweetwood, "Correlates of Dormitory Social Climate," *Environment and Behavior* 5 (1973): 440-464.

26. P. Tamir, "The Relationship among Cognitive Preference, School Environment, Teachers' Curricular Bias, Curriculum, and Subject Matter," *American Educational Research Journal* 12 (1975): 235-264.

27. Joyce L. Epstein and James M. McPartland, "The Concept and Measurement of the Quality of School Life," *ibid.,* 13 (1976): 15-30.

28. Martin Maehr, "Continuing Motivation: An Analysis of a Seldom Considered Educational Outcome," *Review of Educational Research* 46 (1976): 443-462.

29. Harvey Averch *et al., How Effective Is Schooling? A Critical Review of Research* (Englewood Cliffs, N.J.: Educational Technology Publications, 1974); Christopher Jencks, *Inequality: A Reassessment of the Effect of Family and Schooling in America* (New York: Basic Books, 1972).

30. Tricket and Moos, "Personal Correlates of Contrasting Environments: Student Satisfaction in High School Classrooms."

31. Herbert Walberg, "The Social Environment as a Mediator of Classroom Learning," *Journal of Educational Psychology* 60 (1969): 443-448.

32. Michael Paige, "The Impact of the Classroom Learning Environment on Individual Modernity and Academic Achievement in East Java," unpub. diss., Stanford University, 1977).

33. Herbert Walberg, Rampal Singh, and Sue Rasher, "An Operational Test of a Three-Factor Theory of Classroom Social Perception," *Psychology in the Schools,* in press; *id.,* "Predictive Validity of Student Perception: A Cross-Cultural Replication," *American Educational Research Journal* 14 (1978): 45-49.

34. Moos, *Human Context,* chap. 10.

35. Averch *et al.*, *How Effective Is Schooling?* See also Lawrence Bartak and Michael Rutter, "The Measurement of Staff-Child Interaction in Three Units for Autistic Children," in *Varieties of Residential Experience*, ed. Jack Tizard, Ian Sinclair, and R. V. G. Clarke (London: Routledge and Kegan Paul, 1975), 171-202; Jesse Grimes and Wesley Allinsmith, "Compulsivity, Anxiety and School Achievement," *Merrill-Palmer Quarterly* 7 (1961): 247-271.

36. Rudolf Moos and Bernice Moos, "Classroom Social Climate and Student Absences and Grades," *Journal of Educational Psychology*, in press.

37. Moos, *Evaluating Correctional and Community Settings;* Rudolf Moos and Bernice Van Dort, "Student Physical Symptoms and the Social Climate of College Living Groups," *American Journal of Community Psychology*, in press.

38. Alden Wessman, "Scholastic and Psychological Effects of Compensatory Education Program for Disadvantaged High School Students: Project ABC," *American Educational Research Journal* 9 (1972): 361-372.

39. David Johnson and Roger Johnson, "Instructional Goal Structure: Cooperative, Competitive or Individualistic," *Review of Educational Research* 44 (1974): 213-240.

40. Averch *et al.*, *How Effective Is Schooling?*

41. Moos, "Typology of Junior High and High School Classrooms."

42. Gary Anderson and Herbert Walberg, "Learning Environments," in *Evaluating Educational Performance*, ed. Herbert Walberg (Berkeley, Calif.: McCutchan Publishing Corp., 1974), 81-98.

43. Jere Brophy *et al.*, "Classroom Observation Scales: Stability across Time and Context and Relationships with Student Learning Gains," *Journal of Educational Psychology* 67 (1975): 873-881; Herbert Walberg and Susan Thomas, "Open Education: An Operational Definition and Validation in Great Britain and the United States," *American Educational Research Journal* 9 (1972): 197-208.

44. Johnson and Johnson, "Instructional Goal Structure: Cooperative, Competitive or Individualistic"; Maehr, "Continuing Motivation."

45. Rudolf Moos, "Evaluating and Changing Community Settings," *American Journal of Community Psychology* 4 (1976): 313-326.

46. Morton Leiberman, "Relocation Research and Social Policy," *Gerontologist* 14 (1974): 494-501.

47. Daniel Weiler *et al.*, "A Public School Voucher Demonstration: The First Year of Alum Rock — Summary and Conclusions," in *Evaluation Studies Review Annual*, ed. Gene V Glass (Beverly Hills, Calif.: Sage Publications, 1976), 279-304.

48. Alan DeYoung, "Classroom Climate and Class Success: A Case Study at the University Level," *Journal of Educational Research* 70 (1977): 252-257.

49. See Maurice Eash and Harriet Talmage, "Evaluation of Learning Environments," ERIC:TM Rep. 43 (Princeton, N.J.: ERIC Clearing House on Tests, Measurement, and Evaluation, Educational Testing Service, 1975) for an example of the use of student perceptions in feedback and change attempts. See Moos, *Evaluating Treatment Environments*, chaps. 4 and 11, for examples of change studies in psychiatric treatment settings.

50. Moos, *Evaluating Treatment Environments*, chap. 11.

51. See *id., Evaluating Correctional and Community Settings,* chap. 4, for an example of this process.

52. See, for example, B. Swift, "Job Orientations and the Transition from School to Work: A Longitudinal Study," *British Journal of Guidance and Counselling* 1 (1973): 62-78; Barbara Tizard, "Varieties of Residential Nursery Experience," in *Varieties of Residential Experience,* ed. Tizard, Sinclair, and Clarke, 102-121.

53. Herbert Walberg and Kevin Marjoribanks, "Family Environment and Cognitive Development: Twelve Analytic Models," *Review of Educational Research* 46 (1976): 527-551.

54. Alex Inkeles and David Smith, *Becoming Modern: Individual Change in Six Developing Countries* (Cambridge, Mass.: Harvard University Press, 1974).

5. Cooperation, Competition, and Individualization

David W. Johnson and *Roger T. Johnson*

There are instances where traditional practice in schools has gone one way at the same time that empirical research was indicating that another course might be more productive and desirable. Consider the use of cooperative, competitive, and individualistic goal structures for instructional purposes in the United States. For forty years competition among students has been promoted in most schools, and in the past ten years individual effort in the achievement of learning goals has been increasingly encouraged, in spite of the fact that research has indicated that the cooperative goal structure would be more productive than either the competitive or the individualistic ones.

Perhaps one reason for this discrepancy between educational practice and research is the fact that student-student interaction has not been emphasized in the development of curriculum and the preparation of teachers. The role of the teacher and the way students interact with materials have received much more attention than how students should relate to each other while working on instructional tasks, even though student interaction during instruction has powerful and important effects on learning and socialization.

Instructional activities in every classroom are based on a goal structure. A *goal* is a desired state of future affairs (such as the completion of an assignment for a class in mathematics), and a *goal structure* specifies the type of goal interdependence existing among students as they work toward accomplishing an educational goal. There are three goal structures that teachers can use during instruction: cooperative (positive goal interdependence), competitive (negative goal interdependence), and individualistic (no goal interdependence).[1] Within a *cooperative* goal structure, students achieve their goal if and only if the other students with whom they are linked achieve their goals. One example of a cooperative situation is found where a group of students works together to answer a set of comprehension questions after reading a story. Within a *competitive* goal structure students perceive that they can achieve their goals if and only if the other students with whom they are linked fail to achieve their goal. A competitive situation exists when students who have taken a quiz in mathematics are ranked according to the number of questions answered correctly. An *individualistic* goal structure exists when the achievement of a student's learning goal is unrelated to the goal achievement of other students. In an individualistic situation students complete an assignment in mathematics by themselves, with the evaluation of the assignment being based on a criterion-referenced system so that the achievement of one student has no effect (positive or negative) on the achievement of other students.

In the ideal classroom each of these three goal structures would be used at appropriate times. All students would learn how to work cooperatively with other students, how to compete for fun and enjoyment, and how to work autonomously on their own. Most of the time, however, students would work on instructional tasks within the goal structure best suited to the type of task to be done in an effort to produce the cognitive and affective outcomes desired, and the teacher would decide which goal structure to implement within each instructional activity. The way in which teachers structure learning goals determines how students interact with each other and with the teacher, and it is those interaction patterns that determine the cognitive and affective outcomes of instruction. No aspect of teaching is more important than the appropriate use of goal structures.

THE TRADITIONAL USE OF COMPETITION

Once a child enters the first grade there is great concern over whether his performance is equal to or better than that of other children his age. Most educators do not realize how deeply this goal structure is embedded in the daily life of the school. Across the country, students are regularly compared to see who is superior and who is inferior. To know more than someone else is taken as a sign that one is better, more intelligent, and superior. Knowledge is considered a possession that distinguishes between superiority and inferiority. The competitive goal structure has, in fact, pervaded education in the United States to such an extent that it is sometimes difficult to see how society can survive without it, and this constant encouragement of students to outperform their peers has had a strong socializing effect. The children in this country are more competitive than children from other countries, and they become more competitive the longer they are in school or the older they become.[2]

To verify the fact that students recognize this competitive emphasis, elementary and secondary students were interviewed in a series of studies.[3] Most of the students perceived school as being competitive, yet they would have preferred that it be cooperative. It has also been found that this tendency for children to compete often interferes with their capacity to adapt when cooperation is needed to solve a problem and that spontaneous cooperation among students is rare because the educational environment is lacking in experiences that would sensitize the students to the possibility of cooperation.[4] Emphasis on competition can become so overwhelming that a student may be willing to reduce his own reward in order to reduce the reward of a peer,[5] or consider it inappropriate and improper to help someone in distress.[6]

GOAL STRUCTURES AND INSTRUCTIONAL OUTCOMES

The relationship between cooperative, competitive, and individualistic goal structures and the cognitive and affective outcomes of instruction has already been summarized elsewhere.[7] This chapter primarily focuses, instead, on the authors' research on goal structures, and the instructional outcomes examined on that basis are: achievement in a variety of learning tasks, ability to understand the perspectives of others, effects of disagreement among students within a cooperative or a competitive context, students' motivation to learn, students' emotional involvement in learning, students' attitudes toward teachers and other school personnel, students' attitudes toward each other, students' self-esteem, students' psychological health, and the relationship between goal structures and types of teaching methods.

Type of Task

Many studies confirm that the successful mastery, retention, and transfer of concepts, rules, and principles is higher in cooperatively structured learning than in competitive or individualistic learning situations.[8] At the same time other studies have indicated that, in simple, mechanical, previously mastered tasks that require no help from other students, competition promotes greater quantity of output than do cooperative or individualistic efforts. This would indicate that research on achievement should focus on the type of task being studied. In a series of studies involving white first- and fifth-grade students from both urban and suburban settings and black high school students from an urban setting, the relative effects of cooperative, competitive, and individualistic goal structures on the achievement of a variety of school-related tasks were examined.[9] The results were surprisingly consistent. On mathematical and verbal drill-review tasks, spatial-reasoning and verbal problem-solving tasks, pictorial and verbal-sequencing tasks, a knowledge-retention task, and on tasks involving comparison of shape, size, and pattern, cooperation promoted higher achievement than either competitive or individualistic efforts. On a specific knowledge-acquisition task, cooperation and competition both promoted higher achievement than individualistic efforts. These findings are all the more important as care was taken to optimize both competitive and individualistic instruction.

Perspective-Taking

One of the most critical competencies for cognitive and social development is social perspective-taking, that is, understanding how a situation appears to another person and how that person is reacting cognitively and emotionally. A person who lacks social perspective-taking ability is egocentric and becomes wedded to his own viewpoint to the extent that he is unaware of other points of view or the limitations of his own perspective. The acquisition of perspective-taking ability is a central process underlying almost all interpersonal and group skills, and it has been found to be related to effective presentation of information, effective comprehension of information, constructive resolution of conflicts, willingness to disclose information on a personal level, effective group problem solving, cooperativeness, positive attitudes toward others within the same situation, autonomous moral judgment, intellectual and cognitive development, and social adjustment.[10]

What goal structure is most conducive to the development of social perspective? Cooperation appears to be positively related to the ability to recognize the emotional perspective of others,[11] and cooperative learning experiences have, furthermore, been found to promote greater cognitive and emotional perspective-taking ability than either competitive or individualistic learning experiences.[12]

Constructive Conflict

Another important aspect of instruction is the extent to which intellectual disagreements foster conceptual conflict within students and thereby increase motivation to seek out new information or to reorganize what is already known. In a study examining the effects of controversy on motivation within a cooperative or a competitive context,[13] it was found that, where controversy was present, there was greater motivation to seek out new information than there was where controversy was lacking, and the effect was stronger in a competitive than in a cooperative context. Although competition was related to greater conceptual conflict and information-seeking behavior resulting from intellectual disagreement, the competition fostered a closed-minded orientation. Participants felt unwilling to make concessions to other viewpoints, perceived a high level of disagreement between themselves and their opponent, viewed themselves as being opposed to listening to their opponent, and viewed their opponent as having a closed mind. Greater internal distress was experienced when controversy occurred within a competitive (as compared with a cooperative) context.

Degree of Motivation

Motivation is commonly viewed as perceived likelihood of success combined with incentive for success. The more likely one is to succeed and the more important it is to succeed, the higher the motivation. Intrinsic rewards are usually seen as being more desirable for learning than extrinsic rewards. There is evidence to indicate that there is a greater perceived likelihood of success and that success is more important in cooperative than in competitive and individualistic learning situations.[14] The more students cooperate, the more they see themselves as being instrinsically motivated, persevering the pursuit of clearly defined learning goals, believing that it is their own efforts that determine their school success, wanting to be good students and get good grades, and believing that ideas, feelings, and learning new ideas are important and positive.[15] The more students compete, the more they see themselves as being extrinsically motivated in elementary and junior high schools. Competitive attitudes are, however, somewhat related to intrinsic motivation—being a good student and getting good marks in senior high school. Individualistic attitudes tend to be unrelated to all measured aspects of motivation to learn. Experimental evidence also indicates that cooperative learning experiences, compared with individualstic ones, result in more intrinsic motivation, less extrinsic motivation, and less need for teachers to set clear goals for students.[16]

Students' Involvement in Instructional Activities

Students are expected to become involved in instructional activities and to derive as much benefit from them as possible. There is evidence that the more students cooperate, the more they see themselves as expressing their ideas and feelings in large and small classes and as listening to the teacher, while competitive and individualistic attitudes are unrelated to indexes of involvement in instructional activities.[17] Additional evidence shows that cooperative learning experiences, compared with competitive and individualistic ones, encourage a student to discuss ideas with the class,[18] increase willingness to present one's answers, allow a more positive attitude toward one's answers and the instructional experience,[19] and develop more positive attitudes toward the instructional tasks and subject areas.[20]

One finding related to involvement in instructional activities is particularly interesting. While both competitive and individualistic attitudes are related to wanting students to be constrained by teachers (rules enforced, quiet preserved, clear goals set, and full instructions given), they are unrelated to valuing school rules.[21] Cooperativeness, on the other hand, is unrelated to constraining students in junior and senior high school, yet it is consistently related to a positive view of school rules.

Students' Attitudes

Toward School Personnel. The more favorable students' attitudes toward cooperation, the more they believe that (1) teachers, teacher aides, counselors, and principals are important and positive; (2) teachers care about and want to increase students' learning; (3) teachers like and accept students as individuals; and (4) teachers and principals want to be friends with students.[22] These findings hold in elementary and in junior and senior high schools, as well as in rural, suburban, and urban school districts. In suburban junior and senior high schools, student competitiveness is positively related to perceptions of being liked and supported personally and academically by teachers. Individualistic attitudes are consistently unrelated to attitudes toward school personnel. There are also several field experimental studies demonstrating that students who experience cooperative instruction like the teacher better and perceive the teacher as being more supportive and accepting, academically and personally, than do students who experience competitive and individualistic instruction.[23]

Toward Peers. Positive interpersonal relationships among students are necessary for both effective learning and general classroom enjoyment of instructional activities. Cooperative attitudes are related to liking one's peers,[24] and the evidence indicates that cooperative learning experiences, compared with competitive and individualistic ones, promote greater liking for peers[25] and encourage the development of more positive interpersonal relationships characterized by mutual liking, positive attitudes toward each other, mutual concern, friendliness, attentiveness, feelings of obligation to other students, and desire to win the respect of other students.[26]

Cooperative learning experiences, again compared with competitive and individualistic ones, have also been found to strengthen the beliefs that one is liked and accepted by other students and that other students care about how much one learns and want to help.[27] Cooperative attitudes relate to believing that one is liked by other students and wanting to listen to, help, and do schoolwork with them.[28] Individualistic attitudes are related to *not* wanting to do schoolwork with other students, with *not* wanting to help other students learn, with *not* valuing being liked by other students, and with *not* wanting to participate in social interaction.[29]

One of the most important social problems facing our country is prejudice toward groups and individuals that are in some way different from the middle-class white majority. There is a need for instructional strategies that will reduce prejudice among students at the same time that they maximize achievement. There is evidence that cooperative learning experiences, compared with individualistic ones, promote more positive attitudes toward heterogeneity among peers[30] and encourage the liking of peers who are both smarter and less smart than oneself.[31] When stigmatized students are placed in the regular classroom and study individualistically or in competition with other students, interpersonal attraction is more likely to be based on perceived similarity. Cooperative interaction, on the other hand, allows liking for the stigmatized despite perceived differences.[32]

In studies involving students—from different ethnic groups, handicapped and nonhandicapped, male and female—at the junior high school level, the evidence indicates that cooperative learning experiences, compared to competitive and individualistic ones, promote more positive attitudes toward members of different ethnic groups and sexes and toward handicapped peers.[33] Stigmatized students were seen as being more valuable and smarter and as contributing to the learning of nonstigmatized students, as being part of learning groups and after-school activities, and as being friends more frequently following cooperative learning experiences (as compared with competitive or individualistic ones).

Toward Self. Schools are concerned with promoting self-esteem in students for various reasons, which include psychological health and achievement in school and postschool situations. Correlational studies indicate that cooperativeness is positively related to self-esteem in students throughout elementary, junior, and senior high schools in rural, urban, and suburban settings; competitiveness is generally unrelated to self-esteem; and individualistic attitudes tend to be related to feelings of worthlessness and self-rejection.[34] There is also evidence that cooperative learning experiences, compared with individualistic ones, result in higher self-esteem.[35]

Studies of suburban junior and senior high school students examined the relationship between cooperative, competitive, and individualistic attitudes and ways of conceptualizing one's worth from the information available about oneself.[36] Four primary ways of deriving self-esteem are: basic self-acceptance (a belief in the intrinsic acceptability of oneself), conditional self-acceptance (acceptance contingent on meeting external standards and expectations), self-evaluation (one's estimate of how one compares with one's peers), and real-ideal congruence (correspondence between what one thinks one is and what one thinks one should be). Cooperative attitudes are related to basic self-acceptance and positive self-evaluation compared to peers; competitive attitudes, to conditional self-acceptance; individualistic attitudes, to basic self-rejection.

Psychological Health

The ability to build and maintain cooperative relationships is often cited as a primary manifestation of psychological health, yet until recently there has been no evidence that this is so. In a comparison of the attitudes of high school seniors toward cooperation, competition, and individualism and their responses on the *Minnesota Multiphasic Personality Inventory* (MMPI), it was found that there were significant negative correlations between attitudes toward cooperation and nine of the ten MMPI scales indicating psychological pathology. Attitudes toward competition correlated negatively with seven of the ten MMPI psychological pathology scales, and attitudes toward individualism were significantly and positively related to nine of the ten MMPI scales. Since both cooperation and competition involve relationships with other people, while individualistic activities involve isolation from other people, these findings imply that, while an emphasis on cooperative involvement with other people and on appropriate competition during socialization may promote psychological health and well-being, social isolation may promote psychological illness.

Cooperative attitudes are positively related to emotional maturity, well-adjusted social relations, strong personal identity, the ability to resolve conflicts between self-perceptions and adverse information about oneself, amount of social participation, and basic trust and optimism.[37] Competitive attitudes are related to emotional maturity, lack of a need for affection, the ability to resolve conflicts between self-perceptions and adverse information about oneself, social participation, and basic trust and optimism. Individualistic attitudes are related to delinquency, emotional immaturity, social maladjustment, self-alienation, inability to resolve conflicts between self-perceptions and adverse information about oneself, self-rejection, lack of social participation, and basic distrust and pessimism. The ability to build and maintain cooperative relationships, it would appear, is an essential aspect of psychological health and social development. A model of psychological health based on theory and research in cooperative learning has been proposed as a means of developing that ability.[38]

Goal Structures and Teaching Methods

Studies examining the effects of cooperation and competition on students' reactions to didactic versus inquiry teaching methods have been conducted.[39] The results indicate that cooperative or competitive goal structures do not differentially affect student acceptance of and liking for didactic instruction. Inquiry instruction was, however, liked better and accepted more readily when it was cooperative than when it was structured competitively. And inquiry methods were viewed as more positive than didactic methods.

Each of the outcomes of instruction discussed above is important, but the most important of the instructional considerations has not yet been discussed. It is to that subject that we now turn.

BACK TO BASICS: THE IMPORTANCE OF COOPERATIVE LEARNING EXPERIENCES

What competencies are most vital for promoting future success in a career, in building and maintaining a family, in contributing to one's community, and in actualizing one's potential? If the most significant thing for students to learn is how to build and maintain positive relationships with other people in work, leisure, and family situations, then involving students in supportive and meaningful relationships with their classmates and members of the school staff is probably the most important thing schools can do for students.

The importance of cooperative learning experiences goes beyond improving instruction and making life easier and more productive for teachers, although these are worthwhile goals. Cooperation is as basic to humans as the air they breath. It is the ability to cooperate with other people that is the keystone to building and maintaining stable families, successful careers, friendly neighborhoods and communities, important values and beliefs, long-lasting friendships, and worthwhile contributions to society. Technical knowledge and skills are of little use to an engineer, secretary, accountant, or teacher if they cannot be applied while interacting cooperatively with other people on the job, within the family, in the community, and among friends. The most logical way to emphasize cooperative competencies as learning outcomes is to structure the majority of academic learning situations co-operatively. Going back to basics in education means going all the way back to the socialization of students into the competencies needed for cooperating with other people.

Cooperative learning experiences are also important to the school environment. Schools, like all social organizations, require cooperation among people. What would happen if students and school personnel refused to speak the same language, refused to attend classes at the same time, refused to gather in the same building, did not coordinate their actions, or arrived at school randomly during the day and night? Such basic cooperation is taken for granted, and only when it breaks down is it noticed. Schools cannot operate if students and school personnel do not cooperate to achieve educational goals.

Using Goal Structures Appropriately

From a pragmatic point of view, cooperation should be used much more frequently in instructional situations than competitive and individualistic goal structures, for it is the goal structure that should provide the overall context for learning. Whenever it is important for students to be motivated, involved, and alert, whenever it is important for students to master, retain, and apply knowledge and skills, and whenever students' attitudes should be positive, cooperation is needed. Perhaps the only limitation on the use of cooperation is when a task is very simple and can be completed without assistance from another person. Despite the broad effectiveness of cooperative learning, however, there is still a need for competitive and individualistic goal structures in the classroom.

If students can compete for fun and enjoyment, win or lose, competitive drills are an effective change of pace. Conditions under which competition can be used productively are:

—when it is relatively unimportant whether one wins or loses. Winning cannot be a life-or-death matter if competition is to be enjoyed. High levels of anxiety appear when winning becomes too important, along with all the destructive consequences of competition noted by researchers.

—when all students perceive themselves as having a reasonable chance of winning. Motivation to achieve is based on the perceived likelihood of being able to achieve a challenging goal. If students believe they have little chance of winning, they will not compete. By arranging a class into small clusters of evenly matched students, teachers can provide challenging and realistic competition among students and maximize the number of winners in the class at the same time.

3 — when rules, procedures, and answers are an absolute necessity. Ambiguity ruins competition because too much time is spent worrying about what is fair and unfair, what the procedures actually are, and whether or not the answers are correct.

4 — when students are able to monitor the progress of their competitors during the competition so that they can determine whether they are ahead or behind. In competition the only way students can judge their progress is by comparing themselves with their competitors. In athletic events there is a scoreboard to keep players posted, and successful classroom competition requires the same sort of feedback.[41]

Individualistically structured learning activities can supplement cooperation through a division of labor in which each student learns material or skills to be used in cooperative, problem-solving activities. Conditions under which an individualistic goal structure can be productively used are:

1 — when each student has adequate space to study within and all the necessary materials to complete the work. Each student has to be a separate, self-contained learner.

2 — when directions are clear and specific so that students do not need further clarification on how to proceed and how to evaluate their work. In an individualistic situation the teacher is the major resource for all students. If several students need help or clarification at the same time, work grinds to a halt.

3 — when students see the task as relevant and worthwhile. Self-motivation is a key aspect of individualistic efforts. The more important students perceive the learning goal to be, and the more challenging the task, the more motivated they will be to learn. Learning facts and simple skills to be used in cooperation with peers increases the perceived relevance and importance of individualistic tasks.[42]

The Teacher's Role

While the procedures for implementing competitive and individualistic goal structures within instructional activities are commonly used by most teachers, the teacher's role in the cooperative learning situation is often ambiguous. That is why the teacher's role in cooperative instruction is briefly reviewed.[43]

The essence of cooperative learning is assigning a group goal, such as producing a single product or achieving as high a group average on a test as possible, and rewarding every group member on the basis of the quality or quantity of the group product according to a fixed set of standards. The teacher establishes a group goal and a criteria-referenced evaluation system, and rewards group members on the basis of their group performance. Teaching a cooperative lesson, however, involves more than just setting up a cooperative goal structure. It is necessary, as far as possible, to specify the instructional objectives. Then it is important to determine the size of the group most appropriate for the lesson and to select the members of the group. With young students the size of the group may need to be two or three members. With older students larger groups are feasible. The optimal size of a cooperative group also varies according to the resources needed to complete the lesson or project (the larger the group the more resources are needed), the cooperative skills of group members (the less skillful the members of the group, the smaller the group should be), and the nature of the task.

When they assign students to groups, teachers usually wish to include as many different types of students as possible. Random assignment usually ensures a good mixture of males and females, highly verbal and passive students, leaders and followers, and enthusiastic and reluctant learners. Often teachers may wish to assign students to groups so that students with high, low, and average ability are in the same group. At times teachers let students decide for themselves which group they want to join, or the students are grouped according to their interests.

Once the groups are determined, the classroom must be arranged. The groups should be clustered so that one group does not interfere with another. Within the groups students should be able to see the relevant materials, converse with each other, and exchange materials and ideas. A circular seating arrangement is best; long tables should be avoided.

The next step is to provide appropriate materials. When students are first learning how to cooperate or when some students have problems contributing to the efforts of their group, teachers might arrange the materials like a jigsaw puzzle and give each member of the group one piece. In a group writing a report on Abraham Lincoln, for example, each member might have material on a different part of his life. In order for the report to be completed, all members of the group would have to contribute material and ensure that it was incorporated into a single report of the entire group.

After the members of the group have been selected and appropriate materials have been made available, the teacher must explain the task in terms of the cooperative goal structure. The class must realize that there is a group goal, that a criteria-referenced evaluation system will be used, and that all group members are to be rewarded on the basis of the quality of the group's work.

Just because a teacher asks students to cooperate with each other does not mean that they will do so. Much of the teacher's time in cooperative learning situations must be spent observing student groups to detect problems that students are having in functioning cooperatively[44] and intervening as a consultant to help the group solve those problems so that members learn the social skills necessary for cooperating.[45]

Finally, any effort to evaluate the work done by the group requires a criteria-referenced system. The procedures for setting up and using such a system are available.[46]

IMPLICATIONS FOR LEARNING ENVIRONMENTS

The research findings leave little doubt that teachers who master the strategies needed to set up appropriate goal structures in their classrooms and maximize the use of the cooperative goal structure have a powerful and positive effect on their classroom learning environment. A new curriculum is not required. It takes just a few minutes to make clear to students the kind of student-student interaction expected and the appropriate interaction skills needed. All teachers are interested in the achievement gains promised by the research findings, not to mention the more positive attitudes and the increase in the social skills of students. The initial effort required to introduce student-student interaction and the time required to structure it are effort and time well spent. It would be rewarding, when students are asked, "How do you see school?" if the response were: "School is a place where we work together to learn and share our ideas; to argue our point of view unless logically persuaded otherwise; to help each other find the most appropriate answers; and, sometimes, to compete or work on our own. Most of the time, however, we learn together."

The effect on the school environment could be just as dramatic as the effect that goal structuring has had on classrooms, for the school environment is largely the sum of the classroom environments within the school. How children and their parents view school is based on what they see happening in their classrooms and how they perceive the classroom teacher and the other students in the room. When the student-student interaction is predominantly cooperative in most of the classrooms, the school environment will reflect the positive outcomes of the classrooms. Teachers instructing students in the use of cooperative skills will be more inclined to use those same skills when interacting with other staff members. Visualize a school where teachers say: "School is a place where we work together and share our ideas, help each other, and argue our point of view openly and honestly in the hope of finding the most appropriate solutions to our common problems."

This chapter began with a description of how the path of school practice and the research findings in the area of student-student interaction have diverged and gone different ways over the last forty years. The research findings now clearly point out the strategies and skills necessary for cooperative instruction. Let us hope that the gap between educational practice and research can soon be closed.

NOTES

1. Morton Deutsch, "Cooperation and Trust; Some Theoretical Notes," in *Nebraska Symposium on Motivation,* ed. Marshall R. Jones (Lincoln, Neb.: University of Nebraska Press, 1962), 275-320; David W. Johnson and Roger Johnson, *Learning Together and Alone: Cooperation, Competition, and Individualization* (Englewood Cliffs, N. J.: Prentice-Hall, 1975).

2. David W. Johnson and Roger Johnson, *Learning Together and Alone.*

3. *Id.,* "Student Perceptions of and Preferences for Cooperative and Competitive Learning Experiences," *Perceptual and Motor Skills* 42 (1976): 989-990; Roger Johnson, David W. Johnson, and Brenda Bryant, "Cooperation and Competition in the Classroom," *Elementary School Journal* 74 (1974): 172-181, 367-372; Roger Johnson, "The Relationship between Cooperation and Inquiry in Science Classrooms," *Journal of Research in Science Teaching* 13 (1976): 55-63.

4. Linden Nelson and Spencer Kagan, "Competition: The Star-Spangled Scramble," *Psychology Today* 6 (1972): 53-56, 90-91.

5. *Ibid.*

6. Ervin Staub, "Helping a Person in Distress: The Influence of Implicit and Expli-

cit 'Rules' of Conduct on Children and Adults," *Journal of Personality and Social Psychology* 17 (1971): 137-144.

7. David W. Johnson and Roger Johnson, *Learning Together and Alone.*

8. James H. Davis, Patrick R. Laughlin, and Samuel S. Komorita, "The Social Psychology of Small Groups: Cooperative and Mixed-Motive Interaction," in *Annual Review of Psychology*, Volume 27, ed. Mark R. Rosenzweig and Lyman W. Porter (Palo Alto, Calif.: Annual Reviews, 1976), 501-542; David W. Johnson and Roger Johnson, *Learning Together and Alone.*

9. Antoine Garibaldi, "Cooperation, Competition, and Locus of Control in Afro-American Students," unpub. diss., University of Minnesota, 1976; David W. Johnson and Roger Johnson, "Type of Task and Student Achievement and Attitudes in Interpersonal Cooperation, Competition, and Individualization," *Journal of Social Psychology*, in press; *id.* and Linda Skon, "Student Achievement on Different Types of Tasks under Cooperative, Competitive, and Individualistic Conditions," *Contemporary Educational Psychology*, in press.

10. David W. Johnson, "Cooperative Competencies and the Prevention and Treatment of Drug Abuse," *Research in Education* (November 1975). ERIC: ED 108 066.

11. David W. Johnson, "Affective Perspective-Taking and Cooperative Predisposition," *Developmental Psychology* 11 (1975): 869-870; *id.*, "Cooperativeness and Social Perspective-Taking," *Journal of Personality and Social Psychology* 31 (1975): 241-244.

12. Diane Bridgeman, "Cooperative, Interdependent Learning and Its Enhancement of Role-Taking in Fifth Grade Students," paper presented at the American Psychological Association Convention, San Francisco, August 1977; David W. Johnson, Roger Johnson, Jeannette Johnson, and Douglas Anderson, "The Effects of Cooperative vs. Individualized Instruction on Student Prosocial Behavior, Attitudes toward Learning, and Achievement," *Journal of Educational Psychology* 68 (1976): 446-452.

13. Dean Tjosvold and David W. Johnson, "Controversy within a Cooperative or Competitive Context and Cognitive Perspective-Taking," *Contemporary Educational Psychology*, in press.

14. David W. Johnson and Roger Johnson, *Learning Together and Alone.*

15. David W. Johnson and Andrew Ahlgren, "Relationship between Student Attitudes about Cooperation and Competition and Attitudes toward Schooling," *Journal of Educational Psychology* 68 (1976): 92-102; David W. Johnson, Roger Johnson, and Douglas Anderson, "Student Cooperative, Competitive, and Individualistic Attitudes, and Attitudes toward Schooling," *Journal of Psychology*, 100 (1978): 183-199.

16. David W. Johnson *et al.*, "Effective Cooperative vs. Individualized Instruction on Student Prosocial Behavior, Attitudes toward Learning, and Achievement."

17. Johnson and Ahlgren, "Relationship between Student Attitudes about Cooperation and Competition and Attitudes toward Schooling"; Johnson, Johnson, and Anderson, "Student Cooperative, Competitive, and Individualistic Attitudes, and Attitudes toward Schooling."

18. David W. Johnson *et al.*, "Effects of Cooperative vs. Individualized Instruction on Student Prosocial Behavior, Attitudes toward Learning, and Achievement"; Ronald Wheeler and Frank Ryan, "Effects of Cooperative and Competitive Classroom

Environments on the Attitudes and Achievement of Elementary School Students Engaged in Social Studies Inquiry Activities," *Journal of Educational Psychology* 65 (1973): 402-407.

19. Garibaldi, "Cooperation, Competition, and Locus of Control in Afro-American Students."

20. *Ibid.;* David W. Johnson and Roger Johnson, "Type of Task and Student Achievement and Attitudes in Interpersonal Cooperation, Competition, and Individualization"; *id.* and Skon, "Student Achievement on Different Types of Tasks under Cooperative, Competitive, and Individualistic Conditions"; Wheeler and Ryan, "Effects of Cooperative and Competitive Classroom Environments on the Attitudes and Achievement of Elementary School Students Engaged in Social Studies Inquiry Activities."

21. Johnson and Ahlgren, "Relationship between Student Attitudes about Cooperation and Competition and Attitudes toward Schooling"; Johnson, Johnson, and Anderson, "Student Cooperative, Competitive, and Individualistic Attitudes, and Attitudes toward Schooling."

22. Johnson and Ahlgren, "Relationship between Student Attitudes about Cooperation and Competition and Attitudes toward Schooling"; Johnson, Johnson, and Anderson, "Student Cooperative, Competitive, and Individualistic Attitudes, and Attitudes toward Schooling."

23. David W. Johnson *et al.,* "The Effects of Cooperative vs. Individualized Instruction on Student Prosocial Behavior, Attitudes toward Learning, and Achievement"; David W. Johnson, Roger Johnson, and Linda Scott, "The Effects of Cooperative and Individualistic Instruction on Student Attitudes and Achievement," *Journal of Social Psychology,* 104 (1978): 207-216; Roger Johnson, David W. Johnson, and Maxine Tauer, "Effects of Cooperative, Competitive, and Individualistic Goal Structures and Students' Achievement and Attitudes," unpub. MS; Dean Tjosvold, Paul Marino, and David W. Johnson, "The Effects of Cooperation and Competition on Student Reactions to Inquiry and Didactic Science Teaching," *Journal of Research in Science Teaching* 14 (1977): 281-288; Wheeler and Ryan, "Effects of Cooperative and Competitive Classroom Environments on the Attitudes and Achievement of Elementary School Students Engaged in Social Studies Inquiry Activities."

24. Johnson and Ahlgren, "Relationship between Student Attitudes about Cooperation and Competition and Attitudes toward Schooling"; Johnson, Johnson, and Anderson, "Student Cooperative, Competitive, and Individualistic Attitudes, and Attitudes toward Schooling."

25. Garibaldi, "Cooperation, Competition, and Locus of Control in Afro-American Students"; David W. Johnson *et al.,* "The Effects of Cooperative vs. Individualized Instruction on Student Prosocial Behavior, Attitudes toward Learning, and Achievement"; Johnson, Johnson, and Scott, "The Effects of Cooperative and Individualistic Instruction on Student Attitudes and Achievement"; Tjosvold, Marino, and Johnson, "The Effects of Cooperation and Competition on Student Reactions to Inquiry and Didactic Science Teaching."

26. For a review of these studies, see David W. Johnson and Roger Johnson, *Learning Together and Alone.*

27. Lucille Cooper, David W. Johnson, Roger Johnson, and Frank Wilderson, "The Effects of Cooperation, Competition, and Individualization on Cross-Ethnic, Cross-Sex, and Cross-Ability Friendships," unpub. MS; Johnson, Johnson, and Tauer, "Effects of Cooperative, Competitive, and Individualistic Goal Structures on Students' Achievement and Attitudes"; David W. Johnson et al., "The Effects of Cooperative vs. Individualized Instruction on Student Prosocial Behavior, Attitudes toward Learning, and Achievement"; Tjosvold, Marino, and Johnson, "The Effects of Cooperation and Competition on Student Reactions in Inquiry and Didactic Science Teaching."

28. Johnson and Ahlgren, "Relationship between Student Attitudes about Cooperation and Competition and Attitudes toward Schooling"; Johnson, Johnson, and Anderson, "Student Cooperative, Competitive, and Individualistic Attitudes, and Attitudes toward Schooling."

29. Johnson, Johnson, and Anderson, "Student Cooperative, Competitive, and Individualistic Attitudes, and Attitudes toward Schooling"; David W. Johnson and Ardyth Norem-Hebeisen, "Attitudes toward Interdependence among Persons and Psychological Health," *Psychological Reports* 40 (1977): 843-850.

30. Johnson, Johnson, and Scott, "The Effects of Cooperative and Individualistic Instruction on Student Attitudes and Achievement."

31. Johnson and Ahlgren, "Relationship between Student Attitudes about Cooperation and Competition and Attitudes toward Schooling"; Johnson, Johnson, and Anderson, "Student Cooperative, Competitive, and Individualistic Attitudes, and Attitudes toward Schooling."

32. David W. Johnson and Stephen Johnson, "The Effects of Attitude Similarity, Expectation of Goal Facilitation, and Actual Goal Facilitation on Interpersonal Attraction," *Journal of Experimental Social Psychology* 8 (1972): 197-206; Stephen Johnson and David W. Johnson, "The Effects of Others' Actions, Attitude Similarity, and Race on Attraction towards the Other," *Human Relations* 25 (1972): 121-130.

33. Barbara Armstrong, Bruce Balow, and David W. Johnson, "Cooperative Goal Structure as a Means of Integrating Learning-Disabled with Normal-Progress Elementary Pupils," unpub. MS; Cooper et al., "The Effects of Cooperation, Competition, and Individualization on Cross-Ethnic, Cross-Sex, and Cross-Ability Friendships"; Linda Martino and David W. Johnson, "The Effects of Cooperative vs. Individualistic Instruction on Interaction between Normal-Progress and Learning-Disabled Students," *Journal of Social Psychology,* in press.

34. Johnson and Ahlgren, "Relationship between Student Attitudes about Cooperation and Competition and Attitudes toward Schooling"; Johnson, Johnson, and Anderson, "Student Cooperative, Competitive, and Individualistic Attitudes, and Attitudes toward Schooling"; Johnson and Norem-Hebeisen, "Attitudes toward Interdependence among Persons and Psychological Health"; Ardyth Norem-Hebeisen and David W. Johnson, "The Relationship between Cooperative, Competitive, and Individualistic Attitudes and Diffferentiated Aspects of Self- Esteem," unpub. MS.

35. Johnson, Johnson, and Scott, "The Effects of Cooperative and Individualistic Instruction on Student Attitudes and Achievement."

36. Norem-Hebeisen and Johnson, "The Relationship between Cooperative, Com-

petitive, and Individualistic Attitudes and Differentiated Aspects of Self-Esteem."

37. Johnson and Norem-Hebeisen, "Attitudes toward Interdependence among Persons and Psychological Health."

38. David W. Johnson, "Cooperative Competencies and the Prevention and Treatment of Drug Abuse"; *id., Educational Psychology* (Englewood Cliffs, N. J.: Prentice-Hall, 1979).

39. Roger Johnson, "Relationship between Cooperation and Inquiry in Science Classrooms"; *id.,* Frank Ryan, and Helen Schroeder, "Inquiry and the Development of Positive Attitudes," *Science Education* 58 (1974): 51-56; Tjosvold, Marino, and Johnson, "The Effects of Cooperation and Competition on Student Reactions to Inquiry and Didactic Science Teaching"; Wheeler and Ryan, "Effects of Cooperative and Competitive Classroom Environments on the Attitudes and Achievement of Elementary School Students Engaged in Social Studies Inquiry Activities."

40. David W. Johnson and Roger Johnson, *Learning Together and Alone.*

41. *Ibid.*

42. For a more thorough discussion of the teacher's role in structuring cooperative learning and in using competitive and individualistic goal structures to supplement cooperative learning, see *ibid.*

43. For specific procedures for observing, and for specific observation instruments, see *ibid.;* see also David W. Johnson and Frank Johnson, *Joining Together: Group Theory and Group Skills* (Englewood Cliffs, N. J.: Prentice-Hall, 1975).

44. David W. Johnson, *Reaching Out: Interpersonal Effectiveness and Self-Actualization* (Englewood Cliffs, N.J.: Prentice-Hall, 1972); *id., Human Relations and Your Career: A Guide to Interpersonal Skills* (Englewood Cliffs, N. J.: Prentice-Hall, 1978); *id.* and Frank Johnson, *Joining Together.*

45. David W. Johnson and Roger Johnson, *Learning Together and Alone.*

6. Learning in Teams

Robert E. Slavin and *David L. DeVries*

The classroom is a social setting. It is the scene of complex interpersonal behaviors that can have considerable bearing on the ability to educate and socialize students. The traditional model of the classroom begins with the assumption that the relationship between each individual student and the teacher is the only one that is important. Yet we know that peer relationships strongly influence students' attitudes about academic performance, about going to college, and about the appropriateness of such behaviors as studying, cheating, and skipping school.[1] What is worse, we know that students' norms are often opposed to academic achievement, thereby isolating students who strive to do their best academically.[2]

What is needed is a way to use peer influences to assist the educational process, and team techniques, in which students work in small teams and are rewarded as a team for their academic performance, have been suggested as a way to fill this need. When students work in teams, it is to their advantage to encourage their peers, to support rather than oppose academic efforts. Peer relationships can then be a tool in promoting important cognitive and socialization outcomes. Two team techniques—Teams-Games-Tournaments (TGT) and Student Teams-Achievement Division (STAD)—have been extensively evaluated in field experiments, and it is the research on these techniques, as well as on others that employ the same general principles, that is reviewed and discussed in this chapter[3] in an effort to discover the practical and theoretical implications of using teams in classrooms.

TEAM TECHNIQUES

In normal classroom practice there are two essential elements: a *task structure* and a *reward structure*. The task structure refers to instructional activities set up by the teacher, including lecture-discussion, individual worksheets, and small groups working with the teacher. The reward structure refers to the consequences for students of doing school work, that is, the means that teachers use to motivate students to perform school tasks. In most classrooms, the reward structure includes some combination of grades, praise from the teacher, and notes from teachers to parents.

Team techniques change both the task and the reward structure of classrooms. They typically involve students working in small teams (four or five participants) without the teacher being constantly present, and students are rewarded according to the performance of the team as a whole. TGT and STAD use class newsletters to recognize successful teams.

The task structure in a team-learning technique can be termed a "cooperative" one, and the reward structure is also "cooperative." When students perform well in a team, they help their teammates perform and help them to be rewarded. In a traditional classroom, on the other hand, the task structure is one where individual students work alone or listen to the teacher and the reward structure is "competitive" (for example, grading on the curve). When competing for a limited supply of good grades, students seldom help each other.

Do cooperative task and reward structures represent an improvement over traditional ones? In more traditional task structures, students receive little personal attention. Whether prepared or unprepared, a student may go largely unnoticed during an entire class period, and many students, particularly in secondary schools, complain that no one really cares whether they come to school or do their work. The competitive reward structure often found in traditional classrooms has been criticized for many other reasons. Competitive grading has been opposed because it is not sensitive to the efforts of less capable students who may never make an acceptable grade, no matter how hard they try. Competitive grading also sets students against one another because one student's success guarantees another's failure. The result of a competitive reward structure is that many students try not to do their best or to appear to know too many answers, rather than risk losing status among their peers.[4]

Cooperative task structures, on the other hand, ensure that each student gets some attention. Further, research on tutoring peers indicates that students prefer settings in which they teach and learn from other students and that they often learn better in such settings.[5] Finally, cooperative tasks offer an opportunity for active rather than passive learning. As for the cooperative reward structure, the more a student does, the better it is for other members of the team. Coleman has compared peer support for outstanding sports achievement with lack of peer support for outstanding academic achievement.[6] In team sports, where the reward structure is cooperative, a successful individual brings credit to the entire school. In academic situations, where the reward structure is competitive (grading), only one student gets the credit.

Research on cooperative task and reward structures has shown consistently positive effects on several important socialization-related variables, such as liking others, a sense of being liked, cross-racial attraction, and self-esteem. When individuals must rely on one another for rewards, they come to like and help each other.[7] Mutual concern leads in turn to such effects as cross-racial liking when biracial teams are used[8] and growth in self-esteem.[9] It is these effects that are among the most consistent and important outcomes of team techniques. Team techniques used over long periods in schools might improve the mental health and prosocial behavior of students. Could a school experience based on cooperative work and rewards produce a young adult who is more self-confident, friendly, and supportive of society?

Evidence concerning the effects of cooperative task and reward structures on academic achievement is not conclusive. Short-term laboratory studies sometimes show performance effects that favor group task and reward structures, but they favor individual or competitive structures at other times.[10] The effects documented in longer-term classroom studies, which are the ones reviewed in this chapter, are also mixed. TGT has had consistent effects on achievement;[11] STAD has had somewhat less consistent effects,[12] and the Jigsaw method has had effects on achievement among minority students only.[13] Cooperative techniques used with experimental groups at the University of Minnesota have not demonstrated greater effects on achievement than standard techniques used with control groups.[14]

It is apparently not enough to set up a cooperative reward and task structure and wait for achievement to increase. The team techniques that have been most successful in increasing academic performance (TGT, STAD, and the Jigsaw method) require individual accountability on the part of students. In TGT, students compete as individuals with members of other teams to contribute to their team scores, and in STAD and the Jigsaw method students take individual quizzes. The Johnson techniques, on the other hand, do not specifically require individual accountability.

One must recognize that a group reward can allow some students to "drag their feet," forcing others to do the work. Anyone who has had experience with the traditional laboratory or report group to which a single paper has been assigned will recognize this problem — somehow, one student ends up doing most of the work. One of the few studies in which a competitive reward structure produced greater learning than a cooperative one, undertaken by Julian and Perry, involved such laboratory groups.[15] The laboratory group techniques not requiring individual accountability are, however, just as effective as TGT, STAD, and Jigsaw in promoting gains on such variables as mutual attraction, cross-racial friendships, and self-esteem. The study done by Julian and Perry and a study involving the Johnson techniques[16] show the positive effects of both techniques on these variables.

TEAMS-GAMES-TOURNAMENTS

TGT, a team-learning technique developed by David DeVries, Keith Edwards, and others at Johns Hopkins University in 1971, is the most thoroughly researched of the team techniques. It is built around two major components: four- to five-member student teams and instructional tournaments. The teams are the cooperative element, and students are assigned to them according to a procedure that maximizes heterogeneity of ability levels, sex, and race. The primary function of the team is to prepare members to do well in the tournament. After an initial class presentation by the teacher, the teams are given worksheets covering academic material resembling that to be included in the tournament. Teammates study together and quiz each other to be sure that all are prepared.

After the practice session, members of the team must demonstrate their learning in the tournament, which is usually held once each week. During the tournament, students are assigned to three-person "tournament tables" in such a way that competition at each table will be fair—the three students whose past performance was highest are assigned to the first table, the three whose performance was next highest are assigned to the second table, and so on. At the tables, the students compete on simple academic games covering content presented in class by the teacher and again on the worksheets. Students at the tournament tables compete as representatives of their teams, and the score each student earns is added into an overall team score. Because students are assigned to ability-homogeneous tournament tables, each student, regardless of past performance, has an equal chance of contributing a maximum score to the team, as the student who scores in first place at every table brings the same number of points to his or her team. The teacher then prepares a newsletter recognizing successful teams and first-place scorers. While team assignments always remain the same, table assignments change for every tournament according to a system that maintains equality of past performance at each table.

TGT is usually used intensively for six to twelve weeks, and each week usually involves two or three forty-five minute periods of teacher presentation, one or two periods during which the team studies worksheets, and one period for the tournament. For certain review units, however, two tournaments can be scheduled in a week.

Rationale

TGT is based on an expectancy model of student motivation. That is, motivation is a multiplicative function of probability of success given maximum effort and incentive value of success.[17] The TGT model is directed at both components of this relationship. It is designed to increase the probability of success, given maximum effort, through the tournament system. Students compete only against their equals. If they prepare themselves well, they substantially increase their chances of obtaining a good score for their teams. This is in contrast to the traditional class, where some students usually get good grades, while others cannot get good grades no matter how hard they try.

The TGT components directed at maximizing the incentive value of success are the teams and the newsletters. The teams provide peer support for academic performance, since a student who does well is likely to be socially rewarded by other members of the team. For students in the upper grades in elementary schools and those in junior high schools, peer reward may be far more valuable than that provided by adults. There is some evidence that it is peer encouragement more than the opportunity for peer tutoring that makes the team effective in increasing academic performance.[18] The newsletters increase the incentive value of success both by rewarding teams for their successes (thereby motivating them to encourage and reward their members) and by directly recognizing students who have contributed maximum scores to their teams.

Research on TGT has shown positive effects on student self-reports of incentive value of success and probability of success, supporting the usefulness of the expectancy model for explaining TGT effects on academic performance.[19] The same students reported greater peer support for academic performance in a team situation than in a nonteam situation.

The model underlying the effects of TGT on mutual concern, race relationships, and other nonacademic outcomes is a simple one. In any cooperative reward structure, group members grow to like one another more than individuals working independently or competitively.[20] There is no reason why TGT should prove an exception to that rule, as it is built around a cooperative reward structure—the teams.

Research on Outcomes

There have been at least ten studies evaluating TGT in field experiments. These studies, which vary widely in their methodologies, populations, and curriculum areas, have been extensively reviewed elsewhere.[21] The studies involved nearly 3,000 students in grades three through twelve. The settings for the schools were urban and suburban in various parts of the country. Most studies involved random assignment at the individual student or class level. All involved a TGT versus control comparison, and most evaluated variations in TGT components. Table 6-1 summarizes the characteristics and the results of the ten studies.

Academic Achievement. Academic achievement was measured in two ways in most studies. All but one study employed treatment-specific tests, containing a representative sample of items studied in the

Table 6-1
Summary of TGT settings, research designs, and effects on students

Study	Subject area	Grade level	Length (weeks)	Number of students	Level of random assignment	Treatment-specific tests	Standardized tests	Attitude toward school	Mutual concern	Race relations	Peer norms
						Academic achievement		Effects on students			
1	Mathematics	7	9	96	Class	+	+	--	--	+	--
2	Mathematics	7	4	110	Student	+	--	+	+	0	0
3	Mathematics } Social studies	7	12	128	Student	0	--	0	0	+	+ (p<.10)
4	Mathematics	7	10	299	Class	--	+	+	--	+	+
5	Social studies	10 to 12	12	191	Class	+ (p<.10)	0	+	+	+	+
6	Language arts	3	6	60	Student	+	+	0	0	--	--
7	Language arts	3	6	53	Student	+	+	0	0	--	--
8	Reading vocabulary } Verbal analogies	3	5	53	Student	+	--	--	--	--	--
9	Language arts	7 to 8	10	1,742	Teacher	+	0	0	+	--	0
10	Social studies	7 to 9	10	57	Student	0	0	0	+	--	+

Note: + indicates a statistically significant effect (p < .05) in favor of TGT, as contrasted with a control condition.

0 indicates no difference between TGT and control.

-- indicates that the variable was not measured.

TGT and control classes. Eight studies used standardized subject-matter tests. Two studies (numbers 3 and 8) involved two distinct content areas; results for them are reported separately in the table.

The academic achievement results show TGT to be more effective than control treatments in increasing achievement. Eight of the eleven treatment-specific test comparisons and five of the eight standardized test comparisons showed that TGT had positive effects on achievement. One additional study (number 5) showed a marginal effect ($p < .10$) on the treatment-specific test.

Statistically significant effects at the .05 level were obtained neither for the treatment-specific nor for the standardized test in the three studies of social studies classes. This result may be due to possible inefficiency when using TGT with higher-level cognitive material, but it could also be because of the difficulty of specifying a concrete set of measurable objectives for social studies. In mathematics and in language arts (which in the TGT studies focused on grammar and punctuation), it is easier to obtain agreement on objectives. Furthermore, it is more difficult in social studies than it is in mathematics or language to be sure that tests measure what is being taught.

Attitudes toward School. It is obvious to the most casual observer visiting a TGT class that the students enjoy the technique, particularly the tournaments and the team practice sessions. Informal postexperimental talks with TGT classes and reports from teachers confirm this observation. When students responded to the satisfaction scale of the *Learning Environment Inventory* (LEI) and to similar scales derived from the LEI, however, there was failure to discriminate between TGT and control classes in five of the nine occasions in which satisfaction was measured.[22] In most cases, particularly in the two third-grade studies in which satisfaction was measured (numbers 6 and 7), this failure to find effects was because all students, including the control students, expressed positive attitudes toward school on both pretests and posttests.

Mutual Concern. Mutual concern was measured in seven of the TGT studies. Sociometric questionnaires given to students in all seven of the studies asked them to list their friends in the class. The number of friends named was used as a measure of mutual concern. Three other studies used a questionnaire based on a scale derived from the LEI,[23] and the final study (number 9) used the "relationship with peers" subscale from the *Coopersmith Self-Concept Scale.* A plus sign is entered in the table when statistically significant effects were found either for the number of friends named or for the questionnaire scales. Five of the seven studies showed positive TGT effects on at least one of these measures of mutual concern. The two that did not show TGT effects were again the third-grade studies, in which it is possible that a relatively brief intervention (six weeks) was too short to influence well-established friendship patterns.

Race Relations. Four of the TGT studies took place in integrated secondary schools. In these studies two additional questions were asked of the sociometric data: Did TGT, as compared to control treatments, result in a larger *number* of cross-racial friendship choices? Did TGT result in a larger *percentage* of cross-racial friendship choices over all choices? These questions are important in that they indicate the degree to which TGT may be used in integrated settings to break down racial barriers.

The results of the analyses for cross-racial friendship show positive TGT effects on friendship for three of the four studies.[24] The fourth study showed significant effects on the number and percentage of cross-race *helping* choices ("Whom have you helped with their class-work?") but not on friendship choices. The results are quite encouraging as a demonstration of the utility of biracial team techniques as a means of improving race relations in integrated classrooms.

Peer Norms. Peer norms concerning academic performance were measured in five studies. The measures were scales derived from the perceived classmate expectations scale of the LEI (sample item: Students in this class expect me to come to class every day). Positive TGT effects were found on this measure in three studies. That is, TGT students reported more encouragement from their peers to do well in the classroom than did control students. In a fourth study (number 3), marginal effects ($p < .10$) were found in mathematics classes. These results indicate that TGT does have an effect on students' perceptions of others' expectations for their own academic behavior.

Other Measures. Several other measures were taken in various TGT studies. Frequency of peer tutoring was obtained either from behavioral observation or from self-report in seven studies, six of which showed positive TGT effects. The percentage of time spent on the task was observed in study number 10, and it showed positive TGT effects.

The research on TGT shows it be to an effective means of simultaneously increasing academic performance, mutual concern, and pro-academic norms. Of course, the results are not completely replicated; even measures of peer tutoring, virtually an indicator of the degree of implementation of the program, did not always produce TGT effects. But the bulk of the evidence collected supports the usefulness of the team technique.

It is important to note that TGT has been used and is being used by hundreds of teachers all over the country. There is evidence that it has been used in grade three through college, in subjects ranging from home economics to Bible study to foreign language. The TGT teachers' manual and curriculum units (worksheets and games) for mathematics and language arts are commercially available,[25] and many teachers make their own materials for use within the general TGT framework. TGT represents an unusual case in educational research—a technique derived from psychological theory, extensively evaluated in field settings, has been made widely available for practical use.

STUDENT TEAMS-ACHIEVEMENT DIVISION

STAD was developed by Robert Slavin at Johns Hopkins University in 1975. It is based on the most important principles of TGT (team reward, individual accountability, equality of potential team contribution for students of all ability levels), but it was designed to be simpler and more sharply focused on the teams. STAD uses the same four- or five-member heterogeneous teams used in TGT, but replaces the games and tournaments with simple quizzes. After studying in teams, students take simple, fifteen-minute quizzes. The quiz scores are translated into team scores using a system called "achievement division." The quiz scores of the six students highest in past performance are compared, and the top scorer in the group (achievement division) earns eight points for the team, the second scorer earns six points, and so forth. Then the quiz scores of the six students next highest in past performance are compared, and so on. In this way student scores are compared only within ability-homogeneous reference groups instead of within the entire class. A "bumping" procedure changes division assignments from week to week to maintain equality. Students know only their own division assignments; they do not interact in any way with the other members of their division. The achieve-

ment division feature maintains equality of opportunity for contributing to the team score. It also increases the motivation for better
students to tutor those who are not doing as well because the low performers have as much influence on the team score as any other team
members.

Because the quizzes take much less time than the tournaments, two
lessons can more easily be fit into a week. In fact, many teachers have
used STAD in two two-day cycles, leaving the fifth day of each week
for other activities.

The rationale behind STAD is similar to that behind TGT. The
achievement divisions maximize the probability of success given maximum effort, while the teams and the newsletter maximize the incentive value of success. The replacement of games with quizzes, however,
is expected to take all elements of chance out of the effort-reward relationship and to retain focus on what the team does to prepare its
members for a performance setting that is certain and predictable.

Research on Outcomes

Four studies have been conducted to date on STAD. The four
studies involved about 1,250 students in grades four through nine.
Two of the studies took place in urban settings, the other two in rural
areas.[26] Table 6-2 summarizes the settings, designs, and outcomes of
the four STAD studies.

Academic Achievement. Effects on academic achievement were
measured using both treatment-specific and standardized measures.
The results demonstrate generally positive effects on the measures.
Significant STAD effects were found for two studies, although in one
study (number 2) the effects were due primarily to gains made by
black students. White students in the STAD class did only slightly better than their counterparts in the control class.

Attitudes toward School. Positive attitudes toward school were significantly increased in only one of the four studies. It is interesting that
the study was conducted with elementary school children, and the results were the opposite of the pattern observed in TGT research, where
studies at the junior high school level showed a greater effect in attitude toward school.

Mutual Concern. Mutual concern was measured in the STAD
studies both by means of questionnaire scales adapted from the LEI
and by means of sociometric instruments. A plus sign in Table 6-2 in-

Table 6-2

Summary of STAD settings, research designs, and effects on students

| | Settings and designs | | | | | Academic achievement | | Effects on students | | | | |
Study	Subject area	Grade level	Length (weeks)	Number of students	Level of random assignment	Treatment-specific tests	Standardized tests	Attitude toward school	Mutual concern	Race relations	Peer norms	Percentage of time spent on tasks
1	Language arts	7	10	173	Class	0	0	0	+	--	+	+
2	Language arts	7	10	65	Class	+	+	0	0	+	0	--
						(Blacks only)						
3	Language arts	4	12	512	Class	+	+	+	+	--	+	+
4	Language arts	7 to 9	12	480	Class	0	0	0	+	+	+	+

Note: + indicates a statistically significant effect ($p < .05$) in favor of STAD, as contrasted with a control condition.

0 indicates no difference between STAD and control.

-- indicates that the variable was not measured.

dicates effects both on the questionnaire scales and on the increase in number of classmates named as friends. These effects were found in three of the four studies; in the fourth, neither effect was found.

Race Relations. Two of the four studies took place in integrated settings. In both studies significant STAD effects were found in terms of the increase in both the number and the percentage of cross-racial friendship choices made.[27] Also, in study number 4, behavioral observers found greater cross-racial interaction in the STAD classes than in the control classes, both when students were performing the task and when they were not, and a subsequent follow-up found that the increase in cross-racial friendship was maintained over a nine-month period.

Peer Norms. Peer norms concerning academic performance were measured in all four studies by using questionnaire scales adapted from the earlier TGT scales. Positive STAD effects on this measure were found in three of the four studies.

Percentage of Time Spent on Task. In two of the three studies, behavioral observers were trained to indicate whether students were on- or off-task. Both of these studies showed STAD students to be on-task significantly more than control students.

STAD has, in summary, most often proved to be effective in increasing academic performance, mutual concern, positive race relations, proacademic norms, and percentage of time spent on-task. As was the case with TGT, individual findings are not always significantly positive, but the overall trend is clear.

Because TGT and STAD have not been compared in a single study, it is impossible to say whether there is a difference between them in terms of their outcomes. It is possible, however, to contrast the techniques as they appear to the observer. TGT is obviously more fun for students than STAD because the challenge and activity of the games are enjoyed by nearly all students. STAD is more businesslike and efficient in its use of time, so more material can be covered in a STAD than in a TGT unit. Teams appear to be somewhat more important in STAD because the connection between team study and individual success is more obvious. Similarities between the two techniques, however, so far outweigh differences, both in terms of basic structures and outcomes, that the practitioner choosing between them should probably do so on practical grounds.

OTHER TECHNIQUES

In addition to the TGT and STAD research conducted at Johns Hopkins University, there are at least two other research programs investigating team techniques in classrooms. The first, conducted at the University of Minnesota under the direction of David Johnson, is reviewed elsewhere in this volume.[28] The second program, originated by Elliot Aronson, began at the University of Texas at Austin, and it is being continued there and at the University of California at Santa Cruz. This program, which focuses on the "Jigsaw Method,"[29] uses the teams in much the same way that TGT and STAD do. Academic material is broken into as many sections as there are team members. For example, a biography might be broken into "early years," "schooling," "first accomplishments," and so forth. The students study their sections with members of other teams studying the same sections. Then they return to their own team and teach their section to the other members of that team. Finally, all members of the team are quizzed on the entire unit. Quiz scores in this case contribute to individual grades, not to a team score as in TGT or STAD. In this sense, the Jigsaw technique may be seen as a cooperative task structure rather than as a cooperative reward structure where individual performances contribute directly to a group goal. If the Jigsaw technique is used, individual performances contribute only to individual goals. The group is not rewarded as a group; there is no formal group goal. The positive behavior of each team member (learning the sections) does, however, help other group members to be rewarded (because they need each others' information). This means that the essential dynamics of the cooperative reward structure are present, for, when one individual's actions help another to be rewarded, the individuals come to like one another[30] and to expect one another to do well,[31] regardless of whether there is a group goal.

There have been three major studies of the Jigsaw method. Two of them addressed effects on academic achievement. One study failed to find a difference between experimental and control groups.[32] One study found effects for minority students only.[33] One study supported the fact that the Jigsaw method was liked by students,[34] although a second one did not find that this was so.[35] In the two studies that measured self-esteem, Jigsaw effects were found to be positive. The Jigsaw method appears to be useful, particularly for increasing the nonacademic outcomes (interpersonal liking and self-concept) characteristic of team techniques.

PRACTICAL APPLICATION OF TEAM TECHNIQUES

All of the team techniques discussed in this chapter have been used by teachers outside of the research efforts, and all are designed to be used in applied settings. The techniques, although they are similar in conceptual background, are quite different in practice and may best serve different purposes.

The largest family of team techniques are those developed at Johns Hopkins University (TGT, STAD, and several modifications), and these models employ a highly structured set of learning activities. In all of them, the teacher presents material, after which students work in teams on worksheets that reinforce the material presented. Finally, students demonstrate their learning in either a quiz (STAD) or an academic game (TGT). The team's task is to make sure that every team member understands the worksheets so that they will do well on the quiz or game. Most members do this by quizzing each other on worksheet items and explaining rules or principles to one another. Such techniques are most useful in relatively concrete subject areas such as mathematics, language arts, foreign languages, and the factual aspects of social studies and science.

Other team techniques have opposite applications. The Jigsaw method is most useful for social studies areas and some aspects of English and science. Jigsaw requires that there be narrative material capable of being divided into parts. Thus, it is restricted to study in the areas of history and literature, or where there are narrative descriptions of scientific principles. The team techniques developed by David and Roger Johnson are better suited to abstract, conceptual material than to concrete subject matter. It is possible to use more than one technique to cover different parts of the curriculum.[36]

NEXT STEPS

Research has established the effects of team techniques on academic performance, mutual concern, race relations, and proacademic norms. Future research should go in three directions. First, the effects of team techniques should be more extensively measured, possibly by use of more sensitive observation procedures. We know little about what goes on in the teams.

Second, we need to find out whether it is necessary or desirable to spend time teaching students how to be good team members. This is done when the Jigsaw and Johnson techniques are used, but not the TGT or STAD ones. There are related questions, such as: Does a team leader create a more effective group? What are the effects of assigning friends to teams? Is team size important? The answers to these questions would contribute to social psychological theory and have considerable practical importance as well.

Finally, team techniques should be adapted for use as a replacement for, rather than a supplement to, traditional techniques. That is, we need to develop and evaluate team techniques that can become the dominant educational experience of students. The Johnson techniques have been directed toward this goal, but there is more work to be done. For example, could classroom tasks be structured so that all student academic behavior helps both student and team? Could a variety of team techniques be used at the option of the teacher to achieve various learning objectives? If long-term techniques can be developed and proven in field experiments, they may possibly be used to improve substantially the academic performance and socialization of students. The principles and guidelines are in place for such an effort; it is primarily an engineering task that lies ahead.

IMPLICATIONS FOR EDUCATORS

Research on student team techniques in classrooms has had to steer a fine line between basic research on the one hand and the theoretical evaluation of methods on the other. A six- to twelve-week study in a real school, with procedures implemented by real teachers, is not sufficient to test subtle hypotheses. On the other hand, factorial studies using relatively rigid controls and extensive observation and measurement do not simulate the untreated school, and they introduce demand characteristics and experimental bias effects.

Given the difficulties, classroom research on teams has been remarkably successful in adding to scientific knowledge and contributing to practice at the same time. All of the techniques are simple and practical. All have been used voluntarily by teachers outside of the research environment without external assistance. All have contributed to the social psychology of groups as follows:

— The results of the various studies point to the importance of individual accountability in group reward structures. As has been pointed out elsewhere, cooperation can be more effective than competition or individualization only when individuals in a cooperative group have something of value that each must contribute.[37]

— The research on teams and race relations has shown that cooperative rewards can help to break down major interpersonal barriers.

— The results pointing to more positive self-esteem and reduced anxiety as a consequence of participation on teams have major implications for the study of mental health. If schooling could be made a cooperative experience, would we begin to see a decrease in mental health-related problems in children and adolescents? Would a less anxious, more self-confident student be as likely to engage in school violence or vandalism, to be withdrawn, antisocial, or truant? Team-learning research suggests an ecological approach to the problem of mental health—to prevent problems before the labeling process beings to categorize students as "deviant."

— The effects on interpersonal attraction within teams and on race relations suggest that the team concept may be used to overcome other interpersonal barriers. Some particularly relevant situations are the mainstreaming of handicapped, retarded, or emotionally disturbed children and the breaking up of antisocial cliques or gangs.

The research on team techniques demonstrates that social psychologists can bring psychological principles directly into the classroom, and, perhaps more important, they can evaluate techniques in the field without sacrificing the essentials of experimental design. This research has taken the classroom beyond being a convenient source of subjects to being a laboratory that can be used over an extended period to answer questions that have greater external validity than either the short-term experiment or the longer-term correlational design. This is possible because the experiments have been designed both to answer important theoretical and practical questions and to do a better job of teaching. It is this last feature that is vital; few schools would allow social psychologists to implement lengthy experimental treatments that did not promise educational gains.

Fcr the educational practitioner, the implications of research on team techniques should be clear. If a school wants to promote positive race relations, to increase students' academic performance, to encourage mutual concern, and to develop self-esteem, team techniques may be a means of accomplishing those goals. They are practical and inexpensive, require no special training, and generate enthusiasm. Further, they have been extensively researched and field-tested in hundreds of classrooms.

Learning-team techniques may represent a landmark in the history of educational research. They originate from social psychological theory, have been evaluated in numerous field experiments using designs high in both internal and external validity, and have a potential for finding their way into educational practice on a mass scale. The evidence collected on the outcomes of using many of these techniques suggests that, if this mass acceptance does occur, education at all levels and in many subject areas may become more effective in increasing the academic achievement, encouraging the social growth, and protecting the mental health of children.

NOTES

1. Edward McDill and Leo Rigsby, *Structure and Process in Secondary School: The Impact of Academic Climate* (Baltimore, Md.: Johns Hopkins University Press, 1973).

2. James S. Coleman, *The Adolescent Society* (New York: Free Press of Glencoe, 1961).

3. We wish to thank Bernard L. Blackburn, John Hollifield, and Nancy Madden for their comments on this chapter.

4. George Homans, *The Human Group* (New York: Harcourt, Brace and World, 1950).

5. Linda Devin-Sheehan, Robert Feldman, and Vernon Allen, "Research on Children Tutoring Children: A Critical Review," *Review of Educational Research* 46 (1976): 355-385.

6. Coleman, *Adolescent Society.*

7. Morton Deutsch, "An Experimental Study of the Effects of Cooperation and Competition upon Group Process," *Human Relations* 2 (1949): 199-231; David W. Johnson and Roger Johnson, "Instructional Goal Structure: Cooperative, Competitive or Individualistic," *Review of Educational Research* 44 (1974): 213-240.

8. Elliot Aronson *et al.*, "The Jigsaw Route to Learning and Liking," *Psychology Today* 8 (1975): 43-50; David L. DeVries, Keith J. Edwards, and Robert E. Slavin, "Biracial Learning Teams and Race Relations in the Classroom: Four Field Experiments Using Teams-Games-Tournament," *Journal of Educational Psychology* 70 (1978): 356-362; Robert E. Slavin, "How Student Learning Teams Can Integrate the Desegregated Classroom," *Integrated Education* 15 (1977): 56-58; Robert E. Slavin,

"Student Teams and Achievement Divisions," *Journal of Research and Development in Education,* in press.

9. Nancy T. Blaney *et al.,* "Interdependence in the Classroom: A Field Study," *Journal of Educational Psychology* 69 (1977): 121-128.

10. Robert E. Slavin, "Classroom Reward Structure: An Analytical and Practical Review," *Review of Educational Research* 47 (1977): 633-650.

11. David L. DeVries and Robert E. Slavin, "Teams-Games-Tournament: Review of Ten Classroom Experiments," *Journal of Research and Development in Education,* in press.

12 Robert Slavin, "Student Learning Teams and Achievement Divisions."

13. G. William Lucker *et al.,* "Performance in the Interdependent Classroom: A Field Study," *American Educational Research Journal* 13 (1976): 115-123.

14. David W. Johnson, Roger Johnson, and Linda Scott, "The Effects of Cooperative and Individualized Instruction on Student Attitudes and Achievement," *Journal of Social Psychology* 104 (1978): 207-216.

15. James Julian and Franklyn Perry, "Cooperation Contrasted with Intra-group and Inter-group Competition," *Sociometry* 30 (1967): 79-90.

16. David W. Johnson and Roger Johnson, "Effects of Cooperation, Competition, and Individualism on Interpersonal Attraction among Heterogeneous Peers," paper presented at the Annual Convention of the American Psychological Association, San Francisco, 1977.

17. John Atkinson, "Towards Experimental Analysis of Human Motivation in Terms of Motives, Expectancies and Incentives," in *Motives in Fantasy, Action and Society,* ed. *id.* (Princeton, N.J.: Van Nostrand Co. 1958), 288-305; Robert E. Slavin, "A New Model of Classroom Motivation," paper presented at the annual convention of the American Educational Research Association, New York, 1977.

18. Burma H. Hulten and David L. DeVries, *A Study of the Importance of Team Competition and Team Practice to Teams-Games-Tournament,* Baltimore, Md.: Center for Social Organization of Schools, Johns Hopkins University, 1975; Robert Slavin and John S. Wodarski, "Decomposing a Student Team Technique: Team Reward and Team Task," paper presented at the annual convention of the American Psychological Association, San Francisco, 1977.

19. Hulten and DeVries, "A Study of the Importance of Team Competition and Team Practice to Teams-Games-Tournament."

20. Slavin, "Classroom Reward Structure: An Analytical and Practical Review"; David W. Johnson and Roger T. Johnson, "Instructional Goal Structure: Cooperative, Competitive, or Individualistic," *Review of Educational Research* 44 (1974): 213-240.

21. DeVries and Slavin, "Teams-Games-Tournament."

22. Herbert J. Walberg and Gary J. Anderson, "Classroom Climate and Individual Learning," *Journal of Educational Psychology* 59 (1968): 414-419.

23. *Ibid.*

24. DeVries, Edwards, and Slavin, "Biracial Learning Teams and Race Relations in the Classroom: Four Field Experiments Using Teams-Games-Tournament."

25. For information on published TGT materials, please write to Argus Communications, 7440 Natchez Avenue, Niles, IL 60648.

26. Slavin and Wodarski, "Decomposing a Student Team Technique: Team Reward and Team Task"; Robert E. Slavin, "Student Teams and Comparison among Equals: Effects on Academic Performance and Student Attitudes," *Journal of Educational Psychology,* in press.

27. Slavin, "How Student Learning Teams Can Integrate the Desegregated Classroom."

28. See Chapter 5 in this volume. See also David W. Johnson and Roger T. Johnson, *Learning Together and Alone: Cooperation, Competition, and Individualization* (Englewood Cliffs, N.J.: Prentice-Hall, 1975).

29. Aronson *et al.,* "Jigsaw Route to Learning and Liking."

30. Leonard Berkowitz and Louise Daniels, "Responsibility and Dependency," *Journal of Abnormal and Social Psychology* 66 (1963): 429-436.

31. Edwin J. Thomas, "Effects of Facilitative Role Interdependence on Group Functioning," *Human Relations* 10 (1957): 347-366.

32. Aronson *et al.,* "Jigsaw Route to Learning and Liking."

33. Lucker *et al.,* "Performance in the Interdependent Classroom."

34. Aronson *et al.,* "Jigsaw Route to Learning and Liking."

35. Blaney *et al.,* "Interdependence in the Classroom."

36. Information on teachers' manuals and other materials for using TGT, STAD, and Jigsaw may be obtained by writing to the Johns Hopkins Learning Project, 3505 North Charles Street, Baltimore, MD 21218.

37. Slavin, "Classroom Reward Structure."

7. Principals' Competency, Environment, and Outcomes

Chad D. Ellett and *Herbert J. Walberg*

During the past decade, educational administrators have discussed at length the adequacy of research paradigms, the relations between theory and research, and the problems of translating research findings into practice. At the same time, several trends have affected the school principalship: an increasing emphasis on the importance of the principal's role in education, a developing interest in the preservice and continuing education of principals, a growing focus on the use of performance objectives during preparation and training, and a more thorough scrutiny of school system-university partnerships in the search for definitions of effective performance and for ways to relate measures of performance to the preparation of principals.[1] No single model relating theory, research, and practice has yet emerged, which is perhaps as it should be given the open-ended nature of scientific inquiry. The growing significance of the principal's role in education and the demand for accountability, however, require an examination of the relation between principals' on-the-job performance and other variables in the context of the school.

This chapter provides a conceptual framework for research on the principalship. The framework is not an all-encompassing effort to integrate various theories in educational administration; it is, rather, a merging of general assumptions concerning the model for competency-based education (CBE) as it has been applied to the principalship, combined with research on the social environment of learning. An overview of the components of the conceptual framework is provided, and interrelationships are explained through results of a large-scale field test of an assessment system designed to measure the competencies of public school principals. Research findings relating teachers' and students' perceptions of the characteristics of school environment to school outcomes are also discussed because these findings have implications for research on the social environment of learning.

THE PRINCIPALSHIP AND COMPETENCY-BASED EDUCATION

Educators seek programs and training procedures that maximize effectiveness, but traditional approaches have not provided adequate answers to questions concerning the functioning of key school personnel, particularly questions concerning relations between actual performance and school outcomes. Medley's recent review of research on teacher effectiveness and student outcomes makes this point clearly,[2] and there is even less information about the impact of the principal's behavior on school outcomes.

There has, however, been a substantial amount of research and writing on school organization and the principalship based on a variety of theoretical frameworks: social systems theory, role theory, bureaucratic theory, leadership theory, organizational change theory, decision-making theory, management theory, and task analysis models, to name just a few. Using several classification schemes in the evaluation of research studies, Immegart has provided an extensive review and appraisal of research in educational administration during the two decades from 1954 to 1974.[3] Immegart's review and a review by Willower that focuses on the development of theories in educational administration[4] both conclude that the quantity and quality of such research has increased significantly over the twenty-year period.

While research and theories abound, little is really known about the relationship between the specific on-the-job performances of principals and other variables within the school environment. Traditional writings focused on essential "areas of study" or on working role models defined through categories of administrative responsibility, and, by 1940, the professional literature in educational administration had clearly delineated areas of study considered "necessary" for school principals, including financial management and business administration, maintenance of the school plant, curriculum and supervision, public relations, personnel matters related to both teachers and pupils, special school services, and school law. From some fifty different sources it was possible to identify over three thousand different functions, duties, responsibilities, and roles deemed essential for school principals by professional educational administrators.[5] Some of the lists are based on theory, but few derive from actual research findings.

Since the 1940s there has been a tendency to add a "process" approach to educational administration, largely borrowed from business models, whereby operations or processes are considered appropriate and essential to any functioning organization. Some writers have developed more complex models for the principalship that integrate the traditional functional areas of administrative responsibility (for example, curriculum and instruction, pupil personnel, school-community relations) and management processes (for example, communication, decision making, evaluating, and implementing). Bolton has suggested that both classifications be used in a process-product model.[6] The many models developed for conceptualizing the principalship have served as useful guides for preservice training, but few have been operationalized at the performance level and fewer still have been validated (in the measurement sense) through field-based research.

The administrative function in public education has been subjected to critical reanalysis in recent years. Many questions have been raised regarding the essential competencies required to operate a public school effectively. Such questions include: the nature of these competencies; the relationship between competencies and performance; the difference, if any, in competencies required for various administrative roles; and the relationship between performance and school outcomes.

The national movement to develop competency-based teacher education programs has provided a model for a comparable movement in the education of administrators. The basic assumptions and requirements of CBE are not discussed in this chapter because excellent expositions are available elsewhere.[7] Since 1967, when Congress passed the Education Professions Development Act, which was designed to prepare and maintain an adequate supply of competent teachers, competency-based teacher education has proliferated. According to Schmeider, more than five hundred teacher education programs claim to be competency based or are in the developmental stage.[8]

Serious efforts on a national scale toward the specification of administrative competencies began as a result of a conference sponsored by the National Association of Secondary School Principals and the Danforth Foundation. In August 1972 the National Conference of Professors of Educational Administration formed an interest group on the competency-based curriculum in educational administration, and the *CCBC Notebook,* a quarterly publication prepared at the University of Utah, became the primary outlet for information on competency-based school administration.

The literature in educational administration reveals an ever-growing body of information dealing with CBE concepts and the school principal.[9] Many schemes to categorize competencies have been developed, and statements of administrators' competencies have been submitted to practicing principals and other professionals to verify their content and importance. The proliferation of multiple lists of competency statements for the school administrator has become a source of confusion. Those using competency statements for preservice preparation, continuing education, and staff development must sort through lists to find those statements that are appropriate for a particular purpose, or devise new lists for special purposes. To overcome these problems, classification systems and frameworks for competencies have been proposed.[10]

The application of CBE concepts to school principals has at its foundation the idea that principals should be trained to do those things that cause or facilitate constructive learning environments and youth growth. Most research and development efforts have not yet gone beyond the processes of setting priorities and verification, in which lists of administrative performances, knowledges, and attitudes are arrived at through various ranking and consensual agreement procedures. There has been little effort to establish relationships between assessments of principals' competencies and other important variables in the educational context, a conclusion that is supported by a recent review of ongoing nationwide developments in competency-based administration.[11] Without adequate research, the CBE approach to the principalship might well be considered another educational fad and fail to answer critics who claim it is a mechanistic or reductionist model that does not embrace the effectiveness of behavior in reaching measurable goals.

A basic requirement of a CBE system and any other performance-based program is that the performance statements be validated in practice. Research models aimed at validating competencies are inextricably related to the validation of a particular assessment system or methodology. When a set of competencies or an assessment device is validated "in practice," this implies that each has been successfully used for the purpose for which it was designed. This approach to validation is one step removed from undertaking research to establish relationships between competency assessments and meaningful criterion variables in the school environment—a basic research concern.

Gaynor has discussed several instruments that are helpful in measuring administrative performance, all of which have been validated in practice.[12] Two of the instruments, the *Action Analysis Profile* (AAP) and the *Means of Communication Profile* (MCP), have been tested with persons playing the role of the principal in simulated environments. Two others, the *Task Analysis Profile* (TAP) and the *Administrative Style Analysis Profile* (ASAP) have been tested with practicing principals, teachers, and citizens in real school settings. The TAP is designed to assist the respondent in describing his perception of the functional content of the principal's role. The ASAP is designed to help describe perceptions about the process of the principal's role. The AAP was developed to identify patterns of administrative performance in simulated environments. The MCP was designed to provide the principal with feedback about the way in which he communicates with others. Other instruments validated in practice and used to test the theoretical assumptions from which they were derived are the *Leader Behavior Description Questionnaire* (LBDQ),[13] the *Organizational Climate Description Questionnaire* (OCDQ),[14] the *Principal's Profile*,[15] and the *Diagnostic Survey for Leadership Improvement*.[16] The *Croft Leadership Action Folio* reviewed the types of evaluative devices for assessing school principals used nationally, including instruments where evaluation is required by law, instruments where self-appraisal is optional, and instruments that include checklists in selected areas of performance.[17] Several publications by the Educational Research Service have described programs for administrative evaluation and included sample measuring instruments.[18]

Assessment techniques and measuring devices often used for assessing school administrators have thus been validated "in practice" and are considered by their developers as workable and useful. Few attempts have been made, however, to develop instrumentation with content consisting of professionally verified competencies and to validate the instruments through field-based research. Although many such studies related to competency-based teacher education have been completed or are in progress, to our knowledge there have been only two attempts to establish relationships between assessments of principals' competencies and meaningful criterion variables within the school context.[19]

More investigations are needed to improve competencies already developed for school principals, to resolve the arguments between those favoring and those opposing the application of CBE concepts to the principalship, to develop competency assessment instruments and methodologies that have adequate criterion-related validity, to provide data concerning whether or how the principal makes a difference in the school, and to expand theories about an educational context that would include principals' behavior.

There is a fundamental impediment to such research activities. Research on the competencies of principals and on instruments for assessing those competencies requires (as does most research in education) acceptable sample sizes. Since the unit being investigated is the principal and since there is generally only one in each school, statistical analyses to validate a principal's performances against school-related criteria require (with few exceptions) that school means for the criterion measures of students and teachers be utilized. This becomes an expensive and time-consuming research objective. Validity studies on teacher competencies have probably progressed at a more rapid rate because the unit studied is the teacher (there are many teachers in a school), and class means (many classes in each school) can be more practically utilized. There appear to be no simple solutions to this fundamental design problem, but such research can usually be made more cost effective by using sampling procedures when collecting and processing data on criterion variables, and less time consuming by using high-inference measures of principals' performances.

The section that follows describes a framework for conceptualizing relationships between principal behavior, the social environment of learning, and school outcomes. The framework, which is suggested as a possible research paradigm for criterion-related validity studies of measures of principal behavior, is integrated with assumptions and research findings from studies of the school climate and learning environment. Results of a first field test of selected components of the framework are discussed to provide supportive research data. Research findings relating teacher and student perceptions of school environment characteristics to school outcomes are included because they have implications for theories on school environments.

PRINCIPALS' BEHAVIOR IN THE SCHOOL ENVIRONMENT: A THEORETICAL FRAMEWORK

A recent article pointed out several methodological and conceptual difficulties inherent in applying the conventional "treatment-yield" paradigm, which behavioral psychology borrowed from agronomy, to research on teaching.[20] One latent assumption of such models is that teaching can be viewed as a one-way cause of learning. A primary difficulty with this assumption is that it cannot be directly tested through correlational analyses. In addition, it is possible that causality is reversed, or at best circular, when considering the host of variables in the classroom and home environment mediating learning outcomes. The theoretical framework described in this section is performance based and rests on the assumption that causal relations, however complex, exist between principals' behaviors and key variables within the school environment. The causal relations are, however, of the "interactive" type. The framework assumes that the behavior of the principal affects key variables in the school environment that mediate school outcomes and that these consequences, in turn, affect subsequent principal behavior. The principal functions within a highly interactive social system and is affected by the consequences of his own functioning.

A schematic representation of basic components of the theoretical framework and "interactive" causal relations system is presented in Figure 7-1. Solid lines in the figure represent the theoretical impact of principal behavior on other components in the system. Broken lines represent the effects of the consequences of principal behavior on subsequent behavior, as well as the impact of factors within and outside the school on principal behavior. Mediating variables in the figure are conceived as factors associated with cognitive, affective, and behavioral characteristics of key individuals within the school environment

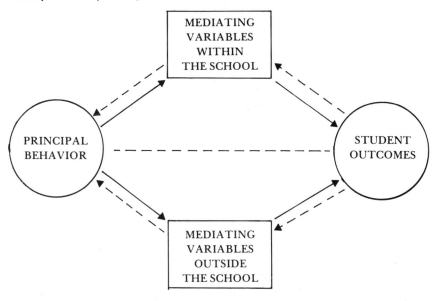

Figure 7-1

Relationship between basic components of the theoretical framework

(teachers and students), and outside the school environment (parents, community members, central office personnel). These variables have been termed "mediating" because they intervene between the principal's functioning and student outcomes. Student outcome variables are attendance, learning, and subsequent achievement. There is no solid line connecting principal behavior with student outcomes because of the assumption that this behavioral effect is indirect, largely mediated by factors within and external to the school environment.

Walberg's model for research on teaching included perceptual, intentional, and behavioral constructs for both teachers and students.[21] This model can be expanded to define further the concepts within the theoretical framework presented in Figure 7-1. Basic constructs permit several causal flows or "paths" to be hypothesized for understanding principal behavior within the school environment, as shown in Figure 7-2.

One path of causal relations goes from 1 (the principal) to 5 (the student). The principal, for example, perceives a situation in the

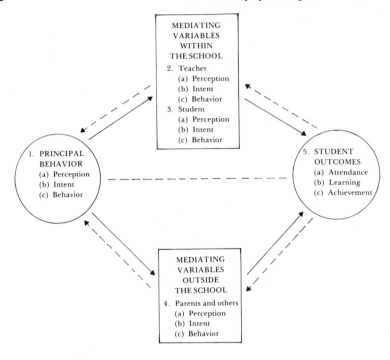

Figure 7-2

Expansion of the theoretical framework to include basic constructs

school, formulates an intention, and acts. This performance may be in relation to any of the other variables, depending upon the original perception and behavioral intention. Principal behavior may be directed at any moment toward teachers, students, or factors outside the school. Or, the long-term intended effect of the behavior might be mediated by its more immediate effect on others. For example, the principal who perceives and acts on a student discipline problem with the intention of changing the student's behavior may do so by discussing the matter with the student's teacher. The teacher's subsequent perception, intention, and behavior impact on the student can mediate the principal's original intention. Similarly, principal behavior directed toward changing parent and community attitudes toward the school may be direct (for example, in a PTA meeting), or indirect and mediated by teachers (parent-teacher conferences), depending upon the original perception and intention.

Another flow of relations is from any component or combination of components (teacher, student, sources outside the school, and student outcomes) toward the principal. This flow depicts the effects of factors within and outside the school on subsequent principal behavior. Thus, the principal affects, and is affected by, complex variables within and external to the school environment.

The constructs are ordered by number because of the assumptions of the theoretical framework proposed. As regards principal-initiated behavior within the school environment, the flow from 1 to 5 is depicted below:

PRINCIPAL → TEACHER → STUDENT → STUDENT OUTCOME

Thus, it would be generally hypothesized that principal-initiated behavior has its primary impact on teachers' perceptions, intentions, and behaviors within the school environment. These teacher characteristics subsequently affect student perceptions, intentions, and behaviors that eventuate in student outcomes. Other causal flows, of course, are possible.

Questions derived from assumptions of the framework are seemingly unending, especially when one considers the circularity of causal relations implied in Figure 7-1. In addition, subsystems and their interacting construct relations could be examined quite apart from the behavior of the principal. Walberg, for example, has provided some suggestions for the study of relationships between teacher and student perception, intention, and behavior in the study of teaching.[22] Research hypotheses could be derived for relationships between principals' behavior and mediating variables outside the school environment, either in terms of how the principal's behavior affects parents and others, or in terms of the effects of the behavior of parents and others on the subsequent performance of the principal.

Ordering relations between components in the theoretical model is admittedly a complex task, particularly when attempting to establish the direction of these relationships. Establishing relationships between a principal's behavior and student outcomes will probably require the application of multivariate techniques to control for the intervening influences of mediating variables within and external to the school environment. Simple two-variable designs are probably impractical — the school environment, like the larger world, is multivariate.

Research studies derived from the theoretical framework will undoubtedly have implications for those who hold traditional conceptions of the process of schooling and the principalship, as well as for those with sociopolitical interests. Should principals be held accountable for student outcomes (attendance, learning, achievement)? If assessments of principal performance are shown to have no relationship to these outcomes, the answer to that question would be "no." As school leaders, should principals be held accountable for fostering an attitudinal and perceptual "tone" in the school environment conducive to learning? If performance assessments are demonstrated to be related to these characteristics and the path and flow of relations is a clear one, then the answer here would be "yes."

If these environmental qualities relate more strongly to teacher effects than to principal behavior, then possibly teachers should primarily be held accountable. If factors external to the school have stronger relations to principal functioning than factors within the school, what are the implications for traditional role models of the principalship? What are the implications for the school-community interface and school politics? What are the implications for preservice and continuing principal education? If teacher assessments of principals' performances have greater reliability and validity than those of superintendents, students, peers, and other sources, what implications are there for states adopting competency-based certification models for leadership personnel? The research strategies needed to answer questions derived from the theoretical framework are complex, but implications of the results would be many. What evidence is there to support basic assumptions of the theoretical framework proposed? The next section describes the results of a large-scale field test of selected components of the framework completed at the University of Georgia.[23]

A TEST OF THE FRAMEWORK

Project ROME (Results Oriented Management in Education) was an ESEA Title III effort sponsored by the Department of Education in Georgia and the Thomas County Schools, Thomasville, Georgia. The general project objectives centered on identifying performance competencies for public school principals, developing an assessment system for those competencies, and establishing the criterion-related validity of the competencies and assessment system through research in the schools. While not specified in as much detail as presented in this chapter, the structural components of the theoretical framework were delineated before the assessment system was field-tested. Results of the field test are of interest because of the magnitude of the project and the implications for the theoretical framework presented in this chapter. Supplemental research findings with selected mediating variable measures are discussed because of implications for understanding relationships between teacher and student perceptions of school environmental dimensions and student outcomes.

Project ROME developed an initial pool of 3,500 to 4,000 statements of competencies, roles, duties, and functions for school principals. This large informational base was reduced to 306 competency statements classified according to a two-dimensional system.[24] A statewide verification of the competencies with school principals further reduced the list to a high-priority set of 80 statements perceived as frequently important for the effective management of a school. Next, 885 performance indicators of the 80 competencies were developed and submitted to a second content verification by a survey to which 290 school principals responded. The large number of indicators was reduced to 338 performance statements perceived as essential or highly desirable for the effective operation of a school by 90 percent of the survey participants.

Principals' Behavior

In the theoretical framework presented in Figure 7-2, principal behavior was considered to relate to student outcomes through the influences of mediating variables within the school environment. Many approaches to performance assessments can be taken within the framework proposed, but most of these can be considered to vary on a dimension of low to high inference. Direct observations of on-the-job performances (for example, time-motion studies, event sampling) utilize low-inference methodology. While considered ideal by some, this technique is usually impractical in terms of time and cost.

In Project ROME, high-inference performance measures were developed for the field test. Each of the 338 verified principal behaviors was assigned to assessment sources on the basis of content. For example, the statement "Observes Teachers in the Classroom to Evaluate Instruction" was a principal performance considered appropriate for assessment by teachers. The following competency assessment sources were utilized; the school principal, teachers, students, central office personnel, and an external observer. Instrumentation was developed for each of these, using Likert-type ratings to assess the perceived frequency and effectiveness with which the school principal carried out performances in the school. Performance assessment instruments were labeled the *Principal Performance Description Survey* (PPDS) — Principal, Teacher, Student, Central Office, and External Observer Forms. These instruments have since been reduced in length and have undergone additional psychometric development.[25]

Mediating Variables within the School

This discussion of components and constructs in the theoretical framework indicates that mediating variables within the school environment are many, and measurement techniques to assess these variables are multiple. Like behavior assessment models, mediating variable measurements can be considered to vary along the high- to low-inference dimension. Project ROME utilized high-inference measures of teacher perceptions of their working environment and student perceptions of characteristics of the school climate-learning environment for their validation research.

Teachers. Work attitudes have been of interest to business and administrative professionals since the 1930s and 1940s, primarily as a result of the classic Hawthorne studies. Mayo[26] and Roethlisberger and Dickson[27] indicate that productivity is related to thoughts and feelings brought to the job by workers that affect work diligence, aptitude, training, skill, and measures of output. Recent well-controlled studies have found positive relationships between work attitudes and performance. Coughlan and Cooke reviewed recent work and showed positive relations between teacher morale and gains in student achievement.[28] Vroom reviewed some twenty investigations in industrial and other organizational settings and found that in most instances higher worker satisfaction was related to better job performance.[29] Several studies report close relationships between actual or perceived behavior of the teacher in the classroom toward students and teachers' attitudes relating to authoritarian-democratic or traditional-progressive dimensions.[30]

In field testing the ROME assessment system, the fourteen-dimension, 118-item *School Survey* was used to measure teachers' perceptions of school environment characteristics. The *School Survey,* developed as a measure of teacher morale or work satisfaction, measures teacher perceptions of school-related factors such as administrative practices, professional work load, supervisory relations, colleague relations, educational effectiveness, performance and development, and materials and equipment.[31] It may be described as a measure of teacher attitudes toward dimensions of their working environment.

Research with the *School Survey* in the Chicago public schools has shown that teachers in schools with the greatest achievement gains perceived their schools as being more educationally effective and themselves as having more constructive supervisory relations with the principal, closer community contact, and a greater voice in the educational program than did teachers in schools with the lowest achievement gains.[32] Subsequent research on this survey instrument demonstrated significant, moderate partial correlations between teacher perceptions and student achievement when school attendance, socioeconomic status, and school size were statistically controlled.[33]

Studies using the *School Survey* as the attitude measure have demonstrated strong canonical correlation relationships between teachers' ratings of principals' competencies and teachers' attitudes toward the school context,[34] and a more recent investigation[35] reported significant multiple correlations between selected factors of the *School Survey* and a semantic differential measure applied to three concepts: "My Role as a Teacher," "My Principal," and "My Students."[36] Positive attitude change on selected factors of the *School Survey* was also found to be significantly greater for teachers working directly with principals on school curriculum projects than for teachers not working directly with the same principals.[37] Other research indicates that positive attitudes of elementary teachers toward administrative practices, school educational effectiveness, and school programs for evaluating students; a voice in determining the school educational program; and opportunities for professional development are significantly negatively correlated with elementary school students' perceptions of classroom difficulty, which in turn correlates negatively with achievement.[38] Thus, the criterion-related validity of the *School Survey,* shown by a variety of studies using different methodologies and criteria, supports hypothesized relations in the theoretical framework proposed and demonstrates that teacher attitudes mediate between the principal and the social environment of learning.

Students. During the past few years, a number of scales have been developed for assessing and evaluating learning environments at different institutional levels. Using Murray's classification of needs as a background, Stern constructed a needs inventory called the *Activities Index.*[39] More recently, Sinclair developed the *Elementary School Survey* for measuring "press" in the elementary school.[40] The most recent theoretical work in this area has been based on Getzels and Thelen's model of the class as a social system.[41] A series of research and evaluation studies was carried out on Harvard Project Physics with the older *Classroom Climate Questionnaire* (CCQ). Because of the redundancy and unreliability of the CCQ scales, a revised instrument was developed and termed the *Learning Environment Inventory* (LEI).[42]

During the past decade, several groups have begun research programs on student perceptions of the sociopsychological characteristics of classroom groups. Reviews of this work demonstrate that student perceptions of the social environment of their classes account for substantial variance in criterion measures of cognitive, affective, and behavioral learning beyond that accounted for by pretests, mental abilities, or both.[43] The predictive validity of these student perceptions has also been replicated in other cultures.[44]

Using partial canonical correlation techniques, Perkins found that elementary student perceptions of the school environment correlated significantly with a school outcome variate of achievement and attendance when variance in teacher attitude was removed from those relations.[45] Significant multiple correlations have been established, using a large sample of secondary students, between the perceptions of goal direction, cohesiveness, lack of competitiveness, and diversity, and a "robustness" semantic differential test applied to the concept "My School."[46] Further research established significant negative correlations between the student perception of the academic difficulty of the school and achievement ($r = -.65$) and attendance ($r = -.55$) in thirty-five elementary schools.[47]

Of all instruments designed to assess students' perceptions of school environments, the most widely used has been the LEI. It has been extensively used in England, Australia, Canada, and the United States in some three hundred investigations. In field tests, the LEI was selected as a mediating criterion measure for the validation of various forms of the Principal Performance Description Survey described above. The

LEI is a 105-item instrument that yields subscale scores for secondary student perceptions for the following school characteristics: cohesiveness, diversity, formality, speed, environment, friction, goal direction, favoritism, difficulty, apathy, democracy, cliquishness, satisfaction, disorganization, and competitiveness. Elementary students were administered a 45-item, 5-subscale adaptation of the LEI called the *My School* (MS) inventory. This inventory was adapted from the original *My Class* inventory[48] by changing the response set of items from "class" to "school." The MS inventory yields scores for the following subscales: satisfaction, friction, competitiveness, difficulty, and cohesiveness.

As in the case of findings for teacher perceptions, past research has demonstrated the discriminant and incremental validity of student perceptions of school environment characteristics using a wide array of criteria. Such research generally supports the construct relations as they fit the theoretical framework discussed in this chapter and suggests that student perceptions of the social environment of learning represent an impȯrtant class of mediating variables against which measures of principal behavior can be examined.

Student Outcomes

For years educators at all levels have debated the goals of American education. As society changes, however, educational goals for children also change. With the recent decline in achievement test scores, a reemphasis on basic skills and a movement toward competency-based education models have been suggested. Alternatives to academic achievement have also been posited as legitimate educational outcomes for students: socialization through the school years,[49] the enhancement of intelligence,[50] humanistic education,[51] attitudes toward the quality of school life,[52] self-responsibility for managing school learning,[53] and the development of an adequate self-concept.[54] Whatever the expressed alternative goals, researchers have attempted to demonstrate relationships between measures of these and academic success in the traditional sense (for example, relationships between attitudes, self-concept, and achievement). It seems that professional discussion of preferred student outcomes varies considerably depending upon one's frame of reference, and, at the same time, that one student outcome of ultimate concern remains student academic learning and achievement.

Within the theoretical framework presented here, student values, attitudes toward school and learning, and perceptions of the school environment, self, and others are all part of the social context in which the school principal functions. When considering principal-initiated behavior within the school environment and its effects on student outcomes, these student-related characteristics take precedence over attendance and achievement. In the field test of the ROME assessment system, student achievement was measured by the *Iowa Tests of Basic Skills* (ITBS) for grades four and eight and the *Tests of Academic Progress* (TAP) for grade eleven. Attendance figures were computed as a percentage of average daily attendance (ADA) for the twenty-day period most closely approximating the time other data were collected.

Results of the Field Test

Space limitations do not permit a detailed discussion of the findings from the field tests of the ROME assessment system to validate measures of principal performance undertaken in 1975 and 1976. A thorough reporting of these results can be found in the project reports. The general results of this research are of interest because they provide preliminary data to test assumptions about relations among selected components of the theoretical model (Figure 7-2).

In the spring of 1975 various forms of the *Principal Performance Description Survey* (PPDS) instruments, the *School Survey* (SS), LEI, and the MS inventory were administered to 3,350 elementary and 3,613 secondary students, 1,200 teachers, and 45 principals in 45 schools (35 elementary, 10 secondary) in Georgia. In addition, student outcome data were collected for the ITBS, TAP, and ADA. Sampling procedures for teachers and students within schools were not used because of the desire to generate stable school means for subsequent statistical analyses.

Using school means as the units of statistical analysis, individual item and subscale correlations were computed for all possible combinations of principal behavior measures (PPDS), teacher and student mediating measures (SS, LEI, MS), and student outcome measures (ITBS, TAP, ADA) for both elementary, secondary, and total school groups. This extremely large number of correlations was summarized for appropriate elementary, secondary, and total school groups in terms of the absolute correlations of variables among and within the principal behavior, mediating variable, and student outcome domains and in terms of the frequency of significant item-subscale correlations between all combinations of principal behavior, mediating variable, and student outcome measures. What were some of the general findings of the first field test of the ROME assessment system, and what significance do they have for the theoretical framework presented here?

In 1975 Payne and his colleagues summarized the many correlations undertaken to examine global relationships between principal behavior, teacher and student mediating measures, and student outcomes. The average percentages of significant (.05 level) item-subscale correlations were computed for elementary, secondary, and combined school groups. For example, the average percentage of item-subscale correlations between elementary principal, teacher, and student and performance ratings by external observers and appropriate subscales of the SS and MS inventories for the thirty-five elementary schools was 18.1 percent. For the ten secondary schools this same index was 12.1 percent. When the data from elementary and secondary schools were combined, the percentage of significant item-subscale correlations increased to 29.2. When this same index was computed for correlations between assessments of principal performance and student outcome variables, the percentage was somewhat less: 9.9 percent for elementary schools, 8.1 percent for secondary schools, and 23.2 percent for total schools. For the mediating variable (SS, LEI, MS)/student outcome (attendance and achievement) index, the average percentage of significant correlations increased considerably to 38.3 percent for elementary schools, 13.5 percent for secondary schools, and 50.2 percent for the total sample of schools.

The results, while certainly not definitive, support the global hypotheses relating principal behavior, mediating variables within the school, and student outcomes presented in the theoretical framework. The data support the general assumption that the impact of principal behavior on student outcomes is mediated through the influences of teacher and student perceptions of characteristics of the school environment. It is also interesting to note that SS was the most predictable mediating criterion measure and that student perceptions of characteristics of the school climate-learning environment (LEI, MS) and teachers' perceptions of school environment (SS) were relatively independent of one another. In addition, the most valid source for assessing principal performances among the four utilized was teachers, particularly when the criterion used was the teacher perception measure (SS).

Several other findings from Project ROME are of interest. There was a general tendency for positive teacher attitudes toward character-istics of their working environment and higher student test perfor-mance to be associated with student reports of a low frequency of interaction with the principal. It was hypothesized that a "student in-dependence" factor would account for these observations with the in-terpretation that in schools where teacher attitudes are positive and student achievement high, the necessity of principal-student interac-tion is minimized.[55] This conclusion was supported by the finding that students' satisfaction with the school climate and learning environ-ment, their perception of school "easiness," and their positive attitude toward lack of structure was associated with student reports of a low frequency of interaction with the school principal. This finding may support the assumption that principal behavior can be affected by its own consequences or other variables (for example, student outcomes). When combined with the finding that teachers in this sample per-ceived the majority of their work environments to be affected posi-tively by the effectiveness with which their principal performed a variety of competencies, these results support the assumption of the theoretical framework that principal behavior affects students through the mediating influence of teachers. Preliminary analyses of data derived from a second field test (60 schools) of the ROME assess-ment system, with an additional 273 principal performance state-ments, have generally replicated the findings of the field test done in 1975.

Of all the variable relationships examined within Project ROME, the strongest and most frequent were those between teachers' percep-tions of characteristics of the school environment and their assessments of the behavior of the principal. In schools where the principal is per-ceived by teachers as frequently and effectively performing important behaviors in the school environment, teachers' attitudes toward a vari-ety of work-related dimensions are positive and often show strong con-nections with student outcomes.

Neither the theoretical framework nor the empirical relations dis-cussed here provide a definitive causal analysis that leads unequivo-cally to a thorough description of ideal principal behavior, teacher attitude, classroom environment, and student learning. When com-pared with other conceptions and evidence, however, what is pre-sented here may represent the most comprehensive, empirically expli-cit, and quantitatively validated description of principal functioning within the school environment.

This description suggests that an ebb and flow of causal functioning runs between principal and teacher and between teacher and student. Although there are exceptions, the teacher mediates between the principal and students, and all three are influenced by factors external to the school environment. The general association of greater principal-student interaction with low test performance by students and general teacher alienation may be attributable to external forces, such as neighborhood-family disruption and associated school behavior problems that cause teacher alienation and require direct principal interventions, or to such internal problems as short-circuiting teachers, which leads to poor staff morale and ultimately to low test performance. Obviously there are many possibilities of causal flow in these and other patterns of relations between principal behavior, the educational environment, and school outcomes.

In psychological terms, a principal requires information to perceive or diagnose the internal and external environments accurately. Then he or she formulates intentions thought likely to improve the situation and behaves in ways that are likely to communicate or accomplish those intentions. There is room for error or loss of information at the stage of perception, intention, and behavior, and parallel processes in teachers and students may also be faulty. To gather adequate information, to be able to reflect carefully enough to arrive at the best intentions, and to determine optimal behaviors that accomplish such intentions and enact them or communicate them with sufficient clarity may be costly in terms of human time and effort. Obviously selective perception, attention, and behavior are required in the chain of events preceding principals' impact on facets of the educational context and subsequent school outcomes. With respect to understanding principal behavior within the school environment, Project ROME offers an explicit rationale and several bases for selectivity:

1. a reasonably comprehensive list of fairly nonredundant competencies that has gone through several stages of refinement by experienced principals;
2. frameworks of categorization of these competencies into a more parsimonious group of constructs;
3. consensual judgments about the relative desirability of the competencies for effective school operation;
4. various methods for measuring the degree to which the competencies are performed by a principal;

5. norms on the median and range of the enactment of the competencies;

6. indications of how degree of enactment of the total set, subsets, or single competencies are associated with the morale of the teaching staff, student perceptions of the classroom environment, and student learning; and

7. beginning, confirmatory evidence, through partial correlation techniques, about the directions of causality.

Since the evidence on these points, summarized above, is available in detail in references cited and in forthcoming works, the interested person can use any one or a combination of these bases for formulating research, training, and practice objectives. On the causal questions, which are vital, one can look with admiration to the wisdom of leading principals and professors of educational administration. Scientific psychology, on the other hand, uses the wisdom of practice as an inspirational and possibly useful starting point—considering it, as Aristotle did, an argument from authority and a weak though often required basis for action.

Much more needs to be learned. It seems even now, however, that causality may not be unidirectional, as has been believed. Relations may be more realistically conceived as being incrementally circular among the elements and processes in the theoretical framework presented here. Astute perception, constructive intention, and effective behavior on the principal's part may constructively increase school effectiveness. At the same time, faulty processes and barriers between student and teacher may detract from school effectiveness. Principals are only one of the key functioning elements within the total school setting, to be sure, but their additional impetus can be assessed, evaluated, better understood, and improved. Once causal relations between principals' functioning, educational and other environments, and school outcomes are better understood, detailed prescriptions for practice can follow.

NOTES

1. Jack A. Culbertson, Curtis Henson, and Ruel Morrison, eds., *Performance Objectives for School Principals* (Berkeley, Calif.: McCutchan Publishing Corp., 1974).

2. Donald Medley, "Effectiveness Research," in *Research on Teaching: Concepts, Findings, and Implications,* ed. Penelope L. Peterson and Herbert J. Walberg (Berkeley, Calif.: McCutchan Publishing Corp., 1979).

3. Glenn L. Immegart, "The Study of Educational Administration, 1954-1974," in *Educational Administration: The Developing Decades*, ed. Luvern L. Cunningham, Walter G. Hack, and Raphael O. Nystrand (Berkeley, Calif.: McCutchan Publishing Corp., 1977), 298-328.

4. Donald J. Willower, "Some Issues in Research on School Organization," paper presented to the UCEA Seminar on Research in Educational Administration, Rochester, New York, May 1977.

5. Jonelle E. Pool, *Compilation of Competency Statements for School Administrators as Derived from the Literature*, Research Report Number 1 (Athens, Ga.: Results Oriented Management in Education, College of Education, University of Georgia, 1974).

6. Dale L. Bolton, "Evaluating School Processes and Products: A Responsibility of School Principals," in *Performance Objectives for School Principals*, ed. Culbertson, Henson, and Morrison, 170-195.

7. W. Robert Houston and Robert B. Howsam, eds., *Competency-based Teacher Education* (Chicago: Science Research Associates, 1972); J. B. Burke *et al.*, *Criteria for Describing and Assessing Competency-based Programs* (Albany, N.Y.: National Consortium on Competency-based Education Centers, 1976).

8. Allan Schmeider, *Competency-based Education: The State of the Scene* (Washington, D.C.: American Association of Colleges for Teacher Education, 1972).

9. Oren B. Graff and Calvin N. Street, *Improving Competence in Educational Administration* (New York: Harper and Brothers, 1956).

10. David A. Erlandson, "The Emergence of Comprehensive Assessment Systems," *CCBC Notebook* 5 (1975): 2-4; David A. Payne *et al.*, *The Verification and Validation of Principal Competencies and Performance Indicators: Assessment Design, Procedures, Instrumentation, Field Test Results*, Volume I, Project Report (Athens, Ga.: College of Education, University of Georgia, 1975).

11. Erlandson, "Emergence of Comprehensive Assessment Systems."

12. Alan K. Gaynor, "Preparing the Organization for Effective Response," in *Performance Objectives for School Principals*, ed. Culbertson, Henson, and Morrison, 54-82.

13. Andrew W. Halpin, *The Leadership Behavior of School Superintendents*, (Columbus, Ohio: College of Education, Ohio State University, 1956).

14. Andrew W. Halpin and Don B. Croft, *The Organizational Climate of Schools* (Chicago: Midwest Administration Center, University of Chicago, 1963).

15. Lee Sprowles, Doyne M. Smith, and James B. Kenny, *The Principal's Profile* (Athens: University of Georgia Press, 1966).

16. David J. Mullin, *Diagnostic Survey for Leadership Improvement* (Athens: University of Georgia Press, 1973).

17. Don B. Croft, *Evaluating School Principals* (Chicago: Croft Publishing Corp., 1969).

18. Educational Research Service, American Association of School Administrators and NEA Research Division, *Evaluating Administrative Performance*, ERS Circular No. 7 (Washington, D.C.: American Association of School Administrators, November 1968); *id.*, *The Evaluatee Evaluates the Evaluator*, ERS Circular No. 5 (Washington, D.C.: American Association of School Administrators, August 1970).

19. Payne *et al.*, *Verification and Validation of Principal Competencies and Performance Indicators*; Chad D. Ellett, *The Continued Refinement and Development of the Georgia Principal Assessment System and Its Application to a Field-based Training Program for Public School Principals: Assessment Design, Procedures, Instrumentation, Field Test Results*, Volume I, Project Report (Athens: College of Education, University of Georgia, 1976).

20. Herbert J. Walberg, "Decision and Perception: New Constructs for Research on Teaching Effects," *Cambridge Journal of Education* 7 (1977): 33-39.

21. *Ibid.*

22. *Ibid.*

23. Payne *et al.*, *Verification and Validation of Principal Competencies and Performance Indicators*; Ellett, *Continued Refinement and Development of the Georgia Principal Assessment System*.

24. Chad D. Ellett, Jonelle E. Pool, and Edward A. Poole, "The R.O.M.E. Competency Classification Model: A Description," *CCBC Notebook* 3 (1974): 3-8.

25. A summary description of the current instruments in the performance assessment system can be found in Chad D. Ellett, *An Informational Guide for Understanding and Using the Georgia Principal Assessment System* (Athens: College of Education, University of Georgia, forthcoming).

26. Elton Mayo, *The Human Problems of an Industrial Civilization* (New York: Harper, 1933).

27. Fritz J. Roethlisberger and William J. Dickson, *Management and the Worker* (Cambridge, Mass.: Harvard University Press, 1941).

28. Robert J. Coughlan and Robert A. Cooke, "Work Attitudes," in *Evaluating Educational Performance,* ed. Herbert J. Walberg (Berkeley, Calif.: McCutchan Publishing Corp., 1974), 295-317.

29. Victor H. Vroom, *Work and Motivation* (New York: Wiley, 1965).

30. Fred N. Kerlinger and Elazar J. Pedhazur, "Educational Attitudes and Perceptions of Desirable Traits of Teachers," *American Educational Research Journal* 5 (1968): 543-560; Henry C. Lindgren and Evelyne P. Singer, "Correlates of Brazilian and North American Attitudes toward Child-centered Practices in Education," *Journal of Social Psychology* 60 (1963): 3-7; Henry M. McGee, "Measurement of Authoritarianism and Its Relation to Teachers' Classroom Behavior," *Genetic Psychology Monographs* 52 (1955): 89-146; Marvin Sontag, "Attitudes toward Education and Perception of Teacher Behaviors," *American Educational Research Journal* 5 (1968): 385-402.

31. Robert J. Coughlan, "Dimensions of Teacher Morale," *American Educational Research Journal* 7 (1970): 221-235.

32. Coughlan and Cooke, "Work Attitudes."

33. Chad D. Ellett and John A. Masters, "The Structure of Teacher Attitudes toward Dimensions of Their Working Environment: A Factor Analysis of the School Survey and Its Implications for Instrument Validity," paper presented at the annual meeting of the Georgia Educational Research Association, Atlanta, 1977; Chad D. Ellett *et al.*, "The Relationship between Teacher and Student Perceptions of School Environment Dimensions and School Outcome Variables," paper presented at the annual meeting of the Southeastern Psychological Association, Miami, Fla. 1977.

34. Jonelle E. Pool, "Canonical Analyses of Teachers' Ratings of Elementary Principals' Competencies and Teachers' Attitudes toward Dimensions of Their Working Environment," unpub. thesis, University of Georgia, 1976; *id.* and Chad D. Ellett, "A Multivariate Analysis of Teachers' Ratings of Principals' Performances and Teacher Attitudes toward Dimensions of Their Working Environment," paper presented at the annual meeting of the Southeastern Psychological Association, Miami, Fla., 1977.

35. Chad D. Ellett and Joseph W. Licata, "The Relationship between Teacher Perceptions of the Robustness of Differential Organizational Roles and Dimensions of Their Working Environment: A Regression Analysis," paper presented at the annual meeting of the American Educational Research Association, Toronto, Canada, 1978.

36. Joseph W. Licata and Donald Willower, "Student Brinkmanship and the School as a Social System," *Educational Administration Quarterly 11 (1975): 1-14.*

37. Joseph W. Licata and Chad D. Ellett, *An Internal and External Evaluation of Project R.O.M.E./FOCUS,* Project Report (Valdosta, Ga.: Valdosta State College, 1976).

38. Ellett *et al.,* "Relationship between Teacher and Student Perceptions of School Environment Dimensions and School Outcome Variables."

39. George G. Stern, *Preliminary Manual: Activities Index; College Characteristics Index* (Syracuse, N.Y.: Psychological Research Center, Syracuse University, 1958).

40. Robert L. Sinclair, "Measurement of Educational Press in Elementary School Environments," paper presented at the annual meeting of the American Educational Research Association, Los Angeles, 1969.

41. Jacob W. Getzels and Herbert A. Thelen, "The Classroom Group as a Unique Social System," in *The Dynamics of Instructional Groups,* Fifty-ninth Yearbook of the National Society for the Study of Education, Part II, ed. Nelson B. Henry (Chicago: University of Chicago Press, 1960), 53-82.

42. Gary J. Anderson, *The Assessment of Learning Environments: A Manual for the Learning Environment Inventory and the My Class Inventory* (Halifax, Nova Scotia: Atlantic Institute of Education, September 1973).

43. Gary J. Anderson and Herbert J. Walberg, "Learning Environments," in *Evaluating Educational Performance,* ed. Walberg, 81-88; Paul M. Insell and Rudolph H. Moos, "Psychological Environments: Expanding the Scope of Human Ecology," *American Psychologist* 29 (1974): 179-188; Rudolph H. Moos, "Conceptualization of Human Environments," *ibid.,* 28 (1973): 652-664; Bikkar S. Randhawa and Lewis L. W. Fu, "Assessment and Effect of Some Classroom Environment Variables," *Review of Educational Research* 43 (1973): 303-323; Herbert J. Walberg, "The Psychology of Learning Environments: Behavioral, Structural, or Perceptual?" in *Review of Research in Education,* Volume IV, ed. Lee S. Shulman (Itasca, Ill.: Peacock, 1976), 142-178.

44. Herbert J. Walberg, Rampal Singh, and Sue P. Rasher, "Predictive Validity of Student Perceptions: A Cross-cultural Replication," *American Educational Research Journal* 14 (1977): 45-49.

45. Mark L. Perkins, "Canonical Correlational Analysis of the Relationships among School Climate, Teacher Morale, and the Educationally Relevant Performance of Fourth-grade Students," unpub. diss., University of Georgia, 1976.

46. Joseph W. Licata, Donald Willower, and Chad D. Ellett, "The School and Environmental Robustness," *Journal of Experimental Education,* in press.

47. Ellett *et al.,* "Relationship between Teacher and Student Perceptions of School Environment Dimensions and School Outcome Variables."

48. Anderson, *Assessment of Learning Environments.*

49. Edward A. Wynne, "Education and Socialization: A Complex Question," *Educational Researcher* 1 (1972): 5-9.

50. Paul R. Lohnes, "Evaluating the Schooling of Intelligence," *ibid.,* 2 (1973): 6-11.

51. Arthur W. Combs, "Educational Accountability from a Humanistic Perspective," *ibid.,* 19-21.

52. Joyce L. Epstein and James M. McPartland, "The Concept and Measurement of the Quality of School Life," *American Educational Research Journal* 13 (1976): 15-30.

53. Margaret C. Wang and Billie Stiles, "An Investigation of Children's Concept of Self-responsibility for Their School Learning," *ibid.,* 13 (1976): 159-179.

54. Benjamin S. Bloom, "Affective Outcomes of School Learning," *Phi Delta Kappan* 59 (1977): 193-198.

55. Payne *et al., Verification and Validation of Principal Competencies and Performance Indicators.*

PART THREE
Instructional Environments

8. Curricular and Longitudinal Effects on Learning Environments

Wayne W. Welch

Many educators are fond of making statements that describe the ebb and flow of the educational environment. For example, one often hears the statement: "Teaching is much different today than it was five years ago." Then there is the frequent question: "How can you, a college professor, know what schools are like when you haven't taught in one for ten years?" And conversations are liberally sprinkled with terms that indicate the swinging pendulum of educational innovation: progressive, open, curriculum development, evaluation, accountability, back to basics, assessment, behavioral objectives, minimum competencies, individualized instruction, to identify just a few. For some, the institution of education is in a constant state of flux; for others, the grinding glacier of educational practice veers little from paths well established during a century of American education.

As in most arguments concerned with education, support could probably be found for both points of view. There are both change and tradition. It is the extent to which each exists that deserves further investigation. Is there evidence to suggest that educational environment remains constant over time, or can changes in the social environment of learning be detected using available instruments?

In the past two decades the study of school environments has emerged as an important area of social science research.[1] Measures of the environment have focused on teacher behavior[2] and on the climate as perceived by students.[3] It is the latter approach that appears to be the most promising one for understanding the educational process because student perception of the learning environment has been shown to be related to student learning.[4] Besides, environmental variables can be predicted from such things as intelligence, student interest, class size, and instructional variables.

Differences in classroom climates associated with various curricula[5] and grade level[6] have been noted, and student perceptions of the learning environment in science classes, as measured by the *Learning Environment Inventory* (LEI), have been shown to be stable across rather short time spans.[7] It is stability or variation in educational environments over longer periods of time that has not, heretofore, been investigated although such investigations would appear to have implications for educational policy makers.

If the learning environment remains stable in spite of perceived institutional demands, sanctions, and expectations, then such things as curriculum materials, instructional techniques, and teacher training change very little across time. Today's teacher could easily function in tomorrow's (or yesterday's) world. If, however, the class environment does vary in response to social pressures or student changes, then the educational system must also change. Curriculum renewal, in-service programs for teachers, and pedagogical revisions take on increased importance.

To what extent do long-term changes on a measure of the social environment of learning affect science and mathematics classes in the secondary school? That is the primary consideration in this chapter. Past research has also suggested some environmental differences related to the curriculum and to the grade level of the student,[8] and these factors have been considered as well. The more specific questions being investigated are: Did student perception of the learning environment in secondary science and mathematics classes (ages twelve to seventeen) change during the four-year period from 1972 to 1976? Do students perceive a different learning environment in science and mathematics classes? Is the learning environment of the junior high school (ages twelve to fourteen) different from that of the senior high school (ages fifteen to seventeen)?

THE SAMPLE

This study is based on a stratified random sampling of all the secondary schools in fifteen states from the western two-thirds of the continental United States.[9] These states were selected because this study is part of a larger evaluation study involving that region.[10] Within each of the schools, either a science or a mathematics teacher was selected at random and then asked to choose a class to participate in the study. A participation rate of 53 percent was obtained in 1972, but this figure dropped to 45 percent in 1976. The drop could reflect the perception many researchers have that it is becoming increasingly difficult to gather school data. Follow-up studies of nonparticipants done for both years suggest that there were few differences between participating and nonparticipating schools.[11]

In the final sample there were 563 classes in 1972 and 558 classes in 1976, and the larger evaluation study required that about 50 percent of the classes participating in 1976 be the same ones that participated in 1972. Each class contained an average of twenty-two students, and, using a randomized data collection procedure,[12] only one-third of the science students and one-half of the mathematics students completed the learning environment instrument. The remaining students in each class were given other instruments. The total number of students in the study exceeded 24,000, but the unit of analysis is the mean of the students in a given class who responded to the LEI. Data were obtained from 1,121 such classes.

THE TEST INSTRUMENT

Student perceptions of the social environment of learning were obtained using the LEI.[13] This instrument was designed to describe the nature of interpersonal relationships as well as the structural characteristics in the class. The LEI meets acceptable levels for reliability, is easily administered, and has been shown to be related to student learning. Testing time limitations, however, required a modification of the original fifteen-scale instrument in that the number of scales was reduced to ten. This shorter version of the LEI (Form F) consisted of ten seven-item scales. The ten scales selected were those shown to be particularly sensitive to differences between mathematics and science classes.[14] Students were asked to express their agreement or disagreement with each statement on a four-point scale. The names of the ten

Table 8-1

Learning Environment Inventory scales—Form F

Scales	Sample statement	Reliabilities	
		Individual scores	Class mean
Diversity	The class divides its efforts among several purposes.	.53	.31
Formality	Students are asked to follow a complicated set of rules.	.76	.92
Friction	Certain students are considered uncooperative.	.72	.83
Goal direction	The objectives of the class are specific.	.85	.75
Favoritism	Only the good students are given special projects.	.78	.76
Difficulty	Students are constantly challenged.	.64	.78
Democratic	Class decisions tend to be made by all the students.	.67	.67
Cliquishness	Certain students work only with their close friends.	.65	.71
Satisfaction	Students are well satisfied with the work of the class.	.79	.84
Disorganization	The class is disorganized.	.82	.92

scales, a sample item from each scale, and the reliabilities of the scales appear in Table 8-1.

The test instrument was administered by teachers in early spring of 1972 and again in 1976. It was part of a larger test battery being used in a national evaluation of in-service programs for teachers. Optically scanned answer sheets were mailed to a central processing facility where they were all checked and scored. Class means on each of the ten variables were obtained and submitted to a three-way multivariate analysis of variance (MANOVA). The main effects due to year (1972,

1976), subject (science, mathematics), and grade level (junior, senior high) were examined with the significance criterion set at the .05 level.

The multivariate procedure is a generalization of analysis of variance when working with several dependent variables. (In this case, the variables are responses of students on the ten LEI scales.) Its purpose is to determine whether statistically significant differences exist between two or more groups on a set of dependent variables. If a statistically significant multivariate F is obtained ($p < .05$), we can reject the null hypothesis of equal group centroids. Subsequent examination of the several univariate F values allows us to determine which of the variables discriminates best between the groups. [15]

RESULTS OF THE STUDY

The multivariate analysis of variance showed statistically significant differences on the ten LEI scales taken together over the four-year period from 1972 to 1976 (the results are shown in Table 8-2), and those differences could not reasonably be attributed to chance. Significant results were also obtained for the comparisons between mathematics and science, and between junior and senior high school students. What these findings suggest is that time, curriculum, and age have an effect on the student's perception of the learning environment.

Three of the four interactions failed to reach the level established for statistical significance. There was, however, a significant multivariate interaction between grade (junior, senior high) and subject (science, mathematics). This suggests that, on some of the LEI scales, the junior-senior high changes are different for science and mathematics.

Examination of the univariate F-values for the LEI scales indicated three significant interactions on the scales labeled "Formality," "Friction," and "Diversity." All were of the same form: senior high scores were lower than those for junior high, but science-mathematics differences were greater for the older students. These interactions are shown schematically in Figure 8-1.

The nature of the interactions is such that it seems reasonable to examine the main effects in more detail. That is, in all cases the science mean is higher than the mathematics mean, and junior high averages exceeded senior high averages. Furthermore, no interactions were noted for the effects of time — the primary concern of this study.

Because multivariate tests of three main effects reached the chosen significance level, univariate F-tests were examined to determine

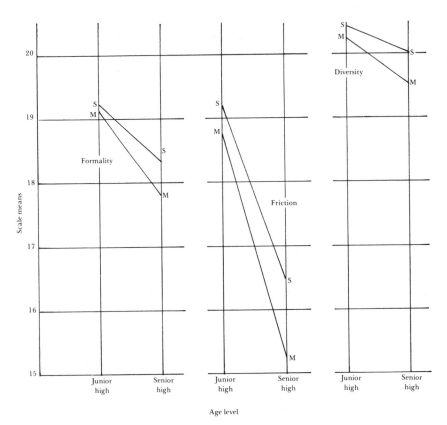

Figure 8-1

Significant interactions by grade level and by subject
(S = Science; M = Mathematics)

which LEI scales showed the greatest differences. A standardized effect contrast was computed for the significant LEI scales by dividing
the main effect differences by the within-group standard deviation.
The significant contrasts across years are shown in Figure 8-2.

Four of the ten univariate tests were statistically significant. Students in 1976 perceived their classes to be better organized and more
formal, goal directed, and satisfying than they had four years earlier.
Disorganization (or its converse, organization) refers to the extent to
which pupils consider the class disorganized. Generally, it is negatively
related to pupil learning. Sample items include: "Many class members are confused during class meetings"; "The work of the class is frequently interrupted when some students have nothing to do."

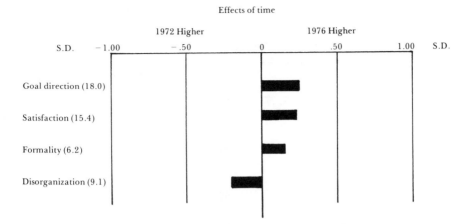

Figure 8-2

Standardized contrasts for significant differences (S.D.) for the effects of time over the years from 1972 to 1976 (*F*-ratios appear in parentheses)

A formal classroom is guided by well-established rules. Students who break the rules know they will be penalized, and there are recognized right and wrong ways of going about class activities. In past studies, the scale has not been related to student learning. Goal direction also refers to the structure of class activities. Recognition of goals and their acceptance by the group characterize classes with high goal direction.

These three variables clearly portray an environment that is shifting toward a more orderly or structured learning climate. A change to a more conservative environment seems to have emerged over the four-year period, and students seemed to find their environment more satisfying.

A second problem of the study was to determine the extent to which differences existed between mathematics and science classes. The effect of subject was shown in Table 8-2 to be statistically significant. To state this more precisely, science students perceived their learning environments differently from mathematics students. The specific subscales of the LEI where this was most pronounced are shown in Figure 8-3.

Nine of the ten LEI scales showed significant differences between mathematics and science. Science classes were seen as being more diverse, disorganized, and formal, and they were thought to possess

Table 8-2

Multivariate *F*-values for analysis of variance on
ten scales of *Learning Environment Inventory*

Source of dispersion	Multivariate *F*-value	Significance of *F*
Main effects		
Year	2.80	.002
Subject	27.71	< .001
Grade level	78.30	< .001
Interactions		
Year by subject	0.54	.866
Year by grade	1.53	.125
Grade by subject	4.94	< .001
Year by grade by subject	0.43	.931

Note: Degrees of freedom 10, 1104

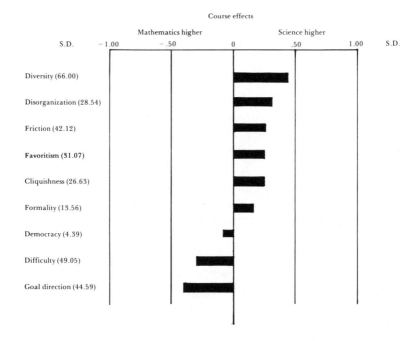

Figure 8-3

**Standardized contrasts for differences (S.D.) for course effects in
science and mathematics, with data for 1972 and 1976 combined
(*F*-ratios appear in parentheses)**

higher levels of friction, cliquishness, and favoritism. Mathematics students perceived their classes to be higher in terms of goal direction, difficulty, and democracy scales. The classes were about equal on the satisfaction scale.

These findings contradict an earlier study by Anderson in which he compared nine mathematics and twenty-six science classes in eight Montreal schools.[16] Five of the differences are in opposition to Anderson's results, only two (formality and difficulty) are in agreement, and two new ones (diversity and democracy) reached the chosen statistical level in the study examined here.

It is interesting to note that Anderson's hypothesized results for a more activity-oriented subject such as science are supported in this study, and yet they are refuted in his own study. Science classes usually contain a substantial laboratory component, vary considerably in their subject matter, and provide many opportunities for social interaction. Accordingly, one might expect the class to be more disorganized and diverse with greater risk of such things as cliquishness, friction, and favoritism.

The conceptual structure and rule-orientation (logic) of mathematics, on the other hand, would suggest a formal, goal-directed, and perhaps difficult climate in class. With the exception of formality, these expectations are borne out in the present study. What is puzzling, in terms of the above reasoning, is that science was seen as more formal in both this and Anderson's study.

The third consideration in this chapter was to investigate climate differences between junior high school classes (ages twelve to fourteen) and senior high school classes (ages fifteen to seventeen). The results of this comparison appear in Figure 8-4.

The multivariate F-value for this comparison was 78.3, and nine of the ten univariate contrasts were significant. The magnitude of the grade-level differences was greater than for the time or subject-matter effects.

Senior high school students saw their classes as more difficult, satisfying, and democratic. On the other hand, junior high school students perceived their classes as more disorganized, diverse, and formal, with higher levels of friction, cliquishness, and favoritism.

In general, these findings tend to support the results of previous work that suggest a more student- and activity-centered environment for junior high classes.[17] Classes apparently are less structured with a

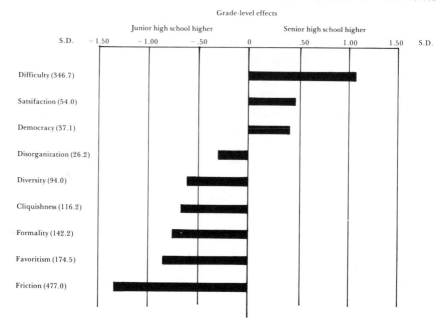

Figure 8-4

Standardized contrasts for significant differences (S.D.) for grade-level effects at the junior and senior high school levels, with data from 1972 and 1976 combined (F-ratios appear in parentheses)

greater variety of activities provided for (or generated by) students. At the same time, there is greater social conflict in the class (favoritism, cliquishness, friction, lack of democracy), which leads to a generally unsatisfying situation.

The volatile characteristics of early adolescents seem to dominate the learning environment in junior high schools. This age group is very active and emotional. These characteristics would tend toward classes that are diverse and disorganized with greater likelihood of disappointing personal interactions, for example, perceived cliquishness.

The higher difficulty scores for the senior high students probably are due to increasingly difficult course content in the higher grades. This seems especially true for science and mathematics with their hierarchical content structures. It may also be related to the concern for "good grades" in the attempt to be admitted to college.

The formality findings seem somewhat surprising. They are, however, consistent with a study done by Shaw and Mackinnon, which found that formality scores declined progressively between the sixth and the twelfth grade.[18] Perhaps classroom rules and procedures become less explicit and confining for the more mature teenager.

IMPLICATIONS OF THE FINDINGS

This study has shown that students' perception of the social environment of learning changed significantly over a four-year period, from 1972 to 1976. The changes are in a conservative direction, with classes seen as being more formal, organized, and goal directed, a learning environment perceived as being more satisfying in 1976.

There were also significant subject and grade-level differences. Perceptions in science classes suggested an activity-oriented environment with considerable student interaction; perceptions in mathematics classes were of a more difficult and goal-directed environment.

The large junior-senior high differences reflect, in general, the volatile nature of early adolescents. Classroom climates mirror quite well the activity and tension presumed to be characteristic of twelve- to fourteen-year-old-children.

Classes in science and classes at the junior high school level were seen as more formal than classes in comparison groups. These results contradict the activity-prone and volatile explanations used in this chapter, and yet they are consistent with previous research.

The return to a more traditional learning environment would appear to have implications for those responsible for educating teachers and developing curricula. The educational pendulum, at least in science and mathematics classes, seems to be moving away from the activist climate of the late 1960s and early 1970s. The return to more conventional texts seems to be a further indication of the change. This study lends strong support to the claims by teachers and administrators that the educational scene is shifting; the perceptions of students seem to reflect the gathering momentum of a back-to-basics movement.

These changes challenge educational policy makers to provide improved education for the youth of this country that is responsive to the changing environment. Teachers using curricula and methodologies appropriate in an earlier setting may now find that those techniques conflict with the current social system. For example, a lesson that relies heavily upon self-discovery or inquiry may pose problems if used in a goal-directed environment. Educators must be sensitive to changes in the learning environment and try to find ways to improve student learning by utilizing predominant environmental characteristics.

Further research is needed to answer questions as to the type of teaching effective in various educational environments. For example, why do students learn more in a climate they perceive to be difficult? To what extend does social conflict (friction and cliquishness) deter learning? How can we maximize learning in the volatile climate of the junior high school? What characteristics of science and mathematics classes are desired goals in and of themselves? Can characteristics of the learning environment in science classes help to explain why enrollments decline at the secondary level?

Answers to these and other questions that grow from analysis of the sociopsychological processes in a classroom as viewed from the learner's perspective should help in reaching the common goal: an optimum learning environment for each child.

NOTES

1. Gary J. Anderson and Herbert J. Walberg, "Learning Environments," in *Evaluating Educational Performance*, ed. Herbert J. Walberg (Berkeley, Calif: McCutchan, 1974), 81-98; H. Dean Nielsen and Diana H. Kirk, "Classroom Climates," *ibid.*, 57-79.

2. Edmund J. Amidon and Ned A. Flanders, *The Role of the Teacher in the Classroom* (Minneapolis: Paul S. Amidon, 1963); Donald M. Medley and Harold E. Mitzel, "A Technique for Measuring Classroom Behavior," *Journal of Educational Psychology* 49 (1958): 86-92,

3. Anderson and Walberg, "Learning Environments"; Joe M. Steele, Ernest R. House, and Thomas Kerins, "An Instrument for Assessing Instructional Climate through Low-Inference Student Judgments," *American Educational Research Journal* 8 (1971): 447-466; George G. Stern, Morris I. Stein, and Benjamin S. Bloom, *Methods in Personality Assessment* (Glencoe, Ill.: Free Press, 1956).

4. Herbert J. Walberg, "Predicting Class Learning: A Multivariate Approach to the Class as a Social System," *American Educational Research Journal* 4 (1969): 529-542.

5. Herbert J. Walberg, "Educational Process Evaluation," in *Educational Evaluation: Analysis and Responsibility*, ed. Michael W. Apple, Michael J. Subkoviak, and Henry S. Lufler, Jr. (Berkeley, Calif.: McCutchan, 1974), 237-268; Wayne W. Welch and Herbert J. Walberg, "A National Experiment in Curriculum Evaluation," *American Educational Research Journal* 9 (1972): 373-383.

6. A. Richard Shaw and Paul Mackinnon, "Evaluation of the Learning Environment" (Burlington, Ontario: Mathematics Department, Lord Elgin High School, 1973), mimeo.

7. Frances Lawrenz, "The Stability of Student Perception of the Classroom Learning Environment," *Journal of Research in Science Teaching* 14 (1977): 77-81.

8. Gary J. Anderson, "Effects of Course Content and Teacher Sex on the Social Climate of Learning," *American Educational Research Journal* 8 (1971): 649-663; Walberg, "Educational Process Evaluation."

9. The states were California, Idaho, Utah, Montana, Wyoming, Colorado, North Dakota, South Dakota, Nebraska, Minnesota, Iowa, Michigan, Indiana, Mississippi, and Alabama.

10. Wayne W. Welch and Arlen R. Gullickson, "A Strategy for Evaluating the NSF Comprehensive Program for Teacher Education," *School Science and Mathematics* 73 (1973): 759-767.

11. Richard S. Sandman, "A Comparison of Participants and Nonparticipants in a National Evaluation Project" (Minneapolis: University of Minnesota, Minnesota Research and Evaluation Project, 1972), mimeo; Sharon Studer, "Comparing Participants and Nonparticipants in a National Evaluation Project" (Minneapolis: University of Minnesota, Minnesota Research and Evaluation Project, 1977), mimeo.

12. Herbert J. Walberg and Wayne W. Welch, "A New Use of Randomization in Experimental Curriculum Evaluation," *School Review* 75 (1967): 369-377.

13. Herbert J. Walberg and Gary J. Anderson, "Classroom Climate and Individual Learning," *Journal of Educational Psychology* 59 (1968): 414-419.

14. Anderson, "Effects of Course Content and Teacher Sex on the Social Climate of Learning."

15. Daniel J. Amick and Kathleen S. Crittenden, "Analysis of Variance and Multivariate Analysis of Variance," in *Introductory Multivariate Analysis,* ed. Daniel J. Amick and Herbert J. Walberg (Berkeley, Calif.: McCutchan, 1975), 208-235.

16. Anderson, "Effects of Course Content and Teacher Sex on the Social Climate of Learning."

17. Shaw and Mackinnon, "Evaluation of the Learning Environment"; Herbert J. Walberg, Ernest R. House, and Joe M. Steele, "Grade Level, Cognition and Affect: A Cross-Section of Classroom Perception," *Journal of Educational Psychology* 64 (1973): 142-146.

18. Shaw and Mackinnon, "Evaluation of the Learning Environment."

9. Curricular Structure

William P. Kuert

This chapter is primarily concerned with the empirical relationship between subject matter (curriculum) and various environmental variables. It should be noted at the outset that many variables comprise the domain of the learning environment. Educational institutions differ widely with respect to level (college, secondary, elementary), cultural and social structures, and the objectives and characteristics of members. Hence, there is no best way of defining "educational environment." It should also be noted that the terms "environment" and "climate" are used interchangeably in the literature. The discussion begins with the presentation of Murray's Need-Press Model, which has been most influential in setting forth the several environmental inventories on which this review is based.

MURRAY'S NEED-PRESS MODEL

The theoretical models and concepts upon which most of the climate studies are based come from social psychology and relate individual needs to social structural variables. In the process, these models have provided researchers with operational definitions of "climate" and have helped to generate theories about the relationship of climate to both antecedent and outcome variables. Murray's Need-Press Model has gained a certain preeminence in this literature.[1] Murray stressed the need to view behavior (B) as an outcome of the relationship between the person (P) and his environment (E), standing firmly on the ground specified in Kurt Lewin's dictum: $B = f(P,E)$. In the Murray model a distinction is made between needs (the P component) and press (the E component). Needs refer to organizational tendencies that appear to give unity and direction to a person's behavior. Needs may be identified "as a taxonomic classification of the characteristic spontaneous behaviors manifested by individuals in their life transactions."[2] The concept of environmental press provides an external situational counterpart to Murray's internalized personality needs. In the ultimate sense of the term, press refers to the phenomenological world of the individual, the unique and inevitable private view each person has of the events in which he takes part. As in the case of needs, descriptions of press are based on inferred continuity and consistency in otherwise discrete events. The concept of press includes conditions that represent impediments to a need as well as those that are likely to facilitate its expression. These conditions, which establish what is commonly referred to as the climate or atmosphere of an institution, are to be found in the structure created or tolerated by others. The components of this structure may be physical as well as social. Press may be defined (like needs) "as a taxonomic classification of characteristic behaviors manifested by aggregates of individuals in their mutual interpersonal transactions."[3] Needs and press are complementary but not necessarily reciprocal concepts. The relationship between any given psychological need and the relevant environmental press (for example, "affiliation") may be said to be isomorphic. The need for affiliation involves the maximization of opportunities to establish close, friendly, reciprocal associations with others; an affiliative press is one in which such opportunities are optimized. It does not follow, however, that persons characterized by a high need for affiliation will behave accordingly under all circumstances, any more than it is to be assumed that a high press for affiliation will elicit affiliative behavior from all people.[4]

INSTRUMENTATION

The two most popular ways of assessing the classroom or school environment are observational systems and the self-report questionnaire. In addition to the actual instrumentation, the climate researcher must consider the degree of inference he wishes to make from the data he collects. In this regard Barak Rosenshine distinguishes between "low-inference" responses and "high-inference" responses.[5] Low-inference responses or variables are those which tap the directly observable, specific, explicit phenomena of the environment. Examples of low-inference responses would be counting the number of teacher statements or asking a student if his teacher ever has students work together in subgroups. High-inference responses are those that ask the subject to determine the meaning of what is going on around him and to interpret his feelings or thoughts about it. Examples of high-inference responses include asking a student to agree or disagree with the statement, "Your teacher likes you," or "Your teacher is friendly toward you."

Observation Instruments

The most widely employed observation instruments in school climate research are "category systems," which in a low-inference manner record and categorize discrete behavioral occurrences. The *Pupil-Teacher Rapport Scale* developed in 1934 by Wrightstone was followed by many other such instruments to be used for measuring student-teacher interaction.[6] The *Pupil-Teacher Rapport Scale* categorized teacher behavior as either "integrative" or "dominative," and the same integrative-dominative dichotomy was also used to study teacher control of pupil behavior in kindergartens.[7] Then the concept of classroom climate was introduced by Withall and operationally defined by a "Climate Index."[8] Using this index, the researcher can categorize a teacher's verbal statements as either "teacher-centered" or "learner-centered," in terms of the way they are categorized on the following continuum: learner-supportive statements, acceptant and clarifying statements, problem-structuring statements, neutral statements, directive or hortative statements, reproving or deprecating statements, and teachers' self-supporting remarks.

As an improvement and expansion of the climate instrument, the *Observation Schedule and Record* (OScAR)[9] was developed. Not only did OScAR classify the teachers' verbal behavior, but also their nonverbal behavior and the classroom social structure according to the following categories: emotional climate, verbal emphasis, and social organization.

Probably the most elaborate and widely employed observational instrument was developed by Flanders, and it is known as the *Interaction Analysis System*.[10] This system, which focuses on teacher influence, differentiates between "direct" and "indirect" influence according to the following ten categories: Teacher Talk — Indirect Influence (1. accepts feeling, 2. praises or encourages, 3. accepts or uses ideas of student, 4. asks questions); Teacher Talk — Direct Influence (5. lecturing, 6. giving directions, 7. criticizing or justifying authority); Student Talk (8. response, 9. initiation); and 10. Silence or Confusion.

The *Interaction Analysis System* has become the point of departure for the development of even more comprehensive instruments like the *Multidimensional Analysis of Classroom Interaction* (MACI) developed by Honigman, which measures not only the affective domain as tapped by Flanders, but also procedural and cognitive dimensions.[11] Cognitive dimensions like the one included in MACI have been emphasized more in climate research in recent years. Two models that have been instrumental in developing cognitive dimensions are the "structure of intellect" model, which categorizes human intellectual activities in terms of "operations," "products," and "contents,"[12] and a model that develops categories of analysis such as "pedagogical moves," "teaching cycles," and "categories of meanings."[13] The measurement of "cognitive" or "intellectual" dimensions has received a significant amount of attention from researchers.[14]

SELF-REPORT QUESTIONNAIRES

In recent years, a number of researchers have been prompted to rely more heavily on the self-reports of students and teachers as a means of assessing the environment. The self-report method of gathering data, in contrast to the observational method, generally requires high-inference responses and conforms more closely to Murray's Need-Press Model.

Murray's concept of need has formed the basis for the development of several objective measures of personality;[15] his concept of press also provides a way of viewing the environment that parallels analytically and synthetically the more familiar methods of dealing with the individual. Objective measures of environmental press have been constructed based on Murray's concept of press.[16]

The *High School Characteristics Index* (HSCI) is one of four indexes constructed to assess environmental press variables.[17] There are three hundred questions on the HSCI that pertain to daily activities, policies, procedures, attitudes, and impressions that are characteristic of high schools in general. The HSCI consists of thirty scales of ten items each, corresponding to the thirty needs in Murray's taxonomy. The thirty scales were factor analyzed and labeled as follows: abasement, achievement, adaptability, affiliation, aggression, change, conjunctivity, counteraction, deference, dominance, ego-achievement, emotionality, energy, exhibitionism, fantasied achievement, harm avoidance, humanism, impulsiveness, narcissism, nurturance, objectivity, order, play, practicalness, reflectiveness, scientism, sensuality, sexuality, succorance, and understanding.

Then there is the *Classroom Environment Scale* (CES), which is also based upon the Murray Need-Press Model.[18] The CES is designed to identify aspects of the psychosocial environment of the classroom. It differs from the *Learning Environment Inventory*, which is discussed later in this chapter, in the specific aspects of the classroom chosen for inclusion in the scale and in test construction.[19] Nine dimensions of classroom climate are identified by the CES, with each dimension represented by ten items. These dimensions are: involvement, affiliation, support, task orientation, competition, order and organization, rule clarity, teacher control, and innovation. The questionnaire consists of ninety statements to which the student answers true or false.

Then there is the *Class Activities Questionnaire* (CAQ) designed to assess both the cognitive and affective dimensions of instructional climate using "low-inference" indicators.[20] The CAQ asks students for a statement of agreement or disagreement on a four-point Likert scale describing general kinds of activities that characterize their class. These activities suggest either levels of thinking or affective classroom conditions. The CAQ can be administered to pupils in grade six and above. The instrument was developed to help evaluate a large-scale, statewide program in Illinois designed for gifted students. Based on a sample of 3,138 elementary and secondary school children, the reliability coefficients range from .76 to .88 for each of the four major dimensions of lower thought processes, higher thought processes, classroom focus, and classroom climate. The cognitive dimensions on the CAQ are based on Benjamin Bloom's taxonomy.[21] There are sixteen additional individual factors on the CAQ whose reliability coefficients range from .58 to .94. The test-retest reliability coefficients for each of the four dimensions of the CAQ ranged from .59 to .91 based on a random sample of 79 students.

The *Learning Environment Inventory,*[22] mentioned earlier, developed from a series of research and evaluation studies carried out by Harvard Project Physics in the late 1960s using secondary school physics classes.[23] Harvard Project Physics was an experimental course employing a variety of new instructional media and stressing the philosophical, historical, and humanistic dimensions of physics.

The first series of studies conducted by Harvard Project Physics used the *Classroom Climate Questionnaire* (CCQ) to assess pupil perception of the learning environment.[24] The construction of the CCQ was based upon the *Group Dimension Description Questionnaire.*[25] This description questionnaire was designed to measure general characteristics of adult groups. Some of the items on the description questionnaire were inappropriate for classroom use, but they suggested a number of dimensions that could possibly be related to learning.[26]

As a result of psychometric studies,[27] the scales of the CCQ were found to be unreliable and redundant, and the task of constructing another instrument called the *Learning Environment Inventory* (LEI) was begun. The LEI, as it was constructed in 1968, consisted of fourteen scales. In 1969 a fifteenth scale was added. In choosing the fifteen climate dimensions, an effort was made to include only concepts previously identified as good predictors of learning, concepts considered relevant to sociopsychological theory and research, concepts exemplifying useful theory and research in education, or concepts intuitively judged relevant to the social psychology of the classroom.[28]

Each of the fifteen scales consists of seven items describing characteristics of classes. The student is asked to indicate, on a four-point Likert scale, his agreement or disagreement on how well each item describes his class. Scale scores are computed by adding the item scores for each scale. A "strongly disagree" is scored "1" and "strongly agree" is scored "4"; hence, the range of scores on a scale is 7 to 28.

The LEI can be administered to pupils in grade seven and above. Based on a sample of 1,048 secondary school children, the alpha reliability coefficients range from .53 to .85. The test-retest coefficients, which were calculated using 139 students in three Boston high schools, range from .46 to .73. The intraclass correlations range from .32 to .92. The intraclass coefficient indicates both the extent to which pupils within the same class respond similarly and the extent to which the scale discriminates among classes.[29]

Unlike "low-inference" measures, which are objective counts of behavior, the LEI scales are "high-inference" measures that require subjective ratings of perceived behavior.[30] Low-inference measures of teacher and class behavior reflect psychology's current behavioristic ethos, and, hence, are far more prevalent. If valid, low-inference measures have the advantage in that they directly suggest changes in specific teacher behavior (for example, "increase the number of questions asked from two to four per minute"). Low-inference scales, however, are generally substantially less valid in predicting learning outcomes than are high-inference measures.[31]

The method of collecting data used in Harvard Project Physics is called a "randomized data collection" system within each class. Random proportions of subjects within each class were given different instruments simultaneously. This procedure increases the number of instruments that can be administered and decreases the amount of testing time for each individual.[32]

DETERMINANTS OF THE LEARNING ENVIRONMENT

After this brief review of the instruments that are available, it is time to turn to specific studies in which the relationship between classroom climate and various educational variables is examined. Either the LEI or CAQ were used as the measure of classroom climate, or the studies are directly related to other studies which did use those two measures, especially at the secondary school level.

In one study Anderson and his colleagues, working with a national sample of 150 high school classes, used the LEI to evaluate the effectiveness of a new curriculum.[33] Physics teachers were randomly assigned to teach either Harvard Project Physics (HPP) or the course they normally taught. Multivariate and univariate statistical tests showed that, as the curriculum developers had hoped, HPP was seen as less difficult, more diverse, and as providing a more stimulating environment than the more traditional approach to high school physics. Also, friction and cliques among class members were perceived as less frequent among HPP students.

In an early attempt at identifying variables that distinguish the press on students in various major fields of study in higher education,

Thistlethwaite analyzed ten measures of student perception on the *Inventory of College Characteristics*.[34] The sample consisted of 1,086 students enrolled at 335 different colleges or universities. Each student was asked to describe the pressures and activities (intellectual and social) that characterized the faculty and students in his major field of study by responding to the 200-item Inventory of College Characteristics. The inventory included ten scales descriptive of the faculty in the student's major field (achievement, affiliation, compliance, directiveness, enthusiasm, humanism, independence, scientism, supportiveness, and vocationalism). Each item asked for either a true or false response. Fifteen major fields of study were included. Physical sciences and mathematics students perceived strong press for scientism, compliance, and vocationalism, but weak press for humanism and independence. Humanities and social studies students perceived strong press for humanism, independence, and enthusiasm, but weak press for scientism, compliance, and vocationalism.

Astin suggested that student perceptions of classroom environment are a useful basis for classifying different subject fields empirically.[35] Ratings of introductory undergraduate courses in nineteen different fields were obtained from 4,109 students majoring in these fields at 246 colleges and universities. The questionnaire, which contained thirty-five items describing the class, was designed primarily to elicit objective information about the instructor's behavior and techniques, the students' behavior in relation to the course, the interaction among students and instructor, and other factors related to classroom environment. Thirty-three of the thirty-five items could be responded to with a "yes" or a "no." A factor analysis of the students' questionnaire responses produced three factors. The first was "Foreign Language" versus "Social Science," with foreign language characterized by enthusiastic instructors who knew their students by name, while social science was characterized by little classroom discussion, little homework, and arguments with the instructor. The second factor was "Natural Science" versus "English and Fine Arts," with the former high on students not speaking in class and the latter high on class discussion, humor, and diverse opinions. The third of the factors was "Business" versus "History," with more testing emphasis, less research emphasis, and duller instructors in business while students in history courses were more likely to know the instructor personally and to take notes in class.

In a study of pupil perceptions of various aspects of school, including subject matter,[36] eight hundred sixth- through ninth-grade students (one hundred of each sex in each grade) were asked to rate four subjects (social studies, language, science, and mathematics) on twelve seven-point, bipolar scales and to rate four people (classmate, parent, teacher, and the pupil himself) on another, but overlapping, set of twelve scales. Each scale consisted of four items. No overall sex differences were found, but, as grade level increased, there was a monotonic decrease in the favorableness of rating on both curriculum and people. Pupil ratings of the four courses resulted in two factors: "Vigor" and "Certainty." Each factor had four scales; namely, Vigor (alivedull, large-small, strong-weak, fast-slow); Certainty (safe-frightening, easy-difficult, usual-unusual, familiar-strange).

In general, mathematics and science courses received equally high scores on "Vigor," whereas social studies and language were significantly lower. Language courses ranked highest on "Certainty," with mathematics, social studies, and science following in that order. Science courses were ranked highest on both "Vigor" and "Certainty" by boys, while girls ranked language courses highest on these two factors. Hence, the learning environment of a classroom appeared to be a function of grade level and subject matter. The sex of the learner had no main effect; but it did interact with grade level and curriculum as a determinant of the learning environment.

In an investigation of the relationship between course content and teacher sex to classroom learning climate,[37] the sample consisted of sixty-two Montreal high school classes in science, mathematics, humanities (English literature and history), and French. There were forty-one male and twenty-one female teachers in the classes, and the pupils were in their tenth or eleventh year of school.

The instrument used to describe the classroom climate was the LEI, which was administered to a 75 percent sample of the students in each class in order to obtain a class mean for climate scores. The remaining 25 percent of the students in each class were given the *Henmon-Nelson Test of Mental Abilities* in order to estimate a mean IQ for each class.

This study revealed that neither the sex of the teacher nor its interaction with subject matter had a statistically significant effect on the learning environment of the classroom. Course content, however, produced three statistically significant dimensions of discrimination. The first discriminant function separated mathematics classes from the others; on the second discriminant dimension, humanities were at one extreme with science at the other; French classes were differentiated from the rest on the third axis. The first discriminant dimension accounted for 49 percent of the variance, while the second and third discriminant functions accounted for 31 percent and 20 percent, respectively.

Mathematics classes were characterized by high scores on friction, favoritism, difficulty, cliquishness, and disorganization and low scores on formality and goal direction. Science classes were perceived as formal and fast-moving, with little friction, favoritism, cliquishness, and disorganization. Humanities (English and history) classes, as compared to the other three subject areas, were paced and easy. On the other hand, French classes were perceived as formal, fast-paced, goal-directed groups without high levels of friction or disorganization.

Olson, who investigated eleven different variables simultaneously, chose variables thought to be associated with the quality of the educational process in the school classroom.[38] For measuring the overall quality of the educational process, Olson used the "indicators of quality" test to assess four major criteria: interpersonal regard, individualization, group activity, and creativity, and trained observers were used to note both teacher and student classroom behaviors as related to the above-mentioned criteria. Included in the sample were 112 largely suburban school districts located in eleven metropolitan regions across the United States. In all, 18,258 separate classroom observations were made (9,961 at the elementary level and 8,567 at the secondary level).

The eleven variables investigated were:

1. Style of educational activity: lecture, discussion, small-group work, question and answer, individual work, demonstration, laboratory work, pupil report, and so forth.
2. Subjects taught.
3. Class size: under 5, 5 to 10, 11 to 15, and so forth.
4. Grade level.
5. Type of teachers: regular teacher, specialist, substitute teacher, student teacher, or teacher aide.
6. Number of adults.
7. Day of the week.
8. Sex of teacher.
9. Half of period: first compared with last.
10. Time of day.
11. Number of nonwhite pupils.

The first seven variables, listed above in their order of importance, explained significant proportions of the criterion score variance at both the elementary and secondary grade levels. That is, these seven variables were found to be highly predictive of the quality of the school system. The last four were found to be insignificant as predictions of the quality criterion.

Another study investigated the effect that grade level had on the cognitive and affective dimensions of classroom climate as measured on the CAQ.[39] This study employed the data base from an earlier study, which consisted of 121 classes in 69 schools that participated in a statewide evaluation study in Illinois.[40] Classes ranged from grades six through twelve and represented the four subject areas of science, mathematics, social studies, and language arts. From the 121 classes, 52 were classified as "gifted" while the remaining 69 were classified as "ordinary." A multivariate regression of mean class perceptions revealed significant linear and quadratic effects of grade level independent of class size, subject matter, giftedness designation, and their interactions. This meant that students in higher grades viewed their classes as less stimulating and enjoyable than did students in the lower grades. High school students also perceived their classes as emphasizing factual memorization, while elementary school students placed greatest emphasis on higher-level cognitive processes such as application and synthesis. The most undesirable classes in the student's perception were at the sophomore and junior levels.

Employing the same data base as the preceding study, Walberg and his colleagues followed up earlier work done by Anderson and compared the classroom climate of four subject matter areas (language arts, social science, science and mathematics), again using the CAQ as the measure of climate.[41] After statistically controlling for class size, grade level, and class type (gifted versus nongifted), three discriminant functions were found to be significant. The first of the functions, which accounted for 69 percent of the variance, was labeled "convergence-divergence" and distinguished language arts from mathematics classes. The variables associated with the language arts side of the dimension had to do with the cognitive operations of interpretation, evaluation, synthesis, and translation as well as the affective processes of student independence and participation in discussion. The items associated with this pole of the discriminant function suggested an openness to, or consideration of, many alternative answers or the creation of new ones. The items associated with mathematics dealt with analysis, memory, the affective conditions of test and grade stress, the absence of humor, and little discussion. The authors thought that these items revealed a converging on a single "right" answer in a methodical, no-nonsense way.

The second discriminant function, which accounted for 17 percent of the variance, was termed "syntax-substance" and separated language arts and mathematics from science and social studies. The function appeared to represent Joseph Schwab's distinction between tool and application subjects.[42] The items associated with mathematics and language arts included the cognitive operations of synthesis, translation, and application. Associated with science and social studies were the cognitive processes of summarizing, memorizing, and evaluating. The pattern of cognitive press on the first two functions was very reminiscent of Anderson's first two functions, despite instrument differences.[43]

The third discriminant function, which accounted for 13 percent of the variance, was labeled "objectivity-subjectivity" and contrasted science with social studies. The items associated with science included independent exploration, learning and memorizing, interpreting, and synthesizing. Associated with social studies were such items as evaluation and absence of humor. It was suggested that this function could have been labeled "doing versus judging."[44]

There was also an attempt to examine the learning environment and the intellectual variables of grades eight and eleven from rural and urban settings representing mathematics, science, social studies, and English courses.[45] Ninety-six classrooms in the province of Saskatchewan were selected. There were forty-six eighth-grade and fifty eleventh-grade classrooms in the sample. Forty-seven of the classrooms were from rural schools and the remaining forty-nine were from urban schools. There were twenty-four mathematics classes, twenty-two science and social studies classes, and twenty-eight English classrooms. The LEI and the *Primary Mental Abilities Test* (PMA) were administered in each classroom so that one-half of the class took the LEI while the other half was taking the PMA. The PMA yields four subscores on verbal meaning, number facility, reasoning, and spatial relations as well as a total score.

Contrary to findings of the previously cited studies, it was found that course content did not affect the learning environment of the classroom, but the other two main effects, locale and grade level, were significant. Grade level was more highly related ($F = 18.78$) to the learning environment of the classroom than was locale ($F = 2.01$).

In a recent study I undertook to synthesize and extend the work of Anderson and of Walberg.[42] I found that measures of cognitive and social climate are sensitive to differences that exist between the core subject areas of a high school curriculum. Two measures of climate (LEI and CAQ) were used to characterize differences in the four subject-matter areas of language arts, social science, mathematics, and science. There were 414 students in eighteen classes who responded to an inventory formed by combining the above-mentioned measures of climate. The results, based on discriminant functions, indicate that students do perceive differences in their learning environments that are related to the subject matter being studied. The first of three significant discriminant functions, which accounted for 54 percent of the variance was labeled "convergence-divergence," and it contrasted mathematics with language arts. The most prominent variable associated with the mathematics side of this dimension had to do with the cognitive operation of analysis.

The most prominent variables associated with the language arts pole of the dimension dealt with the cognitive operations of synthesis and translation and the sociopsychological factor of being hurried or rushed. The second discriminant function, which accounted for 33 percent of the variance, was termed objective-subjective, and it separated science and social science. The third discriminant function, which separated mathematics and language arts from science and social science, was labeled syntax-substance, and it accounted for 13 percent of the variance. Figure 9-1 locates the position of the subjects on the discriminant functions reported in my study with the functions of Walberg and his colleagues and those of Anderson. Zero points are set at science for comparability.

My study is nearly a replication of the work of Walberg and his colleagues. Not only did both studies establish the existence of statistically significant discriminant functions that characterized differences in course content using the CAQ variables, but the two studies were also in basic agreement as to the nature of those differences. In addition, the findings confirm the existence of statistically significant discriminant functions as reported by Anderson and by Welch,[47] both of

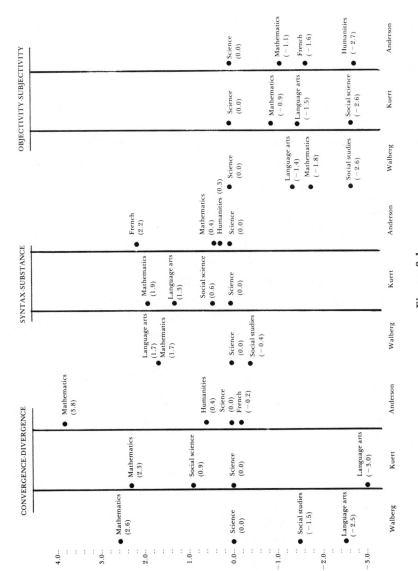

Figure 9-1

Subjects in discriminant space

which characterize differences in course content using the LEI variables, although there are discrepancies concerning the nature of those differences.

The results of my study also showed that cognitive climate variables (CAQ scores) are more sensitive to differences in course content than sociopsychological variables (LEI scores), and that both sets of variables considered simultaneously are more sensitive than either set considered by itself. For example, using a direct discriminant analysis procedure, CAQ scores correctly classified 64 percent of the 414 cases, while LEI scores correctly classified 50 percent. (The percentage of scores correctly classified in discriminant analysis is somewhat analogous to explained variance in regression analyses.) Both sets of scores together correctly classified 77 percent of the cases. These findings indicate that curriculum differences are not only owing to differences in course content, but also to a difference in the cognitive skills emphasized in each area of study. Hence, each subject area can be described in terms of a cognitive climate. Likewise, each subject area possesses a sociopsychological climate that, although not as well defined as the cognitive climate, is nonetheless significant.

In a study reminiscent of Anderson's work, Welch investigated the changes in student perception of the learning environment in secondary (ages twelve to seventeen) science and mathematics classes during the four-year period from 1972 to 1976.[48] He also examined the effect of subject matter (science and mathematics) and grade level (junior high versus senior high school) on the students' perception of the learning environment. A stratified random sample of all the secondary schools in fifteen states situated in the western two-thirds of the continental United States was used, consisting of 563 classes in 1972 and 558 classes in 1976. In all, more than 24,000 students participated in the study. Ten scales of the Learning Environment Inventory were used as the dependent variables. A three-way analysis of variance procedure was employed to analyze the data.

A major finding of the study was that students do perceive the learning environment differently over time. Compared with their counterparts in 1972, students in 1976 perceived their classes to be more organized, formal, goal directed, and satisfying. Significant differences were also reported for comparisons between mathematics and science, and between junior and senior high school students. Moreover, a significant multivariate interaction was obtained between grade (junior high and senior high) and subject matter (science or mathematics). Hence, in addition to subject matter, grade level, and the interaction of the two, this study has introduced the variable of time as another important determinant of the learning environment.

Many studies have failed to show that class size is a consistently significant determinant of classroom climate.[42] Walberg using 149 physics classes and Anderson and Walberg using sixty-one classes in several subject areas found, however, that smaller classes were significantly higher on cohesiveness and difficulty.[50] Olson found that smaller classes produced significantly higher scores on the quality criterion than larger ones.[51] Olson also noted three critical "breakpoints" between class sizes where sharp drops occurred in the performance scores. These class sizes were under five students, over fifteen, and over twenty-five. In contrast, the study done by Walberg and his colleagues found that climate was not significantly related to class size in either its linear or quadratic form.[52] More recently, it has been concluded that small classes are educationally more beneficial than large classes because much previous research relied on measures of superficial educational achievement rather than on measures of deeper understanding.[53]

This chapter has emphasized two self-report approaches to the assessment of the classroom learning environment. One approach is based on students' perceptions of the classroom environment, which reflect the relationship of the students to the subjects being studied, to one another, to the organizational attributes of the class, and to the physical environment as established by references to the *Learning Environment Inventory*. The second approach is based on students' observations of the general kinds of activities that characterize their class, as described by references to the *Class Activities Questionnaire*.

In addition, two basic techniques for determining the classroom learning environment have been examined. Both have their strengths and limitations. For example, observation techniques are good insofar as trained observers are employed to record interaction, manifested during the period of observation, on specified areas of concern. These same techniques are limited in the sense that the observer is a new element in the group, which alters, to a degree, the behavior pattern of the group.

The response of students on questionnaires and inventories has also been used as a measure of environmental perception as seen from the point of view of the inhabitants of the classroom environments. Such responses have been both recommended as useful for research[54] and questioned to some extent.[55] Proponents of such measures regard student responses as realistic and reliable measures of the environment, while critics deride student responses as irresponsible and unrealistic manifestations of feelings with a strong emotive bias.

Finally, of all the variables that have in this chapter been considered possible determinants of classroom climate, course content and grade level appear to be the most important, and those studies dealing with course content were especially interesting. Differences in criteria characterizing subject areas, as well as different ways of grouping areas for analysis, make summary of these studies difficult. Clearly, however, students perceive subject-matter areas differently.

NOTES

1. Henry A. Murray, *Explorations in Personality* (New York: Oxford University Press, 1938).

2. George G. Stern, *People in Context* (New York: John Wiley and Sons, 1970), 7.

3. *Ibid.*, 8.

4. *Ibid.*

5. Barak Rosenshine, "Evaluation of Classroom Instruction," *Review of Educational Research* 40 (1970): 279-300.

6. J. Wayne Wrightstone, "Measuring Teacher Conduct of Class Discussion," *Elementary School Journal* 34 (1934): 454-460.

7. Harold H. Anderson and Helen M. Brewer, "Studies of Teachers' Classroom Personalities. I: Dominative and Socially Integrative Behavior of Kindergarten Teachers," *Applied Psychology Monographs,* No. 6 (Palo Alto, Calif.: Stanford University Press, 1945).

8. John Withall, "The Development of a Technique for the Measurement of Social-Emotional Climate in Classrooms," *Journal of Experimental Education* 17 (1949): 347-361.

9. Donald M. Medley and Harold E. Mitzel, "Some Behavior Correlates of Teacher Effectiveness," *Journal of Educational Psychology* 50 (1959): 239-246.

10. Edmund J. Amidon and Ned A. Flanders, *The Role of the Teacher in the Classroom* (Minneapolis: Paul A. Amidon, 1963).

11. Fred K. Honigman, *Multidimensional Analysis of Classroom Interaction* (Villanova, Pa.: Villanova University Press, 1967).

12. Joy P. Guilford, "The Structure of Intellect," *Psychological Bulletin* 53 (1956): 267-293; *id.*, "The Three Faces of Intellect," *American Psychologist* 14 (1959): 469-479.

13. Arno A. Bellack *et al.; The Language of the Classroom* (New York: Teachers College Press, Columbia University, 1966).

14. Norma F. Furst, "The Multiple Languages of the Classroom: A Further Analysis and a Synthesis of Meanings Communicated in High School Teaching," unpub. diss., Temple University, 1967; James Gallagher *et al.; A System of Topic Classification* (Urbana: Institute for Research on Exceptional Children, University of Illinois, 1966); Laurence Siegel and Lila Siegel, "The Instructional Gestalt," in *Instruction: Some Contemporary Viewpoints,* ed. Laurence Siegel (San Francisco: Chandler Publishing, 1967), 261-290.

15. Allen L. Edwards, *Edwards Personal Preference Schedule* (New York: Psychological Corporation, 1954, 1959); Eric F. Gardner and George G. Thompson, *Social Relations and Morale in Small Groups* (New York: Appleton-Century-Crofts, 1956); David McClelland *et al., The Achievement Motive* (New York: Appleton-Century-Crofts, 1953).

16. C. Robert Pace and George G. Stern, "An Approach to the Measurement of Psychological Characteristics of College Environments," *Journal of Educational Psychology* 49 (1958): 269-277; Joe M. Steele, Ernest R. House, and Thomas Kerins, "An Instrument for Assessing Instructional Climate through Low-Inference Student Judgments," *American Educational Research Journal* 8 (1971): 447-466; Edison J. Trickett and Rudolph H. Moos, "Social Environment of Junior High and High School Classrooms," *Journal of Educational Psychology* 65 (1973): 93-102.

17. George G. Stern, Morris I. Stein, and Benjamin S. Bloom, *Methods in Personality Assessment* (Glencoe, Ill.: Free Press, 1956).

18. Trickett and Moos, "Social Environment of Junior High and High School Classrooms."

19. Gary Anderson and Herbert J. Walberg, "Classroom Climate and Group Learning," *International Journal of Educational Sciences* 2 (1968): 175-180.

20. Steele, House, and Kerins, "Instrument for Assessing Instructional Climate through Low-inference Student Judgments."

21. Benjamin S. Bloom, ed., *Taxonomy of Educational Objectives, The Classification of Educational Goals. Handbook I: Cognitive Domain* (New York: Longman, 1956).

22. Anderson and Walberg, "Classroom Climate and Group Learning."

23. Gary J. Anderson, "Effects of Classroom Social Climate on Individual Learning," *American Educational Research Journal* 1 (1970): 135-152; id., "Effects of Course Content and Teacher Sex on the Social Climate of Learning," *ibid.,* 8 (1971): 649-663; Gary J. Anderson, Herbert J. Walberg, and Wayne W. Welch, "Curriculum Effects on the Social Climate of Learning: A New Representation of Discriminant Functions," *ibid.,* 6 (1969): 315-328; Herbert J. Walberg, "Structural and Affective Aspects of Classroom Climate," *Psychology in the Schools* 5 (1968): 247-253; id., "Predicting Class Learning: An Approach to the Class as a Social System," *American Educational Research Journal* 6 (1969): 529-542; id., "Social Environment as a Mediator of Classroom Learning," *Journal of Educational Psychology* 60 (1969): 443-448; id., "Teacher Personality and Classroom Climate," *Psychology in the Schools* 5 (1969): 163-169; id. and Gary J. Anderson, "Classroom Climate and Individual Learning," *Journal of Educational Psychology* 59 (1968): 414-419.

24. Herbert J. Walberg, "Teacher Personality and Classroom Climate," *Psychology in the Schools* 5 (1968): 163-169.

25. John K. Hemphill and Charles M. Westie, "The Measurement of Group Dimensions," *Journal of Psychology* 29 (1950): 325-342.

26. Walberg, "Structural and Affective Aspects of Classroom Climate."

27. Walberg, "Social Environment as a Mediator of Classroom Learning."

28. Gary J. Anderson, *The Assessment of Learning Environments: A Manual for the Learning Environment Inventory and the My Class Inventory*, 2d ed. (Halifax, Nova Scotia: Atlantic Institute of Education, 1973).

29. *Ibid.*

30. Herbert J. Walberg, Juanita Sorenson, and Thomas Fischback, "Ecological Correlates of Ambience in the Learning Environment," *American Educational Research Journal* 9 (1972): 139-148.

31. Herbert J. Walberg, "Models for Optimizing and Individualizing School Learning," *Interchange* 3 (1971): 15-27.

32. Herbert J. Walberg, "A Model for Research on Instruction," *School Review* 78 (1970): 185-200; Herbert J. Walberg and Wayne W. Welch, "A New Use of Randomization in Experimental Curriculum Evaluation," *ibid.*, 75 (1967): 360-377.

33. Anderson, Walberg, and Welch, "Curriculum Effects on the Social Climate of Learning: A New Representation of Discriminant Functions."

34. Donald L. Thistlethwaite, "Fields of Study and Development of Motivation to Seek Advanced Training," *Journal of Educational Psychology* 53 (1962): 53-64.

35. Alexander W. Astin, "Classroom Environment in Different Fields of Study," *ibid.*, 56 (1965): 275-282.

36. Kaoru Yamamoto, Elizabeth C. Thomas, and Edward A. Karns, "School-Related Attitudes in Middle-School Age Students," *American Educational Research Journal* 6 (1969): 191-206.

37. Anderson, "Effects of Course Content and Teacher Sex on the Social Climate of Learning."

38. Martin N. Olson, "Ways to Achieve Quality in School Classrooms: Some Definitive Answers," *Phi Delta Kappan* 53 (1971): 63-65.

39. Herbert J. Walberg, Ernest R. House, and Joe M. Steele, "Grade Level, Cognition, and Effect: A Cross-Section of Classroom Perceptions," *Journal of Educational Psychology* 64 (1973): 142-146.

40. Steele, House, and Kerins, "Instrument for Assessing Instructional Climate through Low-inference Student Judgments."

41. Herbert J. Walberg, Joe M. Steele, and Ernest R. House, "Subject Areas and Cognitive Press," *Journal of Educational Psychology* 66 (1974): 367-372.

42. *Ibid.*

43. Anderson, "Effects of Course Content and Teacher Sex on the Social Climate of Learning."

44. Walberg, Steele, and House, "Subject Areas and Cognitive Press."

45. Bikkar Randhawa and Julian Michayluk, "Learning Environment in Rural and Urban Classrooms," *American Educational Research Journal* 12 (1975): 265-285.

46. William P. Kuert, "Differences in Course Content at the High School Level

Characterized by Multivariate Measures of Cognitive and Sociopsychological Climate," unpub. diss., University of Tulsa, 1977.

47. See Chapter 8 in this volume.

48. *Ibid.*

49. Anderson, *Assessment of Learning Environments.*

50. Herbert J. Walberg, "Class Size and the Social Environment of Learning," *Human Relations* 22 (1969): 465-475; *id.* and Gary J. Anderson, "Properties of the Urban Achieving Class," *Journal of Educational Psychology* 63 (1972): 381-385.

51. Olson, "Ways to Achieve Quality in School Classrooms."

52. Walberg, House, and Steele, "Grade Level, Cognition, and Effect."

53. Wilbert J. McKeachie and James A. Kulik, "Effective College Teaching," in *Review of Research in Education,* Volume III, ed. Frederick Kerlinger (Itasca, Ill.: F. E. Peacock, 1975), 165-209.

54. Anderson and Walberg, "Classroom Climate and Group Learning"; Anderson, Walberg, and Welch, "Curriculum Effects on the Social Climate of Learning"; Rosenshine, "Evaluation of Classroom Instruction."

55. N.L. Gage, "Teaching Methods," in *Encyclopedia of Educational Research,* ed. Robert L. Ebel, 4th ed. (London: Macmillan, 1969), 1446-1458; George J. Mouly, "Research Methods," *ibid.,* 1144-1152; Donald Musella, "Improving Teacher Evaluation," *Journal of Teacher Education* 21 (1970): 15-21.

10. A Self-Paced Environment

Colin N. Power and Richard P. Tisher

Specifying the nature of classroom learning environments, especially those where "open," "self-paced," or "inquiry-centered" teaching
occurs, has proved to be a difficult task. But, at a time when these
styles of teaching, once regarded as most appropriate for serving the
needs of a variety of pupils, are being challenged, [1] it is essential to obtain descriptions of those environments in which they occur. Only then
can we determine what impact they have on learning and how to vary
them for maximum educational gain.

The mystical qualities of classroom learning environments emerge,
over time, as the result of a complex series of interactions among a
unique mix of persons. Factors within and without a school ensure
that the environments have much in common, but there are variations
that give each classroom distinctive qualities. Pupils and teachers, for
example, relate to each other and to the experiences planned within a
curriculum in separate and varied ways. The challenge for the researcher is to find the distinctive qualities of each classroom learning
environment, to determine the factors that give rise to the variations
between and within environments, and to study the associations between qualities, factors, and learning outcomes.

This challenge is particularly relevant for Australian educationists, for there are definite pressures upon teachers to foster more "open" and "inquiry-centered" teaching in primary and secondary schools. At the secondary level, in particular, there have been attempts to introduce self-paced, inquiry-centered curriculum packages. In mid-1969, for example, Australia's first national curriculum project, the Australian Science Education Project (ASEP) was launched to develop an inquiry-centered junior science course that would allow pupils to work at their own pace, and to provide, at the same time, a rich smorgasbord of curricular offerings. It was divided into forty-seven self-contained curriculum units from which teachers could select as many as they desired. It is not appropriate here to describe the characteristics of ASEP in detail since this has been done elsewhere.[2] It is sufficient to note that each unit usually contains a core of material that all pupils follow, plus a number of options that extend the ideas in the core. Pupils are encouraged to select options designed to take account of different interests, abilities, levels of reading, and rates of working.

The units, tried in various Australian states, became commercially available to schools during 1974. Since then, more than half of the secondary schools in the nation report that they are using one unit or more. It is the use of these materials that has given rise to a series of questions regarding curriculum dissemination and use. For instance, one might ask: What impact does ASEP have on classroom learning environments? And that question can be further divided: What actually happens inside classrooms using ASEP materials? How do these ASEP environments differ from those of classes using existing conventional curriculum materials? In these ASEP classrooms what are some of the associations between key variables such as behaviors, perceptions, and outcomes?

RESEARCH QUESTIONS AND METHODOLOGY

Any attempt to answer such questions requires some knowledge of teachers' educational values, as well as of the characteristics of individual pupils and the class as a group. These aspects, examined in a series of studies carried out at the University of Queensland over a period of several years in the early 1970s, were subsequently replicated at Monash University. In the studies information about self-paced and conventional learning environments was obtained using several techniques. Approximately half of the lessons required to teach the core section of an ASEP unit were videotaped, and the tapes were analyzed using a classroom behavior coding scheme called SABIC (Scheme for Analyzing Behavior in Individualized Classrooms) that was designed especially for the study.[3] SABIC is a forty-category multiple coding system. Events are coded every ten seconds according to the *source* of a message or act, the *target*, or the nature of the act in which the source was engaged, and the *function* of the act. Source and target categories included pupil, group, class, teacher, and materials. Examples of act categories are questioning, giving direction, providing information, reading, writing, observing, and experimenting. Functions are divided into intellectual (stating facts, explaining), instructional (discussion of procedures), affective (positive affect or praise), and noninstructional (task-irrelevant activity) types. Thus, an event coded as pupil-teacher-question-interpreting would indicate that an individual pupil asked the teacher (not the reverse) to interpret the meaning of a substantive statement.

Two ASEP units with quite different purposes were used in two studies in successive years. In the first study, pupils' perceptions of the learning environment associated with the unit "Light Forms Images" were obtained using the *Class Activities Questionnaire* (CAQ) as a posttest.[4] In the second, where the unit "How Many People" was employed, the CAQ, and the *Learning Environment Inventory* (LEI) were administered as pre- and posttests.[5] In addition, attitude and achievement pretests were administered before the teaching of a unit began, and attitude and achievement posttests appropriate to the objectives of the unit were administered when the pupils had completed the core section.

The teachers who participated in the studies were selected so that they represented different value positions about the nature of effective teaching. To determine teachers' values a modified *Teaching Practices Questionnaire*[6] and the *Teacher Opinions Scale*[7] were administered to sixteen ASEP staff members, sixty-eight science teachers in Brisbane, and seventy-three science graduates in the Diploma in Education program at the University of Queensland in the first study, and to forty-two science teachers and seventy-eight science graduates in the Diploma in Education program in the second. In both studies the data were analyzed using a principal components procedure followed by varimax rotation. Factor scores for each individual on the eleven factors extracted were then used in a hierarchical grouping analysis.[8] This technique was used to establish clusters of individuals whose expressed values, based on a combination of the eleven scales measuring beliefs about teaching and curriculum, were similar. Multiple discriminant analysis procedures were then used to determine the manner in which the identified clusters actually differed.[9]

Three basic clusters of individuals were identified and designated. Group I contained those who *opposed* the expressed ASEP style of teaching. The members believed that a whole class, not groups of pupils, should work on an activity and that pupils should not devise or conduct their own experiments. They also believed that the teacher should be dominant in class, controlling, managing, disciplining, demonstrating, and dispensing all the necessary scientific information. The members of Group II were in a *mixed mode* with respect to ASEP. They held some of the beliefs that characterized Group I, but they also shared some of the beliefs that characterized persons in Group III, below. For example, they valued communication among all members in a class, supportive personal relationships between teacher and pupils, and the inclusion of a broad range of scientific subject matter at the same time that they felt the teacher should be dominant in class, controlling, managing, disciplining, demonstrating, and dispensing all the necessary scientific information. In Group III were those people whose values *agreed* with those of ASEP. They valued communication among all members in a school class, supportive personal relationships between teacher and pupils, and the inclusion of a broad range of scientific subject matter. They believed that pupils should have a first-hand experience with phenomena and should devise and conduct their own experiments, preferably in groups. Consequently, a teacher should not be the major dispenser of scientific information nor a dominant disciplinarian or controller of activities.

Forty-one individuals close to the group centroids within each cluster were selected and asked to teach a core of one of the units. Of these, twenty taught the unit "How Many People." The experienced teachers in the sample remained with their ninth-grade science class, whereas the trainees in the Diploma in Education program taught ten to twelve randomly selected ninth-grade pupils from the training schools.

IMPACT OF CURRICULUM MATERIALS

On Pupils' Perceptions

Pupils' perceptions of a learning environment are shaped by a variety of factors. As a first step toward distinguishing how the ASEP environment differed, a comparison was made between pupils' perceptions before and after participation in an ASEP unit. The results are shown in the histograms of Figure 10-1. The X-axis represents the mean score per item for each LEI and CAQ scale on the pre- and posttesting. Only those scales where a difference significant at the level of .05 or better are shown. The hatched tip to the histogram indicates an increase from pre- to posttesting, whereas an open or a blank tip indicates a decrease.

The figure indicates that, compared to earlier science lessons, pupils perceived the ASEP learning environment as being more cohesive, diverse, formal, goal directed, cliquish, satisfying, and entertaining (humor). It was also characterized by less haste (speed), less partiality (favoritism), less disorganization, and less apathy or indifference. That the new environment, characterized by more activity on the part of pupils, was at the same time perceived as more formal may seem somewhat unusual, but the LEI formality scale measures formality in terms of clear standards governing behavior in classrooms rather than in terms of classroom rituals. In an activity-oriented program such as ASEP, the teacher provides explicit guidelines to regulate pupil activity in an effort to reduce accidents and chaos to a minimum. It is not surprising that pupils perceive this environment to be a "formal" one.

The CAQ scale for "Independent Inquiry" does not appear in this figure. Contrary to what might be expected, pupils do not see the ASEP lessons as being more inquiry centered than earlier, more conventional ones. For students, the ASEP settings place as much emphasis on processing information and cramming as conventional settings. This same finding might well be replicated in many "inquiry settings." These data are consistent with data summarized in Table 10-1.

On Classroom Behaviors

In Table 10-1 the first column shows the coding categories, the second and third columns show the mean percentages of time spent on that category in the ASEP lessons, and the last column shows the mean percentages of time in the conventional science lessons.[10] When func-

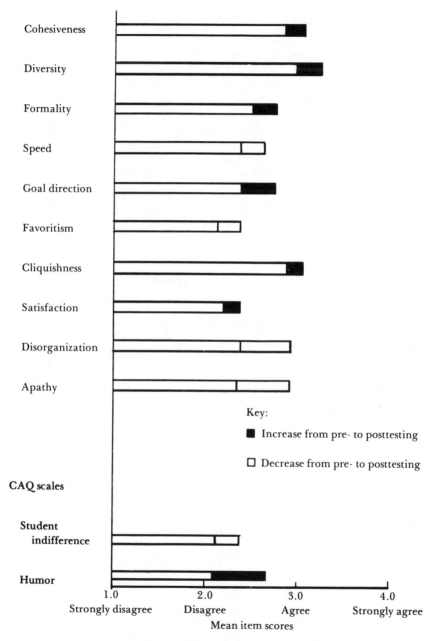

LEI scales

Cohesiveness

Diversity

Formality

Speed

Goal direction

Favoritism

Cliquishness

Satisfaction

Disorganization

Apathy

Key:

■ Increase from pre- to posttesting

□ Decrease from pre- to posttesting

CAQ scales

Student indifference

Humor

1.0 2.0 3.0 4.0
Strongly disagree Disagree Agree Strongly agree
Mean item scores

Figure 10-1

Histogram of mean perceptions before and after use of ASEP unit "How Many People"

Table 10-1

Mean percentage of time spent on behaviors
in ASEP and conventional science classes

| Behavior category | ASEP classes | | Conventional science classes |
	"How Many People"	"Light Forms Images"	
Target of activity			
Pupil	47	28	9
Class	12	14	65
Teacher	12	7	1
Material	24	48	4
Source of activity			
Pupil	55	61	19
Teacher	37	35	73
Interactions			
Pupil-Materials	19	46	3
Pupil-Teacher	10	7	1
Pupil-Pupil	21	6	1
Teacher-Class	11	13	65
Teacher-Pupil	23	22	8
Activities			
Questioning	30	13	25
Informing-directing	41	24	37
Experimenting	7	34	5
Functions			
Fact stating	10	6	48
Describing	4	9	6
Interpreting	4	2	4
Explaining	17	1	18
Procedures	18	21	2
Positive affect	2	1	0.2
Negative affect	0.4	0.5	0.2

tions were classified, facts were stated on 10 percent of the occasions when classes were using the ASEP unit "How Many People," on 6 percent of the occasions when the classes were using "Light Forms Images," and on 48 percent of the occasions when the classes were using more conventional lessons. Using the ASEP lessons, the whole class became the "target" of an activity (for example, questioning or informing) on only 12 or 14 percent of the occasions, whereas, for conventional lessons, this figure increased to 65 percent of the occasions. The table also indicates that, when the source of an activity was identified, teachers were the source more frequently (73 percent) in conventional lessons than they were in ASEP lessons (37 percent and 35 percent, respectively). Also, in ASEP classes pupils interacted more frequently with the curriculum materials, the teacher, and each other. Admittedly there are some differences between the two ASEP environments, but the overall patterns are similar and contrast with the types of activities, functions, and processes found in conventional classes. It appears that ASEP units operate as important determinants of classroom behavior, which more conventional settings do not.

IMPACT OF TEACHERS' VALUES

A survey of the research literature and a general consideration of the nature of educational systems, as well as the specific learning settings within the systems, provide support for the idea that teachers are one of the main sources of stability within schools.[11] Alternative teaching models, where they are presented to teachers, must often be modified or discarded in the face of teachers' needs to adjust to the value systems of the schools where they must shape their careers. Given constraints upon teachers and within schools, however, to what extent are the values held by teachers associated with the characteristics of the learning environment? In particular, are there associations between those values and the characteristics of learning activities in classrooms where identical, self-paced learning materials are used?

Table 10-2 contains *some* of the information on the significant associations found between teachers' values (a maximum of fourteen) and behavior variables (a maximum of thirty-six) used in this study. The information presented must, however, be interpreted circumspectly, for, of 504 possible correlations, 56 were significant at the .05 level, but 25 significant correlations could be expected by chance alone.

Table 10-2

Associations between
teachers' values and classroom activities

Behavior category	Social and personal development	Conceptual schemes	Teacher-centered approach	Behavior orientation	Inquiry orientation	Humanistic values
Target of activity						
Materials	.03	.49	−.08	−.23	.08	−.10
Source of activity						
Group	.49	.19	−.69	.02	.03	.34
Teacher	.30	.45	−.21	−.56	.31	.16
Interactions						
Pupil-Materials	.29	.45	−.38	−.24	−.04	.08
Pupil-Teacher	.46	.07	.02	−.07	.33	.39
Teacher-Materials	−.77	−.39	.44	.56	−.55	−.51
Activities						
Questioning	.44	.18	−.25	−.28	.28	.32
Writing	−.77	−.29	.48	.73	−.71	−.64
Experimenting	−.36	.30	.01	.04	−.19	−.44
Observing	−.77	−.46	.32	.44	−.56	−.49
Functions						
Interpreting	−.21	−.52	.36	.31	−.11	−.03
Purposes	−.69	−.38	.36	.56	−.50	−.49
Progress	−.80	−.37	.52	.63	−.61	−.66
Positive affect	−.50	−.47	.41	.46	−.31	−.28

Note: $r > 0.44$; $p < 0.05$

The data in the table can be interpreted to indicate that in the classes of those teachers who place a premium on the social and personal development of pupils (column 2) and on pupil inquiry (column 6) there are fewer activities involving the discussion of procedures and progress on the learning tasks, fewer occasions involving writing and observing, fewer instances of the teacher consulting the curriculum materials, fewer occasions of positive affect, and a greater number of initiating questions. On the other hand, in classes where teachers place a high premium on directing and controlling classrooms (column 4) there are more occasions involving the discussion of progress in the learning tasks, more occasions involving writing, more instances of the teacher consulting the curriculum materials, and fewer group activities.

It must also be pointed out that those teachers who believed that the fundamental ideas of science (conceptual schemes, column 3) should be emphasized talked more in class, fostered a greater number of interactions between pupils and curriculum materials, and allowed fewer occasions for encouragement (positive affect), observation, and interpretation. Furthermore, those teachers who stated that they rarely encouraged pupils to decide on the correctness of an answer or to probe answers and who reinforced answers (behavior orientation, column 5) appeared to follow the same practices in the ASEP lessons. More time was devoted to recording information, to observing, and to discussing procedures and progress on the learning tests.

Overall, the patterns of relationships are interpretable. Teachers appear, given the cautions expressed above, to foster activities that are congruent with their beliefs about teaching.

ASSOCIATIONS BETWEEN OBSERVED BEHAVIOR AND PUPIL PERCEPTIONS

Two disparate methods of measuring the same educational environment—high-inference measures derived from pupils' responses to the LEI and CAQ scales and low-inference measures derived from the classification of observed behavior using the SABIC system—have been employed. Using the matrix of correlations among environmental variables measured by these two methods (called a multivariable-multimethod matrix), it is possible to check on the extent to which there is significant agreement between the two measurements of the same type of environmental characteristic (convergent validity).

The instruments used in this study were not designed to measure the same constructs. As a consequence, the extent to which the validity of scales can be confirmed using procedures based on the multivariable-multimethod matrix is limited.[12] There should, however, be a close association between at least some of the measures deriving from the two instruments. For example, classes high on task-irrelevant behavior would be expected to rank high on pupil perception of disorganization. In addition to obtaining evidence of convergent validity for selected scales, the correlation matrix can be used to explore the relationship between observations and perceptions, thereby clarifying and refining what each of the environmental variables being measured means.[13]

Evidence of convergent validity was obtained for the following LEI scales in that, as hypothesized, the following relationships were confirmed:

1. Cohesiveness is associated with more information giving (.49) and less criticism (-.53).
2. Diversity is associated with the frequency with which pupils (.55) rather than the teacher (-.54) act as the source of activities.
3. Friction is associated with more criticism (.44) and less frequent discussion of difficulties (-.44).
4. Goal direction is associated with more information giving (.51) and less task-irrelevant behavior (-.53).
5. Satisfaction is associated with more informing (.44) and explaining (.45) and less task-irrelevant behavior (-.65) and less criticism (-.48).
6. Disorganization is associated with more task-irrelevant behavior (.53), more negative affect (.61), and less informing (-.43).
7. Difficulty is associated with the frequency with which difficulties are discussed (.48).
8. Apathy is associated with more directing (.62), less informing (-.56), and more task-irrelevant behavior (.73).

Exploratory analyses assisted in the further clarification of the constraints measured by the LEI scales. A favorable view of the physical environment was, for instance, associated with more time spent in reading and less time spent interacting with the teacher. One interesting result was a negative association between the time spent by pupils in conducting experiments and perceived goal direction (-.48) and satisfaction (-.49). It would seem that, at least in the unit on population ecology, spending a great deal of time on the experiments actually had an adverse effect. On the other hand, it is important that pupils actively discuss ideas and exchange information and that the teacher also contribute to small-group discussions by explaining ecological principles and helping to clarify issues.

In this study, intercorrelations of class mean scores on cohesiveness, satisfaction, and goal direction (between .69 and .91) indicate that pupils who rate their class high on items on one scale tend to rate it high on the items from the other two. Ratings on friction, favoritism, and cliquishness were also found to be closely interrelated (between .74 and .85) and consistently negatively related to cohesiveness, satisfaction, and goal direction (between $-.68$ and $-.85$). Whereas the first analysis provided evidence of reasonable convergent validity, the overall results throw some doubt on the discriminant validity of these six scales. It may be that the dimensions of the environment being measured are not actually independent. But the possibility of a "halo" effect, which is essentially an artifact of the method of measurement, cannot be ignored. This possibility will need to be checked in other studies of the learning contexts using larger numbers of classes.

ASSOCIATION BETWEEN LEI SCALES AND OUTCOMES

Canonical analysis was used to explore the interrelation between the twenty-three environmental variables and the eight outcome variables measured in this study. With the pupil as the unit of analysis (N = 315), three significant canonical relationships were detected, the redundancy of the criteria, given the predictors, being .17.

The first canonical function (Rc = .53, $p < .0001$) links a set of variables measuring the extent to which pupils perceive the classroom as a well-organized place, where pupils are actively participating and enjoying what they see to be meaningful activities, with higher achievement, higher overall satisfaction with the ASEP approach, and more positive attitudes toward the environment. This function parallels that found in another canonical analysis between pretest measures and pupil perceptions of the environment.[14] Together the results suggest that pupils who, prior to the introduction of the ASEP unit, were bright and satisfied tended to perceive the new science program in "rosy" terms; they continued to succeed and to enjoy their science lessons. The data, like those obtained in a previous study,[15] suggest that the introduction of an individualized progam increases the variance in outcomes. This can be explained, in part, because bright students are able to progress more rapidly and to undertake a greater variety of activities than is possible when the pace and the activities provided are dictated by a "steering" group of pupils of lower-middle-range ability.[16]

The second relationship (Rc = .48, $p < .0001$) reveals a link between the degree to which pupils perceive a pressure on the class to keep up (that is, cohesively keeping pace together), on the one hand, and pupil satisfaction with the way the ASEP lessons are organized and with their academic progress, on the other. Given a friendly, cohesive class, it would seem that students expect and respond favorably to a certain degree of pressure to complete activities. Under such circumstances, the pressure is unlikely to generate friction and dissatisfaction.

The third canonical relationship ($Rc = .44$, $p < .0005$) identified was somewhat more difficult to interpret, given the low correlations between the original variables and the derived canonical variates. The relationship was interpreted to suggest an association between a higher cognitive press in environment (perceived pressure to interpret, to apply principles, and to analyze) and the achievement of cognitive goals at the expense of enjoyment of the lessons. Requiring pupils to process evidence for or against environmental protection seems to be a valuable activity so far as the goals of environmental education are concerned; but it cannot be assumed that all students will enjoy the activity.

Canonical analysis provides an indication of the ways several environmental variables are associated with outcomes. There is still, however, a need to discover what contribution an individual's perception of the learning environment makes toward accounting for variance in instructional outcomes, over and above that accounted for in terms of entry characteristics. To obtain relevant information, a series of regression analyses were conducted with the seven pretest scores (ability, measures of prior knowledge, environmental attitudes, satisfaction with science) and the twenty-six environmental measures as predictors—and pupil achievements in ecology, attitudes toward environmental issues, and satisfaction with the ASEP approach as criteria. The results, presented in Table 10-3, indicate that the addition of the environmental measures did not add significantly to the explained variation in individual achievement or change in attitudes toward population growth or use of resources. The environmental measures made a small but significant contribution to the explained variation in satisfaction toward the ASEP approach and to attitudes toward pollution when partial correlations (with pretests held constant) between the various environmental scales and outcomes were calculated. The most consistent relationships were between residual affective outcomes and cohesiveness, goal direction, satisfaction (positive), favoritism, and apathy (negative).

Table 10-3

Correlations and partial correlations (with pretests constant) between environmental scales and posttests.

Environment scale	Achievement				Attitude						Satisfaction					
	1		2		1		2		3		1		2		3	
	r	r^1	r	r^1	r	r^1	r	r^1	r	r^1	r	r^1	r	r^1	r	r^1
Cohesive	.07	.00	.08	.02	.26	.26[b]	.26	.17[b]	.20	.09	.13	.19[b]	.24	.16[b]	.31	.29
Diversity	.07	.01	.03	-.01	.12	.08	.11	.13[a]	.14	.03	.08	-.01	.03	.03	.13	.11
Formality	-.05	.02	-.12	.06	.05	.08	.05	.10	.06	-.03	-.05	.03	.03	.06	.09	.09
Speed	.02	.06	-.04	-.01	.05	.05	.05	.07	.06	-.02	-.02	.08	.05	.13[a]	.12	.13[a]
Environment	.10	.12[a]	.00	-.02	.12	.12[a]	.12	.07	.09	.07	.08	.08	.10	.06	.10	.08
Friction	-.10	-.08	-.09	-.05	-.03	-.03	-.03	-.09	-.12	-.02	-.03	-.22[b]	-.23	-.06	-.06	-.05
Goal direction	.06	.09	.01	.04	.14	.17[b]	.14	.13[a]	.13	.08	.08	.19[b]	.21	.19[b]	.11	.09
Favoritism	-.13	-.08	-.16	-.11[a]	-.16	-.15[b]	-.16	-.12[a]	-.15	-.03	-.08	-.11	-.16	-.02	-.11	-.07
Cliquishness	.01	.02	.00	.02	.00	.00	.04	-.03	-.04	-.03	-.03	-.04	-.04	.01	.01	.01
Satisfaction	.06	.03	.00	-.04	.11	.11[a]	.00	.06	.07	.09	.12	.21[b]	.27	.16[b]	.11	.07
Disorganization	-.21	-.10	-.13	.00	-.11	-.07	-.11	-.07	-.12	-.17[a]	.23	-.17[b]	-.23	-.10	-.08	-.04
Difficulty	.01	.09	-.07	-.03	.02	.06	.02	.08	.04	-.01	-.07	.01	-.04	.04	.11	.15[a]
Apathy	-.28	-.16[b]	-.13	.05	-.15	-.10	-.15	-.10	-.18	-.15[b]	-.24	-.18[b]	-.27	-.14[a]	-.08	-.01
Democratic	.06	.08	-.03	-.02	.01	.02	.01	.00	.01	.08	.09	.08	.09	-.01	-.04	-.05
Competitive	.14	.07	.09	.02	.02	.00	.03	-.05	-.01	-.06	.00	-.05	.00	-.03	.06	.03
Inquiry	.08	.07	-.02	-.04	.06	.05	.06	.08	.09	.08	.11	.02	.06	.03	.09	.06
Indifference	-.16	-.03	-.15	-.05	-.08	-.02	-.08	-.00	-.07	-.12[a]	-.22	-.13[a]	-.23	-.08	-.09	-.02
Humor	.16	.12[a]	.13	.08	-.01	-.05	.01	.07	.00	.02	.09	-.06	-.01	-.09	.00	-.04
Cramming	.15	.06	.07	-.05	.03	-.02	.03	.01	.09	.06	.14	-.01	.06	-.02	.02	-.02
Interpretation	.06	.03	.05	.03	.08	.06	.08	.07	.09	-.03	.01	-.01	.03	.02	.10	.07
Participation	.16	.09	.08	.01	.12	.07	.12	.05	.10	.12[a]	.19	.09	.16	.10	.15	.11[a]
Translation	.07	.03	.10	.09	.14	.10	.14	.06	.09	.09	.14	.04	.08	.04	.14	.11[a]
Information process	.16	.07	.11	.02	.11	.07	.11	.08	.13	.09	.16	-.01	.07	-.05	.13	.08

[a] $p < .05$
[b] $p < .01$

Note: r = correlation; r^1 = partial correlation

Both individually and together the environmental measures contributed little toward explaining the variance in the achievements, attitudes, and satisfactions of pupils studying the unit "How Many People." It should be noted, however, that the pupils' exposure to the ASEP learning environment was quite brief.

In order to discover the contribution made by each environmental measure to the explained variance in class outcomes, regression analysis was employed using the class (N = 20) as the unit of analysis. As there were only a small number of classes, the number of variables in

Table 10-4

Regression analysis for environment versus outcomes
(class as unit of analysis)

Environment scale	Achievement		Attitudes toward environment		Satisfaction with ASEP	
	r	r^1	r	r^1	r	r^1
Cohesive	.33	−.09	.69[b]	.74[b]	.19	−.07
Diversity	.13	−.12	.28	.19	.30	.31
Formality	−.18	−.02	−.02	.22	−.21	−.21
Speed	−.09	−.07	−.27	−.23	−.04	−.02
Environment	.13	−.06	.41	.34	−.04	−.20
Friction	−.06	−.22	−.26	−.50[a]	−.01	.04
Goal direction	.09	.17	.41	.60[b]	.11	.02
Favoritism	−.23	−.09	−.40	−.49[a]	−.06	.10
Cliquishness	−.02	−.13	−.21	−.46[a]	.05	.01
Satisfaction	.12	.18	.33	.43	.18	.03
Disorganization	−.33	−.39	−.43	−.49[a]	−.20	−.07
Difficulty	.06	−.09	.05	.26	.01	.05
Apathy	−.55[a]	−.49[a]	−.49[a]	−.26[a]	−.23	−.05
Democratic	.02	−.29	.00	.12	−.18	−.28
Competitive	.42	.26	.20	−.06	.39	.33
Inquiry	.12	.21	.01	.11	−.23	−.38
Indifference	−.41	−.19	−.48[a]	−.38	−.22	.00
Humor	.58[b]	.18	.55[a]	.38	.64[b]	.58[b]
Cramming	.56[b]	.49[a]	.27	.08	−.02	−.18
Interrelation	.45[a]	.49[a]	.40	.38	−.14	−.28
Participation	.40	.02	.50[a]	.50[a]	.19	.02
Translation	.47[a]	.24	.37	−.14	.09	.00
Information process	.55[a]	.21	.61[b]	.56[a]	−.04	−.25

[a] $p < .05$

[b] $p < .01$

Note: r = correlation; r^1 = partial correlation

the linear regression models was restricted to an appropriate pretest and environmental measure. The results for those LEI scales that made a significant contribution are shown in Table 10-4. The results indicate that almost all of the variances in class achievement can be accounted for in terms of the initial level of understanding of ecology. Higher residual achievement, as indicated by the partial correlations, is associated with perceived academic pressure (or cramming), a press toward requiring students to go beyond the information given and to find trends or consequence (interpretation), and a low level of student apathy. Pupil satisfaction with the ASEP unit was associated with the display of humor. Pupil attitudes toward environmental issues were found to be associated with the cohesiveness of the class and the extent to which the class was seen as being goal directed, demanding active processing of information and high levels of participation. On the other hand, in classes rated high on friction, favoritism, cliquishness, and disorganization, pupil attitudes toward the environment were less likely to alter in the intended direction. It is generally anticipated that cohesive classes exert interpersonal pressure on pupils to conform to class norms. So, given a cohesive class and class "environmental" norms similar to those espoused in the unit "How Many People," an attitude change can be expected to occur in individuals in the direction of the existing environmental norm (or value).[17] Whereas the present study provides support for the position outlined above with respect to attitudinal change, Gary Anderson's study indicates that, where group norms include learning, cohesiveness facilitates achievement.[18]

The regression models described above assume a simple linear relationship between environmental variables and outcomes. It is possible, however, that some relationships may be nonlinear. For example, there may be an optimal level of competitiveness, and too much or too little could inhibit progress. Furthermore, it is conceivable that the impact of the environment on outcomes depends on the interactions between environmental characteristics (for example, difficulty) and pupil characteristics (for example, ability). To investigate some of these possibilities, a series of nonlinear regression analyses were undertaken. In each case the regression model was assigned the form:

$$Z = aX + bY + cXY + dY^2 + K,$$

where Z = the predicted score on the criterion test

X = ability (IQ) measure

Y = the measure on an environmental scale.

Addition of nonlinear terms improved the predictability of outcomes significantly in a number of cases (four out of thirty for LEI analysis), but in each case the magnitude of the increment was small (less than 3 percent); hence, the educational significance of the results are meager. The findings imply that higher levels of class competition and participation tend to facilitate the achievement of less able students slightly more than that of able students.

The Australian studies reported here provide evidence that the introduction of self-paced curriculum materials into conventional learning environments does produce changes in classroom activities and pupils' perceptions of their learning environments. Teachers, however, continue to behave in a manner consistent with their educational values, thereby modifying, to a certain extent, the impact of new curricular materials. The studies also show that there are some intriguing associations among the various environmental variables and outcome measures. Given the short period of treatment to which pupils were exposed, it is not surprising that environmental measures contributed little toward explaining variance in pupils' achievements, over and above pretest measures. Successes using measures of the environment in predicting affective outcomes were, however, achieved, and there was evidence of convergent validity for a number of the LEI scales. The studies, while not definitive on their own, do, when taken together, contribute to the monumental task of unraveling the mysteries of teaching.

NOTES

1. Neville Bennett, *Teaching Styles and Pupil Progress* (London: Open Books, 1976).

2. Australian Science Education Project, *A Guide to ASEP: The ASEP Handbook,* ASEP Teacher Education Materials, Australian Science Education Project (Melbourne: Government Printer, 1973); R. P. Tisher and C. N. Power, "The Learning Environment Associated with an Australian Curriculum Innovation," *Journal of Curriculum Studies* 10 (1978): 169-184.

3. R. P. Tisher and C. N. Power, *The Effects of Classroom Activities: Pupils' Perceptions and Educational Values in Lessons Where Self-Paced Curricula Are Used,* research report (Melbourne: Faculty of Education, Monash University, 1975).

4. Joe M. Steele, Ernest C. House, and Thomas Kerins, "An Instrument for Assessing Instructional Climate through Low-Inference Student Judgments," *American Educational Research Journal* 8 (1971): 447-466.

5. Gary J. Anderson, *The Assessment of Learning Environments: A Manual for the Learning Environment Inventory and the My Class Inventory* (Halifax, Nova Scotia:

Atlantic Institute of Education, 1971).

6. Raymond S. Adams, "Perceived Teaching Styles," *Comparative Education Review* 14 (1970) 50-59.

7. Australian Science Education Project, *Guide to ASEP.*

8. Donald J. Veldman, *Fortran Programming for the Behavioral Sciences* (New York: Holt, Rinehart and Winston, 1967.

9. See R. P. Tisher and C. N. Power, *The Effects of Teaching Strategies in Mini-Teaching Situations Where Australian Science Education Project Materials Are Used,* research report (Brisbane: Faculty of Education, University of Queensland, 1973), and *id., Effects of Classroom Activities,* for details of the procedures used and the results.

10. C. N. Power, "The Effects of Communication Patterns on Student Sociometric Status, Attitudes, and Achievements in Science," unpub. diss., University of Queensland, 1971.

11. William A. Reid, "The Changing Curriculum: Theory and Practice," in *Case Studies in Curriculum Change,* ed. William A. Reid and Decker F. Walker (London: Routledge and Kegan Paul, 1975).

12. Donald T. Campbell and Donald W. Fiske, "Convergent and Discriminant Validation by the Multitrait-Multimethod Matrix," *Psychological Bulletin* 56 (1959): 81-105.

13. Michael L. Ray and R. M. Heeler, "Analysis Techniques for Exploratory Use of the Multitrait-Multimethod Matrix," *Educational and Psychological Measurement* 36 (1975): 255-265.

14. Fisher and Power, *Effects of Classroom Activities.*

15. *Id.; Effects of Teaching Strategies.*

16. Urban Dahllöf, *Ability Grouping: Content Validity and Curriculum Process Analysis* (New York: Teachers College Press, 1971).

17. David Krech, Richard S. Crutchfield, and E. Ballachey, *Individual in Society* (New York: McGraw-Hill, 1962); Richard A. Schmuck and Patricia A. Schmuck, *Group Processes in the Classroom* (Dubuque, Iowa: W. C. Brown Co., 1971).

18. Gary J. Anderson, "Effects of Classroom Social Climate on Individual Learning," *American Educational Research Journal* 7 (1970): 135-152.

11. Evaluation of a Science-Based Curriculum

Barry J. Fraser

How does the instructional environment affect learning? A series of studies, particularly those related to Harvard Project Physics, has convincingly established that the sociopsychological characteristics of the classroom learning environment measured by the *Learning Environment Inventory* (LEI) can be used as both dependent and independent variables when evaluating a curriculum.[1] As dependent variables, LEI dimensions indicate that students following different curricula perceive their classroom learning environments quite differently. As independent variables, LEI dimensions reveal that learning environment variables are good predictors of student cognitive and affective learning outcomes, even after the variance attributable to the corresponding pretest, to general ability, or to both has been removed.

In this study, a modified version of the LEI provided both dependent and independent variables to evaluate an individualized junior high school curriculum. The variables or dimensions of the learning environment were used to judge the relative efficacy of choosing either curriculum materials developed by the Australian Science Education Project (ASEP)[2] or conventional instructional strategies and to predict changes in student learning outcomes in the course of a year's instruction in science.

Both the origins of ASEP and pertinent features of its philosophy and materials have been described elsewhere.[3] What is being considered here are the two main ways in which ASEP provides for individualization. First, particular teachers are free to select units from a range of forty-one ASEP units, each of which occupies approximately a month's teaching time, and to decide the order in which the units are to be presented and how much time should be devoted to each. Second, for a given ASEP unit, students can work individually at their own rate and choose which options within a unit to study and in what order. These provisions for individualization allowed the ASEP instructional treatment to be defined broadly. The only restriction was that ASEP materials were to be used exclusively throughout the study. The control treatment could then be broadly defined as the use of any non-ASEP materials.

The sample contained 541 seventh-grade students in twenty classes, each in a different coeducational high school in the Melbourne metropolitan area. Although the sample was not randomly selected, schools were representative of the various geographic and socioeconomic areas around Melbourne. Of the twenty classes, ten formed the ASEP group; the remaining ten formed the control group.

MODIFICATION OF LEI

Instead of using the original LEI, a modified version was developed. The original version had been developed for use at the senior high school level. Power and Tisher reported that some ninth-grade students experienced difficulty in comprehending numerous items.[4] The original LEI had also been validated in conventional classrooms, which meant that some of the dimensions had little relevance for individualized classrooms, while other dimensions of major importance were not included.

Anderson and Walberg suggested that, instead of always using all fifteen scales in the original LEI, a researcher might exclude those scales of lesser relevance to a particular study.[5] In this case, scales in the original version that had less relevance in individualized classrooms and scales that appeared unsuitable for use with junior high school students, even if the items were reworded, were omitted. The "Democracy" scale, which measured whether class activities were to be decided upon by the class as a whole, was, for instance, deemed inappropriate for an individualized classroom. Another scale, the "Friction" scale, which included items termed "petty quarrels" and "constant bickering," was omitted because it would have been difficult to reword the items to make them easily comprehensible to junior high school students.

The eight scales that remained were "Diversity," "Speed," "Environment," "Goal Direction," "Satisfaction," "Disorganization," "Difficulty," and "Competitiveness." Apart from changes made to improve readability, the wording in the items remained much the same as that in the original version. Of the eight scales, six are linked with advantages commonly claimed for individualized curricula, namely, that students perceive more diversity in the classroom, less emphasis on speed in learning because students work at their own pace, a better environment in terms of availability of materials and resources, more satisfaction because students can follow their own interests, less difficulty since students can follow alternative materials according to their abilities, and less competitiveness since students work on different things simultaneously. The other two dimensions are related to common criticisms of the individualized approach, namely that students could lack goal direction if they worked individually or that they could perceive disorganization if different students in a class were to pursue different activities simultaneously.

The original LEI excluded a dimension of paramount importance in individualized classrooms, namely, the extent to which pupils see their classrooms as individualized in terms of freedom for different students to proceed at their own rate and to make choices according to their own interests and abilities. Items were written to measure this dimension, and the resulting scale was called "Individualization."

The new version of the LEI, a shorter instrument that could be answered by junior high school students in a single class period, was administered to all 541 seventh-grade students who participated in the study approximately six months after the beginning of the school year because students' perceptions at that time could be employed both as predictors of changes in student learning outcomes during the year and as bases for comparing the influence of ASEP and conventional instructional strategies over a period of six months. Data were analyzed to identify certain faulty items,[6] and the subsequent removal of such items enhanced overall scale characteristics. The length of individual scales ranged from four to ten items, and the whole battery of nine refined scales contained fifty-five items in all. Data analyses indicated that the refined scales displayed satisfactory internal consistency (with reliability coefficients ranging from .50 to .80, with a median of .63) and satisfactory discriminant validity (with the magnitudes of the scale intercorrelations ranging from .00 to .48, with a median of .23).

DIMENSIONS OF THE LEARNING ENVIRONMENT AS CRITERION VARIABLES

It is common for the aims and philosophy of many contemporary curricula to be couched, not only in terms of what student learning outcomes are desirable, but also in terms of the type of learning environment to be fostered during classroom use of the curriculum. The statement of philosophical stance issued by the ASEP in 1974 clearly indicates that one of its major orientations is the development of a favorable learning environment.[7] It would follow, then, that any evaluation of ASEP be based in part on the nature of the learning environment promoted in classrooms where ASEP materials are in use.

The effectiveness of ASEP in promoting a more favorable learning environment was measured by comparing the perceptions of the learning environment of students in the sample using ASEP materials with those of students using conventional materials. Since students and teachers in both groups were initially selected so that they were as much the same as possible, it is reasonable to attribute any observed difference in students' perceptions of their learning environment to the influence of the curriculum materials used in science lessons during the six months prior to administering the new LEI scales.

In addition to examining differences between the perceptions of ASEP and control students, a set of student aptitudes was also taken into account. For one thing, a more conservative test of the relationship between the instructional variable (ASEP or control) and perceptions of the learning environment was permitted because differences in students' aptitudes could be controlled. Besides, the relationship between student aptitudes and perceptions of the learning environment could be explored, and, finally, the possibility of interaction between the instructional variable and student aptitude in predicting perceptions of the learning environment could be investigated. The three student aptitudes included in the analysis were socioeconomic status, general ability, and sex.[8] Socioeconomic status was measured using

Congalton's seven-point classification of occupations in Australia,[9] and general ability was measured with a version of the Otis Test.

The actual unit of statistical analysis used in the present investigation was the subgroup within the class formed by grouping students according to similarities in socioeconomic status, general ability, and sex.[10] Each student in the sample was classified as having either high or low socioeconomic status and as having either high or low general ability according to whether individual scores were above or below the median for the entire sample. Each student within a class was then assigned to one of eight possible subgroups according to the student's dichotomous scores on the three variables of socioeconomic status, general ability, and sex. When this procedure was used, it was found that, either because of absences during testing or because of the distribution of socioeconomic status, general ability, and sex in some classes, the total sample consisted of 153 subgroups, which is only seven less than the maximum number possible if each of the twenty schools provided all eight subgroups. When interpreting findings later, however, some caution will be needed since the use of subgroups as sampling units, while it affords a more conservative test of relationships than the use of individual students, provides a less conservative test than if the class were assumed to be the independent unit.[11] An example of another study involving learning environment variables in which subgroups within classes have been employed as the units of statistical analysis has been reported recently.[12]

A multiple regression analysis was performed separately for each of the nine learning environment dimensions using a full regression model containing the following seven terms: the instructional variable (I_i), the three student aptitudes (A_j) of socioeconomic status, general ability, and sex, and the three two-way instruction-aptitude interactions (I_iA_j) possible between instruction and the student aptitudes. (These symbols, I_i, A_j, and I_iA_j, which stand for instructional variables, student aptitudes, and instruction-aptitude interactions, respectively, are those employed in Walberg's model for research on instruction.[13]) Furthermore, statistical power was maximized in these analyses by maintaining socioeconomic status and general ability as continuous variables (instead of reducing them to categories), both when estimating main effects and when forming the instruction-socioeconomic status and the instruction-general ability interactions by taking products of predictor variables.[14]

The multiple regression analyses were based on Overall and Spiegel's Method 2.[15] Using this method, the amount of variance in perceptions of the learning environment associated with the instructional variable was estimated after removal of the variance associated with the block of aptitudes, but not the block of instruction-aptitude interactions. Similarly, the variance associated with the block of aptitudes was estimated after the removal of variance associated with the instructional variable, but not instruction-aptitude interactions. Lastly, the variance associated with the block of instruction-aptitude interactions was estimated after the removal of the variance associated with both the instructional and aptitudinal variables.

Table 11-1 contains the results of the multiple regression analysis for each dimension of the learning environment employed as a criterion variable. This table shows that the amount of variance in scores on each learning environment scale accounted for by the full seven-term model ranged from 6.6 to 18.3 percent, and that a significant relationship ($p < .05$) existed between the set of seven predictors and seven of the nine learning environment scales. Furthermore, after the correction for attenuation in the criterion only was employed to provide estimates in the limiting case of perfect criterion reliability,[16] it was found that the full model accounted for between 10.6 and 35.6 percent of the variance in a learning environment dimension. Results in the table also show that the instructional variable accounted for a significant increase in variance beyond that explained by the block of aptitudes for three learning environment scales, namely, environment, satisfaction, and individualization. On the other hand, the block of aptitudes accounted for a significant increase in variance beyond that explained by the instructional variable for four learning environment scales, namely speed, difficulty, competitiveness, and individualization. The block of instruction-aptitude interactions, however, did not account for a significant increase in variance beyond that explained by the instructional and aptitudinal variables for any of the nine dimensions of the learning environment.

For the three cases in which the instructional variable accounted for a significant amount of variance in perceptions of the learning environment beyond that attributable to student aptitudes, ASEP students perceived a more favorable learning environment than control pupils in all cases. That is, ASEP pupils, relative to control pupils, perceived their classrooms as being characterized by a better environment (in

Table 11-1

Percentage of variance in each dimension of the learning environment accounted for by the full seven-term model, the instructional variable (I_i), student aptitudes (A_j), and instruction-aptitude interactions (I_iA_j)

Learning environment scale	α Reliability	R^2 percent for full seven-term model		Unique R^2 percent for blocks		$\triangle R^2$ percent for block beyond I_i and A_j I_iA_j	Unique $\triangle R^2$ percent for individual A_j variables
		Observed	(Corrected)	I_i	A_j		
Diversity	0.50	10.0[a]	(20.0)[c]	0.1	4.7	4.8	5.0[b] (general ability)
Speed	0.66	13.8[b]	(20.9)	0.9	8.4[b]	4.2	
Environment	0.63	9.2[a]	(14.6)	2.4[a]	3.0	3.6	
Goal direction	0.62	6.6	(10.6)	0.1	5.0	0.5	
Satisfaction	0.80	10.7[a]	(13.4)	4.6[b]	3.1	2.7	
Disorganization	0.66	7.0	(10.6)	0.1	5.0	0.9	
Difficulty	0.50	17.8[b]	(35.6)	1.8	12.8[b]	2.7	9.8[b] (general ability)
Competitiveness	0.53	11.1[a]	(20.9)	1.8	7.1[a]	1.8	4.4[b] (general ability)
Individualization	0.71	18.3[b]	(25.8)	8.6[b]	7.6[a]	1.7	4.6[b] (general ability)

[a] $p < .05$,
[b] $p < .01$
[c] Figures inside parentheses incorporate a correction for attenuation in the criterion.

Note: Full regression model contains seven terms: Pretest, I_i (ASEP or control), three A_j variables (socioeconomic status, general ability, and sex), and three I_iA_j interactions.

terms of availability of materials and resources), greater satisfaction, and more individualization.

In order to facilitate interpretation of the four cases in which the block of student aptitudes accounted for a significant amount of variance in perceptions of the learning environment beyond that attributable to the instructional variable, the variance attributable to the block as a whole was partitioned into contributions accounted for uniquely by socioeconomic status, general ability, and sex. The last column of figures in Table 11-1 shows the variance associated with individual student aptitudes for those cases in which an individual aptitude accounted for a significant increase in variance for a dimension of the learning environment beyond that accounted for by the other two aptitudes and the instructional variable. It was found that, in each of the four cases, general ability was the only individual aptitude that uniquely accounted for a significant increase in variance. The interpretation of these findings is that students having more general ability tended to perceive their classrooms as having less emphasis on speed and being less difficult, less competitive, and less individualized than students with lower general ability in the same classrooms.

In summary, the above analyses have indicated that ASEP students' perceptions of learning environment six months after the beginning of the school year were significantly more favorable than control students' perceptions on several dimensions. Because the ASEP and the control group were initially selected to be as comparable as possible, it can be argued, moreover, that these differences in perceptions could be attributed to the influence of the curriculum materials used during the previous six months.

DIMENSIONS OF THE LEARNING ENVIRONMENT AS PREDICTOR VARIABLES

In addition to being used as criterion variables, perceptions of the learning environment collected six months after the beginning of the school year were also employed as predictors of changes in student learning outcomes occurring during the year. These learning outcomes were measured using a battery of seven cognitive and affective scales administered to each of the 541 students in the sample as a pretest at the beginning of the year and again as a posttest at the end of the same year.

Table 11-2 lists the seven learning outcome measures employed and
shows the α reliability estimate obtained for each scale with a sample
of 1,158 Australian seventh-grade students. As these scales have been
described in more detail elsewhere,[17] only a brief description of the
scope of the aims measured by each scale is provided below. The first
three scales are multiple-choice measures of inquiry skills. While the
first scale consists of nineteen items measuring skill in library usage
and use of the index and table of a book, the second scale consists of
thirty-nine items measuring skill in using and interpreting scales,
tables, and graphs, and the third scale consists of twenty-nine items
measuring skill in designing experimental procedures and drawing
conclusions from experimental data. The fourth scale, which measures understanding of the nature of science, contains thirty multiple-
choice items dealing with philosophical, historical, and social aspects
of science. The fifth scale consists of twenty-one Likert-type items
measuring attitude toward science. The sixth scale contains eight
items that measure attitude toward using inquiry methods to find out
scientific information. The last scale in the table contains eleven items
measuring adoption of scientific attitudes such as curiosity and open-
mindedness.

It should be pointed out also that the set of seven scales shown in
Table 11-2 is divisible into seventeen distinct subscales. Although
analyses have been reported for the seventeen separate subscales elsewhere,[18] it was found that data could be reported in this chapter for
the seven combined scales — with considerable gain in economy and
negligible loss in information yield.

A multiple regression analysis similar to that reported previously,
where each dimension of the learning environment served as the criterion, was conducted for each of the seven learning outcome posttests.
In addition to the seven instructional, aptitudinal, and instruction-aptitude variables included previously, each of the present analyses also
involved the corresponding pretest, the set of learning environment
dimensions, and the set of two-way instruction-environment interactions as independent variables. That is, each full regression model
contained the following twenty-six terms: the corresponding pretest,
the instructional variable (I_i); the three student aptitudes (A_j) of
socioeconomic status, general ability, and sex; the nine learning environment variables (E_k); the three instruction-aptitude interactions
(I_iA_j); and the nine instruction-environment interactions (I_iE_k).

Table 11-2

Percentage of variance in each learning outcome posttest accounted for by the full twenty-six-term model, corresponding pretest, instructional variable (I_i) student aptitudes (A_j), learning environment variables (E_k), instruction-aptitude interactions (I_iA_j), and instruction-environment interactions (I_iE_k)

Learning outcome	α Reliability	R^2 percent for full twenty-six-term model observed	R^2 percent for full twenty-six-term model (corrected)	r^2 percent for pretest	Unique $\triangle R^2$ percent for blocks beyond pretest I_i	Unique $\triangle R^2$ percent for blocks beyond pretest A_j	$\triangle R^2$ percent for block beyond pretest, I_i and A_j E_k	Unique $\triangle R^2$ percent for blocks beyond pretest, I_i, A_j, and E_k I_iA_j	Unique $\triangle R^2$ percent for blocks beyond pretest, I_i, A_j, and E_k I_iE_k	Unique $\triangle R^2$ percent for individual E_k variables	Unique $\triangle R^2$ percent for individual I_iE_k Interactions
Reference materials	0.85	63.1[b]	(74.2)[c]	48.0[b]	0.4	3.4[a]	6.2[a]	1.1	2.1	3.6[b] (Environment)	
Interpreting and processing information	0.91	70.8[b]	(77.8)	57.4[b]	0.0	4.1[b]	2.9	1.1	2.6		
Critical thinking in science	0.85	74.2[b]	(87.3)	57.7[b]	0.6	4.6[b]	5.1[b]	1.2	2.6	1.0[a] (Goal)	
Understanding of nature of science	0.78	58.5[b]	(75.0)	44.5[b]	0.3	4.1[b]	3.4	1.7	2.7	1.1[a] (Competition)	
Attitude toward science	0.89	63.4[b]	(71.2)	23.5[b]	2.2[b]	2.5	22.4[b]	4.0[b]	6.0[a]	1.4[a] (Speed), 1.4[a] (Environment), 6.4[b] (Satisfaction)	1.5[a] (I_i × Diversity)
Attitude toward inquiry	0.72	47.1[b]	(65.4)	22.9[b]	0.2	3.0	9.1[a]	2.0	7.5[a]	2.5[b] (Difficulty), 2.0[a] (Satisfaction)	3.0[b] (I_i × Difficulty), 2.4[a] (I_i × Individuality)
Adoption of scientific attitudes	0.63	51.8[b]	(82.2)	25.2[b]	0.0	6.9[b]	8.0[a]	2.7	7.0[a]	2.0[a] (Speed), 5.0[b] (Difficulty), 1.8[a] (Environment)	2.2[a] (I_i × Diversity)

[a] $p < .05$,
[b] $p < .01$

[c] Figures inside brackets incorporate a correction for attenuation in the criterion.

Note: Full regression model contains twenty-six terms: Pretest, I_i (ASEP or control), three A_j variables (socioeconomic status, general ability, and sex), nine E_k variables (LEI scales), three I_iA_j interactions, and nine I_iE_k interactions.

It has been argued previously that learning environment scores in the present study were determined in part by the instruction during the six months prior to administering the learning environment measures. In examining the relationship between instruction and learning outcomes, therefore, controlling for learning environment would have the deleterious effect of removing an important way in which ASEP and conventional instructional strategies differ. On the other hand, one would want to estimate the variance attributable to instruction after removing what can be explained by student aptitudes. Consequently, in performing the multiple regression analyses, dimensions of the learning environment were entered into the regression equations only after the variance attributable to instruction and student aptitudes had been estimated.

The term entered first into the regression equations was the corresponding pretest because, in curriculum evaluation, one is interested in the changes occurring in student outcomes during the interval between pretest and posttest, while the curriculum is being used. As in the previous analyses, interaction terms were entered only after all main effects. For the reasons given in the previous paragraph, however, learning environment variables were entered only after instruction and student aptitudes.

Table 11-2 shows the results of the multiple regression analyses at each of the four major stages. First, the variance in posttest performance attributable to the corresponding pretest is shown. Second, the variance associated with each of the I_i and A_j blocks is shown as a quantity over and above that attributable to pretest and the other block. Third, the variance attributable to learning environment (E_k) is shown as an estimate over and above that attributable to pretest, instruction, and student aptitudes. Fourth, the variance due to each of the I_iA_j and I_iE_k blocks is shown as a quantity over and above that attributable to pretest, blocks of I_i, A_j, and E_k main effects, and the other block of interactions. Furthermore, in conducting these analyses, statistical power was again maximized by maintaining socioeconomic status, general ability, learning environment variables, and relevant interaction terms as continuous variables.

Data in Table 11-2 indicate that the amount of variance in performance on a learning outcome posttest accounted for by the full twenty-six-term model ranged from 47.1 to 74.2 percent before correction for attenuation, and from 65.4 to 87.3 percent after correction for attenuation. Moreover, the set of twenty-six predictors as a whole was significantly related to posttest performance for all seven learning outcomes ($p < .05$). The third column in the table shows that the variance in posttest performance associated with the corresponding pretest (that is, the square of the simple pretest-posttest correlation) ranged from 22.9 to 57.7 percent for different learning outcomes.

Table 11-2 also shows that instruction (I_i) accounted for a relatively small increase in variance for the learning outcome posttest beyond that attributable to pretest and student aptitudes. In fact, this increase was significant for only one learning outcome, namely, attitude toward science. On the other hand, the increase in variance on the posttest accounted for by the block of student aptitudes (A_j), over and above that attributable to pretest and instruction, ranged from 2.5 to 6.9 percent. Furthermore, this increase was significant for all four cognitive outcomes and the Adoption of Scientific Attitudes scale. The increase in variance for the posttest attributable to the block of learning environment variables (E_k), beyond that attributable to pretest, instruction, and student aptitudes, was relatively large, ranging from 2.9 to 22.4 percent. This increase was also found to be significant for the Reference Materials and Critical Thinking in Science scales and for all three attitude scales.

Results for the blocks of interactions in Table 11-2 indicate that the increase in variance for the posttest accounted for by the block of instruction-aptitude interactions (I_iA_j), over and above that attributable to pretest and I_i, A_j, E_k, and I_iE_k blocks of variables, ranged from 1.1 to 4.0 percent. This increase was, however, found to be significant for only one learning outcome, namely, attitude toward science. The increase in variance for the posttest accounted for by the block of instruction-environment interactions (I_iE_k), over and above that attributable to pretest and I_i, A_j, E_k, and I_iA_j blocks of variables, ranged from 2.1 to 7.5 percent. This increment was significant for each of the three attitudinal outcomes.

The interpretation of the one case in Table 11-2 in which the instructional variable accounted for a significant increment in variance in learning outcome is particularly interesting. It was found that the sample as a whole underwent a decline in positive attitude toward science during the year, but that the magnitude of this decline was smaller in the ASEP group than in the control group. Furthermore, the block of instruction-aptitude interactions also accounted for a significant increase in variance related to scores on attitude toward science. When the variance associated with the block of instruction-aptitude interactions was further partitioned into unique contributions associated with each individual instruction-aptitude interaction, it was found that the instruction-socioeconomic status interaction was the only one significantly related to changes in attitude toward science. The interpretation of this interaction was that, while changes in attitude toward science were almost independent of socioeconomic status in the control group, ASEP students with higher socioeconomic status experienced more favorable changes in attitude toward science than ASEP students with lower socioeconomic status.

Although detailed interpretation of results for individual student aptitudes is outside the scope and purpose of this chapter, it is noteworthy that general ability was a much stronger individual predictor of changes in learning outcomes than either socioeconomic status or sex. On the other hand, detailed interpretation of results for individual E_k and I_iE_k predictors is pertinent to the aims of this chapter. Consequently, for the cases in which the E_k or I_iE_k block accounted for a significant increase in variance of learning outcome, the variance associated with a given block was further partitioned into unique contributions attributable to each individual variable within the block. The last two columns in Table 11-2 show the amounts of variance associated with individual E_k and I_iE_k variables for those cases in which an individual variable uniquely accounted for a significantly increased variance in learning outcome.

The results in Table 11-2 indicate that there were eleven cases in which an individual learning environment dimension uniquely accounted for a significant increment in variance in a learning outcome posttest (beyond that attributable to pretest, instruction, student aptitudes, and the other eight learning environment scales). Furthermore, in ten of these eleven cases, the relationship was in the anticipated direction in that more favorable perceptions of the learning environment were associated with more favorable changes in learning outcomes. The one case in which the relationship was not in the anticipated direction was for the Speed and the Adoption of Scientific Attitudes scales. In this case, it was found that more favorable changes in adoption of scientific attitudes occurred in classes perceived as "speeded." The interpretations of the ten relationships that were in the anticipated direction are given below. More favorable changes in reference materials skills occurred in classes perceived as having a more favorable environment (in terms of availability of materials and resources). More favorable changes in critical thinking in science skills occurred in classes perceived as more goal directed and less competitive. More favorable changes in attitude toward science occurred in classes perceived as being characterized by less emphasis on speed, a better environment, greater satisfaction, and less difficulty. More favorable changes in attitude toward inquiry occurred in classes perceived as better satisfied. More favorable changes in adoption of scientific attitudes occurred in classes perceived as less difficult and having a better environment.

The results in the last column of Table 11-2 show that an individual instruction-environment interaction uniquely accounted for a significant increase in variance in a learning outcome posttest (beyond that attributable to pretest, instruction, student aptitudes, learning environment dimensions, instruction-aptitude interactions, and the other eight instruction-environment interactions) in four cases. The interpretation of the first I_iE_k interaction is that, while changes in attitude toward science were almost independent of perceived diversity in control classes, changes in attitude toward science in the ASEP group were more favorable in classes perceived as more diverse. Whereas changes in attitude toward inquiry in the ASEP group were more favorable in classes perceived as less difficult and less individualized, changes in attitude toward inquiry in the control group were more favorable in classes perceived as more difficult and more individualized. The interpretation of the last interaction is that, while changes in adoption of scientific attitudes were almost independent of perceived diversity in the control group, changes in adoption of scientific attitudes in the ASEP group were more favorable in classes perceived as more diverse.

Some of the salient findings emerging from the analyses reported in Table 11-2 can now be recapitulated and summarized. In terms of the seven learning outcomes considered, the performance of ASEP students differed significantly from that of control students in only one outcome. It was found that ASEP students experienced more favorable changes in attitude toward science than control students, although an instruction-socioeconomic status interaction also emerged for this learning outcome. It was also found that all dimensions of the learning environment considered together accounted for a significant increase in variance accounted for in five of the learning outcome posttests (beyond that attributable to pretest, instruction, and student aptitudes). Further analyses revealed that a single dimension of the learning environment uniquely accounted for a significant increase in variance of learning outcome in eleven cases, and that a single instruction-environment interaction uniquely accounted for a significant increase in variance of learning outcome in four cases.

SIGNIFICANCE OF THE STUDY

This chapter has described the use of student perceptions of sociopsychological aspects of the learning environment in the classroom measured by a modified version of the *Learning Environment Inventory*, as both dependent and independent variables in the evaluation of an individualized junior high school curriculum. The curriculum materials were developed by the Australian Science Education Project, and the sample consisted of some Australian seventh-grade students. Before summarizing findings from the study, the need to qualify these findings is acknowledged because the sample was not randomly chosen and because of other methodological shortcomings discussed throughout the chapter.

The use of dimensions of the learning environment as dependent variables did reveal that, six months after the start of a school year, perceptions of the learning environment were more favorable among students using ASEP materials than among students using conventional materials. When the perceptions of the learning environment were employed as independent variables, they were found to account for an appreciable amount of variance in student cognitive and affective learning outcomes beyond that attributable to pretest, instruction (ASEP or conventional), and the student aptitudes of socioeconomic status, general ability, and sex. Furthermore, some instruction-environment interactions were also found to be significant independent predictors of learning outcomes.[19]

Findings from the present use of a modified version of the *Learning Environment Inventory* replicate the two main patterns emerging from prior research.[20] First, perceptions of the learning environment were again found useful in differentiating between classrooms following different instructional treatments. Second, those perceptions displayed incremental predictive validity in that they were good predictors of student cognitive and affective learning outcomes, even after the removal of variance attributable to pretest, instruction, and student aptitudes. Moreover, the magnitudes of the amounts of variance in learning outcomes found in the present research approximate those in previous studies both in terms of the full models incorporating dimensions of the learning environment and in terms of the amounts associated uniquely with learning environment variables.

Patterns of findings from the present study have implications for curriculum evaluators and decision makers. The finding that classrooms using alternative instructional materials were perceived as having different learning environments demonstrates the general usefulness of dimensions of the learning environment as criteria for weighing instructional effectiveness. Since many contemporary curricula promote the development of a favorable learning environment, it would be desirable for curriculum evaluators to include dimensions of the learning enviroment as dependent variables in their evaluations and for decision makers to base curricular decisions in part upon perceptions of the learning environment. The finding that learning environment variables (both as main effects and, to a lesser extent, as instruction-environment interactions) were good predictors of student cognitive and affective learning outcomes also has implications for curriculum evaluation. This finding, coupled with the observation that students' perceptions of the learning environment are determined in part by the instructional treatment followed, highlights the relevance of including dimensions of the learning environment as independent variables when attempting to evaluate instructional treatments in relation to what students learn.

NOTES

1. Gary J. Anderson and Herbert J. Walberg, "Learning Environments," in *Evaluating Educational Performance: A Sourcebook of Methods, Instruments, and Examples,* ed. Herbert J. Walberg (Berkeley, Calif.: McCutchan Publishing Corp., 1974), 81-98; *id., The Assessment of Learning Environments* (Chicago: University of Illinois Allied Educational Council, 1976); Walberg, "The Psychology of Learning Environments," in *Review of Research in Education,* ed. Lee S. Shulman (Itasca, Ill.: F.E. Peacock, 1976), vol. IV.

2. Australian Science Education Project, *A Guide to ASEP* (Melbourne: Government Printer, 1974).

3. *Ibid.;* A.M. Lucas, "ASEP: A National Curriculum Project in Australia," *Science Education* 56 (1972): 443-451; G.A. Ramsey, "Curriculum Development in Secondary School Science, Parts 1 and 2," *Quarterly Review of Australian Education* 5 (Nos. 1 and 2, 1972), entire issues.

4. C.N. Power and R.P. Tisher, "Variations in the Environment of Self-Paced

Science Classrooms: Their Nature, Determinants and Effects," paper presented to the Annual Conference of the Australian Association for Research in Education, Adelaide, November 1975.

5. Anderson and Walberg, "Learning Environments."

6. Barry J. Fraser, "Measuring Learning Environment in Individualized Junior High School Classrooms," *Science Education,* in press.

7. Australian Science Education Project, *Guide to ASEP.*

8. The term "aptitude" is used here to refer to specific characteristics of the individual known to affect learning.

9. Athol A. Congalton, *Status and Prestige in Australia* (Melbourne: Cheshire, 1969).

10. Barry J. Fraser, "The Impact of ASEP on Pupil Learning and Classroom Climate," in *Research in Science Education,* ed. A.M. Lucas and C.N. Power (Brisbane: Australian Science Foundation Research Association, 1975), vol. V.

11. Percy D. Peckham, Gene V Glass, and Kenneth D. Hopkins, "The Experimental Unit in Statistical Analysis: Comparative Experiments with Intact Groups," *Journal of Special Education* 3 (1969): 337-349.

12. Herbert J. Walberg, Rampal Singh, and Sue P. Rasher, "Predictive Validity of Student Perception: A Cross-Cultural Replication," *American Educational Research Journal* 14 (1977): 45-49.

13. Herbert J. Walberg, "A Model for Research on Instruction," *School Review* 78 (1970): 185-199; *id.,* "Models for Optimizing and Individualizing School Learning." *Interchange* 2 (1971): 15-27.

14. Jacob Cohen and Patricia Cohen, *Applied Multiple Regression/Correlation Analysis for the Behavioral Sciences* (New York: Wiley, 1975).

15. David Kaufman and Robert Sweet, "Contrast Coding in Least Squares Regression Analysis," *American Education Research Journal* 11 (1974): 359-377; I. Newman and M. T. Oravecz, "Solutions to the Problem of Disproportionality: A Discussion of the Models," *Multiple Linear Regression Viewpoints* 7 (1977): 1-51; John E. Overall and Douglas K. Spiegel, "Concerning Least Squares Analysis of Experimental Data," *Psychological Bulletin* 72 (1969): 311-322.

16. Joy P. Guilford, *Fundamental Statistics in Psychology and Education,* 4th ed. (New York: McGraw-Hill, 1965). 487.

17. Barry J. Fraser, "Selecting Evaluation Instruments," in *Research in Science Education,* ed. R. D. Linke, L. H. T. West, and R. P. Tisher (Brisbane: Australian Science Education Research Association, 1974), vol. IV.

18. Barry J. Fraser, "Classroom Climate as Predictor and Criterion in Science Education Research," in *Research in Science Education,* ed. M. N. Maddock and C. N. Power (Brisbane: Australian Science Education Research Association, 1976), vol. VI; *id.,* "An Evaluation of ASEP Involving Learning Outcome, Aptitudinal and Environmental Variables," unpub. diss., Monash University, 1976).

19. Herbert J. Walberg, "The Social Environment as a Mediator of Classroom Learning," *Journal of Educational Psychology* 60 (1969): 443-448.

20. Anderson and Walberg, *The Assessment of Learning Environments;* Walberg, "The Psychology of Learning Environments."

12. A Social Studies Evaluation

H. Russell Cort, Jr.

A large-scale study of an upper elementary social studies program, *Man: A Course of Study,* provided an opportunity to examine some relationships between students' perceptions of the social studies program, on the one hand, and measures of outcomes (achievement and attitude), on the other. The findings are of interest on theoretical as well as practical grounds. There has been increasing attention in education to the characteristics of instruction that facilitate motivation and learning. Studies that simply examine pre- and postmeasures of classes using different programs or methods to achieve the same or similar goals may find differences that are significant, though transient. But they shed little light on why the differences occur. As Wallen and Travers once put the matter: "For the most part, studies which supposedly compare the effectiveness of two teaching methods are generally studies which compare two largely unknown conditions."[1]

This chapter is based on research supported by the National Science Foundation under Grant No. SED 72-06289. Any opinions, findings, and conclusions or recommendations expressed are those of the author and do not necessarily reflect the views of the National Science Foundation.

While students undoubtedly tend to learn what is in the curriculum they study, rather than something else,[2] there is usually substantial variation in learning outcomes even when the curriculum is nominally held constant. The term "nominally" is used advisedly. In an observational study of the teaching of the same single concept in the Biological Science Curriculum Study (BSCS), Gallagher found that there was little uniformity in teaching style,[3] emphasis, or even interpretation among six teachers observed. That finding probably has widespread applicability whether one is interested in the same curriculum operating in different classes or settings, or in different curricula intended to achieve similar goals.

There appear to be two main approaches to understanding the operation of curricula and teaching. One requires careful and extensive observation of classes to obtain measures of behavioral variables considered influential, if not causal, in the learning process.[4] The other seeks measures of students' perceptions of learning activities and the conditions of learning as mediators and predictors of the effects of instruction.[5] The two approaches are not mutually exclusive methodologically. They do, however, have quite different theoretical roots, which are also not necessarily mutually exclusive. The observational approach may be regarded as having a concern with the stimulus ecology in that it is concerned with linkages of the stimulus ecology to responses or behavior (the indicators of learning). Such linkages may or may not be viewed as including intervening organismic variables (for example, perception, motivation, and so forth). The second approach is explicitly concerned with the role of organismic variables, such as perception, intervening between stimuli and responses.

This chapter attempts to combine aspects of both approaches. It leans, however, toward transformational theory (the Gestalt approach) rather than behaviorism (the stimulus-response approach).

MAN: A COURSE OF STUDY

Man: A Course of Study (MACOS) is a social studies curriculum developed by the Educational Development Center of Cambridge, Massachusetts, and now published and sold by Curriculum Development Associates.[6] It was originally designed to be a one-year course for fifth- or sixth-grade students. It was one of the pioneering efforts of the 1960s to revamp social studies in light of mounting dissatisfaction of educators and others with traditional social studies.[7] Its theoretical origin was Bruner's book, *The Process of Education*[8] and, indeed, Bruner became one of the main architects of MACOS. The curriculum became something of a cause célèbre almost from its inception, exciting more response, positive and negative, than any other social studies curriculum of its size and scope in recent times.[9]

MACOS has been described as the "unfinished curriculum," since the course is organized around themes to which there are no final answers: What is human about human beings? How did (do) they get that way? How can they be made more so? The course is replete with concepts, data, and information, but the press of the curriculum is toward keeping questions open, toward recognizing that facts may have a "half-life" that is increasingly short, toward stimulating curiosity in the hope that motivation to keep inquiring will lead to the development in students' minds of higher-order organizing principles to guide further inquiry. The goals, as described by the publishers, are broad, and they agree with the orientations of the developers: "to give pupils confidence in the powers of their own minds; to give them respect for the powers of thought concerning the human condition, man's plight, and man's potential."[10]

The basic pedagogical method used is contrast. Through contrasts it is hoped that students will come to understand more clearly the shaping forces that are said to distinguish human beings from other animals: language, social organization, toolmaking, the management of prolonged dependency of the young (childhood), and the urge to explain the world. The course starts with a unit on the life cycle of the salmon, moves to the herring gull, and then to the baboon. The remainder of the course is a series of lessons about the Netsilik Eskimos. There is no textbook, but, rather, a variety of booklets, filmstrips, records, posters, maps, photomurals, environment boards, and games. But films are the heart of these materials. There are sixteen films in all, nearly six hours worth, many of which were made especially for MACOS. The multimedia approach, along with much emphasis on small-group work and discussion, provides multiple channels of information, reducing students' dependence on the printed word. The materials for the course and the training to teach it encourage teachers to adopt the role of facilitator and resource, partner in inquiry, rather than to assume the didactic role of lecturer.

A formative evaluation of the curriculum, conducted with pilot districts and teachers while MACOS was being developed and tested, avowedly adopted the assumptions of the developers, and yet it nevertheless showed and reported some strengths and weaknesses of the curriculum.[11] The research reported here was based on one underlying question: Once MACOS became operational (was available to school districts on a commercial basis), how did it seem to work?

THE EVALUATION OF MACOS

Design

The focus of this study was to determine what was different and what was similar about MACOS in relation to other social studies curricula. "Different" and "similar" call for contrasts and comparisons. For each MACOS class, therefore, there was a non-MACOS class at the same grade level in the same school district in schools with comparable characteristics. Samples were restricted to public school systems and to fifth and sixth grades or to nongraded equivalent classes. "Non-MACOS" was taken to mean any social studies curriculum that did not include MACOS materials. The school districts, schools, and teachers that eventually participated voluntarily in the study also met criteria besides those just described. For example, districts that volunteered but were using MACOS in all elementary schools at the same grade level were excluded since such districts could not provide classes at the same grade level for comparison. Districts that said MACOS was to be used in a way that spread it over two academic years for the same students were also excluded.

Comparable classes were sought from the same school districts and grade levels as MACOS classes. To the extent possible an effort was made to obtain each MACOS and non-MACOS class within a district from a different school building. No attempt was made to obtain classes using a specific alternative to the non-MACOS curricula. Nor was any attempt made to suggest to MACOS and non-MACOS teachers what should be taught or covered, or how a program should be taught. The interest was in how courses were taught by a variety of teachers in a variety of settings and with what results.

The sample included 108 classes (57 MACOS and 51 non-MACOS) in 76 schools in 15 school districts in 11 states (California, Colorado, Florida, Illinois, Iowa, Nebraska, New Jersey, Pennsylvania, Oregon, Virginia, and Washington). The MACOS group consisted of twenty fifth-grade, twenty sixth-grade, and seventeen equivalent nongraded classes. The non-MACOS group consisted of twenty-four fifth-grade, twenty sixth-grade, and seven equivalent nongraded classes. The classes were in urban, suburban, and rural school districts, although suburban districts predominated.

Variables

The main independent variable was curriculum: MACOS versus non-MACOS. Dependent variables, selected achievement and attitude variables, are described below. It is also useful, however, to consider the results of the study as organized into three main sets of variables: inputs, processes and climate, and outcomes. For purposes of evaluation, outcomes (dependent variables) were compared between MACOS and non-MACOS groups, using inputs and process-climate variables as covariates. In some analyses, process and climate variables were considered to be dependent.

There were three categories of *input variables:* student, teacher, and classroom. Student input variables included pretest measures of achievement and attitudes, and background characteristics such as age, sex, race, economic status, whether or not English was the primary language, and years in the present school. Teacher input variables consisted of attitude and background characteristics (for example, years of teaching experience, years of experience with present program). Classroom input involved such characteristics as size of class, average age of students, standard deviation of students' ages, percentage of fifth-grade students, percentage of white students, percentage of females, percentage of students for whom English was a second language, percentage of students not eligible for free lunch, average reading level of the class, and an index of class stability.

Process variables were activities, emphases, or procedural characteristics of classes. Measures of these variables, obtained at Midtest 2 (February-March 1975), came from ratings made separately by students and teachers.

Classroom climate meant perceived characteristics of classes as measured by the responses of students to items pertaining to apparent satisfaction, apathy of the class, and difficulty of the course. Classroom climate measures came only from students, not from teachers.

At three different times major outcome variables were measured: Posttest (April-May 1975); Follow-up 1 (October 1975); and Follow-up 2 (May 1976). Posttest variables were the same as those measured at pretest. Follow-up 1 variables were those concerned with attitudes toward social studies the year after MACOS, as compared to the previous year and opinions of the extent to which what had been learned (in MACOS) was helpful in the following year. Follow-up 2 variables were primarily achievement and attitude variables measured by instruments that had been used in pre- and posttesting the preceding year. Students in Follow-up 1 and 2 were 50 percent samples from each class that had been given and pre- and posttests. About 80 percent of the students who participated in Follow-up 1 also participated in Follow-up 2.

Interviews

Interviews were conducted with teachers and with samples of students at Midtest 1 (November-December 1974), Midtest 2 (February-March 1975), and Posttest (April-May 1975). Students in Follow-up 1 (October 1975) were also interviewed. The first three interviews with students were conducted with a random sample of four students from each class. The main purposes of the interviews were to provide a means of monitoring classes as to what was being studied and how and to investigate questions about characteristics of classes—questions not easily answered by other means.

Each class was observed during Midtest 1. The observation consisted of having the visitor record the class session on tape. Transcripts of random samples of MACOS and non-MACOS classes were subsequently analyzed by application of the Aschner-Gallagher system.[12] Interviews with teachers and students were recorded on tape. Transcripts were for the most part coded independently by three coders.

Instruments

The following were the main paper-and-pencil instruments used to obtain measures of input, process, climate, and output variables.

A Questionnaire about Animals and People (AP). This two-part, forty-five-item test was made up of items taken or adapted from the MACOS formative evaluation[13] or from the booklet entitled *MACOS: Evaluation Strategies.*[14] One part (AP 1-4) includes items covering concepts, terms, and content found in the parts of MACOS dealing with man and other animals, whereas the second part (AP 5-8) deals with the Netsilik Eskimos. Both parts of this questionnaire were administered as a pretest to a random half of each class and to the same half as a posttest. AP 1-4 was administered to students in Follow-up 2, and is referred to as AP 1-4 F.

The Sequential Tests of Educational Progress (STEP), *Social Studies, Series II, Form 4A.* This is a standardized test of social studies skills such as organizing and evaluating information from a variety of subject areas such as history, economics, and anthropology. It was administered to all students as pretest and as posttest.

The Interpretation of Data Test (IDT). This instrument, developed as part of the Taba curriculum development project is intended to assess the ability to interpret ethnographic information and to use such information to draw logical inferences and conclusions.[15] It was administered as pretest and posttest to the random half of each class that did not respond to the AP questionnaire.

Social Studies Choices (SS Ch). This is a pair comparison instrument intended to provide a measure of preference for social studies in relation to five other subjects: English, reading, spelling, arithmetic, and science.[16] It was administered as a pretest and posttest to all students. A modification of this instrument (SS Ch F) was administered to students in Follow-up 2.

A Child Attitude toward Problem-Solving Inventory (CAPS). This instrument was developed by Richard S. Crutchfield and Martin L. Covington at the University of California (Berkeley). A factor analysis of it, undertaken in this study, identified four subscales: ability of self as problem solver (CAPS-1); interest in problem solving (CAPS-2); tolerance for ambiguity in problem solving (CAPS-3); and creativity of self in thinking (CAPS-4). CAPS was administered as a pretest and posttest to the same half of each class that responded to the questionnaire.

What Would You Think? Parts A and B (WWA, WWB). This instrument, developed for this research, was intended to measure attitudes toward unusual customs or beliefs (WWA) and toward people or groups who would have such customs or beliefs (WWB). It was administered to all students as pretest and posttest and in Follow-up 2. Two similar items were included in Follow-up 2. They will be referred to as WWAPF, and WWBPF.

My Social Studies Class (MSSC) was administered to all students in Midtest 2 (February-March 1974) to obtain measures of perceived classroom processes (activities, emphases) and climate. The instrument included scales adapted from the *Classroom Activities Questionnaire,*[17] and from the *Learning Environment Inventory* and *My*

Class.[18] Some items used in the formative evaluation of MACOS were also included.[19] Teachers completed a questionnaire about their programs at the same time. At pretest, teachers were asked to complete the *Educational Scale* VII (ES VII)[20] and *Teachers at Work* (TAW),[21] as well as a project-developed questionnaire about major goals and objectives. The ES VII and TAW were intended to provide measures of teachers' attitudes toward or beliefs about educational practices. The ES VII provides separate scores for progressivism and traditionalism.

METHODS OF ANALYSIS

Rationale

As noted earlier, a major purpose of the study was to provide profiles of similarities and differences between MACOS and non-MACOS classes with respect to learning and class characteristics. Although learning outcomes are personal, evaluations of main similarities and differences were made using the class as the unit of analysis, that is, measures obtained from students were combined to form class means. There were at least two main reasons for this procedure. First, the procedure helped to retain an independence of units of observation, and, second, the project had little way of determining *directly* just what stimuli acted upon what students and how. Thus, although a class of students could be identified as a MACOS class, or a non-MACOS class, that identification provided only a gross indication of what the instructional input was to individuals within the class. Classes could be treated as units, therefore, and most results pertain to classes, not to individual students.

Four main analyses were employed: analysis of variance; analysis of covariance; fixed-order, set-wise multiple regression; and canonical correlation analysis. The general analytic strategy was to perform an overall multivariate test. If a significant difference (or significant coefficient of determination, R^2) at the .05 level was found, then tests of individual variables or sets of variables were examined. Otherwise, with one exception, further analyses were not made.

Reduction of Variables

Several strategies for reducing the large number of input, process, and classroom climate variables were considered. The method used was to compute principal components for sets of variables. Only the first and second principal components were used, unless the first principal component accounted for more than 50 percent of the variance of the set. In that case, only the first component was used. Sixty-six variables were thus reduced to the following thirteen principal components relating to input, process, and climate.

Input variables: pretest of achievement (ACH); pretest of attitudes of students (Att 1, Att 2); demographic characteristics of classrooms (Class 1, Class 2); experience of teachers (T Demo); and pretest of attitudes of teachers (T Psy 1, T Psy 2).

Process variables: characteristics of classroom process as rated by students (S Proc 1, S Proc 2); characteristics of classroom process as rated by teachers (T Proc 1, T Proc 2).

Climate variable: classroom climate as rated by students (Climate).

Principal components pertaining to students were computed from class means, not from individual scores. For convenience in identifying the source, reference will be made to principal components for students and to principal components for teachers.

MAIN RESULTS

Comparability of MACOS and Non-MACOS Classes at Pretest

Classes were not randomly assigned to treatments; nor indeed was the sample of MACOS and non-MACOS classes nationally representative. To examine the initial comparability of classes, multivariate analyses of variance were made, although it is acknowledged that under such circumstances statistical tests, strictly speaking, do not apply. The independent variable was treatment (MACOS, non-MACOS); the dependent variable was the vector of principal components of input. Two such analyses were made: one using only those principal components for students; the other using principal components for students and teachers. For one of these analyses the sample size was 102 classes; for the other analysis the size was 81 classes. The difference between groups was not significant for either analysis.[22] The two groups of classes thus appeared comparable at pretest with respect to a weighted composite of the principal components relating to the initial characteristics of students, classrooms, and teachers.

Differences between Groups on Outcome Variables

Twenty outcome variables were analyzed simultaneously by a multivariate analysis of covariance. The independent variable was group

(MACOS, non-MACOS), the dependent variables were the twenty outcome variables, and the covariates were the principal components of input and process. There were ten posttest outcome variables, three Follow-up 1 variables, and seven Follow-up 2 outcome variables. Again, two tests were made, one using only the principal components for students and the other using principal components for both students and teachers. The differences between groups were highly significant in both cases.[23] It was concluded that the groups differed in outcomes, and that the outcome variables could be analyzed separately with some confidence that observed differences were not simply due to chance.

On the basis of several univariate analyses, outcome measures could be classified into three categories: measures on which the MACOS and non-MACOS classes clearly and consistently differed significantly (at or beyond the .05 level); measures for which differences between groups were marginal (varied in significance according to the particular analysis) and therefore had to be viewed tentatively; and measures for which there was no indication of a significant difference in any analysis.

MACOS classes, on the average, scored higher at posttest on the MACOS course-specific instrument, the questionnaire about animals and people. A year later, in Follow-up 2, MACOS classes also scored higher, on the average, on the man and animals part of the instrument. In Follow-up 1 (October of the year following the study), MACOS classes, on the average, rated present social studies as less interesting, compared to the previous year, than did non-MACOS classes. The same relationship continued when the scale was used again in Follow-up 2, a year after MACOS. Finally, in Follow-up 1, MACOS classes on the average scored higher than non-MACOS classes on a summated rating of whether various MACOS and general social studies topics had been learned the year before (a scale called "Know").

There were four measures for which there was marginal or tentative evidence of differences in outcomes between the MACOS and non-MACOS classes. At posttest there was some indication that MACOS classes tended to choose more positive reactions than non-MACOS classes on Part A of *What Would You Think?* These were reactions to unusual hypothetical actions, customs, or beliefs. There was general lack of evidence at posttest of a difference between the two groups in ratings on Part B, which asked about attitudes toward people or groups that might have such beliefs or customs. When the instrument was repeated in Follow-up 2, however, there was some indication that the former MACOS classes tended to give more positive reactions toward people who had unusual customs or beliefs than non-MACOS classes. The difference between groups in Follow-up 2 ratings of Part A did not approach significance.

There was marginal or tentative indication at posttest that non-MACOS classes tended to respond more positively to the scale interpreted as measuring perceived ability of self as problem solver. Finally, there was some indication in Follow-up 1 that MACOS classes were more apt to indicate that they had not learned certain skills in social studies the previous year and that it would not be advantageous to them had they done so.

Differences in outcomes between MACOS and non-MACOS classes did not approach significance with respect to the STEP *Social Studies* test, the IDT, SS Ch, CAPS-2 (interest in problem-solving), CAPS-3 (tolerance of ambiguity in problems), and CAPS-4 (creativity in thinking). Nor did the two groups of classes appear to differ significantly in Follow-up 2, a year after MACOS, with respect to a modified version of SS Ch, STEP *Social Studies,* an absolute rating on a four-point scale of how much social studies was liked that year and on two additional items similar to those appearing in *What Would You Think?* These two items concerned attitudes toward unusual behavior of a hypothetical peer.

MACOS classes on the average clearly outperformed non-MACOS classes at posttest, and a year later in Follow-up 2, on the curriculum-specific AP achievement instrument. With respect to the other two measures of achievement that were *not* curriculum-specific (STEP *Social Studies* and IDT), the two groups of classes were comparable at posttest. With respect to attitude measures, the two groups of classes did not differ significantly on measures of general attitude toward social studies. There was a significant difference between the groups when former classes were asked, in Follow-up 1 and also in Follow-up 2, how interesting they found their present course specifically as compared with the previous year's course. Former MACOS classes, on the average, found their present social studies courses less interesting. As with the achievement tests, the more general attitude measures did not differentiate between the two groups of classes as to outcomes. That principle applies to three of the four subtests on problem solving. The interesting exception was on CAPS-1, with the measure being the class mean. On that measure there was an indication that non-MACOS classes were a little more positive than MACOS classes at posttest. One tentative explanatory hypothesis is that the open-ended nature of MACOS does not lead to the perception that the classes are engaged in problem solving since, by definition, problem solving means reaching a solution or finding an answer.

The attitude instrument, WWA or WWB, used at posttest and in Follow-up 2 is not course-specific. Its content (brief descriptions of hypothetical customs, behavior, or beliefs) is more specific and concrete, however, than questions about attitudes toward social studies in general. The instrument is based on the theory that, while one might not like or agree with a custom or belief, one might not condemn out of hand the person or group having it. In terms of the MACOS course, teachers did not expect students to develop a desire to eat fish eyes or raw seal liver; they did expect students to come to see that the Netsilik Eskimos might have had understandable reasons for doing so. Or, as one teacher in the study noted, he hoped to get his students to see that, simply because someone says something with which you may disagree, this does not make that person "an automatic idiot." In one form or another, the goal of developing at least some understanding of differences in beliefs and customs was pervasive in MACOS and non-MACOS classes alike.

It may be noted that both groups, on the average, reacted more positively to WWB at all three testings than to WWA. That is, they reacted more positively toward persons or groups holding to an unusual custom or belief than they did to such customs or beliefs per se. The highest (most positive) average rating on WWA was at least one standard deviation below the WWB average rating. One possible reason for this result is that WWB may elicit more of a tendency to give socially acceptable responses than WWA since the latter involves personal reactions to a specific act or belief.

MACOS classes, as noted above, scored higher on the average than non-MACOS classes on the MACOS-specific instrument. Overall differences, while highly significant statistically, were not large in an absolute sense. AP had a range of possible scores from 0 to 45. Starting from comparable levels at pretest (about 19 raw score points), the MACOS group of classes gained 6.25 raw score points, while the non-

MACOS group of classes gained 3 raw score points. In terms of pretest standard deviation units, that is a gain of about 1.5 units for the MACOS group, and .8 units for the non-MACOS group of classes. An analysis of responses to individual items at posttest shed further light on the effectiveness of the curriculum. This analysis, using the student as the unit, compared percentages of MACOS and non-MACOS students choosing the available alternatives for each item.

The analyses showed, for example, that some of the more abstract concepts or terms of the course, such as the differences between human language and animal signaling, or the concepts of structure and function, were not mastered by large percentages of MACOS students. Mastery here means the ability to use the terms correctly in a matching question, or to identify examples of a concept on the AP test. Of the MACOS as well as non-MACOS students, 62 percent matched "human being" with "the opposite of animal." While proportionately nearly three times as many MACOS students as non-MACOS correctly identified an example of learned behavior, the absolute percentage of MACOS students doing so was 53 percent, and 47 percent chose wrong answers. In general, as measured by responses to items, it appeared that MACOS students learned much factual detail about animals and about the Netsilik Eskimos, but had difficulty with some of the more abstract terms and concepts. Age was partly a factor since sixth graders did better than fifth graders on the average.

Differences in Processes and Climate

Were there differences between the two groups with respect to classroom processes and climate? A multivariate analysis of variance, using class means, was performed, with group (MACOS, non- MACOS) as the independent variable, and the principal components for input, process, and climate as dependent variables. Tests using just the student-based principal components, and then both student- and teacher-based principal components, indicated highly significant differences between groups (p-values of the overall F-tests were .013 and .037, respectively). The principal components on which groups differed on univariate tests were the second student-based process variable (S proc 2), the climate variable, and, when teacher-based principal components were used, the second teacher input variable (T Psy 2) and both teacher-based principal components for process (T Proc 1 and T Proc 2).

Further univariate analyses of variance of student- and teacher-based process and climate variables were performed. Group (MACOS, non-MACOS) again was the independent variable; each original class average for the process and climate variables (from which the principal components were derived) was used in turn as the dependent variable. The groups differed significantly at the .05 level or beyond on the three classroom climate variables. Based on class means, MACOS classes on the average were rated as more satisfying, less difficult, and less apathetic than non-MACOS classes. The three classroom climate variables, however, were highly intercorrelated. The first principal component for the three variables accounted for 82 percent of the total variance. Thus, the three classroom climate variables may reflect a generalized like-dislike attitude toward the particular social studies class rather than more differentiated perceptions. In any case, there was little doubt that MACOS classes, on the average, were the more positive, whether the climate variables were considered separately or as a single weighted composite. Throughout, of course, the qualification is "on the average." Some non-MACOS classes were rated more positively in classroom climate than some MACOS classes. Indeed, *there was no variable in this study on which all classes in one group fell uniformly above or below all classes in the other group.*

Student-based process variables are those in which students rated whether or not they saw their social studies class as emphasizing different types of activities or learning. Using the scales adapted from Steele's *Classroom Activities Questionnaire,* we found that, on five of the fifteen process measures, MACOS classes (as compared with non-MACOS classes) tended to describe the teacher as talking more, but they also rated the classes as having more discussions. They tended to perceive their classes as less grade oriented and as more typically comparing things to see how they were alike or different. Non-MACOS classes more consistently rated synthesis (making up new things from what was learned, such as stories, poems, plays, reports, and so forth, or thinking up new ideas or examples) as a more frequent activity than did MACOS classes. The groups did not appear to differ reliably in perceived emphasis on:

1. memory ("In social studies our teacher really makes us remember the names, new words, and facts that we have learned");
2. translation ("Our teacher always wants us to tell about things in

our own words in social studies class");

3. interpretation ("It isn't enough just to learn facts in social studies; our teacher also makes us decide what the facts mean to us");

4. application ("The things we do and learn in social studies really help me a lot in other classes and outside school too");

5. analysis ("In social studies, we always have to study all the parts or sides of a question before we decide what we think");

6. evaluation ("In social studies, we often have to decide if things in the world are good or bad, or right or wrong, and tell why we think so").

Groups did not differ substantially, on the average, on ratings of the appropriateness of the pacing of the class, of the extent of listening done, and of informality or joking.

MACOS teachers as a group, significantly more than non-MACOS teachers, rated their curriculum higher in emphasizing affective content, application, analysis, and synthesis. They rated their curriculum lower in emphasis on comprehension. On the whole, their ratings were similar to the ratings of non-MACOS teachers in emphasis on memory, evaluation, group activities, and individual activities.

Relationships among Variables

To explore relationships among sets of variables, two types of analyses were performed using principal components for input, process, and climate. First, a fixed-order, set wise multiple regression analysis was done for each outcome variable. The order of entry of variables into the analyses was always as follows: student pretest, demographic characteristics of classrooms, student-based principal components for process, teacher-based principal components for process, and climate. For analyses employing only student-based principal components, the order of entry was as above without the teacher-based principal components. "Group" was entered as a dummy variable last after climate in one set of analyses, and after input in another set. The order of entry as to Group made very little difference in results except with respect to marginal outcome variables (see above). Table 12-1, which shows total multiple R^2 and increments of variance associated with sets of variables for each outcome variable, is typical.

Table 12-1

Increments of proportion of variance in outcome variables associated
with Input, Process, Climate, and Group variables (MACOS, non-MACOS)
using student and teacher PCs[c]

Period	Outcome variable	Pre-post r^2	Total multiple R^2	Increment from Input	Increment from Process	Increment from Climate	Increment from Group (M, N-M)
Posttest	AP	33[b]	64[b]	46[b]	1	0	16[b]
	STEP	81[b]	79[b]	78[b]	0	1[a]	0
	IDT	55[b]	56[b]	53[b]	2	1	0
	SS Ch	35[b]	37[b]	13	9[a]	15[b]	0
	WWA	18[b]	50[b]	30[b]	15[b]	0	4[b]
	WWB	16[b]	33[a]	24[b]	7	1	1
	CAPS-1	32[b]	27	17	2	4	4
	CAPS-2	15[b]	40[b]	31[b]	7	1	1
	CAPS-3	36[b]	55[b]	49[b]	4	2	0
	CAPS-4	26[b]	29[a]	25[b]	2	1	0
Follow-up 1	Skills	.[d]	26	8	12[b]	3	3
	Know	-	34[a]	8	18[b]	1	7[b]
	Interest	-	31[a]	8	17[b]	2	4[a]
Follow-up 2	AP 1-4F	32[b, e]	59[b]	55[b]	1	0	3[a]
	SS Ch F	1[f]	12	6	3	2	0
	SS	-	24	5	7	11	0
	WWAF	1[g]	37[b]	31[b]	6	0	0
	WWBF	14[b, h]	38[b]	33[b]	4	0	1
	WWAPF	-	17	11	4	0	2
	WWBPF	-	19	17	1	0	0

[a] $p \leq .05$

[b] $p \leq .01$

[c] Sample size for all outcomes = 81: MACOS 44, non-MACOS 37. Pre-post correlations, squared, are given for comparison with Multiple R^2. Note that incremental proportions may not add exactly to R^2 due to rounding. Decimals and leading zeroes have been omitted.

[d] A dash indicates there was no pretest for the variable.

[e] Pretest was total AP. For pre AP 1-4 and AP 1-4F, $r^2 = .37$.

[f] Pretest was SS Ch; SS Ch F was a modification of SS Ch.

[g] Correlation is with WWA pre.

[h] Correlation is with WWB pre.

The table is based on the eighty-one classes for which data from all students and teachers were available. It may be seen that most, but not all, multiple R^2s are not significant at or beyond the .05 level; that for most, but not all, outcome variables, the set of input (typically student pretest) variables accounts for the major portion of total variance; and that Group adds a significant increment in the case of AP, WWA, Know, Interest, and AP 1-4F. Group falls just short of significance for CAPS-1, but multiple R^2 for CAPS-1 in this subsample is not significant, unlike in the larger sample; Group falls far short of significance here for Skills and WWBF. It may also be seen that process variables, as a set, add a significant increment of variance for four dependent variables, and the principal component of Climate adds a significant increment for two outcome variables (STEP and SS Ch). The Follow-up 2 variable, SS (an absolute rating of liking social studies), appears to have a large increment for Climate that is not indicated in the table, but note that the multiple R^2 for SS is not significant. Note, finally, that the outcomes in this case for which process variables are statistically significant, or at least relatively large in terms of increments, are attitudinal variables. On the other hand, Climate adds a significant increment for an achievement test (STEP) and for the attitude measure of preference for social studies (SS Ch). Note also that outcome variables for which the process set added a significant increment are in all cases not the variables for which Climate added a significant increment.

What does one make of this? For increments that were significant, a more detailed analysis showed that, with respect to sets of input variables, the significant contributors were almost always pretest achievement or attitudes of students at pretest. There were a few cases in which a demographic principal component for a class or a principal component for teacher background was significant. Where a principal component for teacher background was significant, it suggested that the less traditional and controlling the teacher, as measured by the ES VII traditionalism score, the higher the average score of the class on the outcome. An interesting exception was the case of the MACOS test on animals and people, for which the opposite was the case in Follow-up 2.

With respect to process variables, the situation is more complex. With one exception, it was student-based rather than teacher-based principal components that appeared important (that is, student perceptions, not teacher reports). Even so, perception of the class as traditional as distinct from perception of it as informal, open, and group oriented was important, say, for CAPS-3. The opposite was the case for preference for social studies (SS Ch), WWA, or Interest when the class of the following year was compared to the class of the preceding year.

Climate contributes a significant increment of variance for STEP and SS Ch. Insofar as some instruments are concerned, this may be in part an artifact related to reliability. Climate contributes a significant increment (an R^2 change of .01) to the explained STEP variance because the error term for STEP is very small (basically, $1.00 - .79 = .21$). Precisely the same proportionate increment is not significant for IDT because of the larger error term ($1.00 - .56 = .44$), although degrees of freedom for numerator and for denominator are identical. STEP was in fact more reliable than IDT, as the pre-post correlations squared (r^2) suggest. One conjecture is that the better students feel about a particular class, the more they will try on the tests offered to the class. This conjecture gains some support from the general impressions of project staff administering tests (pre-, post- and follow-up). Not shown here, but indicated by multiple regression analyses of MACOS and non-MACOS classes separately, is the finding that, generally, MACOS classes were less sensitive to variations in processes and climate, insofar as most outcomes were concerned, than the aggregate of non-MACOS classes. Of eleven cases of significant process or climate increments, ten were for the non-MACOS classes, one for the MACOS group.

The multiple regression analyses took sets of variables one at a time and systematically eliminated variance attributable to them. Canonical correlation analyses were used to examine relationships of influence within several sets. Thus, for example, an analysis was performed of the relationships of all principal components for inputs taken as a set to all principal components for process and climate, also taken as a set.

The general pattern found for the two groups combined appeared to be that the older, more affluent, and higher-achieving the class at pretest, and the less traditional the teacher's attitude or point of view, the more the class was perceived by students as being informal, being oriented toward group discussion, and having less emphasis on grades. Also, the classroom climate was perceived to be more positive.

There were some variations in this pattern when the groups of MACOS and non-MACOS classes were analyzed separately. In the MACOS group, years of teaching experience of the teacher also was important (younger teachers were associated more with informality, discussion, and lack of traditional, individual work). That characteristic did not appear influential in the non-MACOS group, where class demographic characteristics and teacher experience seemed less im-

portant in relation to the achievement and attitudes of classes at pretest. Furthermore, whether or not classes were perceived by students as
informal, discussion oriented, and nongrade oriented was less important in the non-MACOS group of classes than whether, for whatever
reason, the class was perceived as having a good climate. The lack of
salience of the particular process characteristics perceived by students
in relation to classroom climate in the non-MACOS group, as compared to the MACOS group, may be in part a consequence of the
greater diversity of curricula in the former. Nevertheless, the general
predictive pattern of more affluent, higher-achieving classes is still
discernible in both groups.

Analysis of relationships for the two groups combined between process and climate variables, on the one hand, and outcome variables,
on the other, suggested that good classroom climate, as well as emphasis by the teacher and the curriculum on group activities, on affective
goals, and on higher-order cognitive skills, were related both to
achievement and attitude at posttest. Of those predictors, *classroom
climate was by far the most salient* (that is, *that* principal component
had the highest correlation with the predictor canonical variate).
Good classroom climate, lack of emphasis on grades, discussions,
evaluation of ideas, and interpretation of the meaning of what was
studied were process characteristics that appeared related to Follow-
up 1 outcomes, particularly to the finding that the follow-up social
studies class was less interesting. Follow-up 2 relationships were
markedly different for the MACOS and non-MACOS groups. For the
MACOS group, if students saw the class as informal, nongrade oriented, not stressing memory or saying things in one's own words, or insis-
tent upon always stating good reasons, *and* if there was any indication
by the teacher of emphasis on remembering, understanding, and individual work and projects, there tended to be a better Follow-up 2 performance on the MACOS-specific test, AP 1-4F. Other Follow-up 2
outcomes were not particularly related to the criterion variate. In the
non-MACOS group, the conspicuous pattern was that emphasis by the
teacher on remembering, comprehension, and individual work, plus
poor classroom climate was associated with negative class average responses on most Follow-up 2 attitude variables. In effect, a similar
pattern of emphasis, based on teachers' ratings, could have different
relationships to students' perceptions of emphases and to outcomes for
MACOS classes, on the average, and for non-MACOS classes. One

implication is that the MACOS curriculum tends to give more leeway to teachers to believe they could stress knowledge and understanding without having students tend to perceive the class as a traditional, work-oriented one.

Correlates of Classroom Climate

Analyses of variables related to classroom climate indicated generally that climate was positively related to teacher attitudinal characteristics and to how students perceived emphases and activities in their classes. Classroom climate in general was not related to pretest *achievement* of students; there *was*, however, a relationship with pretest *attitude*. The more a class perceived itself as interested in problem solving and as creative at pretest, the better the perceived climate. The lower the teachers scored on traditional educational views and on approval of controlling behavior, the better the classroom climate. The less the class was perceived as traditional (emphasis on grades, right answers, facts, individual work, and so forth), the better the climate.

Implementation of MACOS

A word should be said about the implementation of MACOS in the classes in this study. The total percentage of MACOS lessons actually taught by posttest ranged from 16 to 100 percent. From class to class, the curriculum varied in what was emphasized, in how it was supplemented, in the total amount of time spent, and in the amount of time spent on individual lessons or units. Teachers would skip or omit lessons, but they seldom rearranged the sequence from the original sequence (omissions are not included here as rearrangements). The most basic point is that the curriculum, as implemented in this study, was hardly a homogeneous, prescriptive program.

Analysis showed that the percentage of lesson time spent on "Man and Other Animals" was *not* a significant predictor of class performance on the related MACOS subtest (AP 1-4) at posttest, or in Follow-up 2. Pretest and age of student were significant predictors. Sixth-grade classes tended to do better than fifth-grade classes. The "Percentage of Netsilik Eskimo lessons taught" *was* a significant predictor of posttest performance on the related MACOS subtest (AP 5-8). In this case pretest was not a significant predictor; nor was the age of the class.

A canonical correlation analysis was made of the relationship in the

MACOS group of classes between amount of implementation of MACOS and posttest measures considered as a set. The main pattern that emerged was that increased implementation of MACOS was associated with more positive performance on posttest *attitude* measures than on posttest measures of *achievement*. Particularly, this result applied to opinions about unusual customs or beliefs and about people having them (WWA and WWB), preference for social studies (SS Ch), and interest in problem solving (CAPS-2). In effect, it appeared that, when attitude and achievement outcome measures were considered *in conjunction,* it was the attitude outcomes that were more closely associated with amount of implementation of the course. It is possible, of course, that similar relationships would obtain for any other particular curriculum.

Some of the major findings of a comparative, longitudinal study have been discussed. Many findings, particularly those obtained from interviews with students and teachers, have been omitted, although interviews helped to provide concrete detail about classes, as well as to shed light on a number of factors difficult to assess with paper-and-pencil instruments. The data as they have been presented here, as well as other available information, will be used in discussing policy implications.

Many students enjoy MACOS for a variety of reasons. That is a general statement that must be immediately qualified. Some do not. Some classes as a whole do not. Some teachers in our study dropped MACOS when classes clearly were not interested. MACOS appears to have a little more impact on attitudes toward other people and customs (in the abstract) than the conglomerate of other programs. But the impact may be short-lived. One may expect, on the average, that, after taking MACOS, students are likely to find the next year's social studies course a little less interesting. Teachers who make a conscious decision to try MACOS are apt to be stimulated by it, at least for a few years and as long as they find students interested.

Factual information is absorbed by many students in MACOS, as in other courses. We found no evidence that classes taking MACOS developed greater inquiry skills than non-MACOS classes. MACOS students learn particular concepts, but, as was found in the student interviews, they did not appear more astute, perceptive, understanding, or incisive than non-MACOS classes on the whole. They did appear, generally, to be more interested, at least for the moment. There is also no question but that MACOS classes, midway through the year, had a better classroom climate, as measured by students' aggregate perceptions — again, on the average.

MACOS seems particularly suitable for more progressive, experimental teachers, although that has little to do with the teacher's age or experience. It is more effective with older students (for example, sixth graders compared to fifth graders), which, in the context of this study, means simply that older students learned more and liked it better. MACOS seemed, on the average, less sensitive to teacher characteristics and to apparent variations in classroom processes than did the collection of non-MACOS classes. The implication is that if one wants a curriculum that will accommodate a broad range of teacher and pupil characteristics, MACOS is worth considering.

NOTES

1. N. E. Wallen and Robert M. W. Travers, "Analysis and Investigation of Teaching Methods," in *Handbook of Research on Teaching,* ed. N. L. Gage (Chicago: Rand McNally, 1963), 466.

2. Decker F. Walker and Jon Schaffarzick, "Comparing Curricula," *Review of Educational Research* 44 (1974): 83-111.

3. James J. Gallagher, "Teacher Variation in Concept Presentation in BSCS Programs," *BSCS Newsletter,* No. 30 (1967): 8-19.

4. Barak Rosenshine, "Evaluation of Classroom Instruction," *Review of Educational Research* 40 (1970): 279-300; Barak Rosenshine and Norma Furst, "The Use of Direct Observation to Study Teaching," in *Second Handbook of Research on Teaching,* ed. Robert M. W. Travers (Chicago: Rand McNally, 1973), 122-183.

5. Gary Anderson and Herbert J. Walberg, "Learning Environments," in *Evaluating Educational Performance: A Sourcebook of Methods, Instruments, and Examples,* ed. Herbert J. Walberg (Berkeley, Calif.: McCutchan Publishing Corp., 1974), 81-98; H. Dean Nielsen and Diana H. Kirk, "Classroom Climates," in *Evaluating Educational Performance,* ed. Walberg, 57-80; Bikkar S. Randhawa and Lewis L. W. Fu, "Assessment and Effect of Some Classroom Environment Variables," *Review of Educational Research* 43 (1973): 303-321; Herbert J. Walberg, "Psychology of Learning Environments: Behavorial, Structural, or Perceptual?" in *Review of Research in Education,* ed. Lee S. Shulman *et al.* (Itasca, Ill.: Peacock, 1977), 142-178.

6. Curriculum Development Associates, *Man: A Course of Study* (Washington, D.C.: Curriculum Development Associates, 1972).

7. For more on the history of the social studies, see Robert D. Barr, James L. Barth, and S. Samuel Shermis, *Defining the Social Studies,* Bulletin No. 51 (Washington D.C.: National Council for the Social Studies, 1977).

8. Jerome S. Bruner, *The Process of Education* (New York: Vintage Books, 1960).

9. R. A. Bumstead, *"Man: A Course of Study," Educate* 3 (1970): 20-29; Peter B. Dow, *"MACOS:* The Study of Human Behavior as One Road to Survival," *Phi Delta Kappan* 57 (1975): 79-81; *Conflicting Conceptions of Curriculum,* ed. Elliot W. Eisner and Elizabeth Vallance (Berkeley, Calif.: McCutchan Publishing Corp., 1974); George Weber, "The Case against *Man: A Course of Study," Phi Delta Kappan* 57 (1975): 81-82.

10. Curriculum Development Associates, *Man: A Course of Study.*

11. J. P. Hanley *et al., Curiosity/Competence/Community: An Evaluation of "Man: A Course of Study,"* 2 vols. (Cambridge, Mass.: Education Development Center, 1970).

12. *Mirrors for Behavior II: An Anthology of Observation Instruments,* ed. A. Simon and G. E. Boyer (Philadelphia: Classroom Interaction Newsletter in Cooperation with Research for Better Schools, Inc.; 1970), Vol. A.

13. Hanley *et al., Curiosity/Competence/Community.*

14. Education Development Center, *"Man: A Course of Study" Evaluation Strategies* (Cambridge, Mass.: Education Development Center, 1970).

15. N. E. Wallen *et al., The Taba Curriculum Development Project in Social Studies: Development of a Comprehensive Curriculum Model for Social Studies for Grades One through Eight Inclusive of Procedures for Implementation and Dissemination* (San Francisco: San Francisco State College, 1969).

16. W. L. Herman, Jr., *et al.,* "The Relationship of Teacher-centered Activities and Pupil-centered Activities to Pupil Achievement and Interest in Eighteen Fifth-grade Social Studies Classes," *American Educational Research Journal* 6 (1969): 227-239.

17. Joe M. Steele, *Dimensions of the Classroom Activities Questionnaire* (Urbana, Ill.: University of Illinois, 1969).

18. Gary J. Anderson, *The Assessment of Learning Environments: A Manual for the Learning Environment Inventory and the My Class Inventory* (Halifax, Nova Scotia: Atlantic Institute of Education, 1971).

19. Hanley *et al., Curiosity/Competence/Community.*

20. Fred N. Kerlinger and Elezar J. Pedhazur, *Attitudes and Perceptions of Desirable Traits and Behaviors of Teachers,* Final Report, Project No. 5-0330 (New York: New York University, 1967).

21. Elezar J. Pedhazur, "Pseudoprogressivism and Assessment of Teacher Behavior," *Educational and Psychological Measurement* 29 (1969): 377-386.

22. For the analysis using only student input principal components as dependent variables (Ach, Att 1, Att 2, Class 1, Class 2), $F(5, 96) = .631, p < .68$. For the analysis that also included the teacher input principal components (T Demo, T Psy 1, T Psy 2), $F(8, 79) = .287, p < .98$.

23. For the test using just student principal components as covariates, $F(20, 68) = 3.681, p < .001$. For the test using all student and teacher principal components, $F(20, 47) = 3.215, p < 001$.

13. Evaluation of Innovations

Gary J. Coles and *Albert B. Chalupsky*

During the late 1960s and early 1970s hopes were high that intensive, innovative educational programs would exert a dramatic impact on student achievement. Although these hopes have moderated in recent years, many individuals, government officials as well as the general public, still believe that, if schools undergo major change, they will automatically be much more effective. Thus, many efforts continue to be sponsored at the federal and state levels to encourage such change, either through the development of new programs or through increased emphasis on the dissemination or diffusion of innovations by educational "change agents."

The wholesale development, diffusion, and implementation of innovations is an expensive process, and, to date, there has been no comprehensive evidence as to whether or not such added expenditures are justified by improved school effectiveness. The large-scale support of innovation as a national education policy has, therefore, remained an unresolved issue.

PROJECT LONGSTEP

What is the effect of intensive innovation on student performance?

The research upon which this chapter is based was performed under a contract with the Office of Education, U.S. Department of Health, Education, and Welfare (Contract Number OEC-0-70-4789). Points of view are those of the authors and do not, therefore, necessarily represent official Office of Education position or policy.

Is it reasonable to expect that students will achieve more in programs with greater emphasis on innovation than in programs with a lesser emphasis on innovation?

Educators and noneducators alike have shown a growing awareness of both the lack of, and the need for, convincing evidence to demonstrate whether innovative educational practices are indeed better than what are termed more traditional approaches. To investigate such issues, the U.S. Office of Education awarded a contract to the American Institutes for Research (AIR) to develop a design for a study of the overall effectiveness of highly intensive, innovative educational practices on students in grades one through twelve. Emphasis of this study, the Longitudinal Study of Educational Practices (Project LONGSTEP), was on the identification of changes in student achievement that occurred as a result of intensive educational innovation. In the context of the study, an "intensive innovation" was operationally defined as the implementation of a new program encompassing a significant proportion of students, entailing a major alteration of school procedures, and involving a high investment of resources. In short, the study was designed to determine whether investment in intensive educational innovation did, in fact, return a "big bang for big bucks."[1]

The initial design was developed, implemented on a limited basis, and modified during the 1969-70 school year. Full implementation began during the 1970-71 school year and continued through the 1971-72 and 1972-73 school years.

The two major objectives of Project LONGSTEP were, first, to determine as comprehensively as possible over a three-year period of time the impact of intensive innovation upon student performance on standardized achievement tests and on measures of educationally relevant attitudes and, second, to attempt to identify the dimensions of educational components (present in a select sample of highly intensive, innovative programs) that exhibited the greatest impact on student outcomes.

Sample Selection and Description

Through a combination of extensive literature search, interviews with program staff, outside consultant review, and site visiting, schools located in thirteen school districts were selected to participate in the study. No attempt was made to select a representative or random sample of schools in the United States. Rather, the rationale for site selection was that, if innovation in general does have an impact on student performance, then its effects should be most pronounced in schools that are highly innovative. Thus, guidelines for selection emphasized the scope and intensity of the program, instructional content, anticipated continuation of the program, and willingness to cooperate in a multiyear study. Schools and districts were located in nine states widely dispersed throughout the country. Altogether, some 30,000 students, 80 schools, and 1,500 teachers participated in the study over a three-year period.

The thirteen districts voluntarily participating in Project LONG-STEP differed with respect to a number of important school and community characteristics noted during the 1970-71 school year. The communities served by the school districts ranged from 2,500 to over 600,000 in population and varied from rural to urban-metropolitan in setting. Diversity in socioeconomic level was notable, as evidenced by the percentage of students in the participating schools receiving free or reduced-price lunches. This number ranged from less than 1 percent to nearly 30 percent. The reported instructional cost per pupil in the participating school districts, as of the 1970-71 period, varied from a low of $540 to a high of $1,050. The percentage of minority students in the participating schools ranged from less than 1 percent to over 30 percent—another indication of the diversity in the sample.

The educational innovations encompassed by Project LONGSTEP were those that were of particular concern during the late 1960s and early 1970s, and most are still of concern. They included team teaching, multimedia emphasis, unique school design, use of paraprofessionals, variations in scheduling, and use of teacher-developed materials, as well as independent study, student selection of materials, and other practices typically associated with individualized instruction. An overview of the major educational features present in the sample at the time programs were selected, as well as the distribution of such features across districts, is presented in Figure 13-1.

Caution should be exercised in drawing conclusions from this figure since the educational activities listed in the figure were often given their designations by the school districts themselves. Thus the same label may apply to significantly different activities from one school district to another. By the same token, different labels were often applied to very similar activities. For this reason, these labels did not necessarily reflect the underlying educational processes that were the primary concern of this study. Nevertheless, Figure 13-1 does provide a gross indication of the wide variation that existed in the sample of schools present in Project LONGSTEP.

Major educational features	School districts												
	1	2	3	4	5	6	7	8	9	10	11	12	13
Small-group activities	x	x	x	x				x	x	x		x	x
Team teaching	x	x	x	x	x	x	x	x	x				
Multimedia emphasis	x	x	x	x	x	x	x	x	x	x		x	
Ungraded curriculum		x	x	x	x		x	x	x				
Large-group instruction		x	x					x	x	x	x	x	x
Independent study	x	x	x	x	x			x		x		x	x
Unique school design		x	x				x	x					
Differentiated staffing	x	x				x							
Volunteer aides	x	x	x	x	x	x	x	x	x	x			
IPI reading-mathematics		x			x	x			x				
Project PLAN							x		x				
Individualized instruction (other than PLAN or IPI)	x	x		x		x	x	x	x			x	x
Student selection of materials	x	x	x			x		x	x	x			
Modular scheduling	x	x	x	x				x					
Teacher sensitivity training						x							
Intensive guidance and counseling						x							
Home visitation						x							
Traditional-conventional classrooms	x		x	x	x	x	x	x	x	x	x	x	x
Teacher-developed curriculum materials	x	x	x	x		x		x	x	x	x	x	x

Figure 13-1

Overview of major educational features occurring in one or more schools of the districts participating in Project LONGSTEP

Data Collection Instruments and Schedule

The data collection instruments used by Project LONGSTEP provided information on the cognitive performance and characteristics of participating students, on their educational experiences, and on the characteristics of their teachers. Cognitive performance was measured by the *Comprehensive Tests of Basic Skills* (CTBS),[2] Forms Q and R, in grades two through twelve, and the *California Short Form Test of Mental Maturity* (CTMM) for testing in grade one. Background characteristics and attitudes of students and teachers were assessed by means of specially developed questionnaires. Test and questionnaire data were collected during the spring of the 1970-71, 1971-72, and 1972-73 school years.

In order to investigate relationships between educational practices and educational outcomes in a diverse group of schools and programs, a system was needed for describing and quantifying the educational experiences that each student had during a school year. It soon became evident that, although there are a limited number of labels used by school districts to describe educational activities, there are significant differences in practice among educational approaches sharing the same descriptive label. For example, "modular scheduling" is a commonly used term for what are in fact various configurations of class schedules. At the same time, programs bearing different labels often turn out to be very much alike. For example, in one district a program of "individualized instruction" could be much the same as a "nongraded" program in another district. So that meaningful similarities and differences in educational environments could be systematically detected and documented, an Educational Experience Analysis Guide was developed. This guide was designed so that complex educational experiences could be described and quantified with respect to specific observable characteristics (rather than on the basis of variously defined local labels). Each school year, trained AIR staff used this instrument to document the basic educational attributes of the school programs in which participating students were enrolled. Information on educational experiences was gathered from interviews with principals and teachers, from classroom observations, and from existing school documentation.

Use of the guide by AIR staff ensured that all students in a school who were receiving essentially the same basic educational experiences would be identified as belonging to the same "educational experience group" and be distinguished from students receiving different educational experiences, even though both groups of students may have participated in the same school "program." The guide also made it possible to locate the educational experiences of participating students on a number of continuums ranging from traditional to innovative. An illustration of the diversity of the schools participating in Project LONGSTEP and of the kinds of indexes derived from the guide is shown in Figure 13-2. Based upon data aggregated to the district level, this figure shows the differences that existed between two school districts containing third-grade students during the 1972-73 school year with respect to average student socioeconomic status, the number of minutes per day usually spent on language arts activities, and ten indexes from the Educational Experience Analysis Guide.

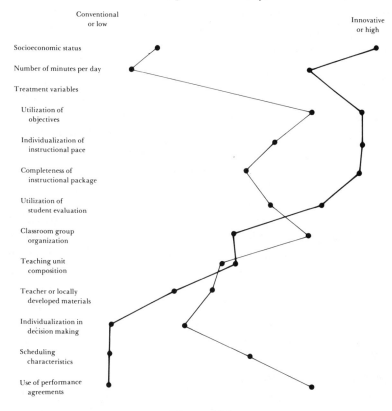

Figure 13-2

Profiles for language arts treatments for two of the five sites
containing third-grade students during the 1972-73 school year

Analysis Methodology

In order to determine whether program emphasis on intensive innovation was related to substantial gains in achievement in Project LONGSTEP's sample of schools, the study hypothesized that, if innovative emphasis did have a dramatic impact on achievement, then the average achievement gains demonstrated by Project LONGSTEP's generally innovative sample of schools should noticeably exceed the gains expected on the basis of national norms, and variation among schools with respect to innovative emphasis, even within LONGSTEP's sample of primarily innovative schools, should be consistently and positively correlated with student achievement.

An integral aspect of this particular analytic approach was the belief that the impact of innovative emphasis was general (that is, an effect that would be present in different classrooms, schools, school districts, and grade levels) and would be consistently present in consecutive school years. Such general hypotheses may seem simplistic to educational researchers who are familiar with the mishmash of findings concerning specific innovative practices gained from numerous studies conducted over the last few years and with the inability of most large-scale evaluations to show meaningful overall impact of programs because of large, within-program variations in the effectiveness of schools and teachers. However, the belief that educational innovation is automatically good and is the panacea for our nation's educational problems still prevails in this country.

Because Project LONGSTEP collected data from students in ongoing school programs, we believed it was essential that the key hypotheses of the study be evaluated from a number of slightly different methodological perspectives in order to minimize the possibility that findings would be highly dependent upon one particular method or upon a single set of assumptions. Conclusions could then be based on converging lines of evidence. For this reason, the analyses were, by design, as intensive as possible within the constraints of time and cost.

Results obtained by means of a given procedure were organized in such a way as to enable us to examine and compare the performance of approximately the same group of students across school years and grade levels and the performance of different student groups at the same grade levels but during different school years. Lastly, we examined the findings to see if there were common trends shown by different analytic methods.

The major school attribute examined in most analyses was a composite measure of emphasis on innovation. This index, called level of innovation, was equal to the sum of ten scales derived from the Educational Experience Analysis Guide. The ten indexes shown in Figure 13-2 were the scales used to define level of innovation. Degree of individualization in the school program, another of the key independent variables, was a component of this level of innovation index and was equal to the sum of four of the ten scales — individualization in decision making, individualization of instructional pace, use of performance agreements, and utilization of student evaluation. A general measure of the experience and training of each student's teacher or teachers, an index called teaching qualifications, was also included in most analyses.

Separate analyses were conducted for reading and for arithmetic for each of the different grades of students present in the study (that is, students who were in grades one through twelve). The measure of the level of innovation and that of teaching qualifications used in each analysis pertained to either language arts or arithmetic, depending upon whether achievement in reading or achievement in arithmetic was being analyzed.[3] Analyses were based upon an examination of growth in achievement between spring 1971 (Year 1) and spring 1972 (Year 2), and between spring 1972 (Year 2) and spring 1973 (Year 3). Analyses of the data for the early elementary grades and high school grades were usually based on from 500 to 900 students per grade. Between 1,200 and 2,000 students per grade were involved in the analyses of students in the upper elementary grades and junior high school grades.

Findings in Review

Reading Achievement. Results of the reading achievement analyses showed that the average reading posttest performance at each grade level was fairly similar, even when different groups of students were involved during different school years. For example, the mean posttest CTBS Expanded Standard Score in reading was 507 for students in the sixth grade during 1972-73, and 505 for students who were in the sixth grade during 1971-72. As shown in Figure 13-3, with the possible exception of growth during the third grade (that is, between grades 2.7 and 3.7) and during the eighth grade, average posttest scores for the Project LONGSTEP analysis samples were not farther from na-

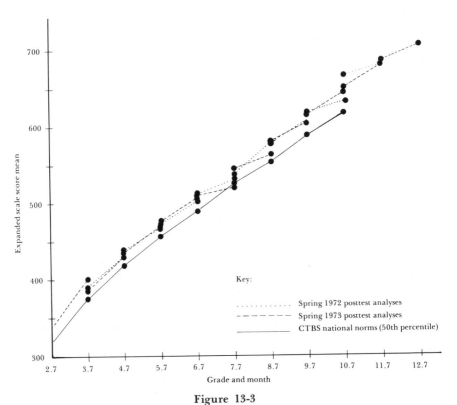

Figure 13-3

Pretest and posttest means and published national norms
(50th percentile for spring testing): **Analyses of total reading scores**

tional norms than the average pretest scores had been. Although average pretest and posttest reading achievement for almost all analysis samples were above national norms, it is obvious that the average gains shown by the set of fairly innovative schools participating in Project LONGSTEP did not notably exceed the growth expected on the basis of CTBS norms.

Although conspicuous growth in achievement was not generally present in Project LONGSTEP's sample, it did seem possible that, in these analyses of changes in average reading scores (shown in Figure 13-3), the poor performance of students who were members of schools with a lesser emphasis on innovation may have offset the unusually good performance of students who were members of more innovative schools. To determine if growth in reading achievement at a given grade level was related to the emphasis on innovation to which students were exposed, we analyzed an educational growth model in which student achievement was related to innovative emphasis in language arts, number of minutes per day (spent on class activities in language arts), student pretest level, student socioeconomic background, and teaching qualifications of students' language arts teachers. Examination of the results showed that there was no consistent relationship between growth in reading achievement and level of innovation, number of minutes per day, and teaching qualifications that held true for a majority of the grades analyzed.

Next, we considered the possibility that program-level emphasis on innovation may not have been substantially related to achievement for the majority of students in a particular school and grade but may have been extremely important for some students. To detect such associations, those students who, for two consecutive school years, achieved much more than was expected on the basis of their particular pretest scores and socioeconomic background were identified. A comparison group was formed from those students who showed notable lack of growth during two consecutive school years. Subsequent analyses showed that underachievement or overachievement was not highly or consistently related to either level of innovation, number of minutes per day, or teaching qualifications across all analyses. These analyses, however, also yielded the following additional but tentative findings:

— Relative to underachieving students, overachieving students who were in elementary and junior high school in Year 1 tended to be members of programs that had a lower level of innovation (on the average) during Year 2 and again during Year 3.
— Overachievers who were in grades one through five during Year 1 were usually exposed to more language arts activities than were underachievers during Year 2 but for less time (relative to underachievers) in Year 3.
— In a number of the analyses, overachievers were exposed to language arts teachers (either during Year 2 or Year 3), who, on the average, had a higher teacher qualification score than did teachers of the underachievers.

Arithmetic Achievement. Average posttest performance in arithmetic was usually fairly similar for different groups of students at the same grade level. With the possible exception of the growth demonstrated during the third grade (that is, between grades 2.7 and 3.7),

however, average posttest CTBS Expanded Standard Scores in arithmetic were not conspicuously farther from national norms than their
average pretest scores. Since one of the major criteria for selection to
participate in Project LONGSTEP was departure from "traditional"
classroom practices, these overall results do not support the hypothesis
that greater program emphasis on innovation is positively related to
notable gains in arithmetic achievement.

As in the analyses of reading achievement, we thought that these
overall analyses of average gains in arithmetic achievement might
have hidden the fact that the most innovative schools within each
grade were having great positive impact and that the overall results
were being diluted by less innovative schools having little impact. Further analyses (that is, analyses of our educational growth model)
showed that emphasis on innovation in arithmetic programs was not
highly related to growth in arithmetic achievement. In fact, the majority of the small associations between achievement and innovative
emphasis in arithmetic were negative. The average number of minutes
per day of arithmetic instruction was fairly constant across all grades.
Within a number of early elementary school and high school grade
levels, however, there was a small but positive association between
achievement growth and number of minutes per day of arithmetic instruction. Lastly, there was a trend in these analyses toward small but
positive associations between growth in arithmetic achievement and
the level of teaching qualifications of students' arithmetic teachers.

We then identified those students who, for two consecutive school
years, had demonstrated unusually large gains in arithmetic achievement (in relation to their particular pretest scores and socioeconomic
background). Students who had shown a notable lack of growth in
arithmetic achievement were also identified. Analyses of these two
groups of students suggested the following tentative conclusions:
—Relative to underachievers, overachievers in arithmetic who were in
  elementary and junior high schools during Year 1 tended to be
  members of programs during Year 3 that, on the average, had a
  slightly lower emphasis on innovation.
—Overachievers in the early elementary and late high school grades
  tended to be exposed to somewhat more instruction in arithmetic
  than underachievers.
—Arithmetic teachers of overachievers had, on the average, higher
  teaching qualifications than arithmetic teachers of underachievers.

The Impact of Schools on Educational Achievement. Even though overall findings showed that dramatic school effects were not associated with intensity of educational innovation, different educational approaches did produce meaningful and important differences in student achievement, especially in the early elementary grades. Unusually large gains in reading, language arts, and arithmetic skills, over and above those expected on the basis of pretest and socioeconomic background, were found in a number of the participating schools. For example, the sixth-grade students in the most effective reading treatment groups had average pretest scores ranging between the 48th and 69th percentiles. At posttest, one year later, their average reading scores ranged between the 63rd and 79th percentiles. Such findings certainly are not surprising to teachers, principals, or parents. They do tend, however, to counter the overly pessimistic conclusions concerning school effects that have been drawn from a number of large-scale educational evaluation studies.

PROJECT LONGSTEP AND NATIONAL EDUCATION POLICY

Because of the current controversy between proponents of traditional educational approaches and proponents of innovative educational practices, Project LONGSTEP has been of great interest to the public, to educators and researchers, and to the news media. For example, the American Institutes for Research and the U.S. Office of Education received almost six thousand requests for Project LONGSTEP final reports during the nine-month period following release of the findings. The findings of the study have also been sensationalized by the media and have been mistakenly interpreted by some as a sweeping criticism of all innovative practices. We believe this particular generalization is unwarranted. However, the findings of Project LONGSTEP and our experiences during the course of the study do indeed have implications for educational policy at both the national and local levels—implications discussed here in the context of four major questions.

Does educational innovation have a dramatic impact on achievement? The most important and well-documented finding of Project LONGSTEP was the lack of either substantial or consistent association between growth in achievement (as measured by standardized achievement tests) and the amount of emphasis the school placed on innovation in either language arts or mathematics programs. In fact, some of the evidence suggested that students who were enrolled in programs where emphasis on innovation was more moderate showed greater improvement in test scores. Further, our analyses showed that, on the average, the findings applied equally well to students at different socioeconomic levels and at different pretest levels. The expectation that there would be substantial average yearly gains in student achievement where school programs were intensive and innovative was not supported by Project LONGSTEP.

The findings imply that educational quality is not synonymous with innovation, and that innovation should not be viewed as the final or complete answer. Rather, Project LONGSTEP data support the more realistic expectation that some changes will be improvements, some changes will be detrimental, and some changes will not matter at all. In short, the findings of Project LONGSTEP suggest that *more* innovation is not necessarily *better* education.

Why did more individualization of instruction not result in better test performance? In retrospect we were somewhat surprised that one particular aspect of much recent innovation, that is, increased individualization of education, was not shown to be clearly and consistently effective in Project LONGSTEP. We would like to discuss some possible explanations for this finding, even though such explanations must be purely speculative. One possibility is that not all modes of "individualization" operate effectively; another is that our index, degree of individualization, may have failed to identify some crucial differences between individualized programs that are effective and those that are not.

The amount of independence and decision making left to the student could also be crucial. Tailoring the educational process or teaching strategy to an individual student's needs or learning style may be very effective, but allowing the student a great deal of independence in selecting the topics to be studied, in deciding the amount of time to be spent on a particular topic, and in establishing the level or standard of attainment during a school year could have a negative impact on performance (as measured by standardized achievement tests) for all but the highly motivated student. Anecdotal experiences gained over years of association with schools participating in Project LONGSTEP suggest that some students tend to lose momentum unless the teacher provides the kind of individual attention that is unlikely except when a sufficient number of qualified assistants are available.

The problem of student motivation was discussed by Lipson in his explanation of the possible reasons why the Individually Prescribed Instruction (IPI) mathematics modules did not produce the dramatic gains that had been expected.[4] His comments have considerable application to a number of other individualized programs. According to Lipson, each student working alone on an instructional module can lessen motivation. In a conventional classroom, however, participation in the group provides competition and lends a feeling of importance to the activities, factors that often motivate students. "The student's relationship to the other members of the class and to the teacher creates a sense of obligation for some level of performance. The rhythm of the class, the rituals of class activity—even when we grumble—give our lives a pattern to follow. The progress of the class is like a tide that carries all the swimmers along even though some are slower and some are faster."[5] In concluding, Lipson expresses the hope that new systems will be developed that "build upon the combined strengths of the classroom approach and the modularized and individualized approaches."[6]

The fact that our degree of individualization index failed to discriminate between successful and unsuccessful educational approaches also suggests the possibility that we overlooked some elements of individualization that occur in conventional classrooms. It could be that individualization is one of the practices that distinguishes good teachers from poor ones, even in traditional educational environments where there is no "experimental" or "innovative" program claiming to be individualized. Perhaps good teachers individualize informally and so naturally that they are not even aware of it in these terms. The good teacher does not treat all children as interchangeable cogs, but, rather, as the individuals they are. This kind of informal individualization, while it would not be noted as a feature of an educational program in Project LONGSTEP, might nevertheless be quite effective.

These speculations, if correct, would extend to the elementary school level the interpretation of some loosely comparable findings at the high school level, based on Project TALENT data. Analyzing Project TALENT retest data, Shaycoft found evidence, as did Project LONGSTEP, that schools differ in effectiveness.[7] She also failed to find that these differences were meaningfully related to available variables in any way that might have been expected.

On the other hand, it is also possible that large, overall educational effects were not demonstrated in Project LONGSTEP (nor in many educational evaluation efforts) because such effects have been attenuated by inappropriate matches between educational approaches and student needs. The undoubtedly dramatic growth in achievement demonstrated during two consecutive school years by a number of students participating in Project LONGSTEP certainly suggests that some near optimal match of student and educational approach may have been one of the reasons for the gains of these students.

Nevertheless, the findings of Project LONGSTEP suggest that educational quality is not synonymous with either innovation or individualization. Individualization of instruction may represent a valuable approach for the improvement of American education, but, as a program strategy, it should not be viewed as a guarantee of improved school effectiveness.

Should education return to the traditional three Rs approach? Our research does not imply that schools should stop experimenting with new school practices or that they should indiscriminately discontinue "innovative" practices and replace them with more "basic" approaches to instruction. It would appear that selected innovative strategies as well as traditional strategies are both valuable. In designing the kinds of educational programs to be implemented in a given community, all important factors in the educational process—the characteristics of students, parents, and teachers, and the available resources—should be considered. We suggest that educators identify and select those strategies that are most appropriate for the educational goals of their communities, recognizing that every change will not necessarily be a change for the better. To ensure that valuable approaches are retained and ineffective strategies are discontinued, educators should be encouraged to gather evidence as to which aspects of their programs are most effective for their students.

What does the experience of Project LONGSTEP suggest for improving educational policy at the national level? Again we would like to emphasize that Project LONGSTEP should not be viewed as providing evidence for the ineffectiveness of all innovative school practices. Neither does it support the value of all traditional approaches. Our experiences, and those of other researchers as well, suggest that there are no automatic guarantees of success in education, no matter what educational program strategies are adopted, whether they be innovative, traditional, or some mixture of new and old educational practices.

We are concerned that education projects will be funded merely because the methods to be used are new or innovative. There is a danger in being preoccupied with the uniqueness or originality of a technique rather than with its effectiveness in solving a significant educational problem. Educational innovation, like the more traditional approaches, should be considered a means to an end and not an end in itself.

That is why we believe financial support should continue to be provided for experimental projects only when there is strong reason to believe that the proposed approach — whether it be totally new, a mixture of new and traditional practices, or an adaptation of traditional approaches — is appropriate for the students, teachers, and parents involved and is likely to achieve an important educational goal.

To ensure that valuable approaches are retained and that ineffective approaches are dropped or modified appropriately, we recommend that all federally funded education projects be rigorously evaluated from the time they start, that sufficient resources be provided to accomplish this goal, and that findings regarding the implementation process and the impact on students be taken into account when making decisions concerning the continued support of these educational approaches.

NOTES

1. Project LONGSTEP reports, all published in Palo Alto, California, by the American Institutes for Research, are available from the ERIC Document Reproduction Service, P.O. Box 190, Arlington, Virginia 22210. The authors and titles of the reports are as follows: Albert B. Chalupsky and Gary J. Coles, *Exploring the Impact of Educational Innovation: Overview of Project LONGSTEP,* October 1976 (ED 132 191); *id., Parental Educational Expectations and Their Impact on Student Outcomes,* Project LONGSTEP Memorandum Report, September 1976 (ED 132 181); Gary J. Coles and Albert B. Chalupsky, *Innovative School Environments and Student Outcomes,* Project LONGSTEP Final Report, Volume II, September 1976 (ED 132 179); *id., Impact of Educational Innovation on Student Performance: Overall Findings for Reading and Arithmetic,* Project LONGSTEP Final Report, Volume I, Supplement, September 1976 (ED 132 193); Gary J. Coles *et al., Impact of Educational Innovation on Student Performance: Project Methods and Findings for Three Cohorts,* Project LONGSTEP Final Report, Volume I, April 1976 (ED 132 177); B.E. Everett, *A Preliminary Study of the Relevance of a Standardized Test for Measuring*

Achievement Gains in Innovative Arithmetic Programs, Project LONGSTEP Final Report, Volume II, Appendix Report, September 1976 (ED 132 180); American Institutes for Research, *Impact of Educational Innovation on Student Performance: Project Methods and Findings for Three Cohorts,* Project LONGSTEP Final Report, Volume I, Executive Summary, April 1976 (ED 132 176).

2. A small substudy was conducted to investigate the extent to which the stated curriculum objectives of the arithmetic programs included in Project LONGSTEP were similar to those underlying the items on the arithmetic subtests of the CTBS. Results showed that arithmetic skills areas tapped by the CTBS were present in the arithmetic programs sampled.

3. Attitude measures were collected and analyzed, but are not reported here. In brief, we were unable to demonstrate any meaningful relationships between attitudes toward school and emphasis on innovation in the school program.

4. J.I. Lipson, "IPI Math: An Example of What's Right and Wrong with Individualized Modular Programs," *Learning* 2 (1974): 60-61.

5. *Ibid.,* 60.

6. *Ibid.*

7. M.F. Shaycoft, *The High School Years: Growth in Cognitive Skills,* Interim Report No. 3 to the U.S. Office of Education, Cooperative Research Project No. 3051 (Pittsburgh: American Institutes for Research and University of Pittsburgh, 1967).

14. Effects of the "Open Classroom"

Robert A. Horwitz

Since the first descriptive reports of the progressive teaching approach in English primary schools appeared in the American press in the mid-1960s, there has been a vast outpouring of literature on what has come to be called "open education," or the "open classroom." Many of the early reports provided rich and vivid descriptions of what was going on in the English schools and stressed how much more humane this approach to teaching seemed to be and how much more sensitive it was to the realities of child development. Other writings analyzed open education in the context of its historical precedents and psychological or philosophical underpinnings and compared the development of the approach in England and in the United States. Still others, with a more practical orientation, provided specific advice on how to implement open education in American schools.

As interest in open education increased, so did demands for systematic evaluation of its effects, to the point where there now exists a fairly sizable body of research on the academic and psychological effects of

This chapter has been submitted in substantially the same form for publication in the *Review of Educational Research.*

open-classroom teaching. In 1975 I reviewed the relevant literature and located over one hundred such studies, which I have summarized in a monograph.[1] While preparing this chapter, I searched the literature again and located nearly one hundred additional studies.

In spite of this outpouring of research, there is still no clear answer to the question of whether the open classroom is significantly more beneficial to students than more traditional approaches. One reason for this is that conflicting findings have emerged for most of the variables that have been assessed. Another reason is that many variables considered important by advocates of open education have not yet been adequately evaluated because they are difficult to measure. Perhaps the most important reason lies in the lingering ambiguity surrounding the definition of "open classroom" — particularly the confusion between "open space" and "open education."

Just what *is* an "open classroom"? Silberman has characterized "openness" as "less an approach or method than a set of shared attitudes and convictions about the nature of childhood, learning, and schooling."[2] Yet some writers who describe "open" classrooms are clearly more concerned with physical space than with attitudes or convictions. To them, the term "open" has primarily an architectural meaning, and "open classrooms" are simply large, open rooms with many children and not many interior walls. What goes on pedagogically in these open spaces may or may not be the same thing as "open education," as Barth, Rathbone, Katz, and others have defined the term.[3] In fact, several studies have shown that the organizational or affective climate in open-space schools is sometimes no more "open" than it is in conventionally built schools. Unfortunately, some of the studies of so-called "open classrooms" have failed to make clear what precisely was open about the classrooms and whether the investigators were measuring effects of building layout, of teacher-student interaction, of both, or of something else.

Although the term "open classroom" has at times been used carelessly and imprecisely, it is important to note that there are a number of observational and questionnaire methods for systematically assessing the degree of "openness" in classrooms. Perhaps the most widely used is the fifty-item scale developed by Walberg and Thomas,[4] which is based in large part on the thoughtful conceptual analysis of open education by Bussis and Chittenden.[5] The Walberg and Thomas instrument has two parallel forms, one for teacher self-rating and one for observer rating, and has been validated on a sample of British and American classrooms. Another popular instrument is the thirty-item *Dimensions of Schooling Questionnaire* (DISC) constructed by Traub and his associates as part of a large-scale evaluation of teaching in open classrooms in Canada.[6] More than twenty other systematic procedures for rating the openness of classrooms have appeared in the literature, in addition to a number of long checklists of characteristics of open classrooms.

With such a plethora of definitions of "openness" and ways of measuring it, it is easy to see why it is impossible to make any unequivocal statement about the effects of teaching in the open classroom. Indeed, some writers have questioned whether the term "open classroom" should even be used any more. Still, the term *is* used, with at least some general understanding within the educational community that it refers to a style of teaching involving flexibility of space, student choice of activity, richness of learning materials, integration of curriculum areas, and more individual or small-group than large-group instruction. Not all of the evaluation studies summarized in this chapter define openness in precisely the same way, and it is certainly not safe to assume that all classrooms described as "open" in these studies are alike. What the classrooms *do* have in common is that they have all been either explicitly labeled "open" or described as having characteristics generally ascribed to "open education."

EARLY RESEARCH

The 1930s and the 1940s

Before summarizing the more recent evaluative studies on open education that have been carried out in the United States, Canada, and Britain, mention should be made of the substantial body of research in the United States undertaken during the "progressive education" era of the 1930s and 1940s. The descriptions of the better of these "progressive" schools make it clear that in many ways they closely resembled the British infant schools that inspired the American "open classroom" approach. Since their appearance in the years following World War I happened to correspond with the burgeoning development of the tests and measurements field, many studies were undertaken to assess quantitatively the impact of progressive schooling on children.

One particularly noteworthy research project evaluating the "activity program" in New York City's public elementary schools was reported in a series of eight articles in the *Journal of Experimental Education* in 1939 and 1941. Activity school children scored slightly lower than the control group in reading and arithmetic achievement tests but surpassed the control group in tests of knowledge of current affairs, progressive social beliefs, personal and social adjustment. In observational studies the activity school group showed more evidence of initiative, experimentation, criticism and appraisal of one another's work, cooperation, and leadership than the control students. The two groups were substantially the same in ratings of classroom conduct and discipline.

Summarizing research studies from across the country, the Progressive Education Association's Informal Committee on Evaluation of Newer Practices in Education reported that, "in general, the evidence shows convincingly that the new methods do not result in a loss of academic proficiency in the usual school subjects and that, where any measures have been applied, there is a definite gain in terms of initiative, skill in dealing with problems, knowledge of contemporary and world affairs, and social participation."[7] Similar general findings were reported in other reviews of research.[8]

The 1950s and the 1960s

By far the most comprehensive single study of the psychological effects of "open" versus "traditional" teaching methods in American schools was a report by Minuchin and her associates at the Bank Street College of Education based on data collected from fourth-grade children in four New York City schools from 1956 to 1958.[9] At that time—after many of the progressive era innovations had disappeared and before the influx of ideas from the British infant schools—it was difficult to find examples of "progressive" or "informal" teaching practice. The Bank Street researchers, who designed their study to assess the impact on nine-year-old children of schools varying on a continuum from very "traditional" to very "modern," had to settle for a rather unusual and expensive private school for their most "modern." The need to do this created serious methodological problems and limited the generalizability of their findings since the three less progressive schools were all ordinary, middle-class public schools. This study remains, however, an important contribution to our understanding of school effects on children, particularly because of its detailed, systematic descriptions of the school environments, its consideration of the influence of parental child-rearing ideologies and practices, and the broad range of cognitive and personality variables that were investigated.

Because of the many dependent measures and the confounding influence of home and parental factors, the findings are complex and difficult to summarize. Generally, there were no significant differences between "modern" and "traditional" schools in group tests of academic achievement or in individual problem-solving tasks, including tests of imaginative thinking. Children from the more "modern" or "open" schools, however, tended to have more "differentiated" self-concepts, that is, they tended to describe themselves in less rigid, more subtle, and more thoughtful ways; they were more invested in their childhood status and less future oriented; they had more open, less conventional or stereotyped conceptions of their social sex roles. In group problem solving, the "open" school children were more cooperative, less competitive, and, in the end, more effective. "Open" school children also had much more positive attitudes toward school.

Although suffering from even more methodological flaws than the Bank Street report, the most important long-term investigation of effects of "open" or "informal" teaching methods to come out of England was the research carried out over some three decades by Gardner at the University of London Institute of Education and summarized in three books.[10] By present standards the Gardner studies seem statistically unsophisticated, but her findings are generally consistent with those of American research: little difference between "informal" and "traditional" schools on measures of academic achievement and numerous advantages for the informal schools on other variables, including some skills and characteristics on which traditional schools are usually believed to place heavier emphasis. In tests administered in the last year of junior school (ages ten to eleven), for example, the informal school children scored significantly higher in descriptive and expressive writing, free drawing and painting, listening and remembering, "neatness, care, and skill," ingenuity and inventiveness, and breadth and depth of out-of-school interests. The informal schools also showed some superiority (although it was apparently not statistically significant) in reading ability, ability to concentrate on an uninteresting task, moral judgment, general information, handwriting, and group cooperation and problem solving. The only area in which the more formal schools showed superiority was arithmetic.

RECENT EVALUATIVE STUDIES

More recent evaluative studies of "open" classrooms have been modest in scope, but great in number. To simplify presentation of their findings, I have grouped studies together according to outcome variables. For each variable, results are tallied in "box-score" form, showing how many studies favored open schools, how many favored traditional schools, how many had mixed results, and how many found no significant differences. While admittedly a rather crude method of summarizing research, the box-score method has the advantage of providing a concise overview of complex data and pointing out general patterns of results across many studies. The disadvantage, of course, is that it is completely nonjudgmental, treating all studies as if they were equal, when, in fact, studies differ considerably in terms of sample size, conceptual design, preciseness of measurement, quality of statistical analysis, and so forth.

What is needed is some "meta-analysis" of the existing studies, perhaps along the lines suggested by Glass.[11] Clearly, some studies are better designed and more valid than others and should, in a sense, "count" more in the overall analysis. Until this enormous and methodologically difficult task of scientifically evaluating the evaluations is completed, however, the box-score approach will have to suffice. Readers interested in details of the studies summarized below can obtain them by writing to me.[12]

Academic Achievement

Of all the variables investigated in evaluations of the open classroom, the one that has received most attention is academic achievement. The overall pattern of findings is quite mixed. Of 102 studies reviewed, 14 favored open schools, 12 favored traditional schools, 29 had mixed results, and 47 revealed no significant differences. While these findings certainly do not show a clear superiority of open or informal methods in the teaching of the basic skills, they do not reveal a clear inferiority either, as might possibly be expected due to the more casual atmosphere and the decreased emphasis on drill. Many writers on open education point out that achievement tests do not adequately measure important aspects of a child's learning and development in school, but whatever other advantages the open classroom may offer to children, the existing research largely suggests that it does not hinder their academic attainment. Unfortunately, the excessive publicity given to a recent study by Bennett that showed superior attainment for children in traditional schools has tended to promote the erroneous impression that open education has been "proved" to be detrimental to achievement.[13] Aside from whatever specific objections can be made on statistical and other grounds to Bennett's study, it is just one of many studies that have addressed the question of academic achievement in the open classroom, and its findings are by no means representative of the prevailing pattern of results.

Self-Concept

Another widely studied variable in evaluations of open education is self-concept. While this is an area of research in child development fraught with serious methodological problems,[14] many investigators have nonetheless endeavored to make use of the various self-concept measures available to test the hypothesis that children in open classrooms feel better about themselves (or at least indicate to adult testers that they feel better about themselves).

The results, once again, are quite mixed. Of 61 studies reviewed, 15 favored open schools, 2 favored traditional schools, 15 showed mixed results, and 29 revealed no significant differences. To what extent this rather inconclusive pattern of results is indicative of measurement problems and to what extent it may reflect a genuinely uneven impact of open schooling on self-concept is not readily apparent. One problem with the studies of self-concept that have been reviewed is that nearly all of them present self-concept as a unitary, linear entity, that is, the self-concepts of children are either high, medium, or low. While lending itself to easily quantifiable data, this notion of self-concept or self-esteem as a single-factor variable is probably inadequate for dealing with the complex question, "What do these groups of children think of themselves?" which the studies purport to ask.

Attitude toward School

A somewhat clearer pattern of findings has emerged in studies investigating attitudes toward school. The observation that open classrooms seem to be more enjoyable for children than traditional class-

rooms has been made by both proponents and critics of open education. The critics generally claim that the school has more important
tasks to accomplish (namely, teaching basic skills) than the amuse-
ment of children; the proponents contend that enjoyment of school is
important in its own right.

Of 57 empirical studies reviewed, 23 found that open-classroom
children held more positive attitudes toward school, compared to only
2 studies favoring traditional classrooms. There were 14 studies that
showed mixed results and 18 that revealed no significant differences.
While certainly not unanimous, the bulk of the evidence does indicate
that, compared to children in traditional classrooms, those in open
classrooms feel at least equally positive, and often more positive, toward their school experience.

Creativity

Writers in the field of creativity have long maintained that schools
can do more than they traditionally have done to foster the development of creative thinking in children.[15] Many of the descriptions of
open classrooms suggest that far more creative activity occurs there
than normally occurs in conventional classrooms. The hypothesis that
children in open classrooms will perform better than children in traditional classrooms on tests of creative thinking has, therefore, been of
considerable interest to researchers. As with studies of self-concept,
however, creativity research has suffered from inadequate definition
and measurement. The whole question of what creative thinking is
and how one can assess and quantify it is fraught with difficulties and
continues to be debated in the literature.[16]

Of 33 studies relating creativity and open education, 12 indicated
that children in open classrooms were more creative than children in
traditional classrooms, 10 showed mixed results, and 11 found no significant differences. No studies favored the traditional classroom.

Independence and Conformity

Independence in thinking and behavior has been frequently mentioned as an important objective of open education. Yeomans has described the teaching approach in the informal or open classroom as
"education for initiative and responsibility."[17] The literature on open
education strongly emphasizes viewing the child as an "active agent"
in his own learning and the classroom as a place to provide maximal
opportunities for fostering self-reliance and autonomy.

Researchers investigating independence in open classrooms have studied the phenomenon in several different ways. Some have used classroom observation and teacher ratings of children's behavior; some have used pencil-and-paper tests; others have devised experimental tasks. A total of 23 studies were reviewed, and, although the findings are not entirely consistent, they tend generally to support the hypothesis that open classrooms do promote greater independence. Only 1 study reported higher independence for a traditional classroom sample, 2 found no significant differences, 2 obtained mixed results. The remaining 18 studies all favored the open classroom.

Curiosity

Since a major aim of the open classroom is to stimulate children's curiosity and to encourage children to develop and explore their own interests, several investigators have attempted to measure whether students in open classrooms are in fact more curious than those in traditional classrooms.

The measurement of curiosity in children poses serious methodological problems. Some researchers, for example, have utilized classroom observation procedures, which fail to distinguish between compliance with teachers' rules and expression of "inherent" curiosity (that is, children may ask fewer questions in a more tightly controlled classroom because they are not allowed to, but may be just as curious in their attitude and behavior outside the classroom as children who are allowed to ask questions in school). Questionnaire measures of curiosity also are of dubious validity, and experimental procedures that involve assigning a child a task, on which he can choose to behave curiously or not, seem to miss the whole point of curiosity as self-directed, self-initiated, exploratory behavior.

For all the methodological difficulties, however, curiosity remains an important dimension worthy of evaluation. Of 14 studies assessing curiosity in open versus traditional classrooms, 6 favored children in open classrooms, 3 showed no consistent or significant differences, and 5 obtained mixed results. No study found evidence of greater curiosity among children in traditional classrooms. More work on the development of instruments and further evaluative studies would seem to be necessary before a satisfactory answer can be given to the question of whether open classrooms do in fact promote greater curiosity than traditional classrooms.

Adjustment and Anxiety

Several investigators have sought to examine whether children in open classrooms appear better adjusted and less anxious than children in traditional classrooms. The results have been quite inconclusive. Of 17 studies dealing specifically with anxiety, 3 found the children in open classrooms to be less anxious, 5 found the children in traditional classrooms to be less anxious, 8 found no significant differences, and 1 obtained mixed results. Of 22 studies dealing more generally with personal adjustment, 7 found evidence of greater adjustment in the open classroom, 4 found no significant differences, and 11 showed mixed results. No studies favored the traditional classroom. This very mixed pattern of findings is difficult to interpret and points to a need for further study of children's emotional reactions to the open-classroom experience.

Locus of Control

Locus of control is a psychological variable referring to the extent to which a person feels he has control over his own destiny. As explained by Knowles,

The feeling of control can be conceived to be spread out along a continuum. At one end, *internal control* connotes the attitude that one can manipulate environments for reinforcements. One that is internally controlled sees himself as instrumental in the outcome of events. On the other end of the continuum, *external control,* the self-attitude is characterized by the feeling that all that happens to the individual is the consequence of chance, luck, fate, etc., all of which are forces and events beyond the subject's control.[18]

The notion that the open classroom is an environment that provides many opportunities for choice and encourages the development of responsibility for one's own actions has led numerous investigators to test the hypothesis that children in open classrooms will show more *internal* control than children in traditional classrooms. The evaluation instruments usually employed were paper-and-pencil, forced-choice questionnaires with items such as: "Suppose you did better than usual in a subject at school. Would it probably happen (*a*) because you tried harder, or (*b*) because someone helped you?"[19] In most of the instruments, measures are made of the child's sense of internal responsibility for both his successes and his failures.

In all, 24 studies were reviewed, and the results were, once again, inconclusive. In 6 studies, results showed greater internal control among children in open classrooms, 1 favored a group in a traditional classroom, 13 found no significant differences, and 4 had mixed results.

Internal control has been shown to be highly correlated with achievement[20] and with a wide range of cognitive and social skills,[21] so research on the impact of open education on the development of internality will likely continue to be of considerable interest.

Cooperation

Because of the informal atmosphere and emphasis on cooperative learning projects in the open classroom, a number of investigators have designed experimental procedures to determine whether children from those classrooms will show a greater tendency than children in traditional classrooms to cooperate in group problem-solving situations outside the classroom setting. Both Minuchin and her colleagues and Gardner utilized such tasks in their studies. The study by Minuchin and her colleagues found greater cooperation among children in progressive schools, while Gardner obtained mixed results.[22] Several of the more recent evaluative studies have utilized similar experimental procedures, while others have employed classroom observation techniques.

Once again, the findings are not conclusive, but lean more in the direction of the open classroom, with 6 studies clearly favoring the open classroom, 1 showing mixed results, and 2 finding no significant differences. No studies favored traditional classrooms.

CONCLUSION: THE OPEN CLASSROOM AND EVALUATIVE FUNCTIONS

Evaluative research on open-classroom teaching is difficult to summarize concisely because the findings are mixed. As indicated in Table 14-1, far more of the studies reviewed favored children educated in open classrooms over those educated in traditional classrooms. Studies showing no significant or consistent differences, however, frequently outnumbered those favoring the open classroom. The overall impression one gets from this research is that the open classroom sometimes appears to have measurable advantages for children and sometimes appears to make no measurable difference, but only rarely appears to do any measurable harm. Even this very general im-

Table 14-1

Overview (by percentage) of results

| Variable (and number of studies) | Results (percent of studies) | | | |
	Open better	Traditional better	Mixed results	No significant differences
Academic achieve- ment (102)	14	12	28	46
Self-concept (61)	25	3	25	47
Attitude toward school (57)	40	4	25	32
Creativity (33)	36	0	30	33
Independence and conformity (23)	78	4	9	9
Curiosity (14)	43	0	36	21
Anxiety and adjust- ment (39)	26	13	31	31
Locus of control (24)	25	4	17	54
Cooperation (9)	67	0	11	22
Overall average	39	4	24	33

pression must be qualified because of the inconsistencies in defining "open classroom" and other variations among the studies, including the age level of subjects, the number of years of exposure to open education, and the type of evaluation instrument utilized.

Before the question of how the open classroom affects children can be more fully answered, much additional research will have to be undertaken. Even as the number of outcome studies on teaching in the open classroom continues to mount, however, there is a growing feeling among educators that alternative forms of evaluation are necessary.

Some of the criticisms that have been made of the more conventional approaches to evaluation deal specifically with the problems of standardized testing. Meier, for example, has criticized standardized reading tests (such as the commonly used *Metropolitan Achievement Test*) for their middle-class bias, their emphasis on speed, the conventional thinking they require, the problems they pose for children who lack confidence or emotional security in competitive situations, and the extent to which they tend to encourage teachers to "teach what the test measures" using methods that are inappropriate for many children.[23] Shapiro argues convincingly that the very nature of the test situation — formal, silent, dominated by adult demands — may discriminate against children in open classrooms who are less accustomed to such a context for school performance than children in traditional classrooms.[24] Carrying Shapiro's point one step further, DeRivera asserts that "the whole format of testing, the very structure of it, contradicts the goals and structure of an open classroom."[25]

Is it reasonable to conclude from these arguments that standardized testing is inappropriate in the evaluation of open-classroom teaching? Are other forms of assessment more appropriate? Ultimately, the answers to these questions lie within a much broader question: What is the evaluation for? The different functions of evaluation — which may be described as teaching, scientific, and political — serve different purposes, and all do not require the same types of assessment procedures.

The Teaching Function

Evaluation performs a "teaching" function when it helps teachers assess their students' progress: to see how much they have learned, to diagnose areas of strength and weakness, to demonstrate the need for additional work. In the area of the teaching function, much has been written that is critical of standardized testing. There no doubt is some truth to the contention that standardized achievement tests are not pleasant experiences for many school children, are not compatible with the philosophy and style of the open classroom, and often do not provide information that classroom teachers find particularly useful.

Many writers have pointed out that, if teachers want to record their students' progress, methods other than formal, standardized testing can provide a more thorough and sensitive picture of their development. One of the most valuable methods is simply to keep folders of representative samples of each child's schoolwork. Another is to keep notes, daily or periodically, on students' activities, interests, language, and social, emotional, and academic skill development. To facilitate this process, the teacher may want to use special evaluation tasks or checklists, or may prefer to make careful anecdotal observations from time to time of the child's experiences in school. Carini and Engel have provided some particularly enlightening examples of the types of observation, description, and documentation procedures that can be utilized by classroom teachers to record children's progress and development.[26]

The Scientific Function

The "scientific" function of evaluation is concerned with description and assessment for the purpose of understanding. It may or may not provide information of immediate practical value to teachers, but should seek to answer important general questions about the process and effects of teaching. Standardized tests certainly have a place in scientific evaluation. Indeed, it is within the scientific realm that standardized, statistically valid and reliable procedures make most sense, particularly if investigators are attempting to compare large samples of children who have been exposed to different teaching approaches.

But standardized tests of academic achievement provide only a limited type of information, and it is the overemphasis on them that has prompted vociferous criticism from proponents of open education. Reading, writing, and arithmetic ability are certainly important in open as well as traditional classrooms, but there is clearly a need to develop reliable measures of other aspects of the child's response to school. Such important but methodologically difficult areas as self-concept, creativity, curiosity, independence, resourcefulness, and sociability are still in need of much further study. Situational, observational, and experimental methodologies as alternatives to the usual pencil-and-paper questionnaires are particularly deserving of further development. Additional research is needed on individual differences in children's responses to open education, and there is room for more descriptive study of the process of teaching in the open classroom, for careful analysis of teacher-pupil interactions, for close investigation of the way in which such key concepts as structure, freedom, and authority are actualized in open as compared to more traditional classrooms. Clarification of the teacher's role in the open classroom is another area in which further research is needed. Gardner, Cass, and Resnick[27] were pioneers in this area with their systematic observation studies, and further efforts along the same line, using diary and interview methods, have been made in the Open Corridor program in New York City. There, teachers have kept logs "reflecting on their organizational changes and curricular developments,"[28] and researchers from the Educational Testing Service have carried out intensive teacher interviews to identify the various modifications in perceptions, beliefs, and attitudes that teachers undergo in moving toward a more open approach.[29] Intensive teacher interviews have also been an important part of the assessment strategy developed by the University of North

Dakota Center for Teaching and Learning, along with interviews with children and parents.[30] Interview studies are still quite rare in open education evaluation, and more are needed. They may well make up in richness and depth what they lack in statistical precision.

The Political Function

Finally, the "political" function of evaluation has to do with the survival of programs, that is, the use of research to decide whether programs "deserve" to be continued.

In the political arena, in spite of the antiachievement test sentiments of some educators, it is mathematics and reading scores that often are deemed most important in decisions to continue or terminate innovative programs. This reality probably explains why achievement tests were utilized far more frequently than any other sorts of measures in the studies reviewed for this chapter. Unfortunately, the mixed pattern of findings on achievement is such that advocates of open education will always be able to cite studies in favor of the open approach, while detractors will always be able to cite evidence against it. As with so many public policy issues, the decision about whether to support or not to support the open classroom ultimately becomes one of values, not science.

It is unlikely that more evaluation studies—however useful to teachers or scientists they may be—will ever resolve the debates between proponents of more "open" teaching styles and advocates of the so-called "back-to-basics" approach.[31] Perrone has suggested rather optimistically that evaluation can serve to counter the back-to-basics movement by "assisting people to understand what open education is about."[32] But there seems little doubt that many opponents of open education already do understand it; they simply do not like it, and they are not likely to be swayed by yet more research.

At this time, the evidence from evaluation studies of the open classroom is not sufficiently consistent to warrant an unqualified endorsement of that approach to teaching over more traditional methods. There is certainly enough evidence, however, to defend open classrooms as viable alternatives where teachers and parents want them.

Evaluation research can continue to play a "formative" role in improving the quality of ongoing programs in open classrooms and a "summative" role in documenting the relative strengths and weaknesses of open and traditional approaches. Although political decisions to support or not to support open education will probably continue to be made regardless of the actual research evidence, the many unanswered questions about the open classroom suggest a need for more and better evaluation.

NOTES

1. Robert A. Horwitz, *Psychological Effects of Open Classroom Teaching on Primary School Children: A Review of the Research,* Monograph of the North Dakota Study Group on Evaluation (Grand Forks, N.D.: University of North Dakota Press, 1976).

2. Charles E. Silberman, *Crisis in the Classroom: The Remaking of American Education* (New York: Random House, 1970), 208.

3. Roland S. Barth, *Open Education and the American School* (New York: Agathon Press, 1972); Charles H. Rathbone, ed., *Open Education: The Informal Classroom* (New York: Citation Press, 1971); Lilian G. Katz, "Research on Open Education: Problems and Issues," in *Current Research and Perspectives in Open Education,* ed. D. Dwain Hearn, Joel L. Burdin, and Lilian G. Katz (Washington, D.C.: American Association of Elementary-Kindergarten-Nursery Educators, 1972), 1-14.

4. Herbert J. Walberg and Susan C. Thomas, "Defining Open Education," *Journal of Research and Development in Education* 8 (1974): 4-13.

5. Anne M. Bussis and Edward A. Chittenden, *Analysis of an Approach to Open Education* (Princeton, N.J.: Educational Testing Service, 1970).

6. Ross E. Traub, Joel Weiss, C.W. Fisher, and Don Musella, "Closure on Openness in Education: Describing and Quantifying Open Education," *Interchange* 3 (1972): 69-84.

7. G. Derwood Baker *et al., New Methods vs. Old in American Education: An Analysis and Summary of Recent Comparative Studies,* by the informal committee appointed by the Progressive Education Association to report on evaluation of newer practices in education (New York: Teachers College, Columbia University, 1941), 52-53.

8. J. Wayne Wrightstone, *Appraisal of Newer Elementary School Practices* (New York: Teachers College, Columbia University, 1938); J. Paul Leonard and Alvin C. Eurich, *An Evaluation of Modern Education* (New York: Appleton-Century-Crofts, 1942).

9. Patricia Minuchin, Barbara Biber, Edna Shapiro, and Herbert Zimiles, *The Psychological Impact of School Experience: A Comparative Study of Nine-year-old Children in Contrasting Schools* (New York: Basic Books, 1969).

10. Dorothy E.M. Gardner, *Testing Results in the Infant School* (London: Methuen, 1942); *id., Long-term Results of Infant School Methods* (London: Methuen, 1950); *id., Experiment and Tradition in Primary Schools* (London: Methuen, 1966).

11. Gene V Glass, "Primary, Secondary, and Meta-analysis of Research," *Educational Researcher* 5 (1976): 3-8.

12. Author's address: Robert A. Horwitz, Ph.D., ACUTE, Hospital of St. Raphael, 1450 Chapel St., New Haven, Conn. 06511.

13. Neville Bennett, *Teaching Styles and Pupil Progress* (London: Open Books, 1976; reprinted by Harvard University Press, Cambridge, Mass., 1976).

14. Chad Gordon, "Self-conceptions Methodologies," *Journal of Nervous and Mental Disease* 148 (1969): 328-364.

15. For example, see Barbara Biber, "The Teacher's Role in Creativity," *American Journal of Orthopsychiatry* 29 (1959): 280-290.

16. Susan B. Crockenberg, "Creativity Tests: A Boon or Boondoggle for Education?" *Review of Educational Research* 42 (1972): 27-45.

17. Edward Yeomans, *Education for Initiative and Responsibility* (Boston: National Association of Independent Schools, 1967).

18. Gerald Knowles, "Open Education and Internal Locus of Control," in *Current Research and Perspectives in Open Education,* ed. Hearn, Burdin, and Katz, 94.

19. Virginia C. Crandall, Walter Katkovsky, and Vaughn J. Crandall, "Children's Beliefs in Their Own Control of Reinforcements in Intellectual-Academic Achievement Situations," *Child Development* 36 (1965): 91-109.

20. James S. Coleman *et al., Equality of Educational Opportunity* (Washington, D.C.: U.S. Government Printing Office, 1966).

21. Virginia C. Crandall, "Locus of Control: Some Important but Neglected Issues," paper presented at the annual meeting of the American Psychological Association, Chicago, September 1975.

22. Minuchin *et al., Psychological Impact of School Experience;* Gardner, *Experiment and Tradition in Primary Schools.*

23. Deborah Meier, "Another Look at What's Wrong with Reading Tests," in *Testing and Evaluation: New Views,* ed. Vito Perrone, Monroe D. Cohen, and Lucy Prete Martin (Washington, D.C.: Association for Childhood Education International, 1975), 32-36.

24. Edna Shapiro, "Educational Evaluation: Rethinking the Criteria of Competence," *School Review* 82 (1973): 523-548.

25. Margaret DeRivera, "Academic Achievement Tests and the Survival of Open Education," *EDC News,* No. 2 (1973): 7-9.

26. Patricia F. Carini, *Observation and Description: An Alternative Methodology for the Investigation of Human Phenomena,* monograph of the North Dakota Study Group on Evaluation (Grand Forks, N.D.: University of North Dakota Press, 1975); Brenda S. Engel, *A Handbook on Documentation,* monograph of the North Dakota Study Group on Evaluation (Grand Forks, N.D.: University of North Dakota Press, 1975).

27. Dorothy E.M. Gardner and Joan E. Cass, *The Role of the Teacher in the Infant and Nursery School* (London: Pergamon Press, 1965); Lauren B. Resnick, "Teacher Behavior in an Informal British Infant School," *School Review* 81 (1972): 63-83.

28. Lillian Weber, "Toward the Finer Specificity," in *Evaluation Reconsidered: A Position Paper and Supporting Documents on Evaluating Change and Changing Evaluation,* ed. Arthur J. Tobier (New York: Workshop Center for Open Education, 1973), 5.

29. Anne M. Bussis, Edward A. Chittenden, and Marianne Amarel, *Beyond Surface Curriculum: An Interview Study of Teachers' Understandings* (Boulder, Colo.: Westview Press, 1976).

30. Vito Perrone, "Report from North Dakota," in *Evaluation Reconsidered,* ed. Tobier.

31. Iver Peterson, "The Newest Innovation: Back to Basics," *New York Times,* January 15, 1975.

32. Gene I. Maeroff, "Liberals Defend Open Classes against Back-to-Basics Forces," *New York Times,* April 20, 1975.

15. Authority Structures

Joyce L. Epstein and *James M. McPartland*

The authority relationship between school teachers and students has frequently been the object of reform movements in education. Educational theorists and practitioners in the United States have been contesting issues related to authority in the school at least since the progressive era of the 1920s.[1] While the long-term trend has been to increase student prerogatives in school decisions, the historical pattern shows inevitable fluctuations. When there has been movement toward minimizing school regulations and maximizing student involvement in decisions, the pendulum often swings back toward stricter uniform standards and stronger control of student behavior.

Recently, there have been reform movements concerned with controls on both the nonacademic and academic behavior of students. In the 1960s, at the height of student demonstrations in high schools, students' political and social rights in nonacademic school affairs were emphasized. Since then there has also been renewed in-

This work was supported in part by National Institute of Education Contract No. 400-76-0046. It does not represent NIE policy, and no endorsement should be inferred.

293

terest in how authority is structured to control student academic behaviors. Contemporary schools take different positions on authority-control issues. Some provide "open" learning environments, while others support "traditional" or "back to basics" programs. But the debate about the most appropriate student-teacher relations in schools remains unresolved and is likely to continue among educational practitioners and theorists.

To learn more about authority structures in the learning process, we undertook a study of open and traditional schools in 1973 and 1974.[2] The study included test and questionnaire data on 7,361 students from grades five, six, seven, nine, and twelve in twenty-three elementary schools, ten middle schools, and six high schools. Two general questions were addressed: What are the defining components of the school authority structure that are successfully implemented in open schools? Which student outcomes are affected most by changes in the school authority structures?

The research was conducted in a rapidly growing suburban school system that had adopted a policy to implement "open education" in many of its new and existing school buildings. Since the school system had been actively pursuing the policy for more than five years, the location provided a valuable research opportunity to learn which particular dimensions of school authority can be most easily changed and which changes are most resistant to successful implementation.

DIMENSIONS OF SCHOOL AUTHORITY

Some differences between the open schools and the traditional schools in the system were apparent. In the traditional buildings there were many self-contained "egg crate" classrooms with fixed rows of seats for twenty to thirty students. In the open schools, in contrast, there were large open spaces containing several instructional areas and a large central area that accommodated one hundred or more students, where the furniture was movable and arranged differently. Instead of a teacher conducting a single lesson from the front of the room, there were many activities going on simultaneously in the open schools, and students were freer to move about the room. Teachers in many of the open schools talked about different staff attitudes toward the role of students in making classroom decisions or about improved student-teacher relationships.

Yet how extensive both the formal and informal differences in authority were among the various schools remained an important empirical question. We did not assume that open-space architecture determined the formal organization of instructional practices; nor that formal classroom practices determined the informal relationships between teachers and students. The first objective of the research was to determine what changes of formal and informal structures had actually been implemented in the schools.

Formal and Informal Structures

The distinction between formal and informal arrangements is a familiar one in many theories of industrial and other goal-directed organizations. The formal organization of official regulations, roles, and purposes may be contrasted with the informal relations, attitudes, and expectations that frequently guide the behavior of individual members. This study used a similar distinction between the formal and informal aspects of school authority structures, rather than beginning with a single definition that combined both aspects.

A variety of definitions have been proposed in previous descriptions and research on open schools. Most of this work focused on elementary schools and included both formal and informal features of classroom arrangements in the definitions of openness without questioning which aspects were most significant in actual practice. Some descriptions of open education stressed the quality of informal life in the classroom and emphasized the informal climate of teacher-student relations in the definition of openness.[3] Other work emphasized the philosophy or attitudes of teachers toward the learning process and included in the definition of openness images of "child-centered education" in which teachers were prepared to follow the natural curiosity, interests, and abilities of individual students.[4] Some research examined the concept of openness in operation by using measures that included both the attitudes of teachers about the learning process and the informal relationships in the classroom, as well as descriptions of the formal arrangements of materials, instructional tasks, and official rules that govern classroom activities.[5]

Two general results from our research help to clarify the definition of openness by identifying those aspects of school authority structures where significant changes can be directly implemented, as well as those aspects where significant changes are not common or occur indirectly.

1. *Open and traditional schools differed greatly on formal organizational aspects of their authority structure, but the same schools did not differ nearly so much on the informal aspects of student-teacher authority relations.*

As part of the procedures to define the specific components that distinguish open and traditional schools, we identified those survey items about classroom practices that showed the most agreement by students in the same school and the least overlap in responses by students from different schools. This criterion of between-school variance was used to learn which specific elements of change had been most successfully implemented in the open schools. We reasoned that, when clear distinctions in students' perceptions of specific school practices depended on the particular school they attended, then these specific practices had taken hold as a defining characteristic of open schools. Conversely, when the distribution of student reports about a school practice was very similar in each school, we argued that this practice was not as successfully changed through the innovation of openness. Results show that a measure that emphasized formal structural properties of openness has much stronger between-school differences than measures of the informal classroom processes.

The features on which schools differed greatly were: *individualization of instruction* (whether the teacher usually permits different individuals or groups of students to work simultaneously on separate assignments), *control of student conversation and movement* (whether the teacher permits students to talk and move freely about during class time), *control of student assignments* (whether the teacher gives students choices of alternative assignments) and *frequency of supervision of student assignments* (whether the teacher permits students to work on their own for extended periods of time). These features are concerned with the formal structure controlling classroom activities. In simplest terms, from the teacher's point of view, the difference in formal structure of open and traditional programs begins with whether a teacher prepares a single lesson for an entire class during a period that starts and ends at a fixed time or whether the teacher prepares alternative activities that differ in content, difficulty, or duration on which different students can work simultaneously. When classroom activities are individualized, the teacher spends less time holding the attention of the entire class and more time assisting particular groups or individual students while other students are busy with separate assignments. From the students' point of view, this often means that fewer controls are placed on their conversation and movement during class, and they have more responsibility for choosing and organizing learning activities without constant teacher direction and supervision.

Such differences in the individualization of the instructional program do not always correspond to the existence of open-space architecture in the school building. In the sample of elementary and secondary schools, only a little more than half of the teachers in open-space buildings reported using a predominantly individualized instructional program, while up to one-quarter of the teachers in traditional self-contained classrooms reported using individualized methods. So although open-space buildings may facilitate the development of a variety of instructional approaches, it is not surprising to find that the architecture of a school by no means determines how teachers will formally structure their classroom learning activities.

Just as the architecture does not determine the formal instructional program, the formal aspects of individualization and control of classroom activities do not determine the informal social relations between teachers and students. We did not find the same large between-school differences on two measures of informal student-teacher relations—students' perceptions of teachers' expectations and teachers' classroom decision-making styles. The first of these measures that failed to distinguish strongly between the various schools was a four-item scale of whether teachers expected originality and personal opinions in students' classwork, or whether teachers expected close conformity to their own directions and ideas. The second measure on which the distribution of student perceptions was nearly equal across the schools was a nine-item scale measuring whether teachers reserved most of the decision-making prerogatives for themselves or extended decision-making opportunities informally to students.

The comparison was striking between measures of the formal and informal aspects of school authority, in terms of their between-school variance. At the secondary level, the average between-school variance for the measure of formal openness of the school program

(36 percent) was more than ten times as large as for the scale of teachers' expectations and more than five times as large as for a scale of teachers' decision-making style. Similar though less dramatic differences were found at the upper elementary level. This means that, while students' reports on the more formal aspects of openness depended strongly upon the particular school they attended, the same was not nearly as true for their perceptions of the informal social processes in the classroom.

It appears that, in implementing open education, it was possible to implement successfully formal changes in the individualization of the instructional program that altered the amount of time students would be under the strict control and close supervision of their teachers, but it was not easy to change teachers' attitudes about their dominant role as the authority in informal encounters. There were teachers located in *every* school who regularly shared authority with students and others who did not. Because informal authority relations may be determined by well-established personality traits or educational philosophies of individual teachers, it may be very difficult to train or recruit a faculty to establish a distinctive style of informal teacher-student relations throughout a school.

These results should not be read to say there were no effects at all of the formal aspects of openness on the informal social processes when teachers and students were in contact. There is evidence of some statistically significant and substantively important relationships between formal and informal aspects of school authority, although these relationships were not very large. This leads to the second important general result of the dimensions of school authority differences.

2. *The small differences between schools on informal aspects of teacher-student authority relations are facilitated by the large formal organizational differences of schools.*

There is convincing evidence that there are some facilitating effects of the openness of the formal instructional program on teachers' informal expectations for student behavior. Using items from the same measure on which we reported a small between-school variance, we examined whether the formal structure of openness is related to specific kinds of teacher expectations. Students were asked about their teachers' expectations for the following four behaviors: "students should listen well and follow directions"; "students should have unusual, imaginative ideas"; "students should do work that is neat and clean"; and "students should speak out with opinions." Students were asked to rate each behavior on a scale ranging from "very important" to "not at all important" to their teachers. Even though student ratings across the sample were positively correlated for all pairs of these four items—teachers who were seen to have high expectations on one behavior were also generally reported high on other behaviors—an interesting set of relationships was found concerning the formal open-school measure. Students in more open schools at all grade levels consistently reported *less* teacher emphasis on strict following of directions or neatness in work and *more* teacher emphasis on creative ideas and expression of students' opinions. These relationships were small but statistically significant and consistent across all grades in the sample. The results suggest that the open-school organization facilitates the development of teacher-student relations that deemphasize uniformity and reward originality and self-expression. Some teachers who wish to foster student individuality may find the open structure more enabling than traditional classroom structures, and other teachers may come to value the freer student expression as a consequence of conducting open instructional programs.

There is also convincing evidence that formal open-school structure facilitates an informal teacher-student sharing of decision-making authority. These analyses involved the same measure of teachers' decision-making style on which we reported a small between-school variance. Although the difference between schools on this measure was very small in comparison to the measure of formal structure of openness, teachers' decision-making style did represent a true difference between the environments of open and traditional schools. We found three times as much between-school variance on the measure of teachers' decision-making style (6 percent) as there was for an exactly parallel measure of parents' decision-making style (2 percent). Since both scales were based on student perceptions, the interpretation of this difference in between-school variances is that the teachers' decision-making scale represents a small but true distinguishing feature of the school environments. Moreover, we found a significant positive relationship between the formal open-school measure and the scale of informal teacher decision-making style. This relationship was examined in general and more specifically by using refined within-school measures of openness and teacher decision-making style for three academic subjects. At every grade level, the formal openness of the instructional measure correlated in a significantly positive direction with the informal decision-making measure, in general and across all subjects in grades nine and twelve, or for particular subjects in grades five, six, and seven, where within-school distinctions between openness of subjects were important. These results suggest that teachers who find it difficult in traditional instructional programs to establish an informal decision-making partnership with students may be able to develop such an informal environment within open instructional programs.

Other research also suggests a facilitating link between the organization of classroom tasks and teacher's style of controlling behavior. In observing elementary school teachers' behaviors, Bossert found that teachers may be limited in the kinds of student behavior and responses they encourage by the more traditional single-lesson method of instruction since that structure requires more teacher control and uniformity in treatment of students.[6] He describes how the same teacher may develop different informal relationships with students, depending upon the formal organization of instruction.

Our results on the dimensions of school authority in open and traditional elementary and secondary schools suggest that the major changes implemented in open schools concern the formal aspects of the program: individualization, control of conversation and movement, control of student assignments and supervision of assignments. Informal aspects of teacher-student relationships, which may be a function of the distribution of teacher personalities or educational philosophies, are not nearly so easily changed. Nevertheless, the formal structure does appear to have a small but significant effect on the probability of informal relationships developing in which teachers give more emphasis to student originality and involve students more frequently in the classroom decision-making process.

The next objective of this study was to examine effects of school authority differences, both effects of the formal program differences that most clearly distinguished the open and traditional school structures and effects of the differences in informal student-teacher authority relations that frequently existed within both open and traditional school structures.

EFFECTS ON STUDENT OUTCOMES

A variety of student outcomes were studied for possible effects from differences in the formal and informal organization of authority in schools. They included students' academic development, as measured by standardized achievement tests and educational aspirations; students' nonacademic development, as measured by selected personality scales; and students' attitudes toward school and school-coping skills, as measured by indexes of student satisfaction and school behaviors. The analyses of the effects of school differences on these outcomes controlled statistically for differences in student background, so that the nonrandom distribution of students among the different school settings would be taken into account. The family background controls included socioeconomic status and family authority relations, as well as race, sex, and ability.

The results can be summarized for three questions about effects on student outcomes: What are the effects of the formal structure of openness? What are the effects of differences in informal processes of authority relations, which may exist in both open and traditional programs? Does the size or direction of school effects depend upon the type of family environment that a student has experienced?

The first general result comes from these analyses.

1. *Positive effects on students resulting from differences in the formal structure of open versus traditional schools are found for nonacademic outcomes and student attitudes but not for academic outcomes. However, even the effects for nonacademic outcomes and student attitudes are small.*

For students' *academic performance,* several extended analyses of relationships between school openness and student performance on standardized tests failed to reveal sizable or consistent effects. Students' standardized achievement scores on the *Iowa Tests of Basic Skills* (ITBS) in grades five, seven, and nine and the reading subtest of the Test of Academic Progress in grade twelve were studied. The degree of openness of the instructional program accounted for less than 2 percent of the variance in test scores and the direction of the relationship was inconsistent across four grades (positive in some grades and negative in others). These inconsistencies appeared to be random and without substantive importance since they were not explained by further detailed analyses of the possible relationships between openness and achievement. Extended analyses showed no orderly trends of achievement scores resulting from duration of attendance in open schools, no evidence that openness of specific subjects within schools is differentially related to achievement on those subjects, and no evidence that openness interacts with individual student variables that would occur if certain subgroups of students are more positively or negatively affected than others by open education. The final conclusion most clearly supported is that, at the elementary and secondary levels, students neither gain nor lose in their performance on standardized achievement tests as a consequence of attending open schools.[7]

Similarly, open-school attendance had no consistent significant effects on students' educational aspirations. A measure of students' college plans analyzed for the secondary school sample failed to show any consistent positive or negative differences related to the type of school program.

For students' *personality development,* the picture was somewhat different on one outcome measure—student self-reliance. An eighteen-item scale was used to measure the degree to which an individual needs strong social approval or explicit direction before taking action. This scale has important properties of reliability and validity: it discriminates among individuals who were named by peers and teachers as independent students, and it shows developmental trends of greater average self-reliance scores. It must be stated that the size of the effect at each grade level is not as impressive as the consistency of the positive direction of effects. At every grade, for two consecutive years, there was a small, positive impact of openness on student self-reliance.

Other general student personality measures of self-esteem and control of environment were not influenced by open-school experiences in any sizable or consistent way across the grades.

Several indexes were used to measure students' *attitudes and school-coping skills.* The *Quality of School Life* scale is a multidimensional measure of students' satisfaction with school, commitment to classwork, and reactions to teachers.[8] In many descriptive accounts of open schools, mainly at the early elementary level, students are described as appearing happier in open schools. To consider the statistical accuracy of the observations, or the generalizability of such findings at the secondary level, our research examined the effect of open schools on student satisfaction in greater detail.

The present research yields one very consistent result: students in more open schools are significantly more positive in their evaluations of their teachers than students in more traditional schools. In grades five, six, and seven this was true when we examined particular subject classrooms, and in grades nine and twelve the pattern was clear in general and in specific subject classrooms. And, at both the elementary and secondary levels, duration of attendance in open schools had positive effects on student evaluation of teachers and school in general. There were, however, no consistent effects of openness on students' commitment to classwork.

The effects of openness of school programs were not present for some other school-coping skills measured in this study. There were no consistent, significant effects of openness on "school anxiety" (feeling tense or lost in school) or on "prosocial school-task behavior" (acting as an "ideal" student). The measure of "school adjustment" (frequency of disciplinary incidents) did present some interesting patterns. Students in more open programs reported being reprimanded in class more frequently for a variety of disciplinary reasons, especially in grades six and seven. At the high school level, there was no significant difference in adjustment between students in open and traditional schools. In addition, analyses of data collected over a two-year period suggest that students with initial disciplinary problems learn to adjust in the open schools; students with adjustment problems one year had fewer problems the next year in more open schools, while in traditional schools more students continued to have discipline problems from one year to the next.

In general, while some selected student outcomes were consistently and significantly related to the formal structure of school openness, none of these effects was very large. Thus, the formal aspects of openness, which were shown to be most easily implemented in schools, had a significant but small impact on certain nonacademic and attitudinal student outcomes, but not on measures of academic development.

The next phase of our study examined the effects of the informal teacher-student authority relationships that vary significantly within both open instructional program schools and traditional schools. The second general result about effects comes from these analyses.

2. *Positive effects on students from differences in informal authority relations in schools are found for all student outcomes,
especially for nonacademic outcomes.*

Earlier research in schools suggests that the way teachers exert
authority in the classroom can affect the development of student
coping skills.[9] Similarly, many years of family research have shown
that authority relationships between parents and children in the
home can have important consequences for child development.[10]
Our research developed parallel measures of teacher-student and
parent-child informal authority relationships to examine the importance of these factors on academic and nonacademic outcomes.

In contrast to the weak effects of the formal structure of school
programs on student outcomes, both the informal teacher-student
and parent-child authority relationships were found to be much
more strongly related to all student outcomes. Student scores on the
parallel scales of teacher decision-making style and parent decision-making style are positively related to most of the student outcome measures. After controlling for other factors, teacher-student
decision-making scale scores were significantly and positively related
to the measures of student self-reliance and to all measures of
school attitudes and coping skills, including student satisfaction,
school adjustment, low school anxiety, and prosocial task-related
behaviors. And, after controlling for other factors, the parent-child
decision-making scale scores were significantly and positively related
to these same outcome measures and to other personality outcomes
of self-concept and control of environment. These effects were present for males and females at all grade levels in elementary, middle,
and high schools. In addition, two patterns of the results of analyses
provide some indications of the complicated causal processes that
link informal authority relationships to student development.

First, the results suggest that student-adult informal authority relationships are more important than students' socioeconomic background for the development of positive nonacademic outcomes. For
example, although students' socioeconomic status was the more
dominant influence in accounting for academic performance on
standardized tests and in explaining differences in students' educational aspirations, students' scores on measures of informal teacher-
student and parent-child decision-making practices were especially
important influences on personality and attitudinal outcomes.[11]

Second, the results indicate that informal authority relationships are not improved simply by eliminating controls on youngsters at home or school, but must reflect the ways in which authority is communicated and decisions are made. A fourteen-item scale of the number of rules in the home (level of regulation) was used in this study in addition to the parent-child decision-making scale to measure family authority relationships. Although these two scales were positively correlated with one another — families with frequent child involvement in decisions tended to have fewer rules — the two scales were often not related to student outcomes in the same direction or degree. Generally, the family decision-making measure was a much stronger positive correlate than level of regulation for most student outcomes. Moreover, when family decision-making style was statistically controlled, infrequency of family rules was related negatively to some student outcomes. The *fewer* the rules, the *lower* the student's perceived quality of school life, school adjustment, school-task behavior, and aspirations. This suggests that low levels of regulation of children's activities without informal practices that encourage decision making may have negative behavioral consequences. This finding is in keeping with other research indicating that the reasoning processes between parents and children are critical features of the authority relationships. [12]

To summarize, we find that informal teacher-student processes have much stronger positive effects on student development than the formal structure of authority of a school program. The indications of the complicated processes linking informal authority relationships to student development may help to explain why it has not been easy to implement successful school changes on these important informal factors.

The final element in this study of school effects was an examination of whether certain types of students are affected differently by variations in the formal and informal structure of school authority. The third general result comes from these analyses.

3. *There is no strong evidence that different combinations of family and school environments interact to influence student outcomes. The effects of differences in school environments do not seem to depend upon student socioeconomic status or family authority practices.*

Both researchers and practitioners have emphasized the need to consider whether certain students would be more likely to benefit from a revised school structure than other students. Although interactions have been difficult to document and replicate in educational research, especially for populations of nondeviant students,[13] there was reason to hypothesize that effects of formal or informal school authority structures would be different for students from particular family backgrounds.

Our study examined closely whether students' experiences at home would make them more or less receptive to the influence of open-school practices or classroom decision-making styles on particular student outcomes. We tested the possibility that *congruence* of family and school learning environments is important for school satisfaction and coping skills,[14] while *incongruence* is important for growth in self-reliance.[15] It is not difficult to imagine that students from "traditional" families in "open" schools may be less satisfied or comfortable in an unfamiliar environment, but yet may benefit most in developing self-reliance because they have received less practice in being self-reliant at home. The study also considered that open schools may be particularly effective for the more economically advantaged students.

The data do not support these hypotheses about family-school interactions. In extensive analyses of the interaction of all family-by-school combinations, there were no significant, consistent, or interpretable interactions for any of the outcomes studied. The results of tests of interactions indicate that students did no better or worse in open and traditional schools because of the matching of particular family and school experiences. Similarly, there were no notable or important special interactive effects found in combinations of informal teacher-student relations and various family environment conditions.

The results of analyses of interactive effects suggest that the congruence or incongruence of school and family environments, per se, is not a primary influence on student development. Although there may be personal or philosophical reasons why parents seek school settings for their children that "match" the family environment, this study concludes that the main effects of school and family practices that encourage students to participate in decision making at school and at home are more important influences than effects of environmental interaction for positive student development.

IMPLICATIONS FOR THEORY AND PRACTICE

Research findings that contribute to educational theory may or may not have direct implications for educational practice. That depends in large part on whether the variables identified by research as important for student development can be purposefully manipulated through practical educational reforms.

Our study of authority structures and student development sought both to identify the types of student outcomes that are potentially most responsive to variations in authority relationships and to suggest important practical considerations for capturing this potential. It is here that the distinction between formal and informal dimensions of school authority structures is of interest.

In our study of effects on student development, we found evidence that the *informal* authority relationships between teachers and students have a strong impact on student outcomes, particularly on students' nonacademic competencies and their attitudes toward school. The results were parallel for authority relations at school and at home: both teacher-student decision-making practices and student-child decision-making processes have sizable positive effects on students' nonacademic attitudes and behavior, controlling for the students' socioeconomic status. Further research is needed to develop detailed theories of the processes at work since our studies confirm earlier research that complicated combinations of decision-making patterns and levels of regulation are involved and the specific causal mechanisms are not all clear.

We also found that it is possible to implement changes in the *formal* aspects of a school's authority structure. Individualization of instruction, fewer restrictions on student movement and conversation, more student choice of assignments, and longer periods of student responsibility for self-direction were all aspects that clearly distinguished between open and traditional schools in our study. These changes had statistically significant but small effects on students' self-reliance and satisfaction with school, not on standardized achievement test performance.

These formal changes also appeared to have a facilitating effect on the informal relationships between teachers and students, and enabled some teachers to reinforce more student self-expression and to involve students more deeply in classroom decision-making processes. Yet these facilitating effects did not produce large overall contrasts between schools in these informal aspects of teacher-student authority relationships. Although schools with open instructional programs had slightly different informal teacher-student authority relationships, each school had a surprisingly similar representation of teachers who reserved most informal authority to themselves as well as teachers who shared more prerogatives and responsibilities with students.

Putting together our results on the major sources of potential effects from authority structures and on the prospects for practical implementation, we find that a major task remains for researchers and educators. The informal aspects of teacher-student authority relationships appear to have strong potential for impact on particular student outcomes, but these aspects are the most difficult to change throughout a school. Conversely, important modifications in the formal authority structure of a school's instructional program can be instituted, but these changes have little direct impact on student outcomes and a limited indirect role in facilitating important informal authority dimensions. To capitalize fully on the potential of authority variables for student development, work is still needed to develop ideas on a variety of possible changes in school authority structures that can both be successfully implemented and have impressive effects on students.

NOTES

1. Lawrence A. Cremin, *The Transformation of the School* (New York: Vintage, 1961).

2. See the following reports from the Center for Social Organization of Schools, Johns Hopkins University, Baltimore, Md.: Joyce L. Epstein and James M. McPartland, "The Effects of Open School Organization on Student Outcomes," Report No. 194 (1975); *id.,* "Classroom Organization and the Quality of School Life," Report No. 215 (1976); *id.,* "Family and School Interactions and Main Effects on Affective Outcomes," Report No. 235 (1977); *id.,* "Sex Differences in Family and School Influence on Student Outcomes," Report No. 236 (1977). See also Joyce L. Epstein and James M. McPartland, "The Concept and Measurement of the Quality of School Life," *American Educational Research Journal* 50 (1976): 13-30; James M. McPartland and Joyce L. Epstein, "Effects of Open School Structure on Student-Student and Student-Teacher Processes," paper presented at the annual meeting of the American Educational Research Association, San Francisco, April 1976; *id.,* "Open Schools and Achievement: Extended Tests of a Finding of No Relationship," *Sociology of Education* 42 (1977): 133-144.

3. Joseph Featherstone, *Schools Where Children Learn* (New York: Liveright, 1971); Charles Silberman, *The Open Classroom Reader* (New York: Vintage Books, 1973).

4. Roland S. Barth, *Open Education and the American School* (New York: Agathon Press, 1972); Anne Bussis and Edward Chittenden, *Analysis of an Approach to Open Education* (Princeton, N.J.: Educational Testing Service, 1970); *Children and Their Primary Schools: A Report of the Central Advisory Council for Education,*

Volumes I and II, ed. Bridget Plowden (London: Her Majesty's Stationery Office, 1967); Lillian Weber, *The English Infant School and Informal Education* (Englewood Cliffs, N.J.: Prentice-Hall, 1971).

5. J. T. Evans, "An Activity Analysis of U.S. Traditional, U.S. Open, and British Open Classrooms," paper presented at the annual meeting of the American Educational Research Association, Chicago, 1972; Bruce W., Tuckman, David W. Cochran and Eugene J. Travers, "Evaluating Open Classrooms," *Journal of Research and Development in Education* 8 (1974): 14-19; Herbert J. Walberg and Susan C. Thomas, "Open Education: An Operational Definition and Validation in Great Britain and the United States," *American Educational Research Journal* 9 (1972): 197-207.

6. Steven Bossert, "Tasks, Group Management, and Teacher Control Behavior: A Study of Classroom Organization and Teacher Style," *School Review* 85 (1977): 552-565.

7. McPartland and Epstein, "Open Schools and Achievement."

8. Epstein and McPartland, "Concept and Measurement of the Quality of School Life." See also Joyce L. Epstein and James M. McPartland, *The Quality of School Life Scale and Technical Manual* (Boston: Houghton Mifflin, 1978).

9. Kurt Lewin, Ronald Lippitt, and Ralph K. White, "Patterns of Aggressive Behavior in Experimentally Created 'Social Climates'," *Journal of Social Psychology* 10 (1939): 271-299.

10. Diana Baumrind, "Early Socialization and Adolescent Competence," in *Adolescence in the Life Cycle,* ed. Sigmund E. Dragastin and Glen H. Elder, Jr. (New York: Halsted Press, 1975), 117-143; Glen H. Elder, Jr., *Adolescent Socialization and Personality Development* (Chicago: Rand McNally, 1968); Martin L. Hoffman and Lois W. Hoffman, eds., *Review of Child Development Research,* 2 vols. (New York: Russell Sage Foundation, 1964 and 1966).

11. Epstein and McPartland, "Sex Differences in Family and School Influences on Student Outcomes."

12. Diana Baumrind, "Socialization and Instrumental Competence in Young Children," in *The Young Child: Reviews of Research,* ed. Willard W. Hartup and Nancy Smothergill (Washington, D.C.: National Association for the Education of Young Children, 1967), 202-224; Wesley C. Becker, "Consequences of Different Kinds of Parental Discipline," in *Review of Child Development Research,* ed. Hoffman and Hoffman, I, 169-208; Elder, *Adolescent Socialization and Personality Development.*

13. David C. Berliner and Leonard S. Cahen, "Trait-Treatment Interaction and Learning," in *Review of Research in Education,* ed. Frederick Kerlinger, (Itasca, Ill.: F. E. Peacock, 1973), I, 58-94; Lee J. Cronbach and Richard E. Snow, *Aptitudes and Instructional Methods* (New York: Irvington Publishers, Inc., 1977); Kenneth A. Feldman and John Weiler, "Changes in Initial Differences among Major-Field Groups: An Exploration of the 'Accentuation Effect'," in *Schooling and Achievement in American Society,* ed. William Sewell, Robert Hauser, and David Featherman, (New York: Academic Press, 1976), 373-407; Gavriel Salomon, "Heuristic Models for the Generation of Aptitude Treatment Interaction Hypotheses," *Review of Educational Research* 42 (1972): 327-344.

14. On preferential treatment interactions, see Salomon, "Heuristic Models for the Generation of Aptitude Treatment Interaction Hypotheses," and Richard E. Snow, "Research on Media and Aptitudes," *Viewpoints* 46 (1970): 63-91.

15. On disequilibrium of treatment, see John W. Atkinson, Willy Lens, and P.M. O'Malley, "Motivation and Ability: Interactive Psychological Determinants of Intellectual Performance, Educational Achievement, and Each Other," in *Schooling and Achievement in American Society,* ed. Sewell, Hauser, and Featherman, 29-60; David E. Hunt, *Matching Models in Education: The Coordination of Teaching Methods with Student Characteristics* (Toronto: Ontario Institute for Studies in Education, 1971).

PART FOUR
Macroenvironments

16. Achievement in the United States

Richard M. Wolf

The International Association for the Evaluation of Educational Achievement (IEA) has conducted a number of multinational studies of educational achievement, and the United States, as one of the founding members of the organization, has participated in virtually all of them. The most recent set of studies was in the areas of reading comprehension, science, literature, civic education, and French and English as foreign languages. The sole subject in which the United States did not carry out testing was English as a foreign language because of its general inappropriateness.

Each subject-area study was handled in a roughly similar way. An international committee was initially established to explore the feasibility of developing multinational tests in a particular area. Each country that was interested in testing in that area appointed a national committee to work with the international committee. The national committees furnished the international committee with copies of syllabi, course guides, texts, and sample tests for the subject under study. These were reviewed, and an international blueprint of the content and objectives for the teaching of the subject was developed. This was circulated to the national committees for review and modification and, after several rounds, resulted in an international blueprint for each subject that set forth both cognitive and affective outcomes for the subject and covered a range of age and grade levels. While not every country would endorse each objective or content topic equally, the blueprint represented an international statement of what is of importance and what should be learned in a particular school subject. Each international blueprint was a rather notable accomplishment in itself.

The international blueprint was then used to develop tests of student achievement at several selected age and grade levels. The process of test development that was followed was similar across subjects. From testing material supplied by the national committees, the international committee developed test questions and exercises for each cell of the blueprint. These were then reviewed by the national committees before tryout. After a suitable amount of testing material had been approved, tryout work began. Typically, each test question was tried out in at least four countries that represented rather different cultural and linguistic settings. Each question was translated into the national language and administered to small samples of students at the appropriate age or grade level. Conventional item statistics were developed, and an item review was undertaken. Between one and three cycles of development, tryout, and review were required to produce acceptable versions of achievement tests in each subject area.

At the same time that the achievement tests were being developed, other international committees were developing other measures. Scales for the measurement of general attitudes toward school as well as attitude scales toward more specific aspects of each subject were developed. In addition, general questionnaires for students, teachers, and school principals were produced and tested. Specific questionnaires relating to teaching and learning in each subject were also produced. Finally, descriptive scales that sought to have the student describe specific instructional practices were developed. All instruments were developed, tried out, and revised, usually several times, until satisfactory versions of final instruments were obtained.

The age and grade levels chosen for study were as follows:

Population I — all students from ten years to ten years and eleven months of age enrolled in school full time.

Population II — all students from fourteen years to fourteen years and eleven months of age enrolled in school full time.

Population IV—all students in the terminal year of full-time secondary education programs that are either preuniversity, that is, university preparatory, or programs of equal length. For the United States, this meant grade twelve.

Multistage sampling procedures were employed to obtain representative samples of schools, and students for each population level are described elsewhere.[1]

Contact was made with the schools selected for study, and arrangements for administration of all instruments were concluded. The actual administration of instruments was carried out in two different years with the time of testing being in March and April. A coordinator in each individual school handled the local arrangements. Completed instruments were returned to the U. S. National Center in New York. Data processing was carried out in New York and Stockholm and included a number of analyses that were standard across countries as well as some that were unique to the United States. Table 16-1 sets forth the number of students, teachers, and schools that were involved in the study at each population level in each subject in the United States.

While a wealth of detailed material is available in both the reports on the international studies,[2] as well as the national report for the United States,[3] it seems important to distinguish between the IEA studies and two other large-scale enterprises—the Equality of Educational Opportunity Survey (the Coleman Report)[4] and the National Assessment of Educational Progress (NAEP).

While the general form of the IEA study closely resembles the Coleman Report, there are several notable differences. First, the achievement measures were carefully developed to measure what was being taught in various academic subjects in the schools. In contrast, the major analyses in the Coleman Report used the score on verbal ability as ". . . the criterion of school achievement."[5] Second, the teaching and learning variables that were used in the IEA studies were developed specifically for each subject area. In contrast, the Coleman Report used a number of rather general measures. In a number of areas there were no measures of instructional procedures and practices. Finally, there were a few major and a number of minor differences in the way in which the data of the two studies were analyzed. These, however, are of no particular concern here.

There are also differences between the IEA studies and those car-

Table 16-1

Number of students, teachers, and schools involved in the IEA study at each population level in each subject

Subject	Population I			Population II			Population IV		
	Schools	Teachers	Students	Schools	Teachers	Students	Schools	Teachers	Students
Science[a]	272	1,632	5,550	160	488	3,530	127	388	2,665
Reading comprehension[a]	272	1,632	5,550	160	500	3,535	127	433	2,703
Literature[b]	--	--	--	160	500	3,535	127	433	2,703
Civic education[b]	--	--	--	132	318	3,232	124	285	3,070
French as a foreign language[b]	--	--	--	195	239	4,420	177	224	3,230

[a] The same sample was tested in science and reading comprehension at Population I. At Populations II and IV the same sample was administered all instruments in reading comprehension and literature.
[b] No testing done at Populaton I.

ried out by the NAEP. These differences stem from the fact that NAEP restricts itself to the testing of student performance in each of a number of school subjects. No information whatsoever is collected regarding any predictors of achievement other than the classificatory variables of age, sex, race, general socioeconomic status of the school, and community size and setting. Thus, it is not possible to relate academic achievement to instructional variables in order to identify those procedures and practices that are related to achievement and, equally important, those that are not.

THE REGRESSION ANALYSES

There have been many analyses of the IEA data. These are reported in international reports and in the national report of the United States, and they include between-nation comparisons, between-region comparisons, differences between predominantly black and predominantly white schools, and multiple regression analyses between schools and between students. It would be impossible to report here even a fraction of the results of the IEA studies, but they already have been reported extensively elsewhere. This chapter concentrates on some of the results of the IEA studies in the United States that bear on issues of learning environments and effects.

The major analyses in the IEA studies that bear on learning environments and effects are the regression analyses. Multiple regression is a statistical procedure for relating variations in a set of predictor variables to variation in a criterion variable. The details of multiple regression analysis are readily available in a number of standard statistical texts and specialized works on the subject.[6]

In the IEA studies, the score on an achievement test served as the criterion variable in each analysis. Predictor variables were grouped into four blocks:

Block 1 — Background variables, primarily indicators of home and family conditions but including sex and age. These represented prior conditions of the student, his family, and his community.

Block 2 — Type of school or type of program in which the student was enrolled. This was a general indicator of previous learning conditions.

Block 3 — School variables, including curricular and instructional organization and procedures and teacher characteristics and behavior.

Block 4 — Kindred variables representing present characteristics of students (activities, interest, and attitudes). These were viewed as concomitants of achievement rather than as causes.

In the regression analyses of French as a foreign language, an additional block of factors associated with time was inserted between Blocks 2 and 3.

The details of the regression analyses for the IEA studies are reported elsewhere[7] and will not be discussed here. Problems involving large numbers of variables (up to 750 per school), limited numbers of schools, and the existence of categorical variables had to be overcome. In some cases, special solutions had to be developed, while, in other cases, generally accepted procedures, for example, dummy variable coding, were applied. Before the results of the analyses can be presented, however, two points need to be made. The first involves the order in which blocks of variables enter into the regression model, and the second concerns the interpretations that can and cannot be made from the results.

The order of entry is a temporal one. Home variables were entered first in the regression equation since they represent the earliest influences on the student. Type of program is entered second since it is to some extent a reflection of success achieved in earlier learning. The block of school variables is entered third since these represent the present conditions of learning. The kindred variables are entered last since the nature of their relationship to achievement is largely unknown and it is often not clear whether they are causes of the achievement to be explained, effects of that achievement, or mere correlates of the achievement.

The issue of order of entry of variables (or, more correctly, blocks of variables) is critical because the predictor variables in the correlation matrix are typically correlated with each other. Thus, the order of entry makes a considerable difference in the proportion of the variation of the criterion variable that is assigned to each block. Variables entering earlier in the analysis take the largest bite out of the explainable variance; those that enter later are left with less to explain. While nothing can be done to overcome this, it is instructive to examine the simple correlations between individual predictor variables and the criterion variable since the regression analyses may underestimate the importance of some, if not many, instructional variables.

The second major point concerns the interpretation of the results of multiple regression analyses. Multiple regression analysis seeks to statistically explain variation in a criterion variable (achievement test performance) by relating it to the variations in a set of predictor variables. The explanation that is sought is statistical, not causal. Furthermore, the magnitude of the relationship of a predictor variable with a criterion variable can be greatly affected by the amount of variability in the predictor. In the most extreme case, a predictor variable that has no variability at all will have a zero relationship with the criterion. It may, however, be extremely important causally. For example, teachers who have had a uniform amount of training may contribute enormously to the education of their students, but amount of training will in fact show no relationship to student achievement. Multiple regression analysis is intended to statistically "explain" *variations* in student performance; it does not explain *level* of performance. Regression analyses of student achievement are greatly influenced by this phenomenon, because, while homes range from very good to very bad, very bad schools are not allowed to exist. Certification and accreditation standards, coupled with local, state, and even federal controls, are intended to ensure that minimum standards of education are met. This reduces the amount of variability of many school-related variables. The reader is thus cautioned against interpreting the absence of relationships as the absence of effects signifying that school variables are of little importance.

RESULTS OF REGRESSION ANALYSES: BETWEEN SCHOOLS

Between-school regression analyses were carried out in three subjects: reading comprehension, literature, and science. The general results of these analyses are summarized in Table 16-2. Two points are especially worth noting about the results displayed in the table. First, in all subjects at all population levels, the largest share of explainable variation in each criterion is accounted for by the Block 1 variables. There are two reasons for this. The first is that these variables were entered first in the regression analysis. Hence, they were able to account for a sizable proportion of the variance in each criterion variable. This result accords with considerable previous research. The second reason is that educators recognize that the home is indeed a powerful influence on the life of the student. The strong relationships between the Block 1 variables and student achievement are no surprise at all.

Table 16-2

Multiple correlations with percentage of added variance
for blocks of variables for reading comprehension,
literature, and science

Subject and population	Blocks							
	1		2		3		4	
	R	Percent-age of added variance	R	Percent-age of added variance	R	Percent-age of added variance	R	Percent-age of added variance
Reading comprehension								
I	.79	63	.80	1	.84	6	.86	3
II	.83	69	.83	0	.86	5	.93	12
IV	.72	53	.72	0	.72	0	.73	1
Literature								
II	.78	61	.78	0	.82	7	.92	17
IV	.56	32	.56	0	.73	22	.78	6
Science								
I	.82	67	.82	0	.86	8	.89	4
II	.82	67	.82	0	.88	11	.89	1
IV	.66	44	.66	0	.79	19	.83	6

The second noteworthy point about Table 16-2 involves the percentage of added variance of the Block 3 variables. The picture is a mixed one with results ranging from zero at Population IV in reading comprehension to twenty-two at Population IV in literature. The median percentages of added variance at Block 3 are: reading comprehension, 5; literature, 14; and science, 11. This generally reflects the extent to which each subject is learned as a result of direct instruction in school as contrasted with school and nonschool learning. Reading is an example of a subject that is learned both in and outside the school. The ready availability of books and other printed materials in the home and society in general and encouragement by parents and others can result in considerable learning in reading. Accordingly, the low level of relationship between Block 3 variables and performance in terms of reading comprehension is not surprising. It is not that schools are powerless; it is that nonschool forces, notably the home, are so powerful.

The results in literature and science are notably different from those in reading comprehension. Here, instructional variables make very real contributions to explaining criterion variance. Furthermore, the contribution increases with increasing age or grade level. That is, the longer students are exposed to school instruction in a subject, the greater the statistical effect of instructional variables in the subject.

The specific Block 3 variables that contribute to explaining criterion variance in literature and science are set forth in Table 16-3 along with the simple correlation between the variable and performance on the achievement tests. The variables listed in the table are rather diverse. There are some commonalities, however. The number of hours of homework per week is substantially related to achievement. This probably attests to the seriousness and rigor associated with study, in addition to affording students the opportuni-

Table 16-3

Block variables that enter in the regression analyses in literature and reading comprehension at Populations I, II, and IV: Between-schools analyses

Subject and population	Variable	Correlation with achievement
Literature—II	Public library	.22
	Years teaching at present school	.11
	Years training of teacher	.20
	Hours of homework per week	.59
Literature—IV	Textbooks purchased or loaned	.10
	Hours of homework per week	.16
	Teaching load of teacher	-.34
	Improve reading speed	-.27
	Teacher judgment in assessing performance	-.16
Science—I	Design own experiments	-.35
	Regular science lessons	.39
	Observations and experiments	.48
Science—II	Male teachers (percent)	.22
	Opportunity to learn science	.16
	Homework in science	.53
	Work environment scale	.49
	Science study	.27
Science—IV	Science study	.54
	Total science homework	.46

ty to increase learning by additional study. Conditions of work are also related to student achievement. Training, length of service in a particular school, lower teaching loads, availability of a public library, and little need to devote instructional time to skills such as reading speed are all associated with higher levels of achievement in literature. The picture in science is even clearer. Having regular science lessons and making observations and performing experiments are associated with higher levels of achievement at Population I. In short, opportunities to engage in the study of science are related to higher levels of achievement. In contrast, a playful approach to science as indicated by having students design their own experiments is associated with lower levels of achievement. The picture at Populations II and IV is essentially the same although the specific variables that enter into the regression model are somewhat different. The amount of homework in science and the total amount of science study are the best predictors of achievement and are closely followed by the school environment scale, a measure of the learning climate in the school, and the total amount of homework in science. Again, seriousness of purpose and learning opportunities are clearly associated with higher levels of achievement in science. The fact that these variables emerged from the regression analysis, after the home and background variables had been entered, attests to the potency of these predictors. The magnitude of the simple correlations of these variables with the criterion underscores their importance.

In summary, the between-schools regression analyses in reading comprehension, science, and literature yielded three important findings. First, the importance of instructional variables was very much a function of the extent to which a subject was learned in school. Science and the study of formal literature showed considerably greater effects from the school than reading comprehension. The results for reading comprehension were similar to those obtained by Coleman, who used score on a verbal ability test as the criterion of school achievement. Second, the powerful influence of home and social background factors emerged in all subjects at all population levels. Third, the particular learning environment variables that emerged from the analyses were indicative of a serious, diligent, and disciplined educational effort.

A series of regression analyses was carried out in which the student constituted the unit of analysis. These analyses were carried out in reading comprehension, science, literature, civic education, French reading comprehension, and French listening comprehension. The results of these analyses are summarized in Tables 16-4 and 16-5.

The results in Table 16-4 are directly comparable to those in Table 16-2. That is, the meaning of each block is the same. Block 3 represents the instructional variables. In Table 16-5 the results are slightly different because a new block (Block 3) representing time factors was introduced. Block 4 in Table 16-5 denotes instructional variables.

There are several noteworthy results in Tables 16-4 and 16-5. The first is that the multiple correlations are considerably lower than those reported in Table 16-2. This is almost exclusively due to the fact that, in Table 16-2 the school was the unit of analysis while in Tables 16-4 and 16-5 the student is the unit of analysis. This is a typical occurrence. Second, the extent to which a subject is learned at school is dramatically demonstrated. Third, the importance of home and background variables is again demonstrated. There is an exception, however. In French, Block 1 variables account for little of the variation in achievement. This is probably due to the fact that those students who elect to study French are relatively homogeneous in terms of home and social background. Thus, correlations are generally low. Fourth, time factors in French account for sizable proportions of the variation in achievement. Fifth, the picture of influence of instructional variables in each subject as one proceeds from Population I to IV is somewhat confused because of two conflicting tendencies. On the one hand, as students progress through school, the effects of instructional variables become clear. This is shown in the results in French, where the proportion of variation in achievement accounted for by Blocks 3 and 4 increases from Population II to IV. On the other hand, about 25 percent of an age group drops out of school before graduation. Since dropouts generally occur from lower socioeconomic groups, this decreases the variability in both the home and social background variables of the population and results in lower correlations. This is consistently demonstrated in the results from Block 1, which appear in Table 16-4.

The major point requiring further comment involves the relationship between the influence of instructional variables and the extent to which a subject is learned at school. Of all the subjects included in the IEA studies, French as a foreign language is the one most clearly learned at school. By and large, students learn French in school or they do not learn it. Accordingly, median percentages of added vari-

Table 16-4

Multiple correlations with percentage of added variance for blocks of variables for science, reading comprehension, literature, and civic education

Subject and population	Blocks							
	1		2		3		4	
	R	Percentage of added variance	R	Percentage of added variance	R	Percentage of added variance	R	Percentage of added variance
Science								
I	.42	18	.43	0	.52	9	.59	7
II	.45	21	.49	3	.55	6	.60	6
IV	.43	18	.52	9	.59	8	.63	4
Reading comprehension								
I	.44	20	.46	1	.50	4	.56	6
II	.47	22	.51	4	.57	6	.65	11
IV	.42	17	.51	9	.53	2	.58	6
Literature								
II	.43	19	.46	2	.53	8	.61	9
IV	.40	16	.44	4	.50	5	.55	6
Civic education								
II	.45	20	.52	7	.55	3	.63	10
IV	.43	18	.52	9	.56	4	.62	7

Table 16-5

Multiple correlations with percentage of added variance for blocks of variables for French reading and French listening

Subject and population	Blocks									
	1		2		3		4		5	
	R	Percentage of added variance	R	Percentage of added variance	R	Percentage of added variance	R	Percentage of added variance	R	Percentage of added variance
French reading										
II	.16	3	.18	0	.27	5	.39	7	.47	7
IV	.23	5	.24	1	.36	7	.51	13	.62	13
French listening										
II	.17	3	.17	0	.31	7	.43	9	.52	8
IV	.19	4	.23	1	.48	18	.73	31	.86	20

ance of instructional variables are 10 and 20 in French reading and listening, respectively. If the Block 3 variables, time factors, are included, these percentages increase to 16 and 32. In contrast, reading comprehension, which is learned both in and out of school, shows a median percentage of 4 for Block 3 variables. Civic education, which is a measure of general and some specialized knowledge about civic and governmental affairs, shows results that are quite similar to those obtained in reading comprehension. Literature and science, which are more school learned, occupy a position between French and civic education. Thus, the question about the importance of school effects cannot be answered simply. The extent of effects depends on the criterion of achievement under study. Coleman's study examined a single criterion, verbal ability test performance. The IEA studies, in contrast, examined a range of criteria, and the results vary considerably. The more a subject is learned in school, the greater the effects of schooling. The greater the opportunity for nonschool learning, the less significant the role of school variables. In such cases, the greater contribution of home variables undoubtedly contains the influence of home instructional variables.[8]

Table 16-6 sets forth a summary list of variables that emerged in the various regression analyses. The list is selective; only variables with correlations of .15 or greater have been included. A full listing of all variables entering into the regression equations is available in the full IEA report for the United States.[9] Inspection of this table indicates that the level of relationship (simple correlations) between Block 3 variables and achievement is modest. The correlations reported here are the highest ones obtained and yet they range from .15 to .40. This accords with previous research suggesting that the influence of single instructional variables on achievement is weak. This simply seems to be the state of affairs. The correlation between smoking cigarettes and incidence of lung cancer, for instance, is only .14, and all variables reported here exceed that reported relationship.

The individual variables can be grouped into three general classes. The first class relates to industriousness and includes the amount of homework done in the subject each week. Science, reading comprehension, and literature—all include these variables in the regression analyses. The second class relates to teacher competence and includes the teacher's perceived ability in French listening, the teacher having lived in a French-speaking country, and the number of years of post-

Table 16-6

Selected Block 3 variables that enter in the regression analyses in reading comprehension, literature, science, civic education, and French reading and listening comprehension at Populations II and IV: Between-student analyses

Subject and population	Variable	Correlation with achievement
Reading comprehension		
II	Hours of homework per week	.25
IV	Hours of homework per week	.25
Science		
II	Hours of homework per week	.19
	Total amount of science studied	.15
IV	Science study and homework	.38
	Amount of science studied	.35
Literature		
II	Hours of homework per week	.24
IV	Percent of class time devoted to literature study	.26
Civic education		
IV	Patriotic rituals in the classroom	−.17
French reading		
II	Methods of teaching grammar	.18
	Frequency of translation	.15
IV	Number of French teachers	.24
	Frequency of speaking English in French class	−.25
French listening		
II	Teachers perceived listening ability in French	.34
IV	Frequency of speaking English in French class	−.40
	Teacher lived in a French-speaking country	.28
	Frequency of translation work in French class	−.28
	Years of postsecondary school study in French	.23

secondary school study in French. These variables only appear in the regression analyses in French. It is here, however, that teacher variability in proficiency is apt to be greatest. The third class consists of variables indicating the extent to which instruction was on target. Included here are: amount of science studied, percentage of time devoted to studying literature in English classes, methods of teaching grammar, frequency of translation in French classes, an absence of patriotic ritual in the classroom (for civic education), lack of conversing in English in French classes, and, for French listening, a lack of translation work. In short, an emphasis on hard work focused on subject-matter learning under the direction of competent teachers is clearly, consistently, and, taken together, highly related to success in learning.

While the material presented here is an extremely terse summarization of results of the IEA studies for the United States, several points are clear. First, effects of the school learning environment have been detected under the most difficult research conditions that could be used. These include: survey research methods, self-report measures, restricted variability, and often crudely conceptualized and measured variables. Second, the influence of home and social background variables on student achievement is strong. The relative influence of school environmental variables versus nonschool variables, however, varies from subject to subject. When what is to be learned is largely or even wholly school based, the school must be the object of inquiry. When learning results from a combination of school and nonschool events, the search for environmental effects must be broadened.

As one moves beyond the specific results for the United States and examines the results across countries, several factors emerge. Instructional time varies considerably from country to country.[10] In the United States, a student spends about 900 hours in school each year. This holds at all three levels of population. In other countries, the time spent in school is considerably greater. At the Population I level, instructional time ranges from 735 hours per year in Japan to 1,212 hours per year in India. At Populations II and IV the range is from 775 hours per year in France to 1,219 hours per year in India. The amount of instructional time accorded students in the United States is on the low side. For example, ten countries provide more hours of instruction to students each year than the United States, while seven offer fewer hours. At Populations II and IV, fifteen countries provide more instructional hours per year, while only two offer fewer. Thus, when it comes to providing students with instructional time, the United States is among the lower countries.

This is still only part of the story, however. Time spent in learning consists of instructional time plus study time. Unfortunately, it is difficult to obtain information on study time outside the school. Students supplied information about the number of hours of homework each week, and this variable entered prominently into a number of the regression analyses. The variability in hours of homework within countries is greatly exceeded by the variability between countries. At Population IV, for example, the average number of reported hours of homework per week in the United States is six. In the other participating countries, the average number of reported hours of homework per week ranges from eight in Chile, Scotland, and Sweden to seventeen in Iran. The median for all other countries is twelve hours. This is *twice* the average in the United States.[11] Assuming a thirty-six-week school year, the average student in the other participating countries will spend 216 hours a year more on homework than a student in this country. Coupled with the relatively low level of instructional time that students in this country receive, this finding helps show why achievement performance in the United States is lower than many expect it to be. Time spent in learning, both in and out of school, has been shown to be related to the level of learning. This is true of the IEA studies as well as a host of other studies undertaken in the United States. It would seem that those concerned with the improvement of learning will need to devote more attention to this crucial variable.

This is not to say that additional study time is the only variable that needs to be manipulated in order to increase learning. There are, of course, many others. Some have emerged in the analysis of the IEA studies, and others have resulted from other efforts. Further study is needed. It is also probably true that simple manipulation of study time will not produce corresponding increments in achievement for all students. For example, if amount of homework were simply increased, some students would refuse to do it. Study time is a complex variable, and it cannot be expected to produce desired effects as a result of simple manipulation. The fact remains, however, that students in the United States experience a lower level of study time (instruction plus homework) than students in almost all other countries participating in the IEA studies. The matter would seem to deserve prompt and serious attention.

NOTES

1. Richard M. Wolf, *Achievement in America* (New York: Teachers College Press, 1977).

2. John B. Carroll, *The Teaching of French as a Foreign Language in Eight Countries* (New York: John Wiley, 1975); L.C. Comber and John P. Keeves, *Science Education in Nineteen Countries* (New York: John Wiley, 1973); Gilbert F. Peaker, *An Empirical Study of Education in Twenty-One Countries* (New York: John Wiley, 1975); Alan C. Purves, *Literature Education in Ten Countries* (New York: John Wiley, 1973); Robert L. Thorndike, *Reading Comprehension Education in Fifteen Countries* (New York: John Wiley, 1973); Judith V. Torney *et al.*, *Civic Education in Ten Countries* (New York: John Wiley, 1975).

3. Wolf, *Achievement in America*.

4. James S. Coleman *et al.*, *Equality of Educational Opportunity* (Washington, D.C.: U.S. Department of Health, Education and Welfare, 1966).

5. *Ibid.*, 234.

6. Fred N. Kerlinger and Elezar J. Pedhazur, *Multiple Regression in Behavioral Research* (New York: Holt, Rinehart and Winston, 1973).

7. Peaker, *Empirical Study of Education in Twenty-One Countries*.

8. Wolf, *Achievement in America*.

9. *Ibid.*

10. A. Harry Passow *et al.*, *The National Case Study: An Empirical Comparative Study of Twenty-One Educational Systems* (New York: John Wiley, 1976). 262.

11. Comber and Keeves, *Science Education in Nineteen Countries*, 94.

17. Poverty in Big Cities

Daniel U. Levine, Cris Kukuk, and *Jeanie Keeny Meyer*

That many students in big-city schools perform poorly on standardized academic achievement tests is hardly news. Numerous books and articles in journals and newspapers have described and discussed the difficult learning conditions and the low levels of academic performance to be found in many big-city schools. Acknowledging the relationship found throughout the world between academic achievement and poverty[1] and recognizing the fact that many big-city schools enroll a substantial number of economically disadvantaged students, one would expect to find unusually low achievement patterns in those school districts. Apart from this generalization, little is known about the relationship between big-city social environments and academic achievement in the public schools.[2]

We have been analyzing data on the neighborhood characteristics of elementary schools in six large cities (Chicago, Cincinnati, Cleveland, Houston, Kansas City, and St. Louis) and on middle-grade reading achievement in those schools. Achievement data were from standardized reading tests. Scores for individual schools were made available by the central office of each district. Data on neighborhoods came mostly from census tract information for 1970, made available by the U.S. Bureau of the Census, but, for some of the cities, additional tract data were obtained from city or regional planning offices. In order to allocate census tracts to schools, we compared school district attendance boundaries with census tract maps for some of the cities, while lists of such allocations were available through research personnel in the school districts for other cities.

Data also were obtained from school district officials who had information on the economic background of the student body as estimated by such indicators as percentage of students eligible for subsidized lunches and percentage of students from families receiving public assistance. These data were treated as descriptive of the neighborhood served by a school inasmuch as most of the students in the school districts attended the school closest to their homes.

Several important findings emerging from our analysis are described below, followed by a discussion of their implications for educational and social policy. Before proceeding to describe the study and the conclusions drawn from it, however, it is important to comment on our measure of academic achievement, standardized reading tests, for which data are reported in grade equivalent units or percentiles in relation to national norms for performance of students. Such scores often are interpreted as representing a student's mastery of basic learning skills. For example, a score of 6.3 grade equivalent units on a test given to sixth graders in the eighth month of the school year frequently is taken to mean that a student with this score is performing about half a year behind the national norm of 6.8. Pupils scoring below grade level in the subject tested are considered to be below the national average in achievement.

Many educators and psychologists believe that standardized tests do not provide a fair or accurate assessment of the academic performance of many students, particularly those from economically or socially disadvantaged families. It is argued that the tests are unfair to students who live in poor neighborhoods or who belong to minority groups because they require experience and knowledge more typical of the middle-class white environment. Economically or socially disadvantaged students might be progressing or performing fairly well in reading, mathematics, or some other subject, but they may be unfamiliar with the terminology of the test or they may not know how to interpret the directions as well as middle-class students. If this happens, test results for disadvantaged students will be invalid because they do not provide an accurate assessment of how well a student can perform in real-life situations.

We share many of the doubts and criticisms concerning the validity of standardized achievement tests as measures of the performance of disadvantaged students. Despite their faults, however, these tests provide information useful in identifying achievement problems in the public schools. This is particularly true for big-city schools, where levels of attainment frequently are so low that there is no way to rationalize poor achievement by claiming that the tests are invalid.

In Kansas City, for example, first-quartile tenth-grade reading achievement on the *Comprehensive Test of Basic Skills* in 1976 was at the eighth percentile on national norms. This means that 25 percent of the district's tenth graders were achieving at or below the eighth percentile. Many were below the fifth percentile, which is below guessing level for the test and is considered functionally illiterate. First-quartile achievement at four of the district's eleven high schools was at the sixth percentile. Similar patterns can be found in the school districts of many other large cities. Whatever one thinks of the tests, it is impossible to deny that many students are failing to acquire fundamental skills in reading and other basic subjects needed to function in school or in society, and that is the basis for the questions considered in this chapter.

NEIGHBORHOOD SOCIOECONOMIC STATUS AND ACHIEVEMENT

In this section we are concerned with the degree to which achievement scores can be predicted using information based on the socioeconomic status of a neighborhood. (In this chapter, use of the term "socioeconomic status" excludes race as a consideration. When race is included, the term "social status" is used.) Certain measures of neighborhood socioeconomic status have consistently had a curvilinear relationship to grade-level achievement scores. A good example of this phenomenon was found by plotting sixth-grade achievement scores for a test administered in 1976 to students in Kansas City's elementary schools against the percentage of students eligible for subsidized lunches that same year. This scatterplot showed that none of the forty-two schools where more than 40 percent of the students were eligible for subsidized lunches had scores above 5.7, whereas thirteen of nineteen schools where the percentage of students eligible for subsidized lunches was below 40 percent had scores higher than 5.7. This means that at least half of the students in the forty-two schools scored below 5.7, which is more than a year below the national norm of 6.8 for the date the test was administered.

The scatterplots showing neighborhood socioeconomic status variables in relation to achievement indicated that the neighborhood variables that consistently showed curvilinear relationships with achievement generally appeared to be measuring *concentrated poverty* or *social disorganization* in neighborhoods served by low-achieving schools. That is, variables such as "percent students eligible for subsidized lunch" appeared to be measuring "threshold" points beyond which poverty had become heavily concentrated (40 percent or more of students eligible for subsidized lunch, as in the example given above), and grade-level achievement averages were almost always low. Other variables curvilinearly related to achievement were "percent housing units with 1.51 or more people per room," a density measure that we also interpret as indicating concentrated poverty since poverty neighborhoods generally have overcrowded housing units, and "percent females separated," which we take to be a measure of disorganization in the social or family structure of urban neighborhoods.

Furthermore, we also found that 1970 census variables that exhibited consistent curvilinear relationships with achievement tended to have relatively uniform threshold points from one city to another. For example, the threshold point denoting low achievement for Chicago elementary schools was about 4 percent on "percent females separated." In 1972, out of a total of 310 schools, 120 out of 121 that had scores above 4.2 percent on "percent females separated" were in the bottom two-thirds of the achievement distribution. (This placed them at a relatively low achievement level since grade-equivalent achievement at the 66th percentile in this distribution was 6.0—more than half a grade below the national average for sixth graders.) Similar threshold points for "percent females separated" in the other five cities were as follows: Cincinnati, 4.4 percent in 1973; Cleveland, 3.5 percent in 1973; Houston, 3.6 percent in 1974; Kansas City, 4.7 percent in 1970; and St. Louis, 4.6 percent in 1973. Based on these data, it appears that, if the range of separated adult females in urban neighborhoods is between 3 and 5 percent, achievement in the schools in those neighborhoods is almost always low. As mentioned above, we regard the percentage of females separated as a measure of social or family disorganization in an urban neighborhood. The meaning and implications of this finding are discussed later in the chapter.

It should be noted, parenthetically, that it is only in school districts where the range of differing status neighborhoods is wide that neighborhood indicators of concentrated poverty and social disorganization seem to have high utility in differentiating schools with high and low achievement. In a large suburban district in the Midwest, for example, we have also been analyzing neighborhood characteristics and reading achievement patterns and have found that there is essentially no relationship between scores on "percent females separated" and fifth-grade reading scores on tests administered in 1974 among forty-nine elementary schools in the district. None of these suburban schools was, however, in a neighborhood where the percentage of females separated was higher than 1.8—far below the big-city threshold points described above. The correlation between the two variables was .11. By way of contrast, "percent females separated" generally correlated between .70 and .85 with reading achievement in the six big-city school districts studied. Other socioeconomic indicators did, however, correlate significantly with achievement in this suburban district. For example, "percent employed persons over 16 years of age who are laborers" correlated with third-grade achievement at .69, and "percent adults who are high school graduates" correlated at .62.

These data indicate that neighborhood socioeconomic status variables can predict with a high degree of accuracy whether students in a big-city elementary school will score relatively high or low in academic achievement. In addition, multiple regression analysis was used to determine how much of the variation in grade-level academic achievement among the schools in a given city could be predicted from socioeconomic status variables. The results indicated that anywhere from about 50 to 90 percent of the variation in achievement scores could be predicted or "explained" by neighborhood information, depending on the type of achievement variable (for example, third grade versus sixth grade) and the nature and utility of the neighborhood data for a given city. Predictions accounting for 80 to 90 percent of the variation in achievement scores such as we obtained in several cities were somewhat higher than have been reported in most previous research relating socioeconomic data on students or neighborhoods to school-level achievement scores.[3] One reason why some of our predictions were so accurate, compared to those of other studies, may have been because we systematically transformed neighborhood variables curvilinearly related to achievement to log, reciprocal, or square root forms in order to maximize their correlation with the achievement measures.[4] Many earlier studies either did not find much curvilinearity in relationships between socioeconomic status variables and achievement, or, for one reason or another, predictor variables were not transformed to allow for nonlinear relationships.

The high degree of accuracy with which achievement can be predicted from information on neighborhood socioeconomic status in big-city school districts is illustrated in Table 17-1, using median sixth-grade reading achievement based on tests administered in 1973 to students in elementary schools in St. Louis. These data show the actual and predicted scores for the first twenty schools in an alphabetically arranged sample of sixty-five schools using the following five neighborhood predictor variables: "percent students from families receiving

Table 17-1

Results of multiple regression analysis on actual and predicted sixth-grade reading achievement scores (1973) for twenty of sixty-five elementary schools in St. Louis

School	Score		Difference
	Actual	Predicted	
1	6.0	5.8	.2
2	5.5	6.0	-.5
3	6.7	6.8	-.1
4	7.0	7.4	-.4
5	5.4	5.5	-.1
6	6.0	6.2	-.2
7	5.5	5.4	.1
8	5.5	5.8	-.3
9	6.7	6.6	.1
10	6.0	5.7	.3
11	7.1	6.6	.5
12	6.3	6.0	.3
13	5.3	5.5	-.2
14	6.6	6.5	.1
15	6.9	6.9	.0
16	5.8	6.1	-.3
17	6.8	6.5	.3
18	6.2	6.5	-.3
19	5.6	5.4	.2
20	5.8	5.7	.1

public assistance (square root)," "male-female ratio for population 15 to 24 years of age," "number separated females per residential acre," "percent owner-occupied housing units valued at less than $15,000 (reciprocal)," "percent owner-occupied housing units lacking plumbing (log)."

The squared multiple correlation (estimate of the percent of variance accounted for in the achievement variable) adjusted for the sample size of sixty-five in this regression analysis was .835. As shown in the data, achievement scores for all of the twenty schools were correctly predicted to within one-half grade level of their actual scores. Predictions nearly as accurate and in some cases even more accurate were obtained for the other five cities, with squared multiple correlations for various reading achievement measures ranging generally in the sixties in Cleveland and in the seventies and eighties in the other cities.[5]

RACIAL COMPOSITION OF NEIGHBORHOODS AND ACHIEVEMENT

Earlier achievement predictions were based on neighborhood socioeconomic status data, but information on the racial composition of neighborhoods or schools was excluded. Since racial composition tends to be related to income, occupational status,[6] and other measures of socioeconomic standing in big-city communities, racial composition is also related to academic achievement in the cities studied. For example, "percent black population" correlated at .69 with median reading scores on tests administered to sixth-grade students in Houston in 1972. Because these correlations may reflect relationships between the low socioeconomic status of predominantly black neighborhoods and achievement, this does not mean that racial composition is independently related to achievement apart from socioeconomic status.

To determine whether racial composition is independently related to achievement, we entered "percent black population" following the best neighborhood socioeconomic status predictors of achievement in regression equations for each city. This procedure controls for the effects of socioeconomic status in order to determine whether racial composition contributes additionally to the prediction of achievement. The results indicated that racial composition generally added nothing at all to the prediction and only occasionally increased the percentage of variance accounted for by as much as one or two points.

Even when "percent black population" was statistically transformed to reflect the curvilinear relationship, it generally added little or nothing to the prediction of achievement.

This finding does not, however, prove that racial composition is unimportant in determining achievement levels in big-city schools. Since racial composition is related to socioeconomic status, it is as plausible to say that correlations between socioeconomic status and achievement reflect relationships between race and achievement as to assume that the latter relationships reflect correlations between race and socioeconomic status. As an alternative approach at this point in our analysis, we decided to study predominantly black and predominantly white schools separately to determine whether socioeconomic status predicts achievement in both sets of schools. If socioeconomic status is as potent a predictor in each set as in a sample in which it is highly confounded with race, it is reasonable to conclude that socioeconomic status is the major determinant of achievement level regardless of how difficult it is to separate the effects of socioeconomic status and race in the latter type of sample.

To conduct this analysis, we selected a set of neighborhood variables including those we had found to be most powerful in predicting achievement either in our total sample of Chicago elementary schools, in a subsample of schools where more than 90 percent of the students were black, or in a subsample where more than 90 percent were non-minority (white) according to the classification of racial-ethnic minority status used by the U.S. Department of Health, Education, and Welfare. Seven neighborhood variables were included: "percent students from families receiving public assistance (square root)," "percent adult females who are separated (log)," "percent owner-occupied housing units valued at less than $20,000 (log)," "percent renter-occupied housing units renting at less than $80 per month (log)," "percent employed persons over 16 years of age who are sales workers," "percent persons over 25 years of age who are high school graduates," and "percent families with income three times or more above poverty level."

The dependent variable in this analysis was median sixth-grade reading achievement as shown by tests administered in 1969. Results of the analysis were as follows: The squared multiple correlation for 288 schools for which we had achievement information was .77. The squared multiple correlation for 61 schools where the enrollment was 90 percent or more black was .69. The squared multiple correlation for 73 schools where the enrollment was 90 percent or more white was .58. The squared multiple correlation for the remaining 154 schools (up to 89 percent black or 89 percent white) was .69.

While the prediction for the total sample (R^2 = .77) was better than for the three subsamples, all four analyses indicated that achievement levels were predictable with a high degree of accuracy from neighborhood socioeconomic data. It seems probable, furthermore, that much or most of the superiority in prediction for the total sample was due to the fact that variables for the total sample had a less restricted range than variables for the subsamples. The standard deviation for reading scores in the total sample of 288 schools, for example, was 1.22 (grade equivalent units), whereas the standard deviation for the 73 white schools was .85.

When we created a new subsample by arbitrarily restricting a regression analysis to schools with reading scores between 4.5 and 7.5, 189 schools were included in the analysis, and the standard deviation of reading scores was .81. The squared multiple regression correlation for this analysis was .68 — about the same as it was for the predominantly black and the racially mixed schools. This pattern suggests that socioeconomic status can account for achievement differences almost as well in predominantly white or predominantly black neighborhoods as in the city as a whole, thereby indicating that race may not be very important in explaining why some schools are high in achievement and others are low.

Further support for the central importance of socioeconomic status in affecting school achievement in big-city neighborhoods also was found in examining scatterplots showing neighborhood socioeconomic variables in relation to achievement for our subsample of predominantly black schools in Chicago. We found a definitely curvilinear relationship between indicators of concentrated poverty and social disorganization on the one hand and academic achievement on the other in the group of schools with 90 percent or more black students: among sixty-four such schools for which data were available on both variables, none of the thirty-six schools in neighborhoods in which 3.2 percent or more of the housing units had 1.51 or more people per room had achievement scores above 5.2, as contrasted with nineteen of twenty-eight schools with lower density scores where the achievement scores were above 5.2. The threshold point of about 3 percent is within the range of 3 to 8 percent that we found for our total sample of schools in six cities. One would not need to know anything about the racial composition of these sixty-four predominantly black schools to predict which of them would be in the lowest part of the Chicago achievement distribution based on information giving the number of people per room in the neighborhoods they serve.

Because predominantly black schools might still score a given increment below the predominantly white schools even after account was taken of people per room and other measures of concentrated poverty and social disorganization, our results do not prove that race makes no contribution to differences in achievement in big-city neighborhoods. To conclude otherwise would be to apply illegitimately the conclusions based on aggregate data to phenomena denoting the performance of individuals.[7] The results do, however, suggest that differences in the socioeconomic status of the neighborhood probably do account for most of the differences in achievement between predominantly white and predominantly black schools.

INTERACTIONS AMONG VARIABLES IN AFFECTING ACHIEVEMENT

We have presented evidence suggesting that race has little or no independent effect on achievement, but this generalization is not definitive and it does not tell us how race interacts with other variables in influencing achievement. In addition, we also want to know about the possible effects of other neighborhood indicators, such as family disorganization, density, and whether housing is owner- or renter-occupied. Does family disorganization have an effect on achievement independent of its correlation with income? Do students in neighborhoods that are high in family disorganization and also high in density achieve less than students in neighborhoods that are high in family disorganization but low in density? Do students in neighborhoods in which housing is largely owner-occupied perform better academically than students in neighborhoods in which most of the housing is rental? Low income is widely recognized as being associated with low achievement in the schools, but relationships between achievement and family disorganization, density, and other neighborhood social characteristics have not been frequently studied. To examine these relationships, we carried out a series of path analyses using at least one dependent achievement variable for each of the six cities in the study.

Path analysis allows an investigator to determine how much "direct" effect a variable has on a dependent variable when the effects of other variables are controlled and the direction of relationships is specified in advance, as compared with its "indirect" effects transmitted through other variables that also are related to the dependent variable.

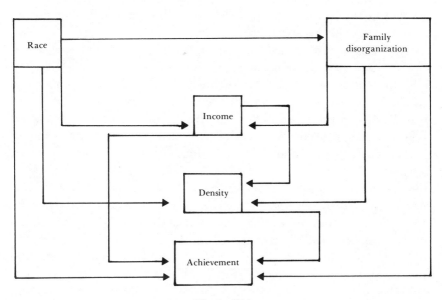

Figure 17-1
Model for path analysis

Path analysis is carried out only after specifying a theoretically-defensible model to be tested against empirical data. The first model we tested against our data is shown in Figure 17-1. Components in the model were measured as follows:

Race — "percent black population in census tracts (log)"

Income — mean family income

Family disorganization — "percent adult females separated (log)"

Density — "percent housing units with 1.51 or more people per room (log)"

Achievement — sixth-grade reading scores

As indicated by the directional arrows, the model postulates the following sequence of relationships:

1. Family disorganization is influenced by race. Black neighborhoods are higher in percentage of females separated than white neighborhoods.

2. Income is influenced by race. Black neighborhoods are lower in income than white neighborhoods.

3. Income is influenced by family disorganization. Neighborhoods with a high percentage of separated females have a high percentage of families headed by females, which tend to have a lower income than families where both parents are present.

4. Density is influenced by race. Black families tend to live in smaller housing units than white families.

5. Density is influenced by income. Low-income families live in smaller housing units than high-income families.

6. Density is influenced by family disorganization. Neighborhoods with a higher percentage of separated females tend to have higher density than neighborhoods with a lower percentage of separated families.

7. Achievement is influenced directly by race, income, family disorganization, and density. Schools in neighborhoods that have high percentages of minority residents, low-income families, separated females, or crowded housing units tend to have low achievement. In addition, some of the influence of race, family disorganization, and income on achievement is transmitted through density, that is, these variables have a particularly significant influence on achievement when combined with density. Part of the influence of race and family disorganization also is transmitted through income.

Results of the path analysis for St. Louis, with standardized partial regression coefficients and associated F levels and probabilities shown in parentheses above the appropriate directional lines, are shown in Figure 17-2. The dotted lines in the figure represent relationships that were not statistically significant at the .05 level. Race, income, and density were not directly related to achievement when other predictors were statistically controlled. Only family disorganization had a direct effect on achievement. Conclusions suggested by the coefficients include the following:

1. The standardized partial coefficient of $-.58$ between family disorganization and achievement means that this variable has direct effects on achievement. After controlling for the effects of race, income, and density, an increase of one standard unit in "percent females

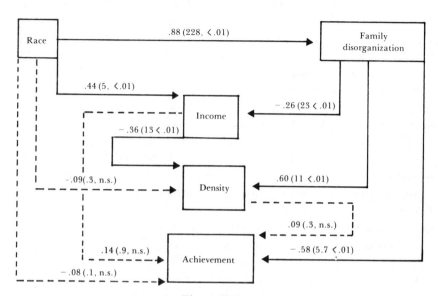

Figure 17-2
Results of path analysis for St. Louis

separated" is associated with a decrease of .58 standard units in achievement.

2. The standardized coefficient of .60 between family disorganization and density means that an increase of one standard unit in "percent families separated" is associated with an increase of .6 standard units in density, after controlling for race and income.

These results agree with our earlier conclusions that race appears to have no independent relationship with achievement when data for the neighborhood and school levels are used to analyze its influence; all its effects are transmitted through family disorganization, income, and density. These results also suggest that family disorganization has a potent separate influence on achievement in the public schools, but density and income do not.

The results of other path analysis runs we carried out did not, however, support these conclusions. Race did have direct effects on achievement in Chicago, Cincinnati, and Kansas City, while density had a direct influence on achievement in all three of these cities, plus Houston. The four cities in which density also had significant direct effects were the four in which it had highest zero-order correlations with achievement. The same tendency was found for other variables: a variable that had a particularly high correlation with achievement in a given city tended to have a direct effect on achievement in that city. In other cities where it did not correlate as highly with achievement, there was no direct effect.

It is possible or even probable that neighborhood social characteristics really are differentially related to achievement and other social phenomena in differing cities, but there is a simpler explanation for the inconsistencies in our findings. Further study of the path analyses indicated that we could manipulate the data to confirm or reject the model described above (as well as other models we also tested) by changing the types and mixtures of variables used in the equations.[8] For example, changing the dependent variable (year in which achievement data were collected) sometimes changed the results, as when race had nonsignificant direct effects for one year, but highly significant direct effects for another year in which it happened to have a higher correlation with achievement. Transforming one or all of the variables to take account of their curvilinear relationships with achievement sometimes resulted in major changes in conclusions, generally by raising the correlation between one of the independent variables and achievement. Substituting one income variable for another sometimes substantially altered the conclusions, as in the case of Cincinnati, where mean family income did not have significant direct effects but the percentage of families three times or more above the poverty level had direct effects of .43, significant at the .05 level of confidence.

In short, we could predetermine whether any given variable, such as race or income or family disorganization, had direct effects on achievement by our choice of variables to analyze, even when using just one or two basic models denoting interrelationships between race, income, social disorganization, density, and achievement. Including additional types of theoretical constructs (for example, educational level of the neighborhood) would affect the results even more.

What do these findings indicate in addition to the conclusion that researchers should be cautious about studies using path analysis techniques to delineate the influence of predictor variables on school achievement? We believe that one reason why our results were inconsistent is because the variables with which we are working generally are so highly intercorrelated. For example, "percent black population" correlates with "percent females separated" between .75 and .89 in all six cities studied. "Percent families three times or more above the poverty level" correlates with "percent housing units with 1.51 or more people per room" and with "percent females separated" at .71 to .86, and correlations between the independent variables and achievement range as high as .88 when statistical transformations are used to account for curvilinearity. Some of the path analysis runs using percentage of families three times or more above the poverty level did not give intelligible results at all, apparently because intercorrelations among the variables made the equations unstable.

The high multicollinearity that we found among our neighborhood predictors suggests that dimensions of social status have become so commingled in big cities that it may be futile to try to separate them. As a result of socioeconomic and racial stratification and segregation in metropolitan areas, substantial parts of big cities are characterized by low income, high family disorganization, high concentration of racial minorities, high density, low occupational status, and very low school achievement relative to other parts of the metropolitan area. We started out by referring to neighborhoods with a high percentage of low-income families as concentrated poverty neighborhoods, but it would be just as accurate to describe most of these neighborhoods in terms of family disorganization, inadequate school achievement, or other problems that arise when social institutions such as the family and the school are confronted with the problems of concentrated urban poverty.

The inability to disentangle completely the effects on achievement of various social status dimensions such as income, race, density, and family disorganization does not, however, mean that path analysis is unable to help us understand something about social conditions that influence academic performance in big cities. To identify supportable generalizations, we have been further analyzing our data using several additional variables and models that we hope will help tease out conclusions about neighborhood conditions and achievement. For example, we have been examining a five-variable model in which "percent owner-occupied housing units" is substituted for density, and "percent females separated" reflects rather than influences income. We also have been examining results with a simplified four-variable model in which race, females separated, and mean income are the only predictor variables. Preliminary conclusions suggested by this analysis have been:

Family disorganization interacts with density in affecting school achievement. In all six cities, there is a significant direct effect of "percent females separated" on "percent housing units with 1.51 or more people per room." In Chicago, Cincinnati, Houston, and Kansas City, density has a direct effect on achievement, but "percent females separated" does not. In Cleveland and St. Louis the situation is reversed: family disorganization has a direct effect on achievement, but density does not. (This pattern appears to arise because density has a higher zero-order correlation with achievement in the first four cities than in the latter two.) These results imply that it is particularly difficult to disentangle relationships between family disorganization and density. Whether one or the other appears to have a direct effect on achievement depends on the correlational data in the sample, but the two clearly interact to affect achievement in the public schools.

Owner-occupied housing has no direct effect on achievement in big-city schools. Some students of urban affairs believe that other things remaining equal, neighborhoods with a high percentage of owner-occupied housing provide better social environments than neighborhoods with mostly rental housing. If so, the percentage of owner-occupied housing might be expected to have a direct effect on achievement in the public schools. Our data show that owner-occupied housing had no direct effect on achievement in any of the cities in our sample. All of its relationship with achievement is either shared with other variables, as when schools in neighborhoods high on this indicator have higher than predicted achievement only if these neighborhoods also are low on family disorganization, or its zero-order correlation with achievement only reflects the influence of other variables, such as high income, with which it also is correlated.

For the most part, these generalizations merely restate and further illustrate and explicate our previous conclusion: indicators of social status in big-city neighborhoods tend to be so intermingled that it is difficult to identify their underlying relationships with school achievement. We believe it is legitimate to refer to this situation in big cities as reflecting the existence of what we have called concentrated urban poverty because we have found that reading achievement is almost universally low in neighborhoods with a high proportion of low-income families. But low achievement in these neighborhoods seems to reflect not just low income, family disorganization, high density, or racial minority status per se, but rather the concentration and interaction of these conditions in particular parts of a city or a metropolitan area.

DISCUSSION

Data on neighborhood socioeconomic status and reading achievement in big-city school districts examined in this chapter have indicated that low achievement is highly correlated with indicators of low social status in neighborhoods. Even more important than this unsurprising conclusion was the discovery that indicators of concentrated poverty and related phenomena such as family disorganization and high density allow one to identify relatively specific threshold ranges beyond which achievement levels in big-city elementary schools are uniformly low. For example, in all six big-city school districts included in the study achievement levels were consistently low in neighborhoods in which 3 to 5 percent of the adult females were classified as separated in the 1970 census.

We also attempted to determine how race, income, family disorganization, density, and owner-renter status in housing interact in affecting achievement. Data on predominantly white and black schools in Chicago suggest, but do not prove, that race makes little difference in and of itself. Path analysis attempts designed to further disentangle the effects of several neighborhood measures were largely unsuccessful, in part because of high intercorrelation among the measures of neighborhood status. We were able, however, to determine that family disorganization and density interact in influencing achievement, and that percentage of owner-occupied housing has no independent, direct influence on achievement.

In effect, what the methodology employed in our studies has done is to identify inner-city neighborhoods that are characterized by multiple, interrelated problems including concentrated poverty and high family and social disorganization. These are the parts of the metropolitan area to which poor and problem-ridden families and individuals have been consigned in unusually heavy concentrations by social and economic forces responsible for the evolution of large metropolitan areas in the United States. Low school achievement is but one manifestation of a larger syndrome of urban decay and deterioration involving the establishment and maintenance of concentrated poverty areas within big cities.

Perhaps it is to be expected that the public schools and other social institutions in inner-city areas are not functioning very successfully in the face of multiple problems that combine to limit their effectiveness.

It is very difficult, for example, for teachers to work successfully with large concentrations of low-status children or for social welfare workers to work effectively with high case loads of extremely poor families living in deteriorating neighborhoods. That is, once the problems characteristic of inner-city neighborhoods reach certain threshold points in severity and frequency, the institutions tend to operate ineffectively or dysfunctionally.

The causes of this dysfunctioning are matters for speculation. Our own belief is that schools—as well as other urban institutions such as hospitals, the police, and the banking system—pass a hypothetical "threshold" point at which the problems associated with poverty become heavily concentrated. And it is at this point that institutional practices, which may work fairly well in other locations, begin to break down. In the inner-city school, for example, teachers may have four or five times as much difficulty providing appropriate instruction for a class with six or eight academically retarded students as teachers in a middle- or mixed-status school with three or four such students. Each additional low-achieving student means an exponential decrease in the amount of time available for other students. Although little research has been conducted comparing classroom dynamics in low-status versus middle-status schools, Deutsch and his colleagues did carry out one study showing that only half as much time was devoted to instruction in inner-city classrooms as in middle-status classrooms.[9] Such differentials probably are related to a variety of considerations, including the degree to which pupils are prepared to handle available materials, the extent to which classroom management problems arise in different types of schools, and the ways in which students encourage and reinforce each other in differing types of behaviors.

As for administrators, counselors, and other school staff, increasing the number of problems to be considered may spread professional resources so thin that few of the problems can be resolved successfully. The problems then feed on themselves. Doubling the number of problems in a school, in other words, may triple or quadruple the difficulty in dealing with them successfully. The result may be dysfunction throughout the institution.

Other social institutions in the inner city face comparable difficulties in handling the multiple problems characteristic of concentrated poverty areas. In a health system, for example, logic suggests that it is many times more difficult to deliver public health services effectively to populations that have few economic resources and are densely concentrated than to wealthy populations spread out in such a way as to lessen the communicability of disease and infection. In a legal system, police and other personnel faced with a particularly high incidence of crime have less time to deal effectively with any given offense. As a result, morale tends to deteriorate, offenders tend to be apprehended and punished relatively less often than in low-crime areas, and young people see evidence that crime and punishment are seldom related in real life. Before long, conditions favor the spread of social behavior fully as destructive and contagious as the illness that reaches epidemic proportions.

Institutions concerned with maintenance of the physical environment are similarly affected by conditions in the inner city. Savings and loan associations, for example, may be unable to make a profit when the default rate on home loans doubles from 2 or 3 percent to 5 or 6 percent. That is why residents of the inner city are unable to obtain loans to maintain or improve their property, except, perhaps, at exorbitant interest rates that lead to still more defaults on payments. Once a few properties on a block deteriorate and become unsalable, property values go down and lending institutions become still more reluctant to approve loans. It is not long before the cycle of deterioration and deflation in the capital stock of the neighborhood passes the threshold point, and it becomes a poverty area.

These examples are admittedly simplistic in that they do not take into account all of the causes and problems involved in the dysfunction of social institutions in concentrated poverty neighborhoods. In particular, a full analysis of institutional dysfunctioning in the inner city also should consider the interrelationships between differing institutions and urban systems, as when abandoned housing provides a breeding ground for delinquency among teenagers or when students who can barely read drop out of school and begin looking for work that requires a higher level of literacy. Inner-city schools, for their part, are faced with the problem of teaching large numbers of students whose main concern frequently is survival in the neighborhood outside the school because housing, health, law enforcement, welfare, and other institutions often do not function successfully in the inner city. Overloaded with too many students who in turn are overloaded with a multitude of individual and family problems, the public schools as traditionally organized and operated may all but cease functioning educationally at all. They become little more than custodial institutions.

An additional point that should be emphasized here involves our finding that the percentage of females separated is one of the best neighborhood predictors of achievement in big-city schools. This variable — and other highly correlated indicators such as the percentage of female-headed families, the percentage of males separated, or the percentage of husband-wife families — is (when high) a primary characteristic of concentrated poverty neighborhoods and a direct reflection of the widespread social disorganization existing in the inner city. From this point of view it is not surprising to find that a high percentage of separated females — or separated males, for that matter — is very closely associated with low achievement levels in the public schools. A high percentage of separated females represents the dysfunctioning of the family as an institution under inner-city conditions, just as low achievement represents the dysfunctioning of the schools. Similarly, a relationship between families headed by females on the one hand and low school achievement or alternate indexes of institutional failure on the other does not in itself indicate that families headed by females are somehow "inferior." As pointed out by Robert Hill of the National Urban League, such statistics do not necessarily support "the view of the Negro family as a causal nexus in a tangle of pathology which feeds on itself. Rather, we view the Negro family in theoretical perspective as a subsystem of the larger society."[10]

A statistical study such as our own, which is based on geographic aggregates, can indicate that students achieve poorly in neighborhoods with a high incidence of poverty and social disorganization; it does not show that students in families headed by females in these neighborhoods achieve more or less than those from intact nuclear families. The results can be interpreted as easily and validly to suggest that many children suffer educational disadvantages associated with environmental conditions in neighborhoods with high proportions of families headed by females as to indicate that such families somehow "cause" low achievement.

Unless urban policies in the future deal directly with the neighborhood-level and institution-level aspects of educational and other problems that burden major social institutions in large cities, they are likely to prove as discouragingly unsuccessful as most previous political experiments in educational or other social reform. If, as our data indicate, low income is closely intertwined with family disorganization, high density, and other variables in generating low school achievement, achievement probably will not be improved much by policies designed only to increase the income of inner-city residents. Some of our path analysis runs for Cincinnati and St. Louis indicated that all of the effects of income on school achievement are transmitted through race, family disorganization, and density. In this context a governmental policy emphasizing incomes but failing to deal with the conditions that relate race, density, and family disorganization to school achievement probably will have little effect on the performance of neighborhood social institutions such as the public schools. Such a policy would give inner-city residents more money to spend, but their neighborhood institutions would still function inadequately and residents would face the same deleterious social conditions that are now associated with concentrated urban poverty.

NOTES

1. Richard D. Noonan, *School Resources, Social Class, and Student Achievement* (New York: John Wiley, 1976).

2. Much research has been conducted to determine whether "physical" resources, such as class size or expenditure per pupil, are more closely related to achievement than "social" resources, such as attitudes or economic background of the student body. Only a few studies, however, such as parts of the reanalysis of the Coleman data (James S. Coleman *et al., Equality of Educational Opportunity* [Washington, D.C.: U.S. Government Printing Office, 1966]) by Mayeske and his colleagues (George W. Mayeske *et al., A Study of the Achievement of Our Nation's Students* [Washington, D.C.: U.S. Government Printing Office, 1973]), have focused on relating social environment to achievement, and fewer still have explicitly examined relationships between big-city environments and achievement.

3. Typical squared multiple correlations (estimates of the variance predicted in a dependent variable), using only socioeconomic data to predict school-level achievement, generally range from about 50 to 80. See Thomas P. Hogan, "Socioeconomic Community Variables as Predictors of Cognitive Test Performance of School Children," unpub. diss., Fordham University, 1970.

4. John W. Tukey, *Exploratory Data Analysis,* Volume I, limited ed. (Reading, Mass.: Addison-Wesley, 1970).

5. Daniel U. Levine *et al.,* "Concentrated Urban Poverty and Reading Achievement in Five Big Cities" (Kansas City, Mo.: Center for the Study of Metropolitan Problems in Education, University of Missouri — Kansas City, 1977, mimeo).

6. In our data on Chicago, for example, "Percent black population" is correlated at .52 with "Percent of families three times or more above the poverty level." In St. Louis, it is correlated at .88 with "Percent of adult females separated."

7. Leigh Burstein and I.D. Smith, "Choosing the Appropriate Unit for Investigating School Effects," *Australian Journal of Education* 21 (1977): 65-79.

8. Daniel U. Levine, Cris Kukuk, and Jeanie Keeny Meyer, "Concentrated Poverty Neighborhoods and Academic Achievement in Big-City Schools" (Kansas City, Mo.: Center for the Study of Metropolitan Problems in Education, University of Missouri—Kansas City, 1977, mimeo).

9. Martin Deutsch *et al., Communication of Information in the Elementary School Classroom* (New York: Institute for Developmental Studies, 1964).

10. Robert B. Hill, "National Urban League Study—The Strength of Black Families," extension of remarks, *Congressional Record,* August 6, 1971, E8985.

18. Achievement in Fifty States

Herbert J. Walberg and *Sue Pinzur Rasher*

Since the publication of *Equality of Educational Opportunity* in 1966, some school boards and educators have begun to doubt the commonsense proposition that schooling makes a difference.[1] This chapter challenges that doubt by describing several recent analyses of school effects that have received less attention than they deserve, by summarizing an extension of earlier analyses of the rate of failure on the Selective Service mental ability test in relation to educational practices in the fifty states,[2] and, finally, by examining the relations of important population characteristics and educational policies in the states.

SCHOOLING DOES MAKE A DIFFERENCE

Perhaps there is confusion over what one means when one says that schooling makes a difference. Any effort to clarify the meaning requires consideration of at least four questions:

Does amount of schooling make a difference? An impressive book, *The Enduring Effects of Education*, provides the most definitive answer to this question.[3] Based on reanalysis of fifty-four national surveys conducted during the years 1949 to 1971 and involving eighty thousand respondents, the results clearly demonstrate differences in knowledge associated with attained levels of schooling. Take just one small example: tabulations of a survey completed in 1966 show that 93 percent of the college graduates knew the meaning of the word "pact," while only 28 percent of elementary school graduates and 77 percent of secondary school graduates could define the word. The association also holds in the humanities, in geography, in science, in civics, and in other fields. Even when social origins were controlled, amount of schooling clearly made great differences. For example, data obtained in 1958 reveal that half of the college graduates with fathers in blue-collar occupations achieved a high score on a test of knowledge of domestic affairs. Of those with professional fathers, only a third of the high school graduates and a fifth of those who attended only elementary school matched that achievement. Although it is difficult to say whether people know more because they attended school longer or attended school longer because they were more capable, it is clear that schools open an avenue to knowledge, even to children of the less well educated.

Does the opportunity to learn make a difference? The work of the International Association for the Evaluation of Educational Achievement is similarly impressive. Another recent volume, *Educational Policy and International Assessment,* draws implications from a survey of 260,000 students in nineteen countries.[4] Of the hundreds of variables surveyed, one cluster of indicators, aside from home background, was most closely related to achievement: the opportunity to learn. Whether indicated by hours of instruction, hours of homework per week, cumulative years of study in the subject, curricular emphasis and challenge, or years of postsecondary preparation of teachers, opportunity to learn is clearly related to test results. Japan's high scores on the most culturally universal subjects in the curriculum, science and mathematics, exemplify national commitment to high and equal levels of educational opportunity.

Does the psychological environment of learning make a difference? Although based on smaller samples (five hundred to a few thousand), recent studies in Australia, Canada, India, and the United States show that student perceptions of the cohesiveness, involvement, goal direction, and democratic practice in their classes are related, with socioeconomic status statistically controlled, to gains on cognitive and affective tests during the course of instruction.[5] Students beyond the ages of ten to twelve can validly rate the extent to which the class works toward the learning goals at hand in productive, satisfying ways.

Do gross indicators of educational quality make a difference? Coleman, Jencks, Mosteller, and Moynihan generally conclude that the answer to this question is negative.[6] Before turning to our analysis, which yields an affirmative answer, several reservations about such research should be mentioned.

First, gross indicators may be only remotely related to test results. It is not the total educational expenditure that may make the difference, but how the money is spent; nor is it small classes as such, but what may be done in a small class. Such variables may then indicate permissive but not sufficient conditions for educational effectiveness.

Second, most of the American research that reached the press was based on Coleman's original survey data. These data systematically underrepresent urban populations because several of the largest city school systems refused to cooperate in the survey. And more than a third of some samples, notably blacks in the South, omitted answers to certain questionnaire items — a fact revealing much about the appropriateness of the survey instruments and the rigor of their administration.

Third, nearly all researchers using Coleman's data and the international data mentioned above underrepresented the effects of schooling by using inadequate analytical techniques. Bowles and Levin, who analyzed the Coleman data more rigorously, show the significant effects of gross indicators on the quality of schooling.[7]

Fourth, in a technocratic society we need to remind ourselves that it does not follow that what is most measurable or most often measured in education is most important. Standardized tests are built not to demonstrate school effects but to reveal student differences — and these in a severely limited sense. Technical problems of practicality, and validity when measuring morality, creativity, social intelligence, and the like may remain insuperable for many years.

RATES OF FAILURE IN THE FIFTY STATES

Notwithstanding these reservations and biases against school effects, our analysis corroborates the significant association, with socioeconomic effects held statistically constant, of gross indicators of school quality and test results. Table 18-1 lists the variables investigated.

Table 18-1

Variable descriptions

Variables	Description	Trans-formation	Mean	Standard deviation
Test failures	Percent of Selective Service draftees examined for military service who failed mental test, 1970	Log Y	1.47	0.90
Adult education	Median school years of education completed by persons 25 years old and above	None	11.85	0.65
Median income	Cost-adjusted personal income per capita	X/1000	3.75	0.46
Black population	Percent of population that is of the black race, according to census definition	$\sqrt{X}$	2.53	1.55
Spanish-origin population	Percent of population that is of Mexican, Puerto Rican, Cuban, Central or South American, or other Spanish origin	$\sqrt{X}$	1.49	0.89
State population	Total population of state in thousands	Log X	7.80	1.06
Density	Population per square mile of land area	Log X	4.07	1.41
Urban residence	Percent of population living in metropolitan areas of more than 100,000 persons	None	51.23	27.63
Rural residence	Percent of population living in areas of fewer than 2,500 persons	$\sqrt{X}$	5.71	1.28
Homicide rate	Number of murder and nonnegligent manslaughter crimes per 100,000 population	$\sqrt{X}$	2.38	0.76
Newspaper subscriptions	Percent of population subscribing to daily newspaper	$\sqrt{X}$	0.52	0.05

Table 18-1 *(continued)*
Variable descriptions

Variables	Description	Trans-formation	Mean	Standard deviation
Public school enrollment	Percent of public school enrollment to population aged 5 to 17	None	0.86	0.05
Pupil-teacher ratio	Ratio of public school pupils to teachers	None	22.24	1.92
School expenditures	Cost-adjusted receipts available from all sources per pupil for public school systems (in thousands of dollars)	1/X	1.05	0.29
Expenditure effort	Ratio of cost-adjusted public school expenditure to personal income per capita	None	0.06	0.01
School size	Ratio of total public school population to the total number of public schools	$\sqrt{X}$	21.12	4.21
Nongraded schools	Ratio of pupils attending ungraded schools to the total pupil population	$\sqrt{X}$	1.26	0.30
One-teacher schools	Ratio of public one-teacher schools to the total number of public schools	Log (X + 1)	-0.63	0.12
Effective attendance	Product of average length of school term with percent average pupil daily attendance	None	167.9	2.69

Source: Herbert J. Walberg and Sue Pinzur Rasher, "The Ways Schooling Makes a Difference," *Phi Delta Kappan* 58 (1977), 703-707. Reprinted by permission.

Regression analysis shows that high rates of failure are significantly associated with low levels of adult education, small population size, and high percentages of black and Spanish-origin residents in the states.[8] The equation, which accounts for 83.9 percent of the variance in rate of failure (with T-values in parentheses), is:

$$8.11 - .37(2.9) \times \text{adult education} + .38(6.5) \times$$
$$\text{black population} - .29(4.1) \times \text{Spanish origin} - .19(2.8)$$
$$\times \text{state population} - 4.54(3.5) \times \text{public school enrollment}$$
$$+ .08(2.2) \times \text{pupil-teacher ratio.}$$

Because the other population indexes—income, density, urban, rural, homicide, and newspapers (Table 18-1)—are disassociated with rate of failure or overlap the other variables in the equation, they are not reliably related to the rate of failure.

Among all school variables and combinations of school variables in Table 18-1, only two are significantly related to rate of failure when controlled for the significant population indexes: either separately or together, higher percentages of children enrolled in public schools and lower pupil-teacher ratios are significantly related to lower rates of failure. None of the other school variables—cost-adjusted expenditures per pupil on public schools, expenditure effort, average school size, nongradedness, attendance, or percentage of one-room schools—carries significant weight in accounting for failure rate.

Despite the variation in expenditure per pupil from \$586 in Mississippi to \$2,084 in Florida, expenditures bear no relation to rate of failure when controlled for the population characteristics; yet the pupil-teacher ratio, varying from 26.8 in Utah to 17.9 in Vermont (Table 18-2) does. A reduction of one pupil per teacher is associated with an estimated 7.9 percent reduction in rate of failure when the other variables are controlled. An interpolation within the range of the data shows a drop of 69 percent in rate of failure associated with a decline from the highest to the lowest pupil-teacher ratio. Although administrative, supportive, and capital expenditures are necessary, smaller classes may pay off because of the intensified, direct services they allow the teacher to provide the children. In particular, small classes permit more individual guidance, small-group work, and discussion without the constraints of authoritarian control often required in large groups.

Research on families [9] and early childhood centers[10] suggests that low child-adult ratios are associated with accelerated cognitive development; moreover, such ratios seem to confer greater benefits to younger and disadvantaged children.[11] Other research on school districts[12] and college classes,[13] more sophisticated than that formerly carried out on class size, supports the value of low pupil-teacher ratios.

A major fault of much of the past research on class size is the use of superficial tests of knowledge, tests that are insensitive to the deeper learning more easily brought about in smaller classes.[14]

We agree with John Corbally's point that the teacher surplus represents underutilization rather than oversupply of talent.[15] Employing recent education graduates to reduce class sizes would be a worthwhile social investment, more worthwhile than allowing federal, state, and local bureaucratic overhead to continue to grow in education.

THE GEOGRAPHY OF ACHIEVEMENT

The differences among the states are not trivial. In South Carolina the rate of failure is 24.6 — thirty-five times higher than that in Minnesota, where the rate is .7 (see Table 18-2). The states most similar to one another in the population and school profile related to test failure fall into five clusters:

Upper Northeast and Northwest. This cluster of states is characterized by high levels of adult education, low percentages of black and Spanish-origin residents, small populations, moderate public school enrollments, and low pupil-teacher ratios. In this cluster the rate of failure is lowest.

Mid-Atlantic and Midwest. This cluster differs from the upper Northeast and Northwest in having higher percentages of black and Spanish-origin residents, larger populations, and lower enrollments. Rates of failure for the cluster on the whole are higher than they are in the upper Northeast and Northwest.

Southwest. This cluster has higher levels of adult education and public school enrollments, lower percentages of black residents, higher percentages of Spanish-origin residents, smaller populations, and higher pupil-teacher ratios than the Mid-Atlantic and Midwest. Rates of failure for the Southwest and the Mid-Atlantic and Midwest, however, are about the same.

Peripheral South. This cluster has higher percentages of black residents and smaller populations, public school enrollments, and pupil-teacher ratios. Rates of failure are higher than they are in the Southwest cluster.

Core South. This cluster has sharply lower levels of adult education, higher percentages of black residents, and larger pupil-teacher ratios than the peripheral South. The rate of failure is higher in this cluster than elsewhere in the country.

Macroenvironments

Table 18-2

Values of failure-associated variables for 50 states

Cluster and state	Adult educa- tion	Black (percent)	Spanish (percent)	Popu- lation (mil- lions)	Percent- age of public school enroll- ment	Pupil- teacher ratio	Test failures	
							Observed	Fitted
Upper Northeast and Northwest								
Minnesota	12.2	.9	1.0	3.8	86	21.0	.7	1.5
New Hampshire	12.2	.3	.3	.7	79	21.3	.8	1.5
Washington	12.4	2.1	1.7	3.4	93	24.5	.9	1.9
Iowa	12.2	1.2	.7	2.8	89	20.2	1.1	1.3
Vermont	12.2	.2	.4	.4	87	17.9	1.2	1.3
Montana	12.3	.3	.9	.7	88	21.0	1.4	1.6
Oregon	12.3	1.3	1.1	2.1	91	22.2	1.5	1.6
Idaho	12.3	.3	2.3	.7	88	22.7	1.7	2.1
North Dakota	12.0	.4	.4	.6	84	19.2	1.8	1.8
South Dakota	12.1	.2	.4	.7	90	19.1	1.9	1.2
Maine	12.1	.3	.2	1.0	90	21.9	2.8	1.3
Mid-Atlantic and Midwest								
Nebraska	12.2	2.7	1.4	1.5	86	19.1	1.1	2.2
Kansas	12.3	4.8	2.4	2.2	86	19.8	2.1	2.8
Wisconsin	12.1	2.9	1.4	4.4	81	21.4	2.2	2.8
Ohio	12.1	9.1	1.2	10.7	84	23.2	3.4	3.9
Pennsylvania	12.0	8.6	.9	11.8	78	22.1	4.4	4.4
Missouri	1.8	10.3	1.3	4.7	87	21.5	4.5	4.2
Michigan	12.1	11.2	1.7	8.9	86	23.4	4.6	4.7
Indiana	12.1	6.9	2.2	5.2	88	24.4	4.7	3.9
Massachusetts	12.2	3.1	1.2	5.7	81	21.1	5.0	2.5
Connecticut	12.2	6.0	2.2	3.0	84	21.1	5.1	3.6
Illinois	12.1	12.8	3.5	11.1	79	21.1	7.1	6.3
New York	12.1	11.9	7.4	18.2	78	19.6	8.3	6.6
New Jersey	12.1	10.7	4.0	7.2	80	20.5	8.9	5.8
Southwest								
Utah	12.5	.6	3.2	1.1	95	26.8	2.6	2.2
Colorado	12.4	3.0	10.2	2.2	94	23.3	2.7	3.4
Oklahoma	12.1	6.7	2.0	2.6	95	22.2	3.6	2.6
Nevada	12.4	5.7	4.2	.5	98	25.7	4.2	4.1
Arizona	12.3	3.0	15.0	1.8	87	23.4	4.6	6.1
California	12.4	7.0	11.9	20.0	92	24.0	4.8	3.9
New Mexico	12.2	1.9	30.3	1.0	87	24.2	9.1	6.9
Peripheral South								
Maryland	12.1	17.8	1.2	3.9	84	22.5	6.1	7.0
Delaware	12.1	14.3	1.6	.5	83	2.0	6.6	9.0
Texas	11.6	12.5	16.4	11.2	89	21.9	7.6	9.5
Florida	12.1	15.3	6.0	6.8	86	22.9	8.0	7.8
Virginia	11.7	18.5	.9	4.6	86	22.5	11.1	7.1

Table 18-2 *(continued)*
Values of failure-associated variables for 50 states

Cluster and state	Adult educa- tion	Black (percent)	Spanish (percent)	Popu- lation (mil- lions)	Percent- age of public school enroll- ment	Pupil- teacher ratio	Test failures	
							Observed	Fitted
Core South								
Tennessee	10.6	15.8	1.3	3.9	86	25.4	8.3	12.9
Arkansas	10.5	18.3	1.3	1.9	89	21.0	10.4	11.4
Louisiana	10.8	29.8	1.9	3.6	80	23.1	13.5	25.1
Alabama	10.8	26.2	1.1	3.4	86	24.4	16.0	17.1
Georgia	10.8	25.9	1.0	4.6	89	25.0	16.4	14.4
North Carolina	10.6	22.2	.9	5.1	88	24.1	16.5	12.7
Mississippi	10.7	36.8	.7	2.2	86	23.7	21.9	24.5
South Carolina	10.5	30.5	.5	2.6	87	22.3	24.6	17.2
Low enrollment, low pupil-teacher								
Rhode Island	11.5	2.7	.8	.9	77	20.9	4.2	4.9
Alaska	12.4	3.0	1.5	.3	80	20.9	5.5	4.3
Hawaii	12.3	1.0	3.2	.8	79	22.6	7.2	4.0
Unclustered								
Wyoming	12.4	.8	4.2	.3	96	19.0	1.9	1.6
Kentucky	10.3	7.2	1.4	3.2	82	23.8	8.1	9.8
West Virginia	10.6	3.9	.5	1.7	90	24.1	8.4	4.7

Source: Herbert J. Walberg and Sue Pinzur Rasher, "The Ways Schooling Makes a Difference," *Phi Delta Kappan* 58 (1977), 703-707. Reprinted by permission.

PUBLIC SCHOOL ENROLLMENTS

Analysis by clusters of states helps to explain why an estimated drop in the rate of failure of 4.5 percent is associated with a one-unit increase in the percentage of children five to seventeen years old attending public schools in the state even though the association is no doubt also partially attributable to dropouts at the age of seventeen or younger. Of the states highest in percentage of public school enrollment (Table 18-2), four are in the upper Northeast and Northwest (Washington, Oregon, South Dakota, and Maine), five are in the Southwest (Utah, Colorado, Oklahoma, Nevada, and California), and two are unclustered (Wyoming and West Virginia). The states lowest in percentage of public school enrollment differ on the average from these high-enrollment states in having greater population density and higher income per capita. (Concentrated population and the ability to pay are, of course, preconditions for private education.) Of the states lowest in public school enrollment, New Hampshire, Rhode Island, Alaska, Hawaii, and Louisiana do not sustain further generalization, but the remaining six states have several common features that tend to distinguish them from the other forty-four.

The six (Wisconsin, Pennsylvania, Massachusetts, Illinois, New York, and New Jersey) are all in the Mid-Atlantic and Midwest cluster and, with the exception of the South, have higher percentages of black residents on the average than other states. They contain several of the major conurbations (Milwaukee-Chicago, Pittsburgh, Boston, and New York-Newark) that are increasingly becoming stratified into a poor minority core with inferior schools and an affluent white suburban ring with superior schools. The mediocre test performance in these metropolitan areas is partially attributable to the immigration of blacks and whites with lower levels of adult education (Table 18-2) from the South to the inner city and the reduction in expenditures, services, and accountability that mark public schools in the city. The fact or threat of busing to achieve racial or social integration in these areas has probably exacerbated the problem it was intended to solve. Influential professionals and members of the middle class move to the suburbs, and industry and retailers follow, which means that articulate demand for quality in the urban public schools weakens. Middle-class whites who do remain in the urban area and who want a good education for their children pay for private schooling in the city; others move to a suburb—choices that are not available to many members of minority groups or the poor.

ENVIRONMENT AND EDUCATIONAL POLICY

The above analysis suggests that there is considerable overlap between the social environmental characteristics in the state and the educational policies associated with failure on the draft test. Socioeconomically advantaged states with relatively small percentages of minority citizens are educationally advantaged. This is one reason why the separate effects of educational policy on test performance are difficult to estimate despite effects found here and in some other research. Since these findings exemplify the rich-getting-richer phenomenon mediated through, or associated with, educational policy to some extent, it may be asked how specific environmental variables relate to educational policy variables.

Table 18-3
Regression analyses of environment variables with educational policy variables

Equation	Dependent variable	Adult education	Median income	Population			Density	Residence		Homicide rate	Newspaper subscriptions	Constant	R^2
				Black	Spanish	State		Urban	Rural				
1	Enrollment	2.52	-3.96[a]	-.97	-.52	.36	-2.31[c]	.11[a]	1.34	2.65[a]	-3.20	63.13	.46
2	Enrollment		-2.15				-2.69[c]	.06[b]	1.13			102.15	.40
3	Enrollment						-2.73[c]	.09[a]	.62			86.29	.39
4	Pupil-Teacher	-.59	-1.25[a]	-.60[a]	-.28	.10	-.66[b]	.10[c]		1.05[a]	-13.05[b]	33.36	.63
5	Pupil-Teacher		-1.55[b]	-.50[a]			-.50	.10[c]	.95[b]	1.13[b]	-12.09[b]	24.21	.62
6	Pupil-Teacher	-.58	-1.19[a]	-.55[a]			-.57[b]	.10[c]	.81[b]	.95[a]	-12.23[b]	31.57	.62
7	Expenditures	20.66[c]	30.05[c]				8.58[c]	-.19				-487.52	.71
8	Expenditure of effort	.47	.67				-.31[b]		.43[b]		-5.48[a]	-.45	.51
9	School size				.51		.89[b]	.10[c]		1.11[b]	-21.59[b]	20.48	.80
10	Nongraded schools		.38[c]				.08[b]				-1.03	.05	.45
11	One teacher schools		9.40[b]				-2.76[b]	-.23[b]				-75.46	.51
12	Effective attendance						-.42[a]			-1.68[c]	-9.27	178.40	.30

[a] $p \le .10$.
[b] $p \le .05$.
[c] $p \le .001$.

Note. The B-Weights for Equations 1-3, 7, 8, and 11 have been multiplied by 100.

The equations in Table 18-3 show the appropriate regressions. Equations 1 to 6 show the association of public school enrollment and pupil-teacher ratio to the exogenous variables. Equations 1 to 3 show that higher-percentage enrollments are found in states with lower median incomes and lower densities. (Equations 1 and 4 include all the variables; equations 2 and 3, 5 and 6, and 7 through 10 include only the most appropriate or predictive variables in Daniel and Wood's sense.[16]) Thus, ability to pay the extra costs and concentrated population in the state or areas within the state are the factors associated with greater attendance in sectarian and independent schools. Higher pupil-teacher ratios (equations 4 to 6) are associated with lower income, fewer newspaper subscriptions, higher homicide rates, and various density indexes.

How are educational policy variables that are not independently linked to test performance associated with the environmental variables? Higher expenditures per pupil are associated with higher adult education, income, and population density. Higher expenditure efforts are also associated with higher adult education and income, although these two variables are so highly correlated that their separate effects cannot be accurately estimated; density indexes also carry significant weight in the equation, but their effects are better estimated using multivariate analysis (see below). School size and the relative incidence of one-teacher schools in the states are also associated with population density indexes. A high attendance rate for students is associated with low homicide rates.

Multivariate Relations

The relations of environment and educational policy can be more parsimoniously accounted for by the condensing power of canonical analysis (Tables 18-4 and 18-5). The first canonical variates show the association of higher public school enrollment, expenditures, one-teacher schools, and effective attendance, lower school size, and nongradedness with lower income, black population, total population, urban population, and density. The first variates contrast such sparsely settled states as South Dakota and Wyoming, mainly in the Northwest, with such densely settled states as New Jersey and New York on the Eastern seaboard.

The second variates show the association of higher pupil-teacher ratios and lower expenditure effort and nongradedness with higher

Table 18-4
Canonical loadings on four pairs of canonical variates

Variables	Loadings			
	1	2	3	4
Dependent				
Public school enrollment	.48	.19	.49	.27
Pupil-teacher	-.23	.65	.54	-.14
Expenditures	.62	-.12	.31	.29
Expenditure of effort	-.39	-.83	.15	.19
School size	-.88	.32	.23	.21
Nongraded schools	-.51	-.44	.20	-.15
One-teacher schools	.68	-.33	.14	-.28
Effective attendance	.42	-.27	-.04	.16
Independent				
Adult education	.05	-.75	.27	.48
Median income	-.41	-.74	.44	-.02
Black population	-.49	.64	-.08	.01
Spanish population	-.25	.07	.44	.40
State population	-.67	.19	-.16	.02
Density	-.88	-.05	-.38	-.12
Urban residence	-.89	-.02	.27	.02
Rural residence	.75	.23	-.30	-.12
Homicide rate	-.30	.52	.40	-.05
Newspaper subscriptions	-.28	-.57	-.06	-.10
Canonical correlation	.95	.89	.80	.62
Probability $\leq$	.0001	.0001	.0007	.1090

Table 18-5

Ranking of top and bottom ten states on predictor canonical variates

Ranking of states	Predictor canonical variates			
	1	2	3	4
1	Montana	Alabama	Nevada	New Mexico
2	South Dakota	Mississippi	Alaska	Delaware
3	North Dakota	South Carolina	Arizona	Florida
4	Wyoming	Arkansas	Utah	Colorado
5	Alaska	Louisiana	Wyoming	Arizona
6	Idaho	Tennessee	Oregon	Mississippi
7	Maine	Georgia	Maryland	Indiana
8	Vermont	North Carolina	Colorado	Virginia
9	New Mexico	Kentucky	Michigan	Oklahoma
10	Nebraska	Utah	California	Vermont
41	Ohio	Montana	New Hampshire	Alaska
42	Illinois	Illinois	Vermont	Oregon
43	California	Massachusetts	New York	North Carolina
44	Massachusetts	New York	Connecticut	Arkansas
45	Delaware	Rhode Island	Maine	Georgia
46	Connecticut	New Hampshire	New Jersey	Nevada
47	New York	Iowa	Massachusetts	Tennessee
48	Maryland	Connecticut	Iowa	West Virginia
49	Rhode Island	Vermont	Mississippi	Rhode Island
50	New Jersey	Alaska	North Dakota	Kentucky

black population and homicide rate and lower adult education, income, and newspaper subscriptions. These variates contrast Mississippi, Alabama, and other states in the South with those in the North. The third variates show the association of higher enrollment and pupil-teacher ratio with higher median education, Spanish-origin population, and homicide rate. These variates contrast the West with the rest of the country. The canonical variates show that the population and environmental characteristics of the states are reflected in their educational policies.

The research summarized and reported above contradicts the view that schooling makes little difference and that improvement in quality and increase in equality of opportunity lie beyond our reach. The case for educational improvement should not, however, rest entirely on social research, for it is too equivocal. Men and women of good will in sociology, economics, and psychology are as yet unable to resolve issues of result and method. The case must be made on the ground of our heritage of equality of opportunity before the law and the state. If it cannot be based on the accomplishment of equality, then it must be based on aspirations to attain the traditional ideal.

We should not let inequalities of educational opportunity weaken the tradition of social advancement through high-quality public schooling. Within states and across the United States, the education of children does not provide an equal chance for success, and the prospect that each child will have an equal chance grows dimmer. To redress the balance may require amendments to state constitutions or, perhaps, as the Education Commission of the States has proposed, to our federal Constitution. The amendments should prevent abridgment of the right to equality of educational opportunity on account of race, sex, religion, economic condition, or place of birth or residence. Although much more needs to be done, research cited and reported here begins to define the aspects of education that seem to allow or make the difference: amount of schooling, opportunity to learn, psychological environment, and even such crude indicators as class size.

NOTES

1. James S. Coleman *et al.*, *Equality of Educational Opportunity* (Washington, D.C.: U.S. Government Printing Office, 1966); Christopher Jencks *et al.*, *Inequality:*

A Reassessment of the Effect of Family and Schooling in America (New York: Basic Books, 1972); *On Equality of Educational Opportunity,* ed. Frederick Mosteller and Daniel P. Moynihan, (New York: Random House, 1972).

2. Herbert J. Walberg and Sue P. Rasher, "Public School Effectiveness and Equality: New Evidence and Its Implications," *Phi Delta Kappan* 66 (1974): 3-9; *id.,* "Improving Regression Models," *Journal of Educational Statistics* 1 (1976): 253-277; idem, "The Ways Schooling Makes a Difference," *Phi Delta Kappan* 58 (1977): 703-707.

3. Herbert H. Hyman, Charles R. Wright, and John S. Reed, *The Enduring Effects of Education* (Chicago: University of Chicago Press, 1975).

4. *Educational Policy and International Assessment: Implications of the IEA Surveys of Achievement,* ed. Alan C. Purves and Daniel U. Levine (Berkeley, Calif.: Mc-Cutchan Publishing Corp., 1975).

5. Herbert J. Walberg, *Evaluating Educational Performance: A Sourcebook of Instruments, Procedures, and Examples* (Berkeley, Calif.: McCutchan Publishing Corp., 1974); *id.,* "Psychology of the Learning Environment: Behavioral, Structural, or Perceptual?" in *Review of Research in Education,* Volume IV, ed. Lee S. Shulman, (Itasca, Ill.: F.E. Peacock, 1976), 142-178. See also chapter 4 in this volume.

6. Coleman *et al., Equality of Educational Opportunity;* Jencks *et al., Inequality; On Equality of Educational Opportunity,* ed. Mosteller and Moynihan.

7. Samuel Bowles and Henry M. Levin, "The Determinants of Scholastic Achievement: An Appraisal of Some Recent Evidence," *Journal of Human Resources* 3 (1968): 3-24.

8. Cuthbert Daniel and Fred S. Wood, *Fitting Equations to Data* (New York: Wiley-Interscience, 1971).

9. Herbert J. Walberg and Kevin Marjoribanks, "Family Environment and Cognitive Development: Twelve Models," *Review of Educational Research* 46 (1976): 527-551.

10. William Fowler, "How Adult/Child Ratios Influence Infant Development," *Interchange* 6 (1975): 17-31.

11. Walberg and Marjoribanks, "Family Environment and Cognitive Development."

12. Charles Bidwell and John Kasarda, "School District Organization and Student Achievement," *American Sociological Review* 40 (1975): 55-70.

13. Wilbert J. McKeachie and James A. Kulik, "Effective College Teaching," in *Review of Research in Education,* Volume III, ed. Frederick N. Kerlinger (Itasca, Ill.: F. E. Peacock, 1975), 165-209.

14. *Ibid.*

15. John E. Corbally, letter in "Backtalk," *Phi Delta Kappan* 56 (1974): 299.

16. Daniel and Wood, *Fitting Equations to Data.*

PART FIVE
Research Methods

19. Research on Educational Effects

James M. McPartland and *Nancy Karweit*

Differences in school environments are not the major causes of differences in students' achievement. Such is the conclusion drawn from the most publicized studies in the last ten to fifteen years by many researchers and critics of American education. But, rather than closing up shop or changing their business, educational researchers and school planners have raised issues of research methodology and interpretation to argue that conclusions on the ineffectiveness of schools are premature or misleading.

Some issues concern the nature of the data on school environments and student outcomes, for example, whether school impacts have been actually addressed with the comparisons being made. Other issues involve the analytic models used to identify school effects, for example, whether the techniques used have been appropriate for separating school effects from other influences on student outcomes. Some of the issues have been raised in counterinterpretations of research findings,

This research is supported by the National Institute of Education, United States Department of Health, Education, and Welfare. The results and opinions of the authors do not necessarily reflect the position of NIE.

some in reanalyses or in reports of new evidence from empirical data, and some in methodological studies using simulated data derivations of analytic formulas under specific assumptions.

Studies with large samples that have been subjected to extensive analyses and reanalyses include the Coleman survey,[1] Project Talent,[2] Youth in Transition,[3] and Hauser's reanalysis of a survey of Nashville schools.[4] The results of the surveys, individually and in combination, have been most frequently interpreted to demonstrate that school differences account for little of the variations in student outcome measures.[5]

Yet each study is based on naturally occurring variations of environments found in existing public schools and uses student samples that are nonrandomly distributed across schools. Because these studies do not meet the scientific standards for controlled experiments, methodological questions on the proper analysis and interpretation of nonexperimental data apply to each of them. The issues, in most general terms, involve the scope of coverage of school environments that is provided by natural variations of existing schools and the separation of school and nonschool influences on students when nonrandom features affect the assignment of students to schools.

SCOPE OF RESEARCH VARIABLES

Because we can only study effects of those school differences on which we have data, it is the scope of school variations studied that limits the possible research conclusions. Closer attention to the actual range of contrasts among schools surveyed in most large-scale studies has raised questions about the proper interpretation of survey results and about the insensitivity of many survey procedures to important educational factors.

As a matter of interpretation, an alternative conclusion can be drawn from the finding that only a small proportion of variation in student outcome measures is due to school differences. Instead of concluding that school influences are weak and ineffective, some would read the same results to mean that school environments present largely the same educational experience for students throughout this country and they are in large part equally effective for most learning outcomes. In other words, school environments do not account for the differences in student outcomes because the schools themselves are not different. According to this interpretation, schools are similar in their programs and equally effective, while other nonschool factors (such as family environments) are more variable in the population and thus have the stronger possibility of correlating with differences in student outcomes. According to this view, schools are not weak influences but simply equal influences.

A similar counterinterpretation holds that the observed relationship between student outcomes and school differences is probably correct but cautions that the generality of the conclusions is limited to the specific range of school contrasts that were studied. For example, if a national sample of schools includes only schools where class size ranges from twenty to forty students per class, we may find that there is little difference in average student achievement across this range, but we cannot conclude that "class size" in general is unimportant. The scope of the study provides no information on the strength of the relationship between achievement and class size outside of its restricted natural range. The same argument for precise interpretation of research results applies to other school factors. Because most studies have measured school variables only within a restricted range of their possible variation, the generality of our knowledge on the effects of these variables is limited. By this reasoning, conclusions on school effects should be carefully expressed in terms of the scope of observed school comparisons, so as not to preclude the possibility of more dramatic effects beyond some unmeasured threshold of school differences.

There appear to be two ways to expand the scope of variations being studied in school environments. One is purposively to select samples that maximize the range of variation on educational practices and environments. A second is to develop more sensitive measures that capture variation in educational environments existing in representative samples of schools and classrooms.

The first strategy explicitly selects samples that provide better comparative data for school effects research. Sampling designs for previous school surveys have rarely attempted to maximize the scope of school contrasts to be studied. More often, the primary objective of the designs has been to achieve a representative sample of major student groups on which to base estimates of average schooling experiences. But, if a major research objective is to examine relationships over a wide range of school contrasts, an appropriate sampling design should be developed. Some researchers have undertaken preliminary screening surveys to locate schools for later intensive study that offer promising comparisons on a selected environmental property or with regard to an unusual record of student performance.[6] Similar efforts are needed in future research studies in an effort to provide data that can increase the generality of our knowledge of school effects.

The second strategy develops more precise measures of differences in educational environments for representative samples of schools and students. This approach assumes that previous studies have failed to detect large differences because they overlooked important environmental variations within the same schools or because they failed to measure the duration of exposure of different students to particular school factors.

A number of researchers have argued that studies of school effects concentrating on measures at the school and district levels have missed important within-school educational differences that affect students.[7] Eric Hanushek showed that linking the characteristics of individual students with the teachers who had actually taught them, rather than with a school average of the teaching faculty, can produce better estimates of instructional effects.[8] Other studies have shown how peer-group influences and normative environments can vary significantly within schools, depending upon a student's curriculum placement, classroom assignments, and other factors.[9] A recent study in Philadelphia was able to find larger school effects, in part by showing how different school resources are targeted for certain students within the school.[10] Thus, there is reason to believe that more careful attention to the differences within schools will show greater variations in educational factors and provide more accurate measures of a student's own learning environment, thereby providing better evidence of the effectiveness of schools.

Another way of being more sensitive to differences in educational experiences is to measure the duration of exposure of students to instructional resources. In other words, we may need to consider differences in the amount of time that students experience instruction to find the most important variations in schooling that account for differences in student learning outcomes.[11] Preliminary studies focusing on the effect of exposure time on achievement, however, have not consistently provided evidence of large effects.[12] The inconsistencies have in part arisen because of the use of different exposure measures, such as the length of the school day, the number of days in the school year, the number of minutes allocated to a particular subject each day, and the percentage of allocated time during which the student's attention is engaged. There have also been differences in these preliminary studies as to the outcome measures used, such as subjective grades assigned by teachers and norm-referenced achievement tests. In addition to resolving measurement issues in future studies, a more comprehensive view of classroom learning is needed to capitalize fully on the potential importance of duration of exposure variables in school effects research.[13]

The learning consequences of additional instructional time may not be the same for all students, for all curricular units, or for all modes of classroom instruction. There are individual differences among students as to how much instruction each one needs to master a particular lesson. Some curriculum tasks are more difficult for all and require longer learning time. The organization of classroom instruction can also affect how the timing and duration of specific learning activities are distributed among the different students in the classroom. In other words, the effectiveness of different amounts of exposure to instruction may depend upon the needs of individual students, the content of the learning material, and the mode of classroom organization. If researchers are to use ideas about time allocation and use to clearly demonstrate the effectiveness of schooling, they should probably conduct studies that incorporate these ideas into more comprehensive views of classroom learning processes.

At this time, there is no guarantee that more variable school samples or more sensitive environmental measures will yield consistent findings of impressive school effects, but current knowledge about the potential impact of school changes is limited because of the narrow range of school contrasts that have been widely studied. Increasing the scope of school variations in future research will increase the generality of our knowledge, and may identify school factors that have sizable effects if they persist for an extended period of time or reach a critical level of intensity.

Just as our current ideas may be limited about potential variable components of school environments, the measures of student outcomes now in use may cover only a limited range of the human talents that schools can foster, or they may be insensitive to effective improvements in an instructional program.

Most school effects research has concentrated on academic achievement, educational aspirations, and a few general personality dimensions (for example, self-concept and locus of control) as the student outcomes to be explained. There may be other student outcomes of schooling important for adult success that have not even been considered in the research on school effects. At this time, however, researchers have neither developed comprehensive lists of the diversity of human talents that schools may influence, nor produced measures of some of the more interesting additional student outcomes that have been suggested.[14]

Even the measures of the student outcomes ordinarily used in school research may not show the true impact of school differences. For example, most measures of academic achievement have selected test items to maximize the discrimination among a student population at a given time, rather than to measure change in performance over time for a student population or to be responsive to specific changes in the school program.[15] There are other technical questions about the proper test metric to be used to measure change in learning, since researchers have presented detailed arguments for and against the use of grade-equivalent scores, percentile scores, raw scores, and standardized scores.[16] In addition, there has been a call for tests that more accurately cover the material actually presented in the classroom since proper school evaluations may need a more careful overlap of curriculum as taught and curriculum as tested.[17] Serious methodological work remains to be done before one can settle upon the best outcome measures to be used in evaluating the effectiveness of different instructional programs.

While methodologists may find ways to improve measures of traditional student outcomes for studies of school effects, other important advances may depend upon educational theorists and researchers who can expand the range of human talents to be considered in future studies. Evidence is emerging that the value of additional schooling for adult success varies for broad classes of occupations, which suggests that many types of jobs value and reward other talents besides academic ones.[18] Research to identify and measure important human competencies and coping skills beyond those ordinarily measured in school effects research may hold an important key to future research on differences in school environment that prove effective in student development.

IDENTIFYING THE SCHOOL AS THE SOURCE OF INFLUENCE

Even if the problems of natural variation were handled with adequate samples and sensitive measures, extremely vexing issues remain in estimating school effects when students are not randomly distributed among the various school settings. These issues involve judging the degree to which effects on student learning should be assigned to school differences or to nonschool influences.

In a sample where all the advantaged students go to one type of school and all the disadvantaged students go to another type, no statistical trick can separate out the influence of the students' family backgrounds versus the type of school on student learning. If the achievement scores are much higher for students from one type of school, these effects may just as well be the consequence of family factors. This represents a case of severe "multicollinearity" between the student background and school environment factors, or total "confounding" between background and school variables. In this case, the data present no way to separate the factors because there is no way to contrast school types for rich students alone or for poor students alone, or to contrast family backgrounds while holding the type of school constant.

The actual nonrandom distribution of any student characteristic across school locations is never this severe. But neither is the problem ever totally absent in nonexperimental situations where students have not actually been randomly assigned to the various schools or classrooms under study. Even if there is no relationship in a sample between school attended and important family background measures such as socioeconomic status, there can be no assurance that some other unmeasured background condition (such as family ambition or student personality) has not contributed to a nonrandom self-selection or assignment of students to schools.

In this chapter we try to describe briefly the approaches followed in prominent school effects studies to identify the relative importance of school and nonschool influences, and to discuss some of the criticisms of the interpretations drawn from these approaches. This is followed by an outline of current efforts to deal with some of the objections.

Assignment of Confounded Variation

To determine the relative influence of school and nonschool factors on student outcomes, when measures of both factors are correlated with one another as well as with the outcome measures, involves judgments on how to assign the proportion of explained variation that is shared by both school and nonschool variables. Nonexperimental studies of school effects have often arrived at these judgments by examining the distribution of outcome scores as school means and variances (between-school and within-school components of variation) and by assuming causal priorities of the school and nonschool variables in models of school effects.

An important piece of evidence is drawn from properties of the distribution of the student outcome variable. By comparing the differences of school means to the overlapping spreads of scores around the school means, the proportion of variation in student outcomes can be uniquely divided into "between-school" and "within-school" components. The proportion of variation in outcome scores that lies "between schools" can theoretically range from zero (if all the school means are exactly equal with equal variances about their means) to 1.00 (if all the school means are different with no variation of student scores within each school). Except in unusual situations, the observed proportion of variance "between schools" provides an upper bound for the relative importance of *all* school factors, because average differences between schools reflect the self-selection or assignment biases as well as the influence of different school programs. In effect, to estimate the relative importance of schools by the proportion of outcome variation found between school means is to assign all overlapping school and nonschool effects to the school. Thus, when the between-school component of variance in student outcome scores is small — and it has been in the range of 10 to 35 percent in most large surveys of student achievement — it is concluded that schools play a relatively minor role in explaining differences in student learning.

Various techniques have been employed in an attempt to further disentangle or partition the between-school variance into the portions attributable to nonschool and school factors. The Coleman study assumed that the nonschool factors (family background) were causally prior to the school factors. Consequently, in estimating the relative importance of school and nonschool variables, all of their shared or confounded variation was assigned to the nonschool factors. The resulting estimates of the amount of variance attributable to school factors was, therefore, conservative. Subsequent reanalyses of the Coleman data recognized this problem and alternative techniques for attributing the shared variance were advocated. As Werts and Linn point out, one can select a technique that gives the most favorable division of shared variation to help support the kind of hypothesis one wishes to advocate.[19] But most of the exercises that use different assignments of the confounded variation have failed to alter the general picture of weak school effects relative to nonschool effects.

Recent Developments: Multi-level Analysis

Recent attention has been given to alternative methods for studying school effects by *separately* analyzing factors contributing to the between-school and within-school components of variation in student outcomes.[20] These approaches recognize that nonschool influences and school effects can operate on student outcomes at different levels of aggregation. Nonschool influences, such as family background and academic ability, are different for each individual student in a classroom or school. Each individual comes from a different family situation, and each individual independently brings to the classroom particular nonschool advantages or disadvantages for learning. On the other hand, the particular variables of classroom or school environment that distinguish one setting from another do not affect individual students independently. To the extent that all students in a classroom or school are provided with the same instructional setting, and to the degree that an individual's reactions to classroom experiences are related to other students' reactions to the common experiences, school or classroom variables have their influences on *groups* of students rather than independently on *individual* students. Indeed, the practical decisions and theoretical issues to be addressed in educational effects research often concern the common programs that can be instituted for students as members of classroom or school groups. The problem becomes how to provide data that allow analyses of these differences between individual-level and group-level effects, and how to develop measures and analytic techniques that are sensitive to these different sources of influence on student outcomes.

In studies such as that done by Coleman, straightforward measures at both the individual and group level were used in the analyses, but the analyses remained solely at the individual level since individual achievement or outcome measures were used. Nonschool variables of family background were measured individually for each student, as were academic achievement and other selected outcomes. School variables, such as instructional resources or social context of the peer group, were measured so that each individual student in the same school received the same resource or context score. The analyses in most early school effects research examined the relationships among *individual* student outcome scores, individual (background) variables, and the group (school resource or context) variables assigned to each individual in the study. Recent criticisms of this approach argue that such an overall between-student analysis that combines individual- and group-level factors into a composite is rarely of substantive interest and may distort significant relationships.[21]

The new approaches being considered and tested for school effects research are concerned with other ways to treat the different units of analysis for (individual) nonschool and (group) school variables. The approaches deal with alternative ways to analyze the within-school and between-school components of variance in student outcomes. Sometimes, the educational group being studied is the classroom or district rather than the school, but the new approaches apply similarly even though the technical complications may be different.

There are two general directions in which this work seems to be heading. One direction is to derive appropriate measures that can be used in separate analyses of within- and between-group effects. A second direction is to consider each school separately, estimate the *relationships* between individual nonschool and outcome measures for each school, and give new interpretations to differences in these relationships across schools. This involves analyses of the "interaction" of school with individual learning processes.[22] Burstein identifies at least seven different approaches to school effects studies that proceed from one or both of these directions.[23]

By analyzing the between-school component of variation in student outcomes separately from the within-school component, researchers are acknowledging that the important practical and theoretical issue often concerns an educational experience or treatment that collectively affects all students in a classroom or school group. The correct number of cases being compared in research on this issue is the number of different classrooms or schools included in the sample, and the correct number of degrees of freedom for statistical tests involves the number of groups not the number of individual students. But it is usually not correct simply to analyze all relationships at the group level. Relationships between student background variables and student outcomes should not be based on group averages because these effects are not generally approximated well in either size or direction by substituting relationships between averages for relationships between individual scores. Various proposals have, therefore, been made to accomplish both an analysis that treats the correct number of cases for school or classroom effects and at the same time takes into account the best estimate of the relationship between individual background and outcome variables.

These alternative techniques propose to analyze between-school components of variation for effects of group factors and to analyze within-school components of variation for effects of individual factors. Different proposals are made for adjusting outcome and school resource means to take into account individual learning processes before school effects are analyzed, and for standardizing individual measures to remove school treatment differences before individual relationships are analyzed. There is still the problem of correctly specifying a model of causal priorities and crucial variables; thus estimates of school effects still depend upon making correct assumptions if student background measures are confounded in the data. But the claim is that separate analyses of between-school and within-school components, under correct assumptions about causal priorities, can be more sensitive to school effects than a combined analysis.

Perhaps the most promising and challenging feature of these approaches is the consideration of new definitions of what constitutes a school effect. There are now more things to look at in the search for evidence that schools have an impact on student development. Up to now, a school effect was indicated by the direct relationship between a school measure and a student outcome measure after background factors had been appropriately taken into account. Now, school effects are being considered if there is evidence that the individual learning process (such as the relationship between student background and achievement) is different in contrasting school situations.[24] For example, notice would be taken of differences among schools in the degree to which learning rates of students depend upon their social-class background or their starting point in terms of academic performance. In this example, schools that show more equal growth in academic performance for all students would be contrasted with those that show the typical pattern of advantaged students growing faster than others to increase their advantages over time. There remain very complicated problems of defining the appropriate statistical parameters to translate into research practice this idea of looking for school effects on relationships (learning processes) as well as on student outcome scores (test performance). At present there is no one accepted way to summarize the existence of such interactions of school with individual learning processes, and very few empirical studies have attempted to analyze the specific school factors that may underly such differences in learning processes.[25] Research methodologists are at work on these problems, using simulated data to learn which alternative approach is most sensitive to particular definitions of school effects and to clarify the analytic problems involved in applying various statistical techniques to nonexperimental data.[26] This statistical work is still in its early stages. At this time we do not even have a good sense of whether there are sizable school-learning process interactions present in educational data that can be the subject of these statistical approaches after they have been more fully developed. Whatever the analytic model and data under investigation, it is certain that substantive assumptions of causal priorities and independent judgments on the specification of appropriate variables will remain as critical issues in nonexperimental research on the effects of schooling.

PROSPECTS FOR RESEARCH ON THE EFFECTS OF SCHOOLING

We have discussed two primary methodological issues in school effects research. Each can be used to argue that previous conclusions on the ineffectiveness of school influences may not be the final word, although there are presently no direct demonstrations that major school effects will be found with specific techniques for dealing with them. The burden of demonstrating impressive school effects remains for those researchers who claim that our knowledge has been limited by the scope of the variables under study or by the ways we define school effects in the face of confounded independent variables or different units of analysis. The complexities of the statistical and measurement models under consideration and the realities of nonexperimental data guarantee that real advances will still depend upon appropriate substantive judgments about the nature of the variables that should be entered into models and their causal sequences. In other words, statistical techniques alone do not hold the key to clearer understanding of questions concerning the effectiveness of schools.

The work on methodological issues has, however, given new impetus to school effects research. It has already raised questions about the generalizability of earlier conclusions on the ineffectiveness of schools and turned attention toward ways of expanding the scope of our knowledge about schools. It has also provided a firmer grasp of how to collect data that will produce the number of cases and sensitivity of measurement required to increase our understanding of the effects of schooling. And methodological work is helping to develop new ways of thinking about those effects that may open up fresh directions for theory and research worthy of serious attention.

NOTES

1. James S. Coleman *et al., Equality of Educational Opportunity* (Washington, D.C.: U.S. Government Printing Office, 1966); *On Equality of Educational Opportunity,* ed. Frederick Mosteller and Daniel P. Moynihan (New York: Vintage Books, 1972).

2. Christopher Jencks *et al., Inequality: A Reassessment of the Effect of Family and Schooling in America* (New York: Basic Books, 1972).

3. Jerald G. Bachman, Swayzer Green, and Ilona Wirtanen, *Youth in Transition:* Volume III, *Dropping Out—Problem or Symptom?* (Ann Arbor, Mich.: Institute for Social Research, 1971).

4. Robert M. Hauser, *Sociometric Background and Educational Performance* (Washington, D.C.: American Sociological Association, 1971).

5. Harvey Averch *et al., How Effective Is Schooling? A Critical Review and Synthesis of Research Findings* (Santa Monica, Calif.: Rand Corporation, 1972); *On Equality of Educational Opportunity,* ed. Mosteller and Moynihan; William G. Spady, "The Impact of School Resources on Students," in *Review of Research in Education,* Volume I, ed. Frederick N. Kerlinger (Itasca, Ill.: F.E. Peacock, 1973), 135-177.

6. R.E. Klitgaard and G.R. Hall, *A Statistical Search for Unusually Effective Schools* (Santa Monica, Calif.: Rand Corporation, 1973); Edward L. McDill and Leo C. Rigsby, *Structure and Process in Secondary Schools: The Academic Impact of Educational Climates* (Baltimore, Md.: Johns Hopkins Press, 1973); James M. McPartland and Joyce L. Epstein, "Open Schools and Achievement: Extended Tests of a Finding of No Relationship," *Sociology of Education* 50 (1977): 133-143.

7. Samuel Bowles and Henry M. Levin, "More on Multicollinearity and the Effectiveness of Schools," *Journal of Human Resources* 3 (1968): 393-400; Marshall S. Smith, "Equality of Educational Opportunity: The Basic Findings Reconsidered," in *On Equality of Educational Opportunity,* ed. Mosteller and Moynihan, 230-342.

8. Eric A. Hanushek, *The Value of Teachers in Teaching* (Santa Monica, Calif.: Rand Corporation, 1970).

9. Ernest Q. Campbell and C. Norman Alexander, "Structural Effects and Interpersonal Relations," *American Journal of Sociology* 71 (1965): 284-289; James

McPartland, "The Relative Influence of School Desegregation and of Classroom Desegregation on the Academic Achievement of Ninth Grade Negro Students," *Journal of Social Issues* 25 (1969): 193-202; McDill and Rigsby, *Structure and Process in Secondary Schools;* Albert Rhodes *et al.,* "Occupational Segregation in a Metropolitan School District," *American Journal of Sociology* 70 (1965): 682-694; James Rosenbaum, "The Stratification of Socialization Processes," *American Sociological Review* 40 (1975): 48-54.

10. Anita A. Summers and B.L. Wolfe, "Which School Resources Help Learning? Efficiency and Equity in Philadelphia Public Schools," *IRCD Bulletin* 11 (No. 3, 1976).

11. David E. Wiley, "Another Hour, Another Day: Quantity of Schooling, a Potent Path for Policy," in *Schooling and Achievement in American Society,* ed. William H. Sewell, Robert M. Hauser, and David L. Featherman (New York: Academic Press, 1976), 225-265; Steven J. Kidder, Robert P. O'Reilly, and Herbert J. Kiesling, "Quantity and Quality of Instruction: Empirical Examples," paper presented at the annual meeting of the American Educational Research Association, Washington, D.C., April 1975.

12. Nancy Karweit, "A Reanalysis of the Effects of Quantity of Schooling on Achievement," *Sociology of Education* 49 (1976): 237-246.

13. W.W. Cooley and G. Leinhardt, "Instructional Dimensions Study," University of Pittsburgh, Learning Research and Development Center, August 1978; J. Alan Thomas, "Resource Allocation in Classrooms," final report of Grant No. NIE 6-74-0037, University of Chicago, Finance and Productivity Center, October 12, 1977; Nancy Karweit, "The Organization of Time in Schools: Time Scales and Learning," prepared for the NIE Conference on School Organization and Productivity, San Diego, January 1978.

14. James S. Coleman, "How Do the Young Become Adults?" *Phi Delta Kappan* 54 (1972): 226-230.

15. Ronald P. Carver, "The Coleman Report: Using Inappropriately Designed Achievement Tests," *American Educational Research Journal* 12 (1975): 77-86.

16. Barbara Heyns, "Models and Measurement for the Study of Cognitive Growth," University of Chicago, Finance and Productivity Center, July 1978; James Coleman and Nancy Karweit, *Information Systems and School Performance Measures* (Englewood Cliffs, N.J.: Educational Technology Publications, 1972).

17. W. W. Cooley and G. Leinhardt, "The Application of a Model for Investigating Classroom Processes," University of Pittsburgh, Learning Research and Development Center, 1975; David C. Berliner, "Studying Instruction in the Elementary School Classroom: Developing Clinical Educational Psychology and Clinical Economics," University of Chicago, Finance and Productivity Center, July 1978.

18. Linda S. Gottfredson, "Differential Educational Payoff Models and Theories of the Diversity of Human Talents," paper presented at the annual meeting of the American Educational Research Association, New York, April 1977; *id.,* "Theories of the Diversity of Human Talents," paper presented at the annual meeting of the American Educational Research Association, New York, April 1977.

19. Charles E. Werts and Robert Linn, "Analyzing School Effects: How to Use the Same Data to Support Different Hypotheses," *American Educational Research Journal* 6 (1969): 439-447.

20. Hauser, *Socioeconomic Background and Educational Performance.*

21. Lee J. Cronbach, "Research on Classrooms and Schools: Formulation of Questions, Design and Analysis," unpub. MS, Stanford Evaluation Consortium, Stanford University, Palo Alto, California, 1976.

22. Nancy Karweit and James Fennessey, "A Pragmatic Framework for Studying School Effects: Estimation Experiments Using Actual and Simulated Data," unpub. MS, 1976.

23. Leigh Burstein, "The Role of Levels of Analysis in the Specification of Educational Effects," University of Chicago, Finance and Productivity Center, July 1978.

24. Karweit and Fennessey, "Pragmatic Framework for Studying School Effects."

25. Paul R. Lohnes, "Statistical Descriptors of School Classes," *American Educational Research Journal* 9 (1972): 547-556.

26. Burstein, "Analysis of Multilevel Data in Educational Research and Evaluation"; Karweit and Fennessey, "Pragmatic Framework for Studying School Effects"; Daniel Luecke and Noel McGinn, "Regression Analysis and Education Production Functions: Can They Be Trusted?" *Harvard Educational Review* 45 (1975): 325-350; Cronbach, "Research on Classrooms and Schools."

20. Causal Research on Teacher Training

Stephen L. Murray and *Nick L. Smith*

A major purpose when evaluating teacher training is to identify how the training affects teacher behavior and subsequent student growth. This becomes particularly difficult when evaluating innovative teacher-training systems because of the developmental nature of such systems and the limited appropriateness of standard evaluation methods.

Innovative teacher-training systems frequently evolve through a cyclical process involving experimentation and revision. The systems are predictably complex as a result of this evolutionary development, as well as the tendency to include multiple strategies in order to achieve maximum impact of training. The primary interest of applied work, it has been claimed, is to effect change; explaining how things operate is of secondary interest.[1] Unfortunately, a training rationale that is ambiguous or unclear as to how training is to affect teacher behaviors and student growth makes it difficult for an evaluator to design an un-

This work was supported in part by National Institute of Education Contract No. 400-76-0046. It does not represent NIE policy, and no endorsement should be inferred.

equivocal assessment of the effectiveness of training.

Although the supporting rationales behind many evaluations of training are as cloudy as the developmental rationales, most evaluations attempt to make causal assessments by relying on experimental designs implemented in field settings. Rossi and Wright comment on the pervasiveness of this causal logic through experimental design in educational evaluation:

If there is a Bible for evaluation, the scriptures have been written by Campbell and Stanley . . . , along with a revised version by Cook and Campbell . . . . The "gospel" of these popular texts is that all research designs can be compared more or less unfavorably to randomized controlled experiments, departures from which are subject to varying combinations of threats to internal and external validity.[2]

Unfortunately, controlled experiments frequently cannot be implemented in the field, although Cook and Campbell have recently suggested strategies for overcoming restrictions on randomization that may help.[3] The experimental approach to evaluating teacher training has a further limitation. Over fifty years of experimental research has failed to show consistent relationships between teacher behavior and student growth.[4] Thus, the most commonly attempted model for evaluating teacher-training systems, the experimental study, can seldom be implemented in the field and has not proved productive in laboratory studies of teacher effects.

Alternative methods for evaluating teacher-training systems need to be considered. Approaches based on the attainment of objectives are currently popular in educational evaluation, but, since many developers employ a cyclical, trial-and-revision strategy, rather than a linear, objectives-based developmental strategy, formally stated objectives provide an unstable and inadequate basis for system evaluation. On the other hand, Scriven's "goal-free" evaluation so effectively bypasses the intentions of developers that it is difficult to see how that method could prompt revision by developers.[5] The responsive approach developed by Robert Stake might be used to produce a thorough description of the training system and its perceived effects, but it would provide little understanding of the underlying causal mechanisms.[6]

What is needed is a methodological approach that enables one to interpret training systems as the developers envision them, thereby providing feedback for revision within the developmental framework. It would also be desirable to have an approach that retained an emphasis on assessing causal mechanisms, but with nonexperimental data that can be collected in field settings. Causal modeling seems to fill these needs. As illustrated below, it can be used as both a design heuristic and a statistical analysis procedure when performing evaluative research on teacher-training systems.[7]

PATH ANALYSIS

There are many forms of causal modeling. For the sake of brevity we focus on just one form, path analysis. Path analysis originated with the work of Sewall Wright in the field of genetics. The method was developed as "an extension of the usual verbal interpretation of statistics, not of the statistics themselves. It is usually easy to give a plausible interpretation of any significant statistic taken by itself. The purpose of path analysis is to determine whether a proposed set of interpretations is consistent throughout."[8]

Path analysis can be characterized as relating primarily to the analysis of nonexperimental data and the absence of laboratory or experimental controls, as employing latent variables that are implied in the relationships with the observable variables, and as utilizing a systems orientation reflected in the use of sets of interacting relational equations.[9] It involves the construction of explicitly formulated alternative structural (causal) models that imply patterns of relationships among variables. The underlying causal reasoning is made explicit in the form of path diagrams and structural equations. Regression analysis is then used to construct "path coefficients" (beta weights). Models inconsistent with the data are rejected, while those not rejected are viewed as plausible causal patterns to be studied further. Causation cannot be unambiguously demonstrated using these techniques, but some causal patterns can be rendered more believable than others.

The first step in the application of path analysis is to construct a path diagram, which is a graphic display of the order in which variables are assumed to affect one another. The variables in a path diagram are referred to as either *endogenous* or *exogenous.* An endogenous variable is one that is dependent upon other variables in the diagramed system, while exogenous variables are those that affect endogenous variables. Since there can be more than one stage of causation displayed in a path diagram (that is, A affects B, which in turn affects C), some endogenous variables may act as exogenous variables for subsequent endogenous variables (that is, B is an endogenous variable with respect to A, but an exogenous variable with respect to C). The initial variables in a diagram, however, are always exogenous to that system.

Conventions for drawing path diagrams are described by Land.[10] Arrows are drawn from variables acting as causes to variables acting as effects. Initial exogenous variables are linked to one another by curved lines with double arrows. For example, suppose one assumes that C is caused by both A and B and that one is not interested in the causes of A or B. This would be represented as in Figure 20-1.

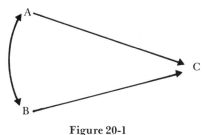

Figure 20-1
A simple causal model

Path models may be recursive (involving only one-way causation) or nonrecursive (involving reciprocal causation). The illustrations presented here deal only with recursive models.

Analysis is designed to produce measures of relationship between a given endogenous variable and each of the exogenous variables on which it is dependent. These indexes are called "path coefficients." The reduction of the effects of an exogenous variable into its *direct effects* (uninterrupted paths of influence between variables), and its *indirect effects* (effects analogous to the effects of an antecedent variable as transmitted through an intervening variable), is a major feature of the path analysis technique.

In applying path analysis, a system of regression equations mathematically representing the causal network is generated. Evaluating the solution to this system of equations is an evaluation of the formal causal model. The isomorphism between the causal model and the mathematical representation is clearly evident in path analysis. In contrast, the usual application of multiple least squares regression results in a single equation that is used to estimate status on the dependent variable as a function of the independent variables. Emphasis is placed on the amount of variance unaccounted for on the dependent variable and the incremental validity resulting from adding independent variables to the equation. Least squares regression gives biased or inappropriate estimates of the causal influence of independent variables whenever there is measurement error, reciprocal causation, or the omission of a causal variable. If none of these conditions obtains, then least squares regression gives suitable parameter estimates.[11] The causal model implicit in multiple regression is, however, only one of a number of models that could be applied to the same set of data. The reader should also be aware of the following assumptions that are made in the use of path analysis:

1. There is a clearly defined, explicitly specified causal system that includes all relevant variables.
2. The model clearly specifies temporal ordering of variables in terms of theory, and the measurement procedures correctly reflect this ordering.
3. Within the structural model, a change in one variable is a linear function of changes in other variables.
4. Dependent variables are uncorrelated with each other.
5. Hypothetical, unmeasured variables are continuous.
6. Measurements have a high degree of reliability and validity (low measurement error).
7. The data meet all multivariate regression assumptions, including interval-scale measurement, homoscedasticity, relatively low intercorrelations among causal variables or predictors, linear and additive effects among variables, uncorrelated residuals with a mean of zero and unit variance, and fixed effects independent variables.

Standard procedures are, of course, available for testing the tenability of most of these assumptions.

Blalock[12] and Duncan[13] introduced causal modeling into sociology, and Land has generalized the method by developing path analysis from basic definitions and assumptions. There are several general discussions of path analysis.[14] Since their introduction into the social sciences, path analysis techniques have been used in research studies on a wide variety of problem areas, including those dealing with job performance,[15] role perceptions,[16] aggression,[17] life satisfaction,[18] social stratification,[19] educational aspirations,[20] educational achievement,[21] teacher characteristics,[22] and college environments.[23] The reader is referred to Land for an extensive discussion of the principles of path analysis, including derivations and interpretations of path coefficients in various types of path models.[24] Spaeth provides a detailed comparison of the logics behind predictive least squares models and totally recursive path models.[25]

CAUSAL MODELING IN TEACHER TRAINING

In applying causal modeling to training evaluation, the developers and evaluators of the teacher-training systems can work collaboratively to establish a network of variables that includes training as a cause and various proximal and distal aspects of teacher and student behavior as consequences of the training. Hypothesized relationships within this network can then be tested. This form of evaluation can be seen as a special instance of construct validation[26] and as being similar to theory testing.[27] Empirical tests of relationships within this network can serve to confirm assumed interrelationships, thus supporting the overall developmental approach, or it can fail to corroborate certain presumptions, thereby identifying breakdowns in design or implementation. Further developmental refinement may be suggested as a result of these analyses.

Teacher training is justified on the basis of its contribution to schooling goals. Conventional evaluations of the impact of training either focus directly on student growth or emphasize the teaching processes through which student growth is facilitated. Causal modeling enables one simultaneously to conceptualize and assess the impact of training on student growth and teacher processes, and it can be used at both a heuristic and statistical level.

As a heuristic device, causal modeling can aid in the design of an evaluation study and in the usefulness of its subsequent findings to developers. We have found that simply mapping the presumed causal relationships is a useful way for developers to share their conception of the training system with evaluators and that the process tends to highlight areas of disagreement between developers. Such mappings are also extremely useful in pinpointing logical inconsistencies in the training design and in identifying the placement of critical relationships within the overall network of training effects. Causal mapping facilitates developer-evaluator communication and enables the evaluator to provide evaluative feedback that is clearly germane to the system's developmental framework.

One of the major strengths of causal modeling as a statistical procedure for evaluating teacher training is that it is one of the few means available for mathematically modeling complex and innovative training systems. Other multivariate approaches do not provide a means of simultaneously testing both the rationale and the effectiveness of the training system. Furthermore, techniques like path analysis enable evaluators to test both direct and indirect training effects within the same study, and they force the consideration of alternative explanatory models. The utility of causal modeling in evaluating teacher training is illustrated in the following example.

AN ILLUSTRATIVE EXAMPLE

Causal modeling and path analysis were applied as part of an evaluation of a newly developed system consisting of materials for training teachers in a five-step generic problem-solving process. Trainees were guided through a sequence of sixteen activities, each consisting of concept papers, group discussions, and exercises, and, as a result, were expected to develop knowledge of and the ability to apply the techniques of problem solving in dealing with classroom situations.

The purpose of the evaluation was to determine what impact the training had on the teachers' application of the problem-solving processes and techniques in the classroom. Analysis of the training materials and interviews with the developers led to the premise that teacher application of the processes and techniques was largely dependent upon the teachers' intention to apply them in a classroom situation. The training was designed to influence this intention in a number of ways. First, the training materials included an extended example of a hypothetical teacher applying the techniques in a classroom situation. Second, the trainees were given practice in using the techniques in their own classrooms. And, finally, encouragement to use the techniques was provided through the materials and the workshop trainer.

The model developed postulated that· teacher training operated upon the teachers' classroom behavior (that is, application) through its impact upon the teachers' intent to apply the techniques in the classroom. This simple three-variable model is presented in the following diagram:

Skill training $\longrightarrow$ Intent to apply $\longrightarrow$ Classroom application

Specific cognitive learning was not seen as a likely or important effect of training. Although the teachers may have learned new techniques during training, the primary emphasis was on the application of relatively simple procedures. Thus, cognitive gain was not included in the causal model.

The evaluation involved sixty fourth-, fifth-, and sixth-grade teachers from the two test sites. A treatment group of thirty-eight teachers participated in two workshops presented in different locations. Twenty-four teachers who had been recruited from the same population of fourth-, fifth-, and sixth-grade teachers in one of the two test areas served as a comparison group. An analysis of background information obtained from these teachers indicated that the composition of the two groups was essentially similar in terms of sex, age, and extent of prior experience in in-service training. Proportionately fewer teachers in the treatment group had received a master's degree.

An attitude survey was developed specifically to measure the teachers' intent to apply the techniques of problem solving. This instrument, the Problem Solving Orientation Questionnaire (PSOQ), was a paper-and-pencil self-report measure in which the respondents were presented with a variety of hypothetical problem situations and asked to estimate the probability of their reacting by using a procedure recommended in the problem-solving training. Responses to the items were made on a five-point scale identical to that for the following sample item:

> Suppose something has gone wrong in your school — something that affects everyone and has everyone upset. What are the chances that you would remain quiet and wait for others to analyze the problem?
>   Almost none (less than 10 percent chance)
>   Maybe (about a 25 percent chance)
>   Possibly (about a 50 percent chance)
>   Almost always (about a 75 percent chance)
>   Definitely (greater than a 90 percent chance)

Thirty-one items were written for situations dealing with: (*a*) interpersonal relationships, (*b*) task accomplishment, (*c*) classroom settings, and (*d*) nonclassroom settings. Sorts by two developers of the training system and four evaluators were conducted to determine if the items could be reliably classified into the two sets of two categories (a and b, c and d). Perfect agreement was reached in assigning all but two items to categories a and b. These two items were not scored in the analysis. For the same reason, two items were left unscored in the classroom setting and nonclassroom setting categories.

Split-half reliabilities corrected by the Spearman-Brown Prophecy formula revealed that only the "task accomplishment" and "classroom situation" scales were reliable enough to warrant use in analysis. The corrected reliabilities for these scales were .71 and .60, respectively. The PSOQ was administered before and after training to the treatment group and at similar times to the comparison group.

Classroom application was measured through four scales adopted from the Student Activities Questionnaire (SAQ).[28] These four scales consist of multiple-choice questionnaire items dealing with various aspects of teachers' behavior in the classroom. Students are the respondents. Thus, the SAQ scales supplied a measure of classroom application employing a source of information operationally independent of the teacher.

The four scales that were adopted for use were selected on the basis of a content analysis of scale items. Scales consisting of items that focused on classroom activities and events rather than subjective reports of student feelings toward the activities were selected. The four scales were "reinforcement of self-concept," "democratic classroom control," "individualization of instruction," and "classroom participation." These scales were administered before and after training to all available students in the treatment and comparison classrooms.

Intraclass correlations[29] ranged from .21 to .79 on the pretest data (based on 84 classrooms and 1,499 students) and from .27 to .72 on the posttest data (based on 73 classrooms and 1,213 students). The intraclass correlation is a function of within-group and between-group variation of student responses and constitutes a measure of consistency for within-class agreement using the classroom as the unit of analysis. "Democratic classroom control" was the most reliable scale in both administrations of the SAQ.

According to the model derived for the evaluation, teachers' intent to apply was seen as a mechanism by which training was expected to affect teachers' classroom behavior. Path analyses were used to evaluate this model. One of the path diagrams used to assess classroom application is presented in Figure 20-1. Based on past research,[30] teacher age, teacher sex, class size, and training (a dummy variable where treatment group = 1 and comparison group = 0) were hypothesized to influence democratic classroom control through their influence on teacher orientation toward task accomplishment. The effect of teacher orientation toward task accomplishment was seen as operating directly on democratic classroom control. The path diagram presented here included only the most reliable measures from the PSOQ and SAQ since the regression procedures used to obtain estimated path coefficients require reliable measurement.

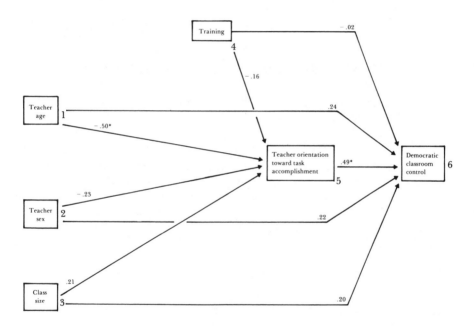

Figure 20-2

Path diagram and standardized partial regression coefficients for the evaluation
of teacher training in terms of its impact on
the level of democratic classroom control

Two recursive structural equations correspond to the path diagram represented in Figure 20-2. The first equation,

$$Z_5 = P_{5,\,1}Z_1 + P_{5,\,2}Z_2 + P_{5,\,3}Z_3 + P_{5,\,4}Z_4 + P_{5,\,a}Z_a$$

represents the influence of the exogenous variables (plus a residual variable a) on teacher intent to apply problem-solving techniques in task accomplishment. By solving this linear regression equation, it is possible to make estimates of the direct effects (path coefficients) of the prior variables on this endogenous variable. While these path coefficients do not in themselves indicate causality, they can be used to assess whether the data are consistent with the prior causal model. Table 20-1 presents the standardized partial regression coefficients or path coefficients for the variables in Figure 20-2 and the multiple correlation obtained for explaining the posttraining intent of teachers to apply the techniques according to the "teacher orientation toward task accomplishment" scale.

It is apparent from examining Table 20-1 that the training did not have a direct effect on teachers' intent to apply as the corresponding coefficient was -.16. The multiple correlation resulting from regressing posttraining task accomplishment on the four variables in the path model was .46. The only significant path coefficient was for teacher age ($P < .01$) indicating that younger teachers saw themselves as having stronger orientations toward task accomplishment.

Table 20-1

Multiple correlation[a] and standardized partial regression coefficients for explaining posttraining teacher orientation toward task accomplishment[b]

Exogenous variable	Standardized partial regression coefficient	p-value
Teacher age	-.50	.01
Teacher sex	-.23	.19
Class size	.21	.23
Training	-.16	.37

[a] $R = .46$
[b] Only subjects for whom there were complete data were used in this analysis (treatment teachers = 26; control teachers = 10).

The second structural equation corresponding to the path diagram represented in Figure 20-2,

$$Z_6 = P_{6,1}Z_1 + P_{6,2}Z_2 + P_{6,3}Z_3 + P_{6,4}Z_4 + P_{6,5}Z_5 + P_{6,b}Z_b$$

represents the influences of all five variables (and a residual variable *b*) on the classroom application variable, democratic classroom control. Table 20-2 includes the multiple correlation and the path coefficients indicating the relationships between each of the exogenous variables and the level of democratic classroom control.

Table 20-2

Multiple correlation[a] and standardized partial regression
coefficients for explaining posttraining
level of democratic classroom control[b]

Exogenous variable	Standardized partial regression coefficient	p-value
Teacher age	.24	.21
Teacher sex	.22	.20
Class size	.20	.24
Training	−.02	.93
Posttraining teacher orientation toward task accomplishment	.49	.01

[a] R = .57
[b] Only subjects for whom there were complete data were used in this analysis (treatment classrooms = 26; students = 650; control classrooms = 10; students = 281).

The multiple correlation of .57 is significant ($P < .05$) and indicates that the model explains 32.5 percent of the variation in the classroom application variable. The path coefficients indicate that the data support the hypothesis that the intent of teachers to apply problem-solving procedures toward task accomplishment (teacher orientation toward task accomplishment) influenced classroom events as perceived by students (democratic classroom control). There was no evidence, however, that training had any impact on student perceptions of classroom events.

In summary, the analysis of the model represented in Figure 20-2 suggests that:
— younger teachers saw themselves as having stronger orientations toward task accomplishment,
— the posttraining orientation of teachers toward task accomplishment influenced classroom application as perceived by students, but
— training had no influence on either teachers' task orientation or classroom application as perceived by students.

When we consider again the original training model

Skill training ⟶ Intent to apply ⟶ Classroom
                                                                                application

we see that, although training had no effect, the assumption that intent to apply is linked to classroom application was supported. The path analysis results thus supported the basic training rationale, while showing that the workshop training was not a sufficiently strong treatment to change teachers' intent. By contrast, analyses of covariance that were conducted showed only that training was ineffective.

The previous example illustrates the use of path analysis with a non-randomized control group to test for direct and indirect training effects and to investigate the causal relationships that were assumed to lead to desired classroom impact. It was not the purpose of the evaluation to sort out which of the possible training influences might operate to affect teacher behavior. In evaluative research, the training program (that is, the independent variable) is often beyond the control of the evaluator, and is likely to confound a number of features assumed to facilitate learning. While such confounding makes pragmatic sense, it limits the opportunity of evaluative researchers to analyze which aspects of training are acting as causal factors.

Greater flexibility and control can be obtained by concentrating upon measuring training effects rather than empirically analyzing the training as a treatment or independent variable.[31] This study made use of path analysis to model the effects of training on teachers' intent to apply and on subsequent application in the classroom.

There are a number of technical and practical problems to contend with in applying path analysis and other causal-modeling approaches. The procedures are more costly and time consuming than simple pre-post testing and require collaborative work with developers to specify structural models that are compatible with the designs of the training system. Furthermore, although the techniques can be used to model complex systems, strong a priori training rationales are needed to restrict the number of structural options; a five-variable system can be portrayed in 1,048,576 possible configurations.[32] Also, when causal modeling is used to evaluate innovative teacher-training systems, the variables employed, while possibly deduced from broader theory, are likely to be defined specifically for the given training program being evaluated, which means that the development of new instruments will likely be required. The uniqueness of the instruments also makes it difficult to relate the results of evaluation studies to similar theory-testing efforts in basic research on teacher effectiveness. Spaeth,[33] Feldman,[34] and Pedhazur[35] have discussed such additional technical problems as specification errors, measurement errors, and multicollinearity in the use of path analysis.

Causal-modeling procedures can be used to assess the effectiveness of teacher training and to show the mechanisms by which such training is assumed to work. In the example presented above, workshop training did not effectively influence the intent of teachers to apply problem-solving skills or students' perceptions of the application of those skills by teachers. The results did, however, support the assumption that specific behavioral intents of teachers do relate to the classroom behavior of teachers, as perceived here by students. Other techniques would also have indicated nonsignificant effects of training, but, by using path analysis, we now also know that the shortcoming lies not in the training rationale, but in the weakness of the treatment. Path analysis thus provides evaluative researchers with a unique capability for studying both the effectiveness of training and causal relationships presumed to underlie training programs. With appropriate designs, evaluators can conduct local decision-oriented studies to revise training at the same time they are investigating more fundamental causal mechanisms — an excellent means of combining field research with field service.

NOTES

1. N.H. Azrin, "A Strategy for Applied Research: Learning Based but Outcome Oriented," *American Psychologist* 32 (1977): 140-149.

2. Peter H. Rossi and Sonia R. Wright, "Evaluation Research: An Evaluation of Theory, Practice, and Politics," *Evaluation Quarterly* 1 (1977): 13. The references in the quotation are to Donald T. Campbell and Julian C. Stanley, *Experimental and Quasiexperimental Designs for Research* (Chicago: Rand-McNally, 1966), and to Thomas C. Cook and Donald T. Campbell, "The Design and Conduct of Quasi-experiments and True Experiments in Field Settings," in *Handbook of Industrial and Organizational Psychology*, ed. Marvin D. Dunnette (Chicago: Rand-McNally, 1976), 223-326.

3. Cook and Campbell, "Design and Conduct of Quasi-experiments and True Experiments in Field Settings."

4. Robert W. Heath and Mark A. Nielson, "The Research Basis for Performance-Based Teacher Education," *Review of Educational Research* 44 (1974): 463-484; Barak Rosenshine and Norma Furst, "Research on Teacher Performance Criteria," in *Research in Teacher Education: A Symposium,* ed. B. Othanel Smith (Englewood Cliffs, N.J.: Prentice-Hall, 1971), 37-72.

5. Michael S. Scriven, "Goal-Free Evaluation," in *School Evaluation: The Politics and Process,* ed. Ernest P. House (Berkeley, Calif.: McCutchan Publishing Corp., 1973), 319-328.

6. *Evaluating the Arts in Education: A Responsive Approach,* ed. Robert E. Stake (Columbus, Ohio: Charles E. Merrill, 1975).

7. The authors wish to acknowledge the assistance of Sue Hiscox, Dean Nafziger, Rachel Rassen, and Stuart Speedie who participated in the evaluation efforts described in this chapter.

8. Sewall Wright, "The Treatment of Reciprocal Interaction, with or without Log, in Path Analysis," *Biometrics* 16 (1960): 444. Other works by Wright on path analysis are: "Correlation and Causation," *Journal of Agricultural Research* 20 (1921): 557-585; "The Interpretation of Multivariate Systems," in *Statistics and Mathematics in Biology,* ed. Oscar Kempthorne *et al.* (Ames, Iowa: State College Press, 1954), 11-33; "The Method of Path Coefficients," *Annals of Mathematical Statistics* 5 (1934): 161-215; "Data Coefficients and Path Regressions: Alternate or Complementary Concepts?" *Biometrics* 16 (1960): 189-202.

9. *Structural Equation Models in the Social Sciences,* ed. Arthur Goldberger and Otis D. Duncan (New York: Seminar Press, 1973).

10. Kenneth C. Land, "Principles of Path Analysis," in *Sociological Methodology: 1969,* ed. Edgar F. Borgatta and George W. Bornstedt (San Francisco: Jossey-Bass, 1969), 3-37.

11. *Structural Equation Models in the Social Sciences,* ed. Goldberger and Duncan.

12. Hubert M. Blalock, *Causal Inferences in Non-experimental Research* (Chapel Hill, N.C.: University of North Carolina Press, 1964); *Causal Models in the Social Sciences,* ed. *id.* (Chicago: Aldine, 1971); *id.,* "The Measurement Problem: A Gap between the Languages of Theory and Research," in *Methodology in Social Research,* ed. Hubert M. Blalock and Ann B. Blalock (New York: McGraw-Hill, 1968), 5-27; *id.,* "Theory Building and Causal Inferences," *ibid.,* 155-198.

13. Otis D. Duncan, "Path Analysis: Sociological Examples," *American Journal of Sociology* 72 (1966): 1-16.

14. Land, "Principles of Path Analysis." General discussions of path analysis also are provided in the following: *Causal Models in the Social Sciences,* ed. Blalock; Duncan, "Path Analysis"; Joe L. Spaeth, "Path Analysis," in *Introductory Multivariate Analysis,* ed. Daniel J. Amick and Herbert J. Walberg (Berkeley, Calif.: McCutchan Publishing Corp., 1975), 53-89; Charles E. Werts and Robert L. Linn, "Path Analysis: Psychological Examples," *Psychological Bulletin* 74 (1970): 193-212.

15. Charles N. Greene, "Causal Connections among Manager's Merit Pay, Job Satisfaction, and Performance," *Journal of Applied Psychology* 58 (1973): 95-100; Ed-

ward E. Lawler, "'A Correlational-Causal Analysis of the Relationships between Expectancy Attitudes and Job Performance," *ibid.*, 52 (1968): 462-468; John P. Wanous, "A Causal-Correlational Analysis of the Job Satisfaction and Performance Relationship," *ibid.*, 59 (1974): 139-144.

16. Robert H. Miles, "An Empirical Test of Causal Inference between Role Perceptions of Conflict and Ambiguity and Various Personal Outcomes," *Journal of Applied Psychology* 60 (1975): 334-339.

17. Leonard D, Eron *et al.*, "Does Television Violence Cause Aggression?" *American Psychologist* 27 (1972): 253-263.

18. Robert R. Sears, "Sources of Life Satisfaction of the Terman Gifted Men," *ibid.*, 32 (1977): 119-128.

19. Peter M. Blau and Otis D. Duncan, *The American Occupational Structure* (New York: Wiley, 1967).

20. William H. Sewell and Vimal P. Shah, "Social Class, Parental Encouragement, and Educational Aspirations," *American Journal of Sociology* 73 (1968): 559-572.

21. James G. Anderson and Francis B. Evans, "Causal Models in Educational Research: Recursive Models," *American Educational Research Journal* 11 (1974): 29-39.

22. *Ibid.*

23. Charles E. Werts, "The Study of College Environments Using Path Analysis," *National Merit Scholarship Research Reports* 3 (1967): 1-40.

24. Land, "Principles of Path Analysis."

25. Spaeth, "Path Analysis."

26. Lee J. Cronbach and Paul E. Meehl, "Construct Validity in Psychological Tests," *Psychological Bulletin* 52 (1955): 281-302.

27. C.T. Fitz-Gibbon and L.L. Morris, "Theory-based Evaluation," *Evaluation Comment* 5 (1975): 1-4.

28. R.L. Ellison *et al.*, "The Measurement of Academic Climate in Elementary Schools," paper presented at the meeting of the American Psychological Association, Montreal, August 1973).

29. Ernest A. Haggard, *Intraclass Correlation and the Analysis of Variance* (New York: Dryden Press, 1958).

30. Bikkar S. Randhawa and Lewis L.W. Fu, "Assessment and Effect of Some Classroom Environment Variables," *Review of Educational Research* 43 (1973): 303-321.

31. Cook and Campbell, "Design and Conduct of Quasi-experiments and True Experiments in Field Settings."

32. Jerald W. Young, "The Function of Theory in a Dilemma of Path Analysis," *Journal of Applied Psychology* 62 (1977): 108-110.

33. Spaeth, "Path Analysis."

34. Jack Feldman, "Considerations in the Use of Causal-Correlational Techniques in Applied Psychology," *Journal of Applied Psychology* 60 (1975): 663-670.

35. Elezar Pedhazur, "Analytic Methods in Studies of Educational Effects," in *Review of Research in Education,* Volume III, ed. Frederick N. Kerlinger (Itasca, Ill.: F. E. Peacock, 1975), 243-286.

Index

Academic achievement. *See* Achievement, academic

Academic guidance, as press variable, 18

Achelpohl, Clark, 76

Achievement, academic: in arithmetic, and innovation, 267-268; in big cities, 331-352; and family environment, 17-18, 27, 30, 31; in the fifty states, 353-368; geography of, 359-361; interaction among variables affecting, 340-346; and learning conditions, 354-355; motivation for, 17, 18, 20, 23, 33; multinational studies of, 313-317; and open classrooms, 280-281, 286; as outcomes, 301-302; and public school enrollments, 361-362; and race, 337-340, 341, 342, 343, 344, 345, 351; in reading, and innovation, 265-267; in social environment, 83-84; and socioeconomic status, 333-337; and standardized tests, 332-333; team learning related to, 122-123, 125-127, 130-131, 133; and time factors, 328-329; in United States, 313-330

Action Analysis Profile (AAP), 144

Activeness of family, as press variable, 18, 20-21

Activities Index, 154

Activity-environmental interaction, as press variable, 19

Adams, Anne H., 76

Adams, Raymond S., 217

Adjustment, and anxiety, and open classrooms, 284, 286

Administrative Style Analysis Profile (ASAP), 144

Affective characteristics, of family environment, 23-27, 32

Affiliation, in social environment, 83, 92, 94, 95

Affiliation orientation, in social environment, 86, 87-88

Ahlgren, Andrew, 116, 117, 118

Akers, Roger, 76

Alabama, achievement in, 361, 366, 367

Alaska, achievement in, 361, 362, 366

Alexander, C. Norman, 383

Alice Heim General Intelligence Test (AH4), 31

Allen, Vernon, 137

Allinsmith, Wesley, 99

Amarel, Marianne, 292

American Institutes for Research (AIR), 259, 262, 269, 273

American Medical Association, 61

American Psychiatric Association, 61